Systematic
Software Testing

Rick D. Craig
Stefan P. Jaskiel

Artech House
Publishers

Boston ● London

Systematic Software Testing

Library of Congress and British CIP information available on request.

Artech House Publishers

685 Canton Street   46 Gillingham Street
Norwood, MA 02062   London SW1V 1AH
(781) 769-9750   +44 (0)171 973-8077

International Standard Book Number: 1-58053-508-9

Printed in the United States of America

First Printing: May 2002

Trademarks

Warning and Disclaimer

Reviewers & Contributors

Heidi Amundson
Rob Baarda
Bev Berry
Rex Black
Steve Boycan
Renee E. Broadbent
Lee Copeland
George Flynn
Cheryl Happe
Tim Koomen
Claire Lohr
Clare Matthews
Amanda McCrary
Anne Meilof
Wayne Middleton
Wilton Morley
Eric Patel
Dale Perry
Martin Pol
Cristina Raszewski
Bill Scoffield
Steven Splaine
Marjolein Steyerberg
Laurie F. White
Pamela Young

Cover Designer

Jamie Borders

Indexer

Bill Graham

From Rick,

▪▪▪▪▪▪▪▪▪▪▪▪▪▪▪▪

To my daughter Crissy,
my mother Phyllis, my sisters Pam and
Beth, and my brothers Ed and Mark for
always being there when I needed you.

~

To the mentors in my life: my father Richard
Craig, Jim Gleason, and Mark Caldarello. I
learned more from you than any book I
could ever read.

From Stefan,

▪▪▪▪▪▪▪▪▪▪▪▪▪▪▪▪

To my parents, Maria and Walter, for
teaching me how to choose the best road
to follow among life's many choices.

~

To my sisters Halina and Anita, and my
brothers George and Frank, for always
"listening" and helping me find my way.

Table of Contents

Chapter 5 – Analysis and Design 145

Chapter 7 – Test Execution...................................239

Chapter 8 – The Test Organization 293

Foreword

When I wrote *Managing the Testing Process*, that book joined a fairly slender collection of books on testing. Happily, over the last few years, the collection of published resources for test professionals has grown steadily. As I work on the second edition of *Managing the Testing Process*, and my new book, *Critical Testing Processes*, I now find I have lots of material I can recommend to my readers for further ideas. *Systematic Software Testing* will show up in lots of footnotes in my current and future books. Attendees of my test management course often ask me to recommend books on various testing topics. I plan on including *Systematic Software Testing* in the short list of books that I preface with the remark, "If you only have time to read one book on testing, pick one of these."

While the number of books on testing has grown considerably over the last few years, this is not a "me too" testing book. *Systematic Software Testing* offers a complete roadmap for test professionals looking to institute or improve the way they test software. The title says that the book will outline a systematic method, and it does. I expect that many test professionals – myself included – will find this book occupies a frequently-accessed part of their professional library. I'm sure a dog-eared and annotated copy of this book will accompany me on a number of my consulting forays.

I first learned that Rick Craig and Stefan Jaskiel were working on this book about six months ago, and I was excited to hear it. Along with Rick and some of his other colleagues at Software Quality Engineering, I teach the Systematic Software Testing course, and I had long thought that the excellent course materials needed a full-length book to delve deeper into the details. This book fills that need perfectly. When Rick and Stefan asked me to write this foreword, I was excited and happy to have been asked. Back when Rick recommended me as a teacher of the Systematic Software Testing course, he said, "Rex is smart – he thinks like me!" (I think he might have been joking a little bit.) I was glad that Rick's opinion of me hadn't changed, and that he'd been able to convince Stefan of my talents, too.

But I was also a little apprehensive. I have a huge pile of books in my office that I know I *should* read. I mean, I'm sure there are good ideas that I need to absorb in them, but for some reason I just can't get to the point where the books move out of that huge pile and into my hands for a long enough period of time to learn from them. Some books have made it out of that pile for a short period, only to return to it with a lonely bookmark stuck near the front cover when something else comes up. I was somewhat concerned that perhaps this might somehow be such a book, one that I had to force myself to read. Those concerns were unfounded. I simply flew through this book in four days. Good ideas – lots of them, one after another – are presented and fully explained, but never belabored. The topics are brought to life throughout with anecdotes and case studies. (While some look down their noses at "anecdotal evidence," I found the stories rang true for me. As the saying goes, "The plural of anecdote is data.") Rick and Stefan's senses of humor leaven the material; I even found myself laughing out loud a time or two.

Just because I was smiling doesn't mean I wasn't learning, though. Rick and Stefan led me on a soup-to-nuts tour of the issues that confront the tester and test manager. Heard good things about risk-based testing and looking for a way to start? There's a simple yet effective approach outlined right in here. Looking to learn how to write actionable, useful, well-received test plans? Just keep reading. Wondering about whether change management and release management can be improved at your company? You've found the book you need. Metrics? Yep. A synopsis of various black-box and white-box test design techniques? It's here. How to go from being merely in charge of testing to being an effective leader of a test team? The chapter on test management, especially Rick's lessons on leadership gleaned from experience as a United States Marine Corps officer, makes the book worth purchasing for that chapter alone.

Throughout the discussion, Rick and Stefan remind the reader that the correct answer to any hard question about how to tackle some thorny testing problems is, "It depends." They're careful to discuss the contextual issues that affect testers and test managers, which will help those implementing the ideas in this book to avoid the landmines. And speaking of landmines, there are plenty of honest comments about where some of the common testing landmines live. People new to testing can use this book to avoid stepping on them.

If I'm a smart guy – and after all, Rick tells people that I am – then I should be able to make a few predictions. I predict you'll learn a lot from this book if you read it. I predict that you'll laugh from time to time, you'll nod in recognition at some of the anecdotes, and you'll stroke your chin thoughtfully more than once. And I predict that you'll return to this book for sage advice from two seasoned test professionals even if you, like me, consider yourself a seasoned test professional, too. This is good stuff, well written, entertaining, and insightful. If I may be so bold as to offer some advice in someone else's book, I recommend that you read on, enjoy, and learn new ways to be more systematic about your software testing.

Rex Black
President of Rex Black Consulting Services, Inc.

Preface

We wrote this book because many of our clients and students, through Software Quality Engineering (SQE), told us that it would be useful to capture the information that we present in our classes. And we saw an opportunity to share some of the information that we've learned from our audiences over the years. In the beginning, we specifically didn't want to write a cookbook with prescriptive instructions and lists of processes. One thing we have learned from our clients is that one size definitely does not fit all. What works well at one company is not necessarily the right fit at another. We even jokingly tell our students that one good answer to any question is "it depends," in recognition of the fact that every organization, project, and release is different.

When the book was done, however, we had done just the opposite and created a comprehensive reference with specific directions on how to conduct risk analysis, create inventories, write test plans, and so forth. These practices represent the basis of what we have found to work most of the time. It may be that some of you will be able to use the processes described in this book "as is" or "off the shelf." Good for you! It's more likely, though, that most readers will have to use the described processes as a starting point to build their own unique processes and infrastructure. Please feel free to take our step-by-step instructions and modify them to meet your own particular corporate culture and situation. While you're at it, don't get too complacent once you find something that works. Without a doubt, you'll need to continuously update and improve your processes as your culture and environment change.

How Is This Book Organized?

Standalone Chapters

This book was written so our readers could read any chapter independently of all of the other chapters. However, the chapters are organized in such a way that reading the book sequentially beginning with Chapter 1 and finishing with Chapter 12 will lead the reader through a more or less chronological journey through the software testing process. The choice is yours – you can read this book from cover to cover, or keep it as a handy reference guide.

References

This book was developed based on the IEEE Std. 829-1998 Standard for Software Test Documentation and the IEEE Std. 610.12-1990 Glossary of Terms, The Systematic Test and Evaluation Process (STEP^{TM}): An Introduction and Summary Guide, magazine articles, books, Web sites (e.g., www.StickyMinds.com), and many years of personal experiences. All of these references are presented in an alphabetized list at the end of the book.

SST and TM Courses

Much of the content within this book was developed based on the topics covered in the *Systematic Software Testing (SST)* and *Test Management (TM)* Courses offered by Software Quality Engineering, Inc. While these courses provided the foundation for this book, our students' comments, stories, and suggestions really brought this book to life.

Case Studies

The case studies are a combination of Rick's real-life adventures and our clients' experiences. In the case studies that are based on our colleagues' experiences, we've given credit where credit is due. Although we hope that you'll find some of our case studies entertaining, they're also important because they represent real-life examples of how people behave, why some processes fail, why some processes succeed, and lessons we've learned over the years. In other instances, we use "Case Study" boxes to explain calculations or processes via examples.

■■■■■■■■■■■■■■■■■
Case Study

Not all testers need all of the same skills.

They say I tell a great many stories. I reckon I do; but I have learned from long experience that plain people, take them as they run, are more easily influenced through the medium of a broad and humorous illustration than in any other way...

– Abraham Lincoln

Key Points

Important ideas, concepts, definitions, reminders, and other things that need extra emphasis are highlighted in the "Key Point" boxes throughout this book. In some cases, we also use these boxes to provide our readers with a synopsis of the topic explained in the corresponding paragraph. Readers of Stefan's other book, *The Web Testing Handbook*, find these informative boxes useful for quickly locating topics of interest by just "flipping pages."

■■■■■■■■■■■■■■■■■
Key Point

Finding our the level of maturity of a vendor's software engineering process can help you draw conclusions about the quality of their testing software.

Terminology

We've purposely chosen to use an informal and conversational writing style in this book that we hope you'll find easy to read and understand. Throughout this book, we use the words "we," "our," and "us," to describe our combined knowledge and/or experiences. Whenever a story, topic, or belief pertains only to one of us, we've identified that person by name. We've referred to you, our readers, as "testers" even though we understand that many of you may not be full-time testers. You may, in fact, be developers, users, managers or just someone interested in software testing. (Our family and friends have pledged to read the book just to figure out what it is that we actually do for a living.) For the time you spend reading this book, we dub you honorary testers.

Throughout this book, we use software terminology as defined by the Institute of Electrical and Electronics Engineers (IEEE) Standard 610.12-1990 Glossary of Software Engineering Terminology. In some cases, we use other terms that have gained popularity through different sources. David Gelperin, cofounder of Software Quality Engineering, Inc., for example, coined the term "testware" to describe all software testing-related work products including test procedures, test data, test specifications, and test reports, among other things. "Testware" and other terms used in this book are defined in the Appendix – *Glossary of Terms*.

During the development of this book, some of our reviewers were concerned about our occasional use of "slang" as opposed to "engineering terminology." For example, we use the (slang) word "bug" interchangeably with its more formal cousin "defect." To be consistent with our informal and conversational writing style, we made a conscious decision to use the terms "defects" and "bugs" synonymously. Although some of our colleagues may disagree with this usage, we believe that these terms have evolved to be one and the same after years of usage throughout the software industry.

Who Should Read This Book?

This book is designed to be used by testers, test managers, developers, and other people who interact with testers or need to understand testing. Specifically, this book is useful to software engineers who:

- are just beginning their careers and need to understand how software testing works
- are seasoned professionals and want to refresh their knowledge of software testing and test management
- want to substantiate that they're already doing the right things
- want to try a new approach to testing

■■■■■■■■■■■■■■■■■

Key Point

StickyMinds.com is an excellent online resource for testing articles, papers, message boards, tools info, and other resources.

The book covers a wide range of software testing topics, but it does not provide a comprehensive explanation of everything. Instead, we try to provide an introduction to each topic along with recommended procedures and supporting examples. That way, you'll be able to immediately apply our techniques and also gain a strong foundation for continuing your own comprehensive research into the specific topics that interest you.

Who Are the Authors?

The back cover of this book says that Rick Craig is a professional speaker, tester and test manager, consultant, author of numerous articles, technical editor for StickyMinds.com, and of course the co-author of this book. What the back cover doesn't mention, though, is that Rick is also a proud father, a

Colonel in the United States Marine Corps Reserve, a restaurant owner, an after-dinner speaker, and a member of Mensa. For over 15 years, Rick has entertained audiences with stories from these various facets of his life by somehow relating them to software testing. Repeat visits to the same client sites often result in, "Rick, tell us about the time you…" We've included a few of these stories and hope that you enjoy them and, at least occasionally, get the point.

– *Stefan*

Stefan Jaskiel is a manager, technical writer, author, consultant, and entrepreneur. Stefan keeps insisting that he'll *"take a long vacation after just one more project,"* but that hasn't happened in the 16 years that we've known each other. Wow, time really flies when you're a workaholic! While assisting me in the development of this book, Stefan has also led the development of the graphical user interface, documentation, and marketing literature for a revolutionary network security system based on a military radar metaphor, and worked on several other security- and surveillance-related projects. In his spare time, Stefan dreams about taking a ski trip to Colorado or traveling through Europe. Maybe his next consulting assignment will take him there… Hey, wait a minute, isn't that still considered work?

– *Rick*

Acknowledgments

Software Testing is a dynamic interdisciplinary subject that spans the entire breadth of software engineering. We believe that no one person or even group of people could possibly write a comprehensive text on such a broad subject. Indeed, even in this broad, but admittedly incomplete text, we had to rely heavily on our colleagues, students, clients, and the authors of other books, articles, and Web sites for support.

We would like to thank our colleagues (especially Rex Black, Lee Copeland, Claire Lohr, and Dale Perry – who also teach various SQE courses) who contributed to the work by providing insight, reviewing various stages of the book, and providing content on subjects where our own knowledge was inadequate. We offer a special thanks to the authors of our principal references:

- *The Systematic Test and Evaluation Process (STEP): An Introduction and Summary Guide*
  by Dr. Bill Hetzel
- *The Systematic Software Testing (SST) Course*
  by Dr. David Gelperin
- *The Test Management Course*
  by Steven Splaine and Rick Craig

Additionally, we would like to acknowledge that many of our reviewers supported us not only with their insightful reviews, but also, in some cases, by also allowing us to use their words and ideas. Finally, we would like to acknowledge our family, friends, clients, and colleagues who really didn't see us very often during the development of this book.

– Rick and Stefan

Chapter 1 –
An Overview of the Testing Process

"Few things are harder to put up with than the annoyance of a good example."

— Mark Twain

For several years, our clients have told us that we should write a book about the processes and methods that we use to test software, so, with a lot of help, that's what we've done. Specifically, the processes we use are based upon a methodology called STEP™, which was created by Dr. Bill Hetzel and Dr. David Gelperin as a way to implement the original IEEE-829 Standard for Test Documentation.

A Brief History of Testing

STEP was originally developed out of a frustration that, although the IEEE standard did a good job of specifying what testing documents needed to be built, they didn't describe how to create them or how to develop the processes (planning, analysis, design, execution, etc.) needed to use them.   The STEP methodology (and therefore this book) doesn't establish absolute rules that must be followed but rather describes guidelines that can and should be modified to meet the needs and expectations of the software engineers using them.   Even as we write this book, thousands of our past and present clients and students are using their own version of the STEP methodology and its underlying processes to build and implement quality software.

However, before we launch into the ins and outs of STEP, it's instructional to review the state of software testing prior to the launch of STEP, during its creation, and today. A good starting point is to review the definitions of testing (shown in Table 1-1) published by the authors at each of these times.

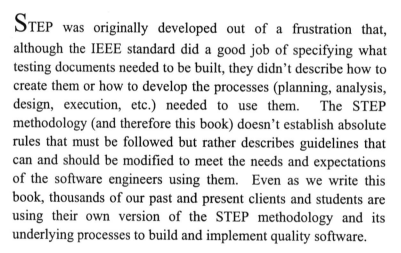

Key Point

"Innovate! Follow the standard and do it intelligently. That means including what you know needs to be included regardless of what the standard says. It means adding additional levels or organization that make sense."

– IEEE Computer Society Software Engineering Standards Collection

Table 1-1   Definitions of Testing Over the Years

Year	Definition
1979	Testing is the process of executing a program or system with the intent of finding errors.
1983	Testing is any activity aimed at evaluating an attribute of a program or system. Testing is the measurement of software quality.
2002	Testing is a concurrent lifecycle process of engineering, using, and maintaining testware in order to measure and improve the quality of the software being tested.

In 1979, Glenford Myers explained, "Testing is the process of executing a program or system with the intent of finding errors," in his classic book, *The Art of Software Testing*. At the time Myers' book was written, his definition was probably the best available and mirrored the thoughts of the day. Simply stated, testing occurred at the end of the software development cycle and its main purpose was to find errors.

If we skip forward to 1983, we find that the definition of testing had changed to include an assessment of the quality of the software, rather than merely a process to find defects. In *The Complete Guide to Software Testing*, Bill Hetzel stated that, "Testing is any activity aimed at evaluating an attribute of a program or system. Testing is the measurement of software quality."

Myers' and Hetzel's definitions are still valid today because they each address a particular facet of software testing. But, the problem with these definitions is scope. To resolve this problem, we offer the following definition of testing that will be used throughout this book:

■■■■■■■■■■■■■■■■■
Key Point

Philip Crosby's definition of *quality* is "conformance to requirements. Lack of conformance is lack of quality."

Dr. Joseph M. Juran's definition of *quality* is "the presence of that which satisfies customers and users and the absence of that which dissatisfies."

Testing is a concurrent lifecycle process of engineering, using and maintaining testware in order to measure and improve the quality of the software being tested.

Notice that no direct mention was made of finding defects, although that's certainly still a valid goal of testing. Also note that our definition includes not only measuring, but also improving the quality of the software. This is known as preventive testing and will be a consistent theme throughout this book.

Preventive Testing

Preventive testing uses the philosophy that testing can actually improve the quality of the software being tested if it occurs early enough in the lifecycle. Specifically, preventive testing requires the creation of test cases to validate the requirements before the code is written. Suppose, for example, that the user of an Automated Teller Machine (ATM) specified the following requirement:

A valid user must be able to withdraw up to $200 or the maximum amount in the account.

We know that some of you are already thinking, "What a horrible requirement." But we also know that many of you are thinking, "Wouldn't it be nice to have such a good requirement?" And, some of you are even thinking, "So that's what a requirement looks like?" Whatever you think about our sample requirement and no matter how good your requirement specifications are, they're certain to have inaccuracies, ambiguities, and omissions. And problems in the requirements can be very expensive to fix, especially if they aren't discovered until after the code is written, because this may necessitate the rewriting of the code, design and/or requirements.

■■■■■■■■■■■■■■■■
Key Point

Preventive testing uses the philosophy that testing can actually improve the quality of the software being tested if it occurs early enough in the lifecycle.

Preventive testing attempts to avoid this situation by employing a very simple notion: the process of writing the test cases to test a requirement (before the design or code is completed) can identify flaws in the requirements specification.

Now, let's get back to our ATM example. Table 1-2 briefly describes two (of many) test cases that you might write.

Table 1-2   Sample Test Cases for an ATM

Test Case	Description	Results
TC01	Withdraw $200 from an account with $165 in it.	???
TC02	Withdraw $168.46 from an account with $200 in it.	???

Should TC01 pass? It depends on how you interpret the "or" in the requirement: *A valid user must be able to withdraw up to $200 or the maximum amount in the account.* Some people will interpret it to mean that the ATM user can withdraw the lesser of the two values ($165), while other people will interpret it to mean they can withdraw the greater of the two values ($200). Congratulations, you've discovered an ambiguity in the requirements specifications that can lead to many problems down the road.

Should TC02 pass? It should according to the specification. But do you really think that the bank wants the ATM to dispense coins to the users? Well, maybe, but we doubt it. Some of you may be saying that no programmer would ever write the code to do this. Think again, this is a real example and the programmer did indeed write the code to allow the withdrawal of odd amounts.

By writing the test cases before the code was written, we were able to find some (in this case, obvious) problems. We found them early enough that it's a relatively simple and inexpensive job to correct them. An added benefit of creating the test cases before the code is that the test cases themselves help document the software. Think how much easier it would be to write code if instead of just having requirements specifications to base your code on, you could also use the test cases that were created to test the system as part of the system documentation.

■■■■■■■■■■■■■■■■
Key Point

An added benefit of creating the test cases before the code is that the test cases themselves help document the software.

Where Are Most Companies Today?

After reading the example above, we hope that most of you will think that the philosophy of preventive testing is clearly sound. Preventive testing is certainly not a new idea, so everyone must be using it, right? Well, not exactly. Our experience at most of the organizations we visit each year is that software is still developed using some kind of sequential model where the requirements are built, then the design, then the code, and *finally* the testing begins. The most famous of the sequential models of software development is the Waterfall model shown in Figure 1-1.

■■■■■■■■■■■■■■■■
Key Point

Our experience at most of the organizations we visit each year is that software is still developed using some kind of sequential model where the requirements are built, then the design, then the code, and *finally* the testing begins.

Although at first it appears that once a phase is complete there's "no going back," this is not necessarily true. There are usually one or more returns to a previous phase from a current phase due to overlooked elements or surprises. The difficulty arises when you have to back up more than one phase, especially in later phases. The costs of rework, re-testing, re-documenting, etc. become very high and usually result in shortcuts and bypasses. As Steve McConnell explains in his book *Rapid Development*, "late changes in the Waterfall model are akin to salmon swimming upstream – it isn't impossible, just difficult."

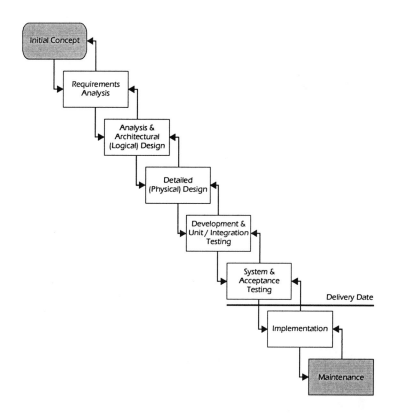

■■■■■■■■■■■■■■■■■
Figure 1-1

Waterfall Model of
Software
Development

When a sequential model like the Waterfall model is used for software development, testers should be especially concerned with the quality, completeness, and stability of the requirements. Failure to clarify and define requirements at the beginning of the project will likely result in the development of a software design and code that's not what the users wanted or needed. Worse, the discovery of these defects will be delayed until the end of the lifecycle (i.e., test execution).

There are actually a few advantages to the Waterfall model, the most obvious one being that the resources are largely focused on one activity at a time, and the next activity has the (hopefully) completed artifact from the previous stage to use as the basis for the next stage. However, as you will see, in addition to a few good features, the Waterfall model has many problems.

Sequential models are, in particular, difficult to use successfully from the testing viewpoint. You can see in Figure 1-1 that in the Waterfall model, testing is largely ignored until the end, and indeed that's exactly how it works today in many companies around the world. If testing occurs only (or largely) after the product has already been built, then the most that the testers can hope to accomplish is to find bugs in the finished product. (This would be like discovering you forgot to put the chocolate chips in the cookies until you were testing – eating – them. Sure, you could take a bite of the cookie and then throw down a couple of chocolate chips, but the effect is really not the same. You would have to settle for chocolate chipless cookies or start over.) If testing occurs only at the end, there's a lot of "starting over" going on.

Key Point

The Waterfall model is particularly difficult to use successfully from the testing viewpoint.

Another problem with the Waterfall model is that the testers will almost always find themselves on the critical path of delivery of the software. This is exacerbated because all too often the software is delivered to the testers late, and the schedule is cast in stone and cannot be changed. The result, of course, is that the window of opportunity for testing is constantly shrinking.

The STEP process described in this book can be used with any software development methodology (e.g., XP, RAD, Prototyping, Spiral, DSDM). If used with a sequential model of software development like the Waterfall model, many of the problems described earlier can be overcome (i.e., the use of the STEP testing methodology will transform a sequential model into an iterative model).

Why Is Testing So Difficult?

To the uninitiated, testing software seems like one of the easiest things imaginable. You try the software and either it works or it doesn't. But there has to be more to it than this or companies wouldn't spend 20, 30, 40, 50 percent or more of the software development budget on testing. So why is testing so difficult? We've already encountered some of the difficulties in testing: ambiguous and incorrect requirements, and tight time schedules. There are, unfortunately, many more difficulties in testing.

Why Is Testing Difficult?

When we ask a group of testers the question, "Why is testing difficult?" we get fairly consistent (and lengthy) answers. The reply we received from our friend Clare when we asked her to give us a fresh perspective on an early version of this book sums up many of the difficulties in testing:

Sure! Not only can I give you a fresh perspective, but by being in the trenches every day, I can offer a reality check quite well. I am sadly well-versed in doing whatever it takes to test, which includes working with ridiculous time frames, bad to no requirements, testers who need to be trained in testing, politics in test responsibility, providing data in as neutral a way as possible when notifying development and marketing of the state of the product. You name it... I think I've experienced it all.

— *Clare Matthews*

Case Study 1-1

Different testers may have different reasons why they think testing is difficult, but they all seem to agree that IT IS DIFFICULT!

Clare is not the only tester experiencing difficulties in testing, so let's get to work. We'll start by describing a high-level overview of STEP and where each of the facets of this methodology is covered in this book.

STEP Methodology

The Systematic Test and Evaluation Process (STEP) was first introduced in 1985 as part of the course material for the Systematic Software Testing seminar series. It has since been revised many times and field-tested through consulting engagements and the shared experience of many individuals and organizations. STEP is built upon the foundation of the IEEE Std. 829-1983 Standard for Software Test Documentation and subsequently updated based on the latest version (IEEE Std. 828-1998) of this standard and the IEEE Std. 1008-1987 Standard for Software Unit Testing. While retaining compatibility with these standards, this methodology has grown in scope and now stands as one of the leading models for effective software testing throughout the industry.

Key Point

Much of this section was reprinted from the STEP Guide with permission from Software Quality Engineering.

Scope and Objectives of STEP

STEP covers the broad activity of software evaluation. Evaluation is defined as that sub-discipline of software engineering concerned with determining whether software products do what they are supposed to do. The major techniques employed in evaluation are analysis, review and test. STEP focuses on testing as the most complex of the three, but stresses overall coordination and planning of all aspects of evaluation as a key to success. It stresses the prevention potential of testing, with defect detection and demonstration of capability as secondary goals.

Key Point

Evaluation is defined as the sub-discipline of software engineering concerned with determining whether software products do what they are supposed to do.

Early views saw testing as a phase that occurred after software development, or "something that programmers did to get the bugs out of their programs." The more modern view sees testing as a process to be performed in parallel with the software development or maintenance effort (refer to Figure 1-2) incorporating the activities of planning (determining risks and selecting strategies); analysis (setting test objectives and requirements); design (specifying tests to be developed); implementation (constructing or acquiring the test procedures and cases); execution (running and rerunning the tests); and maintenance (saving and updating the tests as the software changes).

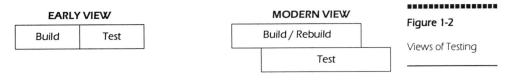

Figure 1-2

Views of Testing

This lifecycle perspective of testing represents a major change from just a few years ago, when many equated testing with executing tests. The contribution of planning, analyzing, and designing tests was under-recognized (and still is by many people), and testing was not seen as really starting until tests started running. Now we understand the evaluation power of test planning and analysis. These activities can be more powerful than test execution in defect prevention and timely detection. We also understand that an accurate interpretation of the situation when "all tests are running successfully" requires a clear understanding of the test design.

The lifecycle model for testing that has emerged borrows heavily from the methodology we've grown accustomed to for software. Considering that a test set is made up of *data* and *procedures* (which are often implemented as executable test programs), it should not come as a surprise that what it takes to build good software is also what it takes to build good testware!

Elements of STEP

STEP draws from the established foundation of software methodologies to provide a process model for software testing. The methodology consists of specified tasks (individual actions); work products (documentation and implemented tests); and roles (defined responsibilities associated with groups of tasks), as shown in Figure 1-3, packaged into a system with proven effectiveness for consistently achieving quality software.

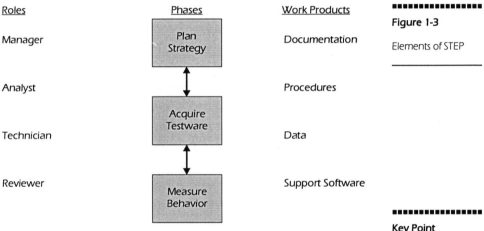

■■■■■■■■■■■■■■■■■
Figure 1-3

Elements of STEP

The STEP methodology is not tool dependent and does not assume any particular test organization or staffing (such as independent test groups). It does assume a development (not a research) effort, where the requirements information for the product and the technical design information are comprehensible and available for use as inputs to testing. Even if the requirements and design are not specified, much of the STEP methodology can still be used and can, in fact, facilitate the analysis and specification of software requirements and design.

■■■■■■■■■■■■■■■■■
Key Point

Even if the requirements and design are not specified, much of the STEP methodology can still be used and can, in fact, facilitate the analysis and specification of requirements and design.

STEP Architecture

Figure 1-4 shows how STEP assumes that the total testing job is divided into levels during planning. A level represents a particular testing environment (e.g., unit testing usually refers to the level associated with program testing in a programmer's personal development library). Simple projects, such as minor enhancements, may consist of just one or two levels of testing (e.g., unit and acceptance). Complex projects, such as a new product development, may have more levels (e.g., unit, function, subsystem, system, acceptance, alpha, beta, etc.).

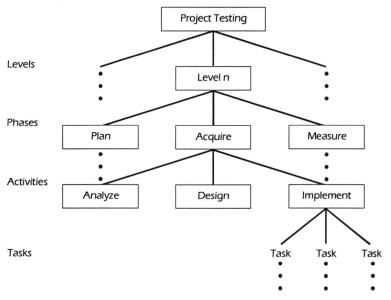

Figure 1-4

Activity Timing at
Each Level of Test

STEP provides a model that can be used as a starting point in establishing a detailed test plan. All of the components of the model are intended to be tailored and revised, or extended to fit each particular test situation.

The three major phases in STEP that are employed at every level include: planning the strategy (selecting strategy and specifying levels and approach), acquiring the testware (specifying detailed test objectives, designing and implementing test sets), and measuring the behavior (executing the tests and evaluating the software and the process). The phases are further broken down into eight major activities, as shown in Table 1-3.

Table 1-3 STEP Activities & Their Locations in This Book

Step 1	**Plan the Strategy**	Covered In
P1	Establish the master test plan.	Chapters 2 and 3
P2	Develop the detailed test plans.	Chapter 4
Step 2	**Acquire the Testware**	
A1	Inventory the test objectives (requirements-based, design-based, and implementation-based).	Chapter 5
A2	Design the tests (architecture and environment, requirements-based, design-based, and implementation-based).	Chapter 5
A3	Implement the plans and designs.	Chapter 6
Step 3	**Measure the Behavior**	
M1	Execute the tests.	Chapter 7
M2	Check the adequacy of the test set.	Chapter 7
M3	Evaluate the software and testing process.	Chapter 11

NOTE: Chapters 8, 9, and 10 cover the testing organization, the software tester, and the test manager, respectively. Chapter 12 provides a review of critical testing processes.

Timing of STEP Activities

STEP specifies when the testing activities and tasks are to be performed, as well as what the tasks should be and their sequence, as shown in Figure 1-5. The timing emphasis is based on getting most of the test design work completed before the detailed design of the software. The trigger for beginning the test design work is an external, functional, or black box specification of the software component to be tested. For higher test levels (e.g., acceptance or system), the external specification is equivalent to the system requirements document. As soon as that document is available, work can (and should) begin on the design of the requirements-based tests.

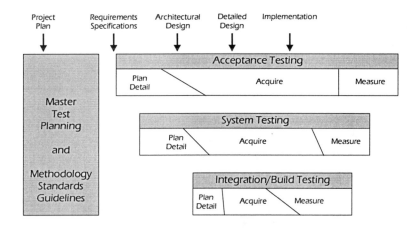

The test design process continues as the software is being designed and additional tests based on the detailed design of the software are identified and added to the requirements-based tests. As the software design process proceeds, detailed design documents are produced for the various software components and modules comprising the system. These, in turn, serve as functional specifications for the component or module, and thus may be used to trigger the development of requirements-based tests at the component or module level. As the software project moves to the coding stage, a third increment of tests is designed based on the code and implementation details.

■■■■■■■■■■■■■■■■■■

Key Point

The goal at each level is to complete the bulk of the test design work as soon as possible.

Test inventory and design activities at the various levels overlap. The goal at each level is to complete the bulk of the test design work as soon as possible. This helps to ensure that the requirements are "testable" and well thought out and that defects are discovered early in the process. This strategy supports an effective software review and inspection program.

Measurement phase activities are conducted by level. Units are executed first, then modules or functions are integrated and system and acceptance execution is performed. The sequential execution from small pieces to big pieces is a physical constraint that we must follow. A major contribution of the methodology is in pointing out that the planning and acquisition phases are not so constrained; and furthermore, it's in our interest to reverse the order and begin to develop the high-level test sets first – even though we use them last!

The timing within a given test level is shown in Figure 1-6 and follows our natural expectation. Plans and objectives come first, then test design, then implementation, then finally execution and evaluation. Overlap of activities is possible.

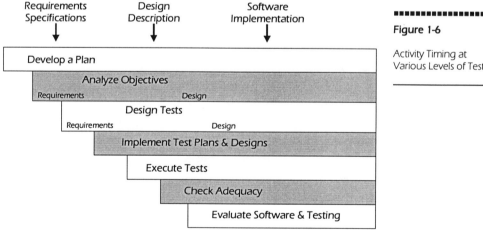

Figure 1-6

Activity Timing at Various Levels of Test

Work Products of STEP

Another aspect of the STEP process model is the set of work products produced in each phase and activity. STEP uses the word "testware" to refer to the major testing products such as test plans and test specification documents and the implemented test procedures, test cases, and test data files. The word "testware" is intentionally analogous to software and, as suggested by Figure 1-7, is intended to reflect a parallel development process. As the software is designed, specified, and built, the testware is also designed, specified, and built.

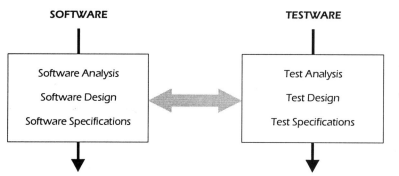

SOFTWARE

- Software Analysis
- Software Design
- Software Specifications

TESTWARE

- Test Analysis
- Test Design
- Test Specifications

Figure 1-7

Parallel, Mutually Supportive Development

These two broad classes of work products support each other. Testware development, by relying on software work products, supports the prevention and detection of software faults. Software development, by reviewing testware work products, supports the prevention and detection of testware faults.

STEP uses IEEE standard document templates as a recommended guideline for document structure and content. Figure 1-8 lists the documents that are included in this book.

IEEE Std. 829-1998 Standard for Software Test Documentation
Template for Test Documents

Contents

1. Test Plan
   Used for the master test plan and level-specific test plans.

2. Test Design Specification
   Used at each test level to specify the test set architecture and coverage traces.

3. Test Case Specification
   Used as needed to describe test cases or automated scripts.

4. Test Procedure Specification
   Used to specify the steps for executing a set of test cases.

5. Test Log
   Used as needed to record the execution of test procedures.

6. Test Incident Report
   Used to describe anomalies that occur during testing or in production. These anomalies may be in the requirements, design, code, documentation, or the test cases themselves. Incidents may later be classified as defects or enhancements.

7. Test Summary Report
   Used to report completion of testing at a level or a major test objective within a level.

■■■■■■■■■■■■■■■■■
Figure 1-8

Template for Test Documents from IEEE Std. 829-1998.

The templates for many IEEE documents are presented in this book, but we recommend that you purchase the complete guidelines from the IEEE at:

www.ieee.org

Implementations are the actual test procedures to be executed along with their supporting test data and test files or test environments and any supporting test code that is required.

Roles and Responsibilities in STEP

Roles and responsibilities for various testing activities are defined by STEP. The four major roles of manager, analyst, technician, and reviewer are listed in Table 1-4.

Table 1-4   Roles and Responsibilities

Role	Description of Responsibilities
Manager	Communicate, plan, and coordinate.
Analyst	Plan, inventory, design, and evaluate.
Technician	Implement, execute, and check.
Reviewer	Examine and evaluate.

These roles are analogous to their counterpart roles in software development. The test manager is responsible for providing overall test direction and coordination, and communicating key information to all interested parties. The test analyst is responsible for detailed planning, inventorying of test objectives and coverage areas, test designs and specifications, and test review and evaluation. The test technician is responsible for implementation of test procedures and test sets according to the designs provided by the analyst, for test execution and checking of results for termination criteria, and for test logging and problem reporting. The test reviewer provides review and oversight over all steps and work products in the process.

The STEP methodology does not require that these roles be filled by different individuals. On small projects, it's possible that one person may wear all four hats: manager, analyst, technician, and reviewer. On larger projects and as a test specialty becomes more refined in an organization, the roles will tend to be assigned to different individuals and test specialty career paths will develop.

■■■■■■■■■■■■■■■■
Key Point

On smaller projects, it's possible that one person may wear all four hats: manager, analyst, technician, and reviewer.

Summary of STEP

STEP has been introduced through Software Quality Engineering's (SQE) Systematic Software Testing classes to hundreds of organizations. It's a proven methodology offering significant potential for improving software quality in most companies.

Key differences between STEP and prevalent industry practices are highlighted in Table 1-5. First is the overall goal of the testing activity. STEP is prevention oriented, with a primary focus on finding requirements and design defects through early development of test designs. This results in the second major difference of when major testing activities are begun (e.g., planning timing and activity timing). In STEP, test planning begins during software requirements definition, and testware design occurs in parallel with software design and before coding. Prevalent practice is for planning to begin in parallel with coding and test development to be done after coding.

■■■■■■■■■■■■■■■■
Key Point

In STEP, test planning begins during software requirements definition and testware design occurs in parallel with software design and before coding.

Another major difference between STEP and prevalent industry practices is the creation of a group of test cases with known coverage (i.e., mapping test cases to inventories of requirements, design, and code). Finally, using the IEEE documents provides full documentation (i.e., visibility) of testing activities.

Table 1-5   Major Differences Between STEP and Industry Practice

Methodology	Focus	Planning Timing	Acquisition Timing	Coverage	Visibility
STEP	Prevention & Risk Management	Begins During Requirements Definition	Begins During Requirements Definition	Known (Relative to Inventories)	Fully Documented & Evaluated
Prevalent Industry Practice	Detection & Demonstration	Begins After Software Design	Begins After Software Design (or Code)	Largely Unknown	Largely Undocumented with Little or No Evaluation

STEP also requires careful and systematic development of requirements and design-based coverage inventories and for the resulting test designs to be calibrated to these inventories. The result is that in STEP, the test coverage is known and measured (at least with respect to the listed inventories). Prevalent practice largely ignores the issue of coverage measurement and often results in ad hoc or unknown coverage.

A final major difference lies in the visibility of the full testing process. Every activity in STEP leads to visible work products. From plans, to inventories, to test designs, to test specs, to test sets, to test reports, the process is visible and controlled. Industry practice provides much less visibility, with little or no systematic evaluation of intermediate products.

These differences are significant and not necessarily easy to put into practice. However, the benefits are equally significant and well worth the difficulty and investment.

■■■■■■■■■■■■■■■■■
Key Point

Calibration is the term used to describe the measurement of coverage of test cases against an inventory of requirements and design attributes.

Chapter 2 –
Risk Analysis

"If you do not actively attack risks, they will actively attack you."

— Tom Gilb

There's no way we can ever guarantee that a software system will be "perfect," because failures may come from many unexpected directions. A *latent* defect in a system that has run well for many years may cause the system to fail unexpectedly. Hardware may fail or defects may remain undetected for years, then suddenly become *unmasked*. These effects may be amplified as changes to interfaces and protocols in one part of the system begin to interfere with legacy software in another part. Multiplying numbers of users may stress the system, or changes in the business model may cause them to use it in ways that were never originally foreseen. A changing operating environment may also pose risks that can undermine a sound software design, creating implementation and operational problems.

In his article "Chaos Into Success," Jim Johnson reported that only 26% of projects met the criteria for success – completed on time, on budget, and with all of the features and functions originally specified. Unfortunately, the disaster stories behind these statistics are often more difficult to digest than the numbers themselves. In an article in *IEEE Computer* magazine, Nancy Leveson and Clark Turner reported that a computerized radiation therapy machine called Therac-25 caused six known incidents of accidental overdose between June 1985 and January 1987, which resulted in deaths and serious injuries. According to *Space Events Diary*, corrupted software may have been the cause of the failure of the upper stage on a Titan 4B spacecraft on April 30, 1999. The malfunction caused the upper stage of the rocket to misfire and place its payload (a communications satellite) in the wrong orbit. A review of newspapers, magazines, and Web sites will show that these are only a few of the documented incidents caused by defective software. Thousands of undocumented incidents occur every day and affect nearly every aspect of our lives.

■■■■■■■■■■■■■■■
Key Point

A *latent* defect is an existing defect that has not yet caused a failure because the exact set of conditions has never been met.

A *masked* defect is an existing defect that hasn't yet caused a failure, because another defect has prevented that part of the code from being executed.

Most software testing managers and engineers realize that it's impossible to test everything in even the most trivial of systems. The features and attributes of a simple application may result in millions of permutations that could potentially be developed into test cases. Obviously, it's not possible to create millions of test cases; and even if a large number of test cases are created, they generally still represent only a tiny fraction of the possible combinations. Even if you had created thousands of test cases, and through a concerted effort doubled that number, millions of other combinations may still exist and your "doubled" test set would still represent only a tiny fraction of the potential combinations, as illustrated in Figure 2-1. In most cases, "what" you test in a system is much more important than "how much" you test.

■■■■■■■■■■■■■■■■■■
Key Point

A GUI with 10 fields that can be entered in any order results in a set of 3,628,800 combinations that could potentially be tested.

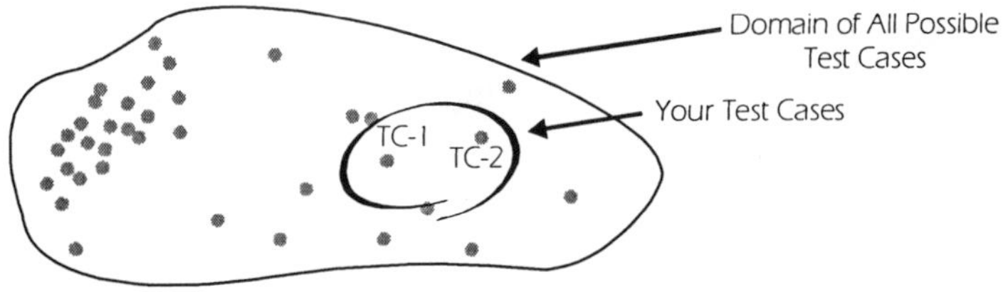

Domain of All Possible Test Cases

Your Test Cases

TC-1
TC-2

Figure 2-1

Domain of All Possible Test Cases (TC) in a Software System

Tight time schedules and shortages of trained testers serve to exacerbate this problem even further. In many companies, the testers begin work on whatever components or parts of the system they encounter first, or perhaps they work on those parts that they're most familiar with. Unfortunately, both of these approaches typically result in the eventual delivery of a system in which some of the most critical components are untested, inadequately tested, or at the very least, tested later in the lifecycle. Even if problems are found later in the lifecycle, there may be inadequate time to fix them, thereby adding to the risk of the software. Changing priorities, feature creep, and loss of resources can also reduce the ability of the test team to perform a reasonably comprehensive test.

What Is Risk?

Webster's dictionary defines risk as *"the chance of injury, damage, or loss; a dangerous chance; a hazard."*   In other words, risk involves the probability or likelihood of an event occurring and the negative consequences or impact of that event. For the purposes of this book, we will use the words likelihood and impact as the two components of risk.

Everyone subconsciously performs risk analysis hundreds of times a day.   If you were living or working in downtown Manhattan and were late for a meeting, for example, you might decide to take a risk and dash across a busy street. Consciously, you might not even think much about it, but subconsciously, you're probably thinking, "What is the likelihood that I'll be hit by a yellow cab and if I'm hit by the cab, what is the impact (no pun intended)?" Obviously, the impact could be catastrophic to you personally, so you would only dart across the street if you were reasonably confident that you wouldn't be hit by a cab. This is just one example of how risk analysis impacts our daily lives. The good news is that all of these daily decisions that you've made have helped prepare you, as a tester, for analyzing software risk. Still, having said this and after visiting hundreds of companies as management consultants over the years, we've found that very few companies make any attempt at conducting even a semi-formal software risk analysis. A risk analysis is one of the most important activities that can occur on any software development project, especially if schedules are tight and/or resources are scarce.

There is an entire body of information about and many professionals who specialize in *risk management*, which is composed of risk analysis, avoidance, and control. However, the

For more information on Risk Management, refer to the following books:

Software Risk Management by Barry W. Boehm

Software Engineering Risk Analysis by Robert Charette

Risk Management for Software Projects by Down, Coleman, and Absolon

IEEE Tutorial on Software Risk Management by Barry Boehm

A Manager's Guide to Software Engineering by Roger S. Pressman

Key Point

Risk Management is the process of controlling risk and monitoring the effectiveness of the control mechanisms.

Risk Analysis is the process of identifying, estimating, and evaluating risk.

primary focus of this chapter is on *risk analysis* and, to a lesser degree, risk avoidance and control. Even though the risk analysis techniques explained in this book are focused on software testing, they can also be useful tools in other areas of the development project, especially if no other risk analysis has been undertaken. If another group, such as developers or users, has already conducted a risk analysis, you may be able to use their results to help plan and prioritize your tests.

IEEE Standard for Software Test Documentation (IEEE Std. 829-1998) identifies a section in the test plan template called *Risks and Contingencies*. We've taken this a step further by separating risk analysis into two key activities: *software risk analysis* and the analysis of *planning risks and contingencies*.

■■■■■■■■■■■■■■■■■
Key Point

Risk Analysis can be separated into two key activities:

- software risk analysis
- analysis of planning risks and contingencies

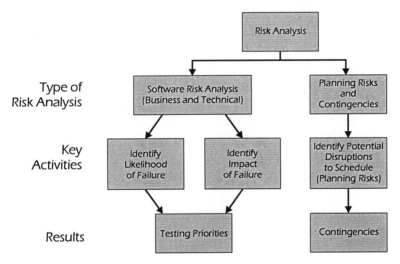

■■■■■■■■■■■■■■■■■
Figure 2-2

Risk Analysis Activities

This separation of activities provides a clear distinction between the risk associated with the failure of a feature or attribute of the system and the risk associated with the implementation of the test plan.

Software Risk Analysis

The purpose of a software risk analysis is to determine what to test, the testing priority, and the depth of testing. In some cases, it may also include determining what *not* to test. A risk analysis can help testers identify high-risk applications that should be tested more thoroughly, and potentially error-prone components within specific applications that should be tested more rigorously than other components. The results of the risk analysis can be used during the test planning phase to determine the testing priorities for the software under test.

■■■■■■■■■■■■■■■■■
Key Point

The purpose of a *software risk analysis* is to determine what to test, the testing priority, and the depth of testing.

Who Should Do the Analysis?

You might argue that it would be logical to have the users or customers perform a software risk analysis – and you would be right. Or, you might argue that if the users don't do the risk analysis, the developers should do it – and you would be right again. Developers who are responsible for software maintenance, for example, can derive great benefits from doing a risk analysis. So why did we include this topic in a software testing book? Because users and developers rarely perform a risk analysis or, at least, fail to do one in sufficient detail to help the tester. So even if you think it's not your job, you can't do your job well if a risk analysis isn't done first.

Ideally, the risk analysis should be done by a team of experts from various groups within the organization. Likely candidates may include developers, testers, users, customers, marketers, and other interested, willing, and able contributors.

■■■■■■■■■■■■■■■■■
Key Point

Ideally, the risk analysis should be done by an interdisciplinary team of experts.

When Should It Be Done?

A risk analysis should be done as early as possible in the software lifecycle. A first cut at a risk analysis can usually be done as soon as the high-level requirements are known. The risk analysis doesn't have to be completely re-done for every release, but should be revisited based on the changes that are being implemented. Also, keep in mind that the results of the analysis may have to be reviewed occasionally during the course of a project since the requirements, resources, and other factors may change.

How Should It Be Done?

We have outlined the ten-step process (illustrated in Figure 2-3) that we use for conducting a software risk analysis. Depending on the structure of your organization, you may have encountered one or more variations of this process. Some organizations may combine several steps into one, while others may include additional steps. However, the overall objective remains the same – to determine what to test, the testing priority, and the depth of testing.

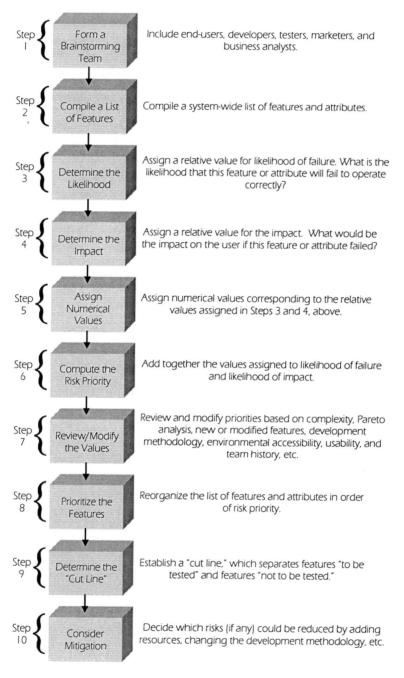

Step 1 — Form a Brainstorming Team — Include end-users, developers, testers, marketers, and business analysts.

Step 2 — Compile a List of Features — Compile a system-wide list of features and attributes.

Step 3 — Determine the Likelihood — Assign a relative value for likelihood of failure. What is the likelihood that this feature or attribute will fail to operate correctly?

Step 4 — Determine the Impact — Assign a relative value for the impact. What would be the impact on the user if this feature or attribute failed?

Step 5 — Assign Numerical Values — Assign numerical values corresponding to the relative values assigned in Steps 3 and 4, above.

Step 6 — Compute the Risk Priority — Add together the values assigned to likelihood of failure and likelihood of impact.

Step 7 — Review/Modify the Values — Review and modify priorities based on complexity, Pareto analysis, new or modified features, development methodology, environmental accessibility, usability, and team history, etc.

Step 8 — Prioritize the Features — Reorganize the list of features and attributes in order of risk priority.

Step 9 — Determine the "Cut Line" — Establish a "cut line," which separates features "to be tested" and features "not to be tested."

Step 10 — Consider Mitigation — Decide which risks (if any) could be reduced by adding resources, changing the development methodology, etc.

Figure 2-3

Software Risk Analysis Process Overview

NOTE

Each of these steps will be explained in detail on the following pages.

Step 1 – Form a Brainstorming Team

The first step in performing a risk analysis is to form a brainstorming team. Typically, you should include users (or pseudo-users such as business analysts), developers, testers, marketers, customer service representatives, support personnel, and anyone else that has knowledge of the business and/or product, and is willing and able to participate. Too many teams fail because not enough or the wrong people participate.

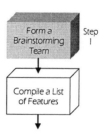

In their excellent book *Exploring Requirements: Quality Before Design*, Donald Gause and Gerald Weinberg lay out guidelines for conducting a brainstorming session. We've only included an outline of their suggestions here. For a more complete description, we recommend you obtain a copy of their book.

The purpose of Part One of a brainstorm session is to increase the number of ideas that the group generates. As a general rule of thumb:

- Do not allow criticism or debate.
- Let your imagination soar.
- Shoot for quantity.
- Mutate and combine ideas.

The purpose of Part Two of the brainstorming session is to reduce the list of ideas to a workable size. As a general rule of thumb, the methods for doing this include:

- Voting with campaign speeches
- Blending ideas
- Applying criteria
- Using scoring or ranking systems

The software risk analysis process that we've outlined will take care of Part Two of Gause and Weinberg's guidelines, but we've included them here in case you want to apply brainstorming techniques elsewhere (e.g., inventories: refer to Chapter 5).

Step 2 – Compile a List of Features

The brainstorming team should gather any available documentation such as requirements specifications (if they exist), functional specifications, change requests, defect reports, design documents, etc. Once these documents have been collected, the team should compile an inventory of features (initially at a high level), attributes, or business functions for the entire system. Later, as time allows, the list can be made more complete and detailed. If a given development effort or release is being done on only a subset of the system or on a sub-system, the analysis can be focused just on that area. However, in addition to the included features, all interfaces should be identified and listed because they may also need to be tested.

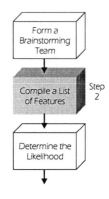

In our classes, we often use an Automated Teller Machine (ATM) as an example for demonstrating how a risk analysis works, since almost everyone is familiar with ATMs. An ATM application has a variety of features. Some of the features that our students typically identify include withdraw cash, deposit cash, check account balance, transfer funds, purchase stamps, and make a loan payment. In most cases, global attributes are also identified and considered in the risk analysis. Some of these global attributes include accessibility, availability, compatibility, maintainability, performance, reliability, scalability, security, and usability, which are applicable to most systems.

■■■■■■■■■■■■■■■■■
Key Point

Examples of attributes to consider may include:

- accessibility
- availability
- compatibility
- maintainability
- performance
- reliability
- scalability
- security
- usability

Step 3 – Determine the Likelihood

The next step in the risk analysis process is to assign an indicator for the relative likelihood of failure. We typically assign H for a relatively high likelihood of failure, M for medium, and L for low. When the brainstorming team assigns a value of H, M, or L for each feature, they should be answering the question, "Based on our current knowledge of the system, what is the likelihood that this feature or attribute will fail or fail to operate correctly?" Usually, the likelihood indicators are caused by systemic characteristics (e.g., complexity, number of interfaces, etc.) of the system, which makes developers and other technically oriented members of the team useful during this part of the risk analysis. For example, most students quickly assign a likelihood value of H for the *withdraw cash* feature. When asked why, they invariably point out that in order to withdraw cash, the system must go through various software interfaces, software/hardware interfaces, and human activities (load the cash). Other values typically identified for the likelihood of failure of selected ATM features and attributes are listed in Table 2-1.

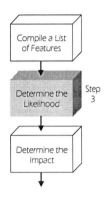

Key Point

Based on our current knowledge of the system, what is the likelihood that this feature or attribute will fail or fail to operate correctly?

Table 2-1   Likelihood of Failure for ATM Features/Attributes

| ATM Software | | Likelihood |
Features	Attributes	
Withdraw cash		High
Deposit cash		Medium
Check account balance		Low
Transfer funds		Medium
Purchase stamps		High
Make a loan payment		Low
	Usability	Medium
	Performance	Low
	Security	Medium

It's very important that the brainstorming team begin by assigning an initial value for the (relative) likelihood of a failure for each feature or attribute. Even though some team members may not agree on the initial value, it's important to get something committed to paper as soon as possible to stimulate the thought process. It's not important for the team to be precise in their rankings or in total agreement at this point in the risk analysis process. In fact, the entire process up to this point is fairly subjective, based on the experience and knowledge level of each of the team members.

Suppose that four members of your team think that a feature has a *high* likelihood of failure, one thinks it's *medium*, and one thinks it's *low*. You should assign a likelihood of *high* or *medium* and move on. It's critical that the team doesn't become bogged down early in the process. Later they'll discover that they're not trying to prioritize every feature 1 through *n*, but are simply trying to put each feature into a few "buckets" or broad categories. Later, if time allows, the team can go back and modify the first likelihood analysis by using one or more of the likelihood indicators outlined in Step 7.

Step 4 – Determine the Impact

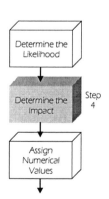

Once again the brainstorming team should use the same high, medium, and low rating system that they used for the likelihood of failure. Here, the team should ask themselves the question, "What would be the impact on the user if this feature or attribute failed to operate correctly?" Our students typically assign a value of H for *withdraw cash*, since most users of ATMs would consider the apparatus worthless without this feature. The impact of failure for other features and attributes in our ATM example is highlighted in Table 2-2. Although you may be tempted to also consider the impact of a failed function on the development of the rest of the system (i.e., the critical path) at this point, you should resist doing this as part of the software risk analysis. You should focus only on the features and attributes that directly impact the user, not necessarily the testing effort. Concerns regarding the impact on the testing schedule will be addressed in a later section of this chapter, *Planning Risks and Contingencies*.

■■■■■■■■■■■■■■■■■

Key Point

What would be the impact on the user if this feature or attribute failed to operate correctly?

Table 2-2   Impact of Failure for ATM Features/Attributes

ATM Software		Likelihood	Impact	
Features	Attributes			
Withdraw cash		High	High	
Deposit cash		Medium	High	
Check account balance		Low	Medium	
Transfer funds		Medium	Medium	
Purchase stamps		High	Low	
Make a loan payment		Low	Medium	
	Usability	Medium	High	
	Performance	Low	Medium	
	Security	Medium	High	

The users are particularly important for this part of the risk analysis because the impact is usually driven by business issues rather than by the systemic nature of the system. One word of caution: many users will insist that every feature has a high failure impact. This is especially true if the system is large enough that you need several users who each possess different areas of expertise. Obviously, it doesn't help in prioritizing risks if virtually every feature is ranked the same (i.e., high). If you experience this phenomenon, you might want to limit each user to assigning a specific number of Hs, Ms, and Ls.

■■■■■■■■■■■■■■■■■

Key Point

The users are particularly important in assigning values for impact, since the impact is usually driven by business issues rather than by the systemic nature of the system.

Testers who have worked in the industry for a substantial amount of time are often very good at determining the impact of failures. In fact, we have found that at many companies, experienced testers have the broadest knowledge of how the systems relate to the business. Especially in larger systems, many users may only be experts in one particular area of functionality, while experienced testers often have a much broader view. It is this broad view that is most useful in determining the relative impact of failure.

Step 5 – Assign Numerical Values

In this step of the risk analysis, the brainstorming team should assign numerical values for H, M, and L for both likelihood and impact. While these values can be any sequence of descending numbers, for the sake of simplicity, we usually assign a value of 3 for H, 2 for M, and 1 for L. Some people like to get a greater "spread" by assigning 10 for H, 3 for M, and 1 for L, or various other schemes. Weighting scales will vary from organization to organization depending on how they perceive the relative risk. Once a scale has been selected, you must use that same scale throughout the entire risk analysis.

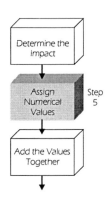

Key Point

If your system is *safety-critical*, it's important that those features that can cause death or loss of limb are always assigned a high priority for test even if the overall risk was low due to an exceptionally low likelihood of failure.

If your system is *safety-critical* (i.e., people's lives may be endangered by the malfunction of the system), it's important that those features that can cause death or loss of limb are always assigned a high priority. You can accomplish this in a variety of ways such as "flagging" those safety-critical features or by assigning a special high value to their impact. Suppose, for example, that you were working on a nuclear control system and there was a function called the "nuclear shut-off switch." In reality, this switch probably doesn't exist, but hopefully you get the idea that this would be a very risky function indeed! You would always want to ensure that this function was given a high priority even if the overall risk was low due to an exceptionally low likelihood of failure.

Step 6 – Compute the Risk Priority

Next, the values assigned to the likelihood of failure and the impact of failure should be added together. If a value of 3 is used for H, 2 for M, and 1 for L, then five risk priority levels are possible (i.e., 6, 5, 4, 3, 2) as illustrated in Figure 2-4. The overall risk priority is a relative value for the potential impact of failure of a feature or attribute of the software weighted by the likelihood of it failing.

Assign
Numerical
Values

Compute the
Priority

Step
6

Review/Modify
the Values

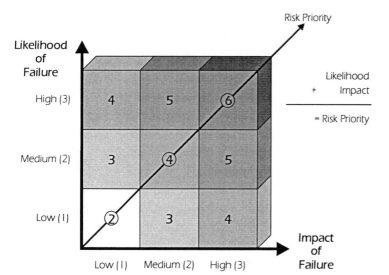

Likelihood
+   Impact

= Risk Priority

■■■■■■■■■■■■■■■■■■

Figure 2-4

Risk Priority

Notice that the feature *withdraw cash*, which has a relatively high likelihood of failure (value 3) and a relatively high impact of failure (value 3), has a risk priority of 6 (i.e., 3+3=6) in Table 2-3. The *deposit cash* feature has a priority of 5, and so forth. This isn't the only possible method for determining risk priority, however. Even though we prefer to add the values for likelihood of failure and impact of failure together, some organizations choose to multiply these values together, which has the effect of amplifying the risky areas.

Table 2-3   Summed Priorities for ATM Features/Attributes

ATM Software		Likelihood	Impact	Priority	
Features	**Attributes**				
Withdraw cash		High	High	6	
Deposit cash		Medium	High	5	
Check account balance		Low	Medium	3	
Transfer funds		Medium	Medium	4	
Purchase stamps		High	Low	4	
Make a loan payment		Low	Medium	3	
	Usability	Medium	High	5	
	Performance	Low	Medium	3	
	Security	Medium	High	5	

Step 7 – Review/Modify the Values

In Step 3 of the risk analysis process, a value was assigned to the likelihood of failure for each feature or attribute based upon the experience and perception of the brainstorming team. After the team has initially reached a consensus on the likelihood of failure for each feature or attribute based upon their brainstorming session, it's possible that these values may be modified based on additional information or analyses that may be available. Some examples of *likelihood-of-failure indicators* include team history, complexity, usability, new or modified features, features developed using new technology, defect history, and those features that are difficult to test due to constraints in the (test) environment.

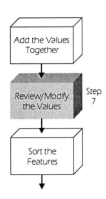

For example, most of us know that certain developers or development teams produce better code than others. If you have knowledge about the relative skill or experience of the teams developing the system, it might be prudent to plan to test the code of the less experienced teams more than the code developed

■■■■■■■■■■■■■■■■■
Team History

Experience of the developers can affect testing priorities.

by the more experienced teams. So, if a new team is assigned to work on the *check account balance* feature, for example, the brainstorming team may agree to raise the initial "low" likelihood rating of that feature (refer to Table 2-3) to medium or even high. This, of course, will eventually have the effect of raising the risk priority of that feature.

A word of caution is needed here. Although understanding the relative skill or effectiveness of various development teams would be useful in planning the testing priorities, collecting metrics about the relative effectiveness of developers or teams can bring unwanted political problems to the table and can ultimately undermine your relationship with the developers. Developers (like testers, or anyone else for that matter) don't like to feel that they are being measured. So your best intentions may do more harm than good. Since we have no knowledge of the culture of your organization, we offer no advice here, but if you choose to collect metrics about individual or team efficiency, please proceed cautiously.

Another indicator of the likelihood of failure is the relative complexity of the components or features of the system. Tom McCabe, who has done a substantial amount of work on software complexity, has devised a metric known as cyclomatic complexity that is based on the number of decisions in a program. He, along with others, has shown that those parts of the system with high cyclomatic complexity are more prone to defects than those with a lower value. For our purposes, we would assign those features a higher likelihood of failure. Tools are available to assist in this analysis. Of course if the system has not yet been coded, complexity cannot be measured because there's nothing yet to measure.

Some organizations use the complexity measures as the sole input into the assignment of the likelihood value (probably because it's fairly simple to do). We recommend that you assign

■■■■■■■■■■■■■■■■■
Complexity

This is one of the most commonly used likelihood-of-failure indicators.

■■■■■■■■■■■■■■■■■
Key Point

Tom McCabe noted that modules with high cyclomatic complexity are harder to understand and have a higher probability of defects than modules with smaller values. He recommended limiting cyclomatic complexity to 10. Later, Victor Basili noted that modules with cyclomatic complexity exceeding 14 are more defect prone.

– From *Practical Software Metrics for Project Management and Process Improvement* by Robert B. Grady.

the initial value during the brainstorming session and use the complexity analysis as a way to modify these initial values.

Increasing the "user-friendliness" of a system (or part of a system) generally increases the complexity of the software and ultimately increases the likelihood of failure. This problem is amplified because it may also be difficult to replicate the end-user environment or even know who the end-user is. One of the problems with the statement "The user is always right" is defining "Who is the user?" Companies that make and sell commercial software dedicate a lot of resources, thought, and money to this issue. All users aren't the same and they have different needs. Some users want to have a powerful system devoid of annoying prompts such as "Do you really want to delete this file?" Other users are a little more timid and, after deleting their newly written version of *War and Peace*, would welcome a question that requires confirmation.

■■■■■■■■■■■■■■■■

Usability

Increasing the "user-friendliness" of a system can increase the complexity of the software.

Usability labs attempt to simulate these users' requirements and the conditions under which they'll be using a particular feature of the system. If you have a usability lab, it can be useful for determining those features that have a high likelihood of failure due to the user-friendliness of the system. Refer to *Chapter 4* for more information on usability labs.

Parts of the system that are new (e.g., enhancements) or those modules that have experienced changes are usually more prone to defects than those modules that remain unchanged. Ironically, features that have had just a one- or two-line code change often have a higher rate of error introduction per line changed than modules with more extensive changes (probably because they have less rigorous regression testing). You would have to analyze your own defects versus changed lines of code in order to determine if this is true on your software. A useful metric is the number of bugs introduced per fix or the number of bugs introduced per changed line of code, as shown in Figure 2-5.

■■■■■■■■■■■■■■■■

New or Modified Features

This is one of the most commonly used likelihood-of-failure indicators.

This is often used as a measure of the effectiveness of maintenance programming.

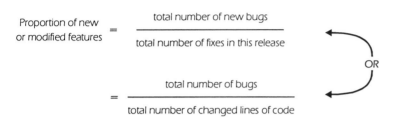

$$\text{Proportion of new or modified features} = \frac{\text{total number of new bugs}}{\text{total number of fixes in this release}}$$

OR

$$= \frac{\text{total number of bugs}}{\text{total number of changed lines of code}}$$

Figure 2-5

Formulae for Measuring the Ratio of Bugs to Fixes

Unfortunately, fixing problems may not necessarily make your software more reliable. On the contrary, serious new problems may arise. According to an article by Alan Joch, after changing three lines of code in a signaling program containing millions of lines of code in 1991, the local telephone systems in California and along the Eastern seaboard came to a halt. One company that we visited learned that they had introduced more bugs (and in some cases with greater severity) than they had fixed in a project for three releases in a row! It seems that more than just their software was broken.

In the course of conducting project reviews at many companies, we've frequently encountered the situation where certain functions or features were written (or rewritten) using some new or unfamiliar technology. For example, the organization may have gone from COBOL to C++, introduced object-oriented design techniques, developed a new database structure, or introduced a new development/testing methodology such as Extreme Programming. Obviously, as testers we are concerned about these changes and want to focus additional testing on those affected features (i.e., raise the likelihood value). This is especially true if the change was sudden or not supported by adequate training.

Key Point

Features developed using new technology, methods, techniques, or languages may require extra testing.

As an aside, we have also noted that many companies introduce multiple technology changes on the same project at the same time (often due to a new VP or CIO coming onboard). If this is the case, the tester should beware! Conventional wisdom for implementing change is to limit the number of new processes introduced on a given project. Refer to Chapter 11 for more information on process improvement.

In some systems, it's difficult to replicate the production environment in the laboratory, which can increase the software risk for certain features or attributes, or for the entire project. For example, it may be difficult to replicate the loads experienced on a Web application or have as many clients as would normally operate in a client/server environment. It's probably not feasible to launch the space shuttle just to test some new code. Similarly, if you were working on a weather prediction system, you couldn't just conjure up a hurricane to assist you in the testing effort.

Environmental Accessibility

The realism of the test environment may affect testing priorities.

Those features that are difficult to test due to environmental accessibility have a higher likelihood of failure and should receive a higher priority for testing to allow for the additional time that may be required to create simulators, conduct beta testing, etc. These features are also candidates for mitigation (refer to *Step 10* of the *Risk Analysis Process*).

Pareto Principle (80-20 Rule)

According to *Software Risk Management* by Barry W. Boehm, "Many software phenomena follow a Pareto distribution: 80% of the contribution comes from 20% of the contributors."

One example: 20% of the modules contribute 80% of the errors (not necessarily the same ones).

One type of analysis that we strongly recommend is the analysis of the trends and patterns of defects. If defects from previous releases or earlier levels of test and/or inspections are documented, they can be analyzed to determine particular areas of the system that have a "clumping" of bugs. Testers routinely call this type of analysis a "Pareto analysis," although it may not rigorously meet the definition assigned by statisticians. Anyone who has ever been a maintenance programmer knows that they are repeatedly called in to fix the same feature or module. In almost every case, areas of a system that have proven to be buggy in the past, will very likely continue to be buggy in the future and should be assigned a higher likelihood of failure. This clumping of bugs often occurs because certain parts of the system may be unusually complex, or written from a poor specification, etc.

There are many factors that affect the likelihood of failure such as usability, new features, complexity, etc., and many people would like to choose one of these as the sole method of determining likelihood of failure. However, the preferable approach is to allow the brainstorming team to assign these values as described in Step 4 and then use these other techniques, like complexity, to validate or modify their choices. For example, if your brainstorming team has found that the *withdraw cash* feature has a low (L) likelihood of failure, but the developer tells you that the underlying code has a very high complexity, you might want to change the "L" to an "M" or even an "H." Similarly, you can apply the same logic using Pareto analysis, inventory of changes, or one of the other likelihood-of-failure indicators.

Step 8 – Prioritize the Features

In this step of the risk analysis process, the brainstorming team should reorganize their list of features and attributes in order of risk priority. Table 2-4 shows the features and attributes of an ATM application in order of risk priority. Since the *withdraw cash* feature has the highest risk priority, it appears first in the list. Although the impact of releasing the software with *poor performance* is medium, the likelihood of failure is low. Consequently, *performance* is assigned a relatively low risk priority of 3 and therefore appears last in the list. Consider entering the risk data into a software tool that is "sort-friendly" to assist in the prioritization.

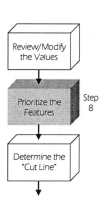

The sorted list of priorities provides a clear view of which risks need the most attention. As you may have noticed, one deficiency of this technique for prioritization is that it doesn't take into account the testing dependencies. For example, even though the *check account balance* value is assigned a relatively low priority, it will very likely be tested early on since the system must check the account value prior to withdrawing cash. We urge you to ignore these dependencies until after the first draft of the software risk analysis is complete.

■■■■■■■■■■■■■■■
Key Point

The sorted list of priorities provides a clear view of which risks need the most attention.

Table 2-4 Sorted Priorities for ATM Features/Attributes

ATM Software		Likelihood	Impact	Priority
Features	**Attributes**			
Withdraw cash		High	High	6
Deposit cash		Medium	High	5
	Usability	Medium	High	5
	Security	Medium	High	5
Transfer funds		Medium	Medium	4
Purchase stamps		High	Low	4
Make a loan payment		Low	Medium	3
Check account balance		Low	Medium	3
	Performance	Low	Medium	3

Step 9 – Determine the "Cut Line"

After the priorities have been sorted, a "cut line" may be established to indicate the line below which features will not be tested (if any) or tested less. In order to determine where the cut line should go, it's necessary to estimate the amount of testing that is possible with the available time and resources. Refer to *Chapter 7* for more information on estimating time and resources. The dotted line in Table 2-5 represents the cut line that the brainstorming team established for the ATM project. The *check account balance* feature and the *make a loan payment* feature will not be tested on this release due to the relatively low risk and limited availability of time and resources.

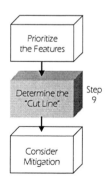

Table 2-5 "Cut Line" for ATM Features/Attributes

ATM Software Features	Attributes	Likelihood	Impact	Priority	
Withdraw cash		High	High	6	
Deposit cash		Medium	High	5	
	Usability	Medium	High	5	
Transfer funds		Medium	Medium	4	To Be Tested
Purchase stamps		High	Low	4	
✂	Security	Low	High	4	
Make a loan payment		Low	Medium	3	
Check account balance		Low	Medium	3	Not to Be Tested (or tested less)
	Performance	Low	Medium	3	

Of course, as time goes by and estimates are "honed," the cut line may have to be moved up or down (or the *amount* of testing of lower-risk features or attributes may be reduced). If the system is very risky and it's unacceptable to have features go untested, additional time and/or resources must be allocated. Wishful thinking doesn't work here. An important job of the test manager is to present the information and decide what can and can't be done with the resources that are available. The software risk analysis is a wonderful tool to use with upper management to gain buy-in for schedules, budgets, and allocation of resources.

Step 10 – Consider Mitigation

Some companies like to add a column to their software risk analysis called *mitigation*. If the *withdraw cash* feature is rated a 6 (i.e., high likelihood and high impact) the test or development group may decide to consider a way to lower or mitigate the risk. For example, the mitigation might be that all of the code and design associated with the *withdraw cash* feature will undergo

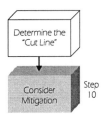

rigorous code and design inspections. Or, maybe a prototype of the *deposit cash* feature will be built early in order to allow users to provide early feedback on the usability of this feature. This may be accomplished with a "paper" prototype or by using a more formal prototype in a usability lab. Another mitigation might be to add an extra layer of test such as beta testing (refer to *Chapter 4*). Table 2-6 includes a column for mitigated priorities. Notice that only the *withdraw cash* feature, *deposit funds* feature, and *usability* attribute were mitigated for this particular project. Some projects may warrant the inclusion of a *mitigation* column, while others don't – the choice is yours and may vary depending on the project. Notice that the mitigation activities may require action by developers, users, testers, or others, which is another reason why the risk analysis team should include people from these groups. Whether implicitly or explicitly, you should somehow account for mitigation during the creation of your test plan.

■■■■■■■■■■■■■■■■■
Key Point

Risk mitigation helps reduce the likelihood of a failure, but does not affect the impact.

Table 2-6   Mitigated List of Priorities for ATM Features/Attributes

ATM Software		Likelihood	Impact	Priority	Mitigation
Features	**Attributes**				
Withdraw cash		High	High	6	Code inspection
Deposit cash		Medium	High	5	Early prototype
	Usability	Medium	High	5	Early user feedback
	Security	Medium	High	5	
Transfer funds		Medium	Medium	4	
Purchase stamps		High	Low	4	
Make a loan payment		Low	Medium	3	
Check account balance		Low	Medium	3	
	Performance	Low	Medium	3	

At this point, you should have completed the first draft of your software risk analysis. This means that you've already accomplished something that most test groups fail to do. The software risk analysis will have to be revisited occasionally in order to update it as changes in requirements, scope, design, schedule, and other factors occur. When you move to the next version of software, you can use the current risk analysis as the basis for the new analysis. Without a doubt, you'll find that on subsequent releases the risk will naturally be higher for those components undergoing change. Although this isn't a hard and fast rule, subsequent revisions to support new releases often require greater changes to the likelihood column than the impact column unless major functionality changes have been introduced.

Planning Risks and Contingencies

Now, let's go on the other side of risk management and take a look at planning risks, which are unscheduled events or late activities that occur which may jeopardize the testing schedule. The purpose of this risk analysis is to determine the best contingencies in the event that one of the planning risks occurs. This is important because the scope and nature of a project almost always change as the project progresses. Most test managers find that during the planning phases, the users and developers are much more likely to sit down and make rational decisions on what to do if one of the planning risks occurs. If the decision is made in "the heat of battle" near the end of the project, emotions and politics are much more likely to be the primary drivers of the decision-making process.

Most of us have taken part in projects where the schedule is at best ambitious and at worst impossible. Once an implementation date has been set, it's often considered sacred. Customers may have been promised a product on a certain date, management's credibility is on the line, corporate reputation is at stake, or competitors may be breathing down your neck. At the same

Key Point

Planning risks are unscheduled events or late activities that may jeopardize the testing schedule.

Some common planning risks include:

- Delivery dates
- Staff availability
- Budget
- Environmental options
- Tool inventory
- Acquisition schedule
- Participant buy-in
- Training needs
- Scope of testing
- Lack of requirements
- Risk assumptions
- Usage assumptions
- Resources
- Feature creep
- Poor quality s/w

time, as an organization, you may have stretched your resources to the limit. Planning risks are anything that adversely affects the planned testing effort. Perhaps the start of the project is slightly delayed, or a major software vendor releases a new version of the operating system that the application will run on. It's not our purpose here to address the many reasons why we so often find ourselves in this unenviable spot. Rather, we would like to talk about what can be done about it. Case Study 2-1 describes a common scenario in many organizations along with some possible contingencies.

The Deliverable Is the Date

Consider the following scenario. Your VP has promised the next release of your product on a certain date. The date seems very aggressive to you in light of the available resources and the need to release a high-quality product (after the last release failed spectacularly). Then, the unthinkable happens. Jane Doe takes a job with your competitor, leaving a huge gap in your company's knowledge base (or a key component is late, or the requirements change, or some other planning risk occurs). What was once an ambitious schedule now appears to be impossible. What are your choices or contingencies?

1. Alter the schedule – which marketing says can't be done...
2. Reduce the scope – but we promised our customers...
3. Reduce quality, which usually means reduce testing or allow more defects in the final product – but our last release failed!!!
4. Add resources (including overtime) – but there are none to add and everyone is already working around the clock...
5. Punt...

Unfortunately, all of the choices listed above seem bad and, all too often, management decides that they're all unacceptable. If management does not make proactive decisions during the planning stage, the technical staff will often end up making the choices by default. Initially, more resources may be added in the form of overtime. If this doesn't solve the problem, the team will begin to

■■■■■■■■■■■■■■■■■
Case Study 2-1

Suppose Jane Doe resigned and your ambitious schedule suddenly became impossible. What would you do?

take shortcuts -- eliminating a document here, a review there, or eliminating an entire set of tests. Of course, the quality suffers.

If the project is still in jeopardy, functionality that is not absolutely essential will be rescheduled for a later release or the date may be slipped. Eventually, the new target date may be met when a watered-down system of poor quality is delivered to the customer late, by a very frustrated development team. Sound familiar?

Identifying planning risks and contingencies helps you make intelligent, informed decisions. Almost every project team can identify the planning risks that cause concern: late requirements, test environment problems, late delivery of software, etc. Our goal is to decide in advance what to do if one of these planning risks comes true. In our opinion, the only possible contingencies that exist are:

- reduce the scope
- delay implementation
- add resources
- reduce quality processes

However, you may encounter many different "flavors" of these four contingencies, depending on your organization and the details of the project. For example, "add resources" might mean overtime for the prime staff or it could mean bringing in additional testers. Case Study 2-2 lists some examples of planning risks and contingencies.

Key Point

The major focus of the section *Planning Risks and Contingencies* in the IEEE Standard 829-1998 is on planning risks (as opposed to software risks).

Although not universally used, planning risks and contingencies are more commonly used than software risk analysis.

Sample Planning Risk

The user introduces a major requirements change late in the software lifecycle.

Sample Contingency #1

Ask the user group to contribute more users to the testing effort (i.e., add more resources).

Case Study 2-2

Sample Planning Risk and Contingencies

Sample Contingency #2

Decide not to implement a low-priority feature until a later release (e.g., reduce the scope).

Sample Contingency #3

Decide not to test (or at least to test less) some of the low-risk features identified in the course of the software risk analysis (i.e., reduce quality processes).

Sample Planning Risk

The size of the project keeps growing – this is a double whammy. Not only do testing resources need to grow because of the increased size of the project, but productivity rates for software development and testing typically decrease as the size of the project increases.

Sample Contingency #1

Add resources (e.g., outsource, add users, add developers, authorize overtime).

Sample Contingency #2

Reduce the scope of the project. Choose a strategy of incremental delivery to the customer.

Sample Contingency #3

Reduce testing of some of the lower-risk modules (i.e., reduce quality processes).

Sample Contingency #4

Delay implementation.

■■■■■■■■■■■■■■■■■

Case Study 2-3

Sample Planning Risk and Contingencies

As you can see, all of the contingencies in Case Studies 2-2 and 2-3 involve compromise. But without planning risks and contingencies, the developers and testers are forced to make these choices on the fly. The *software risk analysis* and the analysis of the *planning risks and contingencies* work together. Recall our Automated Teller Machine (ATM) example from the previous section. The risk analysis process helped us identify the software risks, which, in turn, helped us focus and prioritize our testing effort in order to reduce those risks.

The planning risks help us to do the "What if..." and develop contingencies. For example, what if Jane Doe really does leave and her departure causes the software to be delivered to the test group late? One of the contingencies was to reduce quality (this usually means less testing). If this contingency befalls us, we would probably want to go back to the software risk analysis and consider reducing the testing of the least critical components (i.e., moving the cut line up). Refer to *Step 9* of the *Software Risk Process* for information on the cut line.

It should be apparent at this point that planning risks, software risks, features/attributes to be tested, features/attributes not to be tested, and indeed the entire testing strategy are built around the concept of using risk to prioritize the testing effort.

Project Assumptions

Some project plans and even some test plans have a section called *Assumptions*. In many cases, these assumptions will become planning risks if they turn out to be false. Suppose, for example, management assumes that the very experienced Team X will be developing the *transfer funds* feature for your ATM software. If this feature is outsourced to another company with an unknown track record instead, the likelihood of failure may increase or decrease, depending on the skills of this outside resource. Consider the following as another example. If you assume there will be 10 testers, but in reality there are only 5 available, this is a planning risk even though it may have been originally recorded as an assumption.

While there are many different ways to perform a risk analysis, this chapter has identified two distinct types of risk analysis that have worked well for our clients, students, and colleagues over the years. Software risk analysis helps you decide what features and attributes should be tested and helps you assign priorities to these items. Planning risk analysis helps you decide what to do in the event that an unplanned problem arises. Effective risk analysis is a joint effort of developers, testers, subject-matter experts, marketers, and other willing and able participants. Unfortunately, in many companies, risk analysis is not done in any formal sense. After reading this chapter, we hope that you'll have a clear understanding of how to perform or improve risk analysis within your organization and understand its benefits to you and your organization.

■■■■■■■■■■■■■■■■
Key Point

Planning risk analysis helps you decide what to do in the event that an unplanned problem arises.

Chapter 3 – Master Test Planning

"Make no little plans; they have no magic to stir men's blood."

— Daniel Hudson Burnham

"Plans must be simple and flexible. Actually, they only form a datum plane from which you build as necessity directs or opportunity offers. They should be made by the people who are going to execute them."

— George S. Patton

Test planning is one of the keys to successful software testing, yet it's frequently omitted due to time constraints, lack of training, or cultural bias. A survey taken at a recent STAR conference showed that 81% of the companies participating in the survey completed test plans. That doesn't sound too bad, but our experience has shown that many of those 81% are calling the testing schedule the test plan, so the actual percentage is probably much less. Testing without a plan is analogous to developing software without a project plan and generally occurs for the same reason – pressure to begin coding (or in this case, testing) as soon as possible. Many organizations measure progress in development by modules completed or lines of code delivered, and in testing by the number of test cases run. While these can be valuable measures, they don't recognize planning as a worthwhile activity.

■■■■■■■■■■■■■■■■
Key Point

" Planning is the art and science of envisioning a desired future and laying out effective ways of bringing it about."

– Planning, MCDP5
U.S. Marine Corps

Levels (Stages) of Test Planning   ■ ■ ■ ■ ■

Test planning can and should occur at several levels or stages. The first plan to consider is the Master Test Plan (MTP), which can be a separate document or could be included as part of the project plan. The purpose of the MTP is to orchestrate testing at all levels. The IEEE Std. 829-1998 Standard for Software Test Documentation identifies the following levels of test: Unit, Integration, System, and Acceptance. Other organizations may use more or less than four levels and possibly use different names. Some other levels (or at least other names) that we frequently encounter include beta, alpha, customer acceptance, user acceptance, build, string, and development. In this book, we will use the four levels identified in the IEEE and illustrated in figure 3-1.

■■■■■■■■■■■■■■■■
Key Point

Test planning CAN'T be separated from project planning.

All important test planning issues are also important project planning issues.

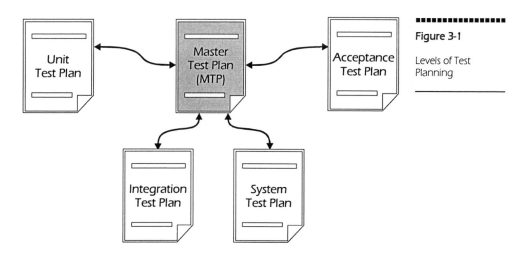

Figure 3-1

Levels of Test
Planning

The test manager should think of the Master Test Plan as one of his or her major communication channels with all project participants. Test planning is a process that ultimately leads to a document that allows all parties involved in the testing process to proactively decide what the important issues are in testing and how to best deal with these issues. The goal of test planning is not to create a long list of test cases, but rather to deal with the important issues of testing strategy, resource utilization, responsibilities, risks, and priorities.

Key Point

Test planning
SHOULD be
separated from test
design.

In test planning, even though the document is important, the process is ultimately more important than the document. Discussing issues of what and how to test early in the project lifecycle can save a lot of time, money, and disagreement later. Case Study 3-1 describes how one company derived a great benefit from their Master Test Plan, even though it was never actually used.

Key Point

*" We should think of
planning as a
learning process – as
mental preparation
which improves our
understanding of a
situation... Planning
is thinking before
doing."*

– Planning, MCDP5
U.S. Marine Corps

The "Best" Test Plan We Ever Wrote

*I once had a consulting assignment at a major American company where I was supposed to help them create their first ever Master Test Plan. Following up with the client a few months later, the project manager told me that the creation of the Master Test Plan had contributed significantly to the success of the project, but unfortunately they hadn't really followed the plan or kept it up to date. I replied, " Let me get this straight. You didn't use the plan, but you felt that it was a major contributor to your success. Please explain." The project manager told me that when they began to fall behind, they dispensed with much of the project documentation, including the test plan (sound familiar?). But because they created the plan early in the project lifecycle, many testing issues were raised that normally weren't considered until it was too late to take action. The planning process also heightened the awareness of the importance of testing to all of the project participants. Now, I believe that keeping test plans up to date is important, so that's not the purpose of telling you this story. Rather, I'm trying to stress the importance of the testing **process**, not just the document.*

— Rick Craig

■■■■■■■■■■■■■■■■
Case Study 3-1

If the Master Test Plan was so great, why didn't they use it?

───────────────

■■■■■■■■■■■■■■■■
Key Point

Ike said it best: "The plan is nothing, the planning is everything."

– Dwight D. Eisenhower

───────────────

In addition to the Master Test Plan, it is often necessary to create detailed or level-specific test plans. On a larger or more complex project, it's often worthwhile to create an Acceptance Test Plan, System Test Plan, Integration Test Plan, Unit Test Plan, and other test plans, depending on the scope of your project. Smaller projects, that is, projects with smaller scope, number of participants, and organizations, may find that they only need one test plan, which will cover all levels of test. Deciding the number and scope of test plans required should be one of the first strategy decisions made in test planning. As the complexity of a testing activity increases, the criticality of having a good Master Test Plan increases exponentially, as illustrated in Figure 3-2.

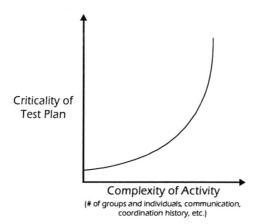

■■■■■■■■■■■■■■■■■■
Figure 3-2

Importance of Test
Planning

Detailed level planning is explained in Chapter 4 – *Detailed Test Planning*. For the most part, the major considerations for detailed test plans are the same as those for the master test plan, but differ in scope and level of detail. In fact, it's normally desirable to use the same basic template for the detailed test plans that you use for the master test plan.

Audience Analysis   ■■■■■

The first question you must ask yourself when creating a test plan is, "Who is my audience?" The audience for a Unit Test Plan is quite different than the audience for an Acceptance Test Plan or a Master Test Plan, so the wording, use of acronyms, technical terms, and jargon should be adjusted accordingly. Also keep in mind that various audiences have different tolerances for what they will and will not read. Executives, for example, may not be willing to read an entire Master Test Plan if it's 50 pages long, so you might have to include an executive summary. In fact, you may want to avoid making the test plan prohibitively long or no one will read (and use) it. If your test plan is too long, it may be necessary to create a number of plans of reduced scope built around subsystems or functionality. Sometimes, the size of your test plans can be managed and limited by the judicious use of references. If you decide to use references, though, you should carefully consider the implications. Most people don't really want to gather a stack of documents just so they can read a single test plan.

Since we can't predict how long a document your audience is willing to read, we can't say that your test plan should not exceed any particular length such as 5, 10, 15, or 100 pages. Instead, we recommend that you survey the potential audience of your test plan to determine how long a document they are willing to read and use. Some military organizations, for example, may be accustomed to using documents of 100 pages or more, while members of a small entrepreneurial firm may only tolerate 10 pages or less.

Activity Timing ■■■■■

Test planning should be started as soon as possible. Generally, it's desirable to begin the Master Test Plan at about the same time the requirements specifications and the project plan are being developed. Figure 3-3 relates the approximate start times of various test plans to the software development lifecycle.

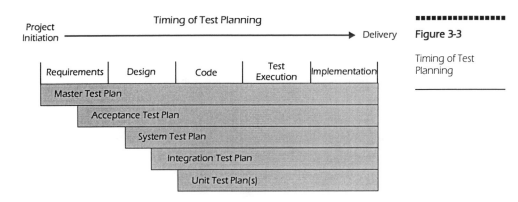

■■■■■■■■■■■■■■■■■
Figure 3-3

Timing of Test
Planning

If test planning is begun early enough, it can and should have a significant impact on the content of the project plan. Acceptance test planning can be started as soon as the requirements definition process has begun. We have one client, for example, that actually includes the acceptance test plan and high-level test scenarios as part of the requirements specification. Similarly, the system, integration, and unit test plans should be started as early as possible.

Test planners often get frustrated when they begin their planning process early and find out that all of the information needed is either not available or in a state of flux. Experienced test planners have learned to use TBD (To Be Determined) when they come to a part of the plan that is not yet known. This, in itself, is important because it allows planners to see where to focus their efforts and it highlights what has yet to be done. It's true that plans that are written early will probably have to be changed during the course of the software development and testing. Sometimes, the documenting of the test plan will precipitate changes to the strategy. This change process is important because it records the progress of the testing effort and helps planners become more proficient on future projects.

■■■■■■■■■■■■■■■■■
Key Point

As a rule of thumb, when using TBD (To Be Determined), it's desirable to record who's responsible for resolution of the TBD and a target completion date.

Standard Templates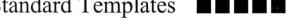

It's important that an organization have a template for its test plans. The templates used in this book are based on the IEEE Std. 829-1998 for Software Test Documentation, which provides a good basis for creating your own customized template. In many cases, you may find that the IEEE template meets your particular needs without requiring modifications.

If a template doesn't meet your particular requirements, you should feel free to customize it as necessary. For example, we use a slightly modified version of the IEEE test plan template in this book because we believe that risk should be divided into two sections, rather than the one section included in the standard template. Refer to *Chapter 2 – Risk Analysis* for a detailed explanation.

Over time, it's likely that you'll find some of the required items on your template are always left blank. If you're confident that those items are not germane to your organization, there's no need to maintain those fields in your template, so remove them. If the wording in certain sections is constant from plan to plan, then you must first decide if you've really addressed the issue. If you're confident that you've adequately addressed the issue, then maybe that section should become part of your standard methodology and be removed from the test plan. Remember that a test plan should consider the unique situation of a given project or release and may need to be customized for some projects. Since different sizes and types of projects require different amounts of documentation, it may be wise to identify some sections of the template as optional.

Key Point

Since different sizes and types of projects require different amounts of documentation, it may be wise to identify some sections of the template as optional.

Case Study 3-2 describes a strategy that some companies use to improve the usability of their templates and, consequently, recognize their employees for their outstanding achievements.

A Mark of Pride

One good idea that we've seen at several companies is the inclusion of sample documents such as test plans and supporting material for the template. You could include one sample each from a small, medium, and large project. If your organization has different types of applications, you might consider having a sample template for each of them (e.g., client/server, Web, etc.). In one company, it was regarded as a "mark of pride" if your test plan was chosen to be included as a sample in the template.

■■■■■■■■■■■■■■■■
Case Study 3-2

What do your company's templates have in common with employee morale?
_____

Sections of a Test Plan ■■■■■

There are many issues that should be considered in developing a test plan. The outline that we describe (refer to Figure 3-4) and recommend is a slightly modified version of the IEEE Std. 829-1998 document for test planning. The modifications that we've made to this template include breaking the standard IEEE section *Risks and Contingencies* into two sections: *Software Risk* and *Planning Risks and Contingencies*. Furthermore, we've added sections for *Table of Contents*, *References*, and *Glossary*, which aren't included in the IEEE Standard. The parts of the template in Figure 3-4 that we've added to the IEEE template are shown in italics. Please feel free to modify this template (or any other template) to meet your needs. This outline is useful for creating any kind of test plan: Master, Acceptance, System, Integration, Unit, or whatever you call the levels of test planning within your organization.

■■■■■■■■■■■■■■■■

Figure 3-4

Template for Test
Planning from IEEE
Std. 829-1998

IEEE Std. 829-1998 Standard for Software Test Documentation

Template for Test Planning

Contents

1. Test Plan Identifier
2. *Table of Contents*
3. *References*
4. *Glossary*
5. Introduction
6. Test Items
7. *Software Risk Issues*
8. Features to Be Tested
9. Features Not to Be Tested
10. Approach
11. Item Pass/Fail Criteria
12. Suspension Criteria and Resumption Requirements
13. Test Deliverables
14. Testing Tasks
15. Environmental Needs
16. Responsibilities
17. Staffing and Training Needs
18. Schedule
19. Planning Risks and Contingencies
20. Approvals

1.0 – Test Plan Identifier

In order to keep track of the most current version of your test plan, you should assign it an identifying number. If you have a standard documentation control system in your organization, then assigning numbers should be second nature to you. A test plan identifier is a unique company-generated number used to

identify a version of a test plan, its level, and the version of software that it pertains to.

Keep in mind that test plans are like other software documentation – they're dynamic in nature and, therefore, must be kept up-to-date. When we're auditing the testing practices of an organization, we always check for the test plan identifier. If there isn't one, this usually means that the plan was created but never changed and probably never used. In some cases, it may even mean that the plan was created only to satisfy International Standards Organization (ISO) or Capability Maturity Model (CMM) guidelines, or simply because the boss said you had to have a plan. Occasionally, we even encounter a situation where the test plan was written after the software was released. Our colleague, Lee Copeland, calls this "post-implementation test planning."

■■■■■■■■■■■■■■■■■■
Key Point

Due to the dynamic nature of test plans, it may be more efficient to disseminate and maintain the documents electronically.

2.0 – Table of Contents

The table of contents should list each topic that's included in the test plan, as well as any references, glossaries, and appendices. If possible, the table of contents should be two or more levels deep to give the reader as much detail about the content of each topic as possible. The reader can then use this information to quickly review the topics of interest, without having to read through the document from beginning to end.

Section
2.0

3.0 – References

In the IEEE Std. 829-1998 Standard for Test Documentation, references are included in the *Introduction*, but we've separated them into their own section to emphasize their importance.

Section
3.0

References recommended in the IEEE include:
- Project Authorization

- Project Plan
- QA Plan
- Configuration Management Plan
- Relevant Policies
- Relevant Standards

The IEEE standard also specifies that in multi-level test plans, each lower-level plan must reference the next higher-level plan. Other references to consider are requirements specifications, design documents, and any other documents that provide additional related information. Each listing in this section should include the name of the document, date and version, and the location or point of contact. References add credibility to your test plan, while allowing the reader to decide which topics warrant further investigation.

4.0 – Glossary

A glossary is used to define any terms and acronyms used in the document. When compiling the glossary, be sure to remember who your audience is and include any product-specific terms as well as technical and testing terms. Some readers, for example, may not understand the meaning of a "level" as it pertains to test planning. A glossary provides readers with additional information, beyond the simple meaning of a term derived from its usage.

Section
4.0

5.0 – Introduction (Scope)

There are two main things to include in the Introduction section: a basic description of the *scope of the project* or release including key features, history, etc., and an introduction that describes the *scope of the plan*. The scope of the project may include a statement such as:

- "This project will cover all of the features currently in use, but will not cover features scheduled for general availability in release 5.0."

The scope of the plan might include a statement such as:

- "This Master Test Plan covers integration, system, and acceptance testing, but not unit testing, since unit testing is being done by the vendor and is outside the scope of this organization."

Figure 3-5 illustrates some of the considerations when deciding the scope of the Master Test Plan (MTP). For embedded systems, the MTP might cover the entire product (including hardware) or only the software. The MTP might include only testing or might address other evaluation techniques such as reviews, walkthroughs, and inspections. Similarly, a project may have one MTP, or large projects may have multiple plans organized around subsystems.

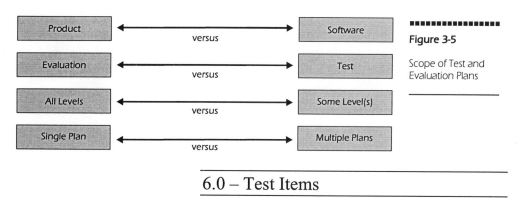

Figure 3-5

Scope of Test and Evaluation Plans

6.0 – Test Items

This section of the test plan describes programmatically *what* is to be tested within the scope of this test plan and should be completed in collaboration with the configuration or library manager and the developer. This section can be oriented to the level of the test plan. For higher levels, this section may be organized by application or by version. For lower levels, it may be organized by program, unit, module, or build. If this is a

Section 6.0

Master Test Plan, for example, this section might include information pertaining to version 2.2 of the accounting software, version 1.2 of the user manual and version 4.5 of the requirements specification. If this is an Integration or Unit Test Plan, this section might actually list the programs to be tested, if they're known. The IEEE standard specifies that the following documentation be referenced, if it exists:

- Requirements Specification
- Design Specification
- User's Guide
- Operations Guide
- Installation Guide
- Incident Reports that relate to the test items

Items that are to be specifically excluded from testing should be identified.

7.0 – Software Risk Issues

The purpose of discussing software risk is to determine what the primary focus of testing should be. Generally speaking, most organizations find that their resources are inadequate to test *everything* in a given release. Outlining software risks helps the testers prioritize what to test and allows them to concentrate on those areas that are likely to fail or have a large impact on the customer if they do fail. Organizations that work on safety-critical software can usually use the information from their safety and hazard analysis as the basis for this section of the test plan.

Section
7.0

We've found, though, that in most companies no attempt is made to verbalize software risks in any fashion. If your company doesn't currently do any type of risk analysis, starting simple is the recommended approach. Organize a brainstorming session among a small group of users, developers, and testers to find out what their concerns are. Start the session by asking the group, "What worries you?" We don't use the word *risk*, which we find can be intimidating to some people. Some examples of software risks include:

- Interfaces to other systems
- Features that handle large sums of money
- Features that affect many (or a few very important) customers
- Highly complex software
- Modules with a history of defects (from a defect analysis)
- Modules with many or complicated changes
- Security, performance, and reliability issues
- Features that are difficult to change or test

You can see that the risk analysis team needs users to judge the impact of failure on their work; as well as developers and testers to analyze the likelihood of failure. The list of software risks should have a direct effect on what you test, how much you test, and in what order you test. Risk analysis is hard, especially the first time you try it, but you will get better, and it's worth the effort. Risk analysis is covered in depth in Chapter 2.

■■■■■■■■■■■■■■■■
Key Point

What you test is more important than how much you test.
_____

8.0 – Features to Be Tested

This section of the test plan includes a listing of what will be tested from the user or customer point of view as opposed to test items, which are a measure of what to test from the viewpoint of the developer or library manager. If you're testing an Automated Teller Machine (ATM), for example, some of the features to be tested might include withdraw cash, deposit cash, check account balance, transfer funds, purchase stamps, and make a loan payment. For lower levels of test, the features to be tested might be much more detailed. Table 3-1 shows how the risk analysis described in Section 7.0 is based on analyzing the

Section 8.0

relative risk of each feature identified in the *Features to Be Tested* section.

Table 3-1 Prioritized List of ATM Features/Attributes with "Cut Line"

Features	Attributes	Likelihood	Impact	Priority	
ATM Software					
Withdraw cash		High	High	6	
Deposit cash		Medium	High	5	
	Usability	Medium	High	5	
Transfer funds		Medium	Medium	4	To Be Tested
Purchase stamps		High	Low	4	
✂	Security	Low	High	4	
Make a loan payment		Low	Medium	3	
Check account balance		Low	Medium	3	Not to Be Tested (or tested less)
	Performance	Low	Medium	3	

One benefit of using the list of features to be tested as the basis for software risk analysis is that it can help determine which low-risk features should be moved to Section 9.0 – *Features Not to Be Tested*, if your project falls behind schedule.

9.0 – Features Not to Be Tested

This section of the test plan is used to record any features that will not be tested and why. There are many reasons why a particular feature might not be tested. Maybe the feature wasn't changed, it's not yet available for use, or it has a good track record; but whatever the reason a feature is listed in this section, it all boils down to *relatively* low risk. Even features that are to be shipped but not yet enabled and available for use pose at least a certain degree of risk, especially if no testing is done on them. This section will certainly raise a few eyebrows among managers and users, many of whom cannot imagine consciously deciding not to test a feature, so be careful to document the reason you

Section 9.0

decided not to test a particular feature. These same managers and users, however, will often approve a schedule that doesn't possibly allow enough time to test everything. This section is about intelligently choosing what not to test (i.e., low-risk features), rather than just running out of time and not testing whatever was left on the ship date.

Politically, some companies that develop safety-critical systems or have a corporate culture that "requires" every feature to be tested will have a hard time listing any features in this section. If every feature is actually tested, then that's fine. But, if resources don't allow that degree of effort, using the *Features Not to Be Tested* section actually helps *reduce* risk by raising awareness. We've met many test managers who have obtained additional test resources or time when they clearly spelled out which features would not be tested! Case Study 3-3 describes one company's claim that they test every feature of their software.

Key Point

Choosing features not to be tested allows you to intelligently decide what not to test, rather than just running out of time and not testing whatever was left on the ship date.

Here at XYZ Company, "We Test Everything"

Once, I was giving a series of Test Management courses at a large software company. I gave the same two-day lecture three times in a row! I thought I deserved a medal for that, but the real medal belonged to the VP of Testing (yes, they had a Testing VP) for sitting through the same class three straight times. Anyway, the only guideline he gave me was that I couldn't talk about "features NOT to be tested" because at his company, everything was tested! Well, of course I forgot what the VP told me and I began talking to his staff about features not to be tested. The VP quickly stood up and said, "Rick, you know that here at the XYZ Company, we test everything." Meanwhile, behind him, all of his managers were mouthing the words, "No, we don't." Apparently, the only person who thought that everything was being tested was the VP. The moral of the story is this: even if you think your company tests every feature of their software, chances are they don't.

— *Rick Craig*

Case Study 3-3

Does your company really test every feature?

Another important item to note is that this section may grow if projects fall behind schedule. If the risk assessment identifies each feature by risk, it's much easier to decide which additional features pose the least risk if moved from Section 8.0 – *Features to Be Tested* to Section 9.0 – *Features Not to Be Tested* of your test plan. Of course, there are other options other than reducing testing when a project falls behind schedule, and they should be included in Section 19.0 – *Planning Risks and Contingencies.*

10.0 – Approach (Strategy)

Since this section is the heart of the test plan, some organizations choose to label it *Strategy* rather than *Approach*. This section should contain a description of how testing will be performed (approach) and explain any issues that have a major impact on the success of testing and ultimately on the project (strategy). Figure 3-6 illustrates some typical influences on strategy decisions.

Figure 3-6

Influences on Strategy Decisions

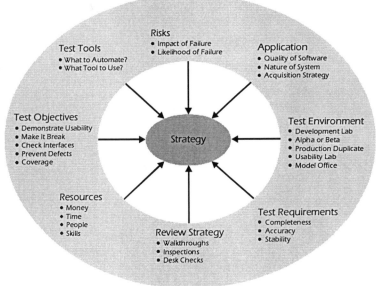

For a Master Test Plan, the approach to be taken for each level should be explained, including the entrance and exit criteria from one level to another. Case Study 3-4 describes one company's approach to testing.

ABC Company's Approach to Testing

System testing will take place in the test labs in our London Office. The Testing effort will be under the direction of the London test team, with support from the development staff and users from our New York office. An extract of production data from an entire month will be used for the duration of the testing effort. Test plans, test design specs, and test case specs will be developed using the IEEE Std. 829-1998 Standard for Software Test Documentation. All tests will be captured using our in-house tool for subsequent regression testing. Tests will be designed and run to test all features listed in section 8 of the system test plan. Additionally, testing will be done in concert with our Paris office to test the billing interface. Performance, security, load, reliability, and usability testing will be included as part of the system test. Performance testing will begin as soon as the system has achieved stability. All user documentation will be tested in the latter part of the system test. The system test team will assist the acceptance test team in testing the installation procedures. Before bug fixes are reintroduced into the test system, they must first successfully pass unit testing, and if necessary, integration testing. Weekly status meetings will be held to discuss any issues and revisions to the system test plan, as required.

Exit Criteria from System Test include:
- All test cases must be documented and run.
- 90% of all test cases must pass.
- All test cases dealing with the Billing function must pass.
- All Medium and High defects must be fixed.
- Code coverage must be at least 90% (including Integration and Unit testing).

Case Study 3-4

Example of the Approach Section in a Master Test Plan

Methodology Decisions

Many organizations use an "off-the-shelf" methodology, while others have either created a brand-new methodology from scratch or have adapted someone else's. Methodology decisions require management to answer many questions:

- When will testers become involved in the project?
- When will test execution begin?
- How many (if any) beta sites will be used?
- Will there be a pilot (i.e., a production system executed at a single or limited number of sites)?
- What testing techniques (e.g., "buddy" testing, inspections, walkthroughs, etc.) will be utilized?
- How many testers will be required for planning? Design? Execution?
- What testing levels (e.g., Acceptance, System, Integration, Unit, etc.) will be used?

Key Point

Refer to Chapter 4 – *Detailed Test Planning* for more information on buddy testing.

The left-most column of Figure 3-7 shows the standard levels identified in the IEEE 829-1998 Standard for Software Test Documentation. Many organizations always try to use the same levels on every project and every release, but some organizations may choose to occasionally or always combine levels, delete levels, add levels, or call them by different names.

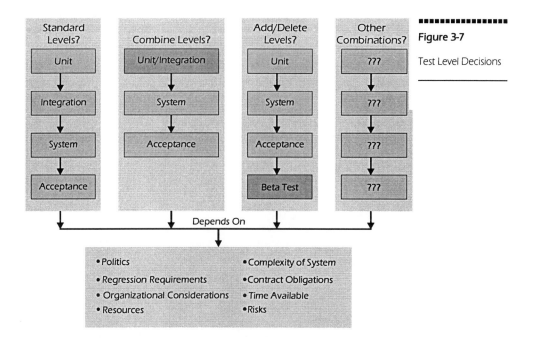

■■■■■■■■■■■■■■■■■
Figure 3-7

Test Level Decisions

Figure 3-8 illustrates the test levels identified in IEEE Std. 829-1998 Standard for Test Documentation. Each level is defined by a particular environment, which may include the hardware configuration, software configuration, interfaces, testers, etc. Notice that as you move to higher levels of test, the environment becomes increasingly more realistic. The highest level of test, in this example acceptance testing, should mirror the production environment as closely as possible since the system will be fielded upon successful completion of the testing.

■■■■■■■■■■■■■■■■■
Key Point

As you move to higher levels of test, the environment becomes more realistic.

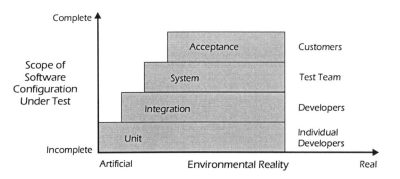

■■■■■■■■■■■■■■■■■

Figure 3-8

Typical Test Levels

_____

Using the Test Planning Process to Create a Methodology

As consultants, we are often asked to help create a testing methodology for organizations that don't even have a rudimentary testing process in place – or at least not one that is documented. We've found that many people who are used to actually doing the coding and testing are frustrated by the process of sitting around trying to help us document a testing methodology – they feel like they should be doing "real" work. This frustration often leads to a documented process that no one wants to use.

So, an alternate approach is to use the test planning process as a way to create a methodology from the bottom up. That is, we choose a pilot project and create a master test plan. The decisions made while creating the master test plan for the pilot project are declared to be Version 1.0 of the organization's testing methodology.

■■■■■■■■■■■■■■■■■

Case Study 3-5

Many people who are used to actually doing the coding and testing are frustrated by the process of sitting around trying to help us document a testing methodology – they feel like they should be doing "real" work.

_____

Resources

The best-laid plans of test managers can easily be sabotaged by either of two events: development is running late and will not be able to provide the testing team with the builds as originally scheduled, or the ship date has been moved forward (often due to competitive pressure). Unfortunately, the test manager has little

10.0
Approach

control over these events and should therefore ensure that the testing schedule contains contingencies to accommodate these possible scenarios.

Another strategy decision might be where the testing resources will come from. If your organization has a dedicated test group, you may already have sufficient resources. If the testing group is understaffed or has other priorities, it may be necessary to look for other resources in the form of developers, users, college interns, contractors, support staff, and others. Unfortunately, adding resources can also become a political issue in some organizations. Some users may want nothing to do with the testing effort, while others may be "miffed" if they aren't included in the project. You can usually maximize efficiency by adequately staffing your project from the beginning. However, you should avoid the scenario in which high-priced testing consultants are just sitting around (using up the testing budget) waiting for development to provide them with something to test. Conversely, bringing on additional testers late in the project can actually slow down the process due to the steep learning curve.

■■■■■■■■■■■■■■■■■

Key Point

According to Frederick Brooks' *The Mythical Man-Month,* "adding more people to a late software project makes it later."

Test Coverage Decisions

Several types of coverage measures are used in software testing. Perhaps the best-known form of coverage is code coverage, which measures the percentage of program statements, branches, or paths that are executed by a group of test cases (i.e., a test set). Code coverage requires the assistance of a special tool to instrument the code. These tools have been around for years and help the programmers and testers understand what parts of the code are or are not executed by a given group of tests. They are also useful for identifying "dead" or unexecutable code.

10.0 Approach

Based on our experiences, code coverage tools still don't enjoy widespread use. While it is not totally clear why these tools are not used more often, we believe the following issues may be factors:

- Code coverage requires the purchase and subsequent training on a new tool.
- Code coverage metrics are foreign to some functional level testers.
- Code coverage is almost a moot point for organizations that have entire programs or even subsystems that are not addressed by the tests due to time or resource constraints or lack of system knowledge.

Other measures include coverage of requirements, design, and interfaces. Requirements coverage measures the percentage of business requirements that are covered by a test set, while design coverage measures how much of the design is covered. Interface coverage measures the percentage of interfaces that are being exercised by a test set. Coverage will be explained in more detail in Chapter 7 – *Test Execution*.

■■■■■■■■■■■■■■■■■

Key Point

Requirements coverage measures the percentage of business requirements that are covered by a test set, while *design coverage* measures how much of the design is covered.

Walkthroughs and Inspections

10.0
Approach

The major focus of this book is on testing and analysis, but as you can see in Figure 3-9, software evaluation also includes another category called *reviews*. Reviews of requirements, design, and code are examples of verification techniques, which are an important part of software quality assurance (known as evaluation in the STEP methodology). While they are not testing activities, they are complementary activities that can significantly affect the test strategy and should be included in the *Approach (Strategy)* section of the Master Test Plan. Specifically, they can have an impact on the quality of the software being tested and on the resources available for testing.

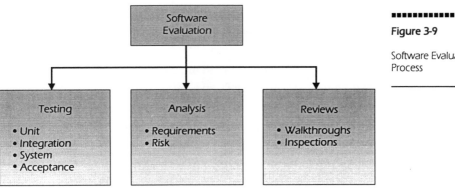

■■■■■■■■■■■■■■■■■
Figure 3-9

Software Evaluation
Process

Two of the most common types of reviews are walkthroughs and inspections. It is not clear to us when and where the term "walkthrough" originated, but walkthroughs have been in use longer than their more rigorous cousin, software inspections. Software inspections as we know them today were developed and popularized by Michael Fagan while he worked for IBM in the 1970s.

A walkthrough is a peer review of a software product that is conducted by "walking through" the product sequentially (line by line) to judge the quality of the product being reviewed and to discover defects. Most walkthroughs that we've taken part in are led by the developer of the product being reviewed. Inspections are also peer reviews, but are much more rigorous and, in addition to finding defects in the product being inspected, typically employ statistical process control to measure the effectiveness of the inspection process and to identify process improvement opportunities in the entire software development process.

The IEEE Std. 729-1983 Standard Glossary of Software Engineering Terminology defines an *inspection* as: a formal evaluation technique in which software requirements, design, or code are examined in detail by a person or group other than the

■■■■■■■■■■■■■■■■■
Key Point

The IEEE defines an *inspection* as a formal evaluation technique in which software requirements, design, or code are examined in detail by a person or group other than the author, to detect faults, violations of development standards, and other problems.

author to detect faults, violations of development standards, and other problems. It also states that the objective of software inspections is to detect and identify defects in software elements.

The information in Table 3-2 reflects our thoughts on the differences between walkthroughs and inspections. The various books on walkthroughs and inspections have surprisingly different views on the exact definition, purpose, and rigor of the two techniques.

Table 3-2 Comparison of Walkthroughs versus Inspections

	Walkthroughs	Inspections
Participants	Peer(s) led by author	Peers in designated roles
Rigor	Informal to formal	Formal
Training Required	None, informal, or structured	Structured, preferably by teams
Purpose	Judge quality, find defects, training	Measure/improve quality of product and process
Effectiveness	Low to medium	Low to very high, depending on training and commitment
References	*Handbook of Walkthroughs, Inspections, and Technical Reviews* by Daniel P. Freedman and Gerald M. Weinberg *Structured Walkthroughs* by Edward Yourdon *Software Reviews and Audits Handbook* by C.P. Hollocker	*Software Inspection* by Tom Gilb and Dorothy Graham *Handbook of Walkthroughs, Inspections, and Technical Reviews* by Daniel P. Freedman and Gerald M. Weinberg *Design and Code Inspections to Reduce Errors in Program Development* by Michael E. Fagan

Inspections and, to a lesser degree, walkthroughs are very labor and thought intensive and require a lot of resources to conduct them well. For many projects, it may not be possible to perform inspections on everything. The tester and/or the developer may decide to do inspections only on highly complex code, modules that have had many lines of code changed, code that's been

■■■■■■■■■■■■■■■■■
Key Point

To learn more about software inspections, we recommend the book *Software Inspection* by Tom Gilb and Dorothy Graham.

problematic in past releases, or high-risk requirements and design specifications. *What* has been inspected will have a great impact on the testing strategy. Those modules that have undergone successful inspections may require less testing than other modules. On the other hand, if the inspection reveals many bugs, testing should be delayed until the code or specification is repaired or more time may need to be allocated for testing those parts of the system. An inspection is a rigorous, formal peer examination that does the following:

- Verifies that the software elements satisfy the specifications.
- Verifies that the software element(s) conform to applicable standards.
- Identifies deviations from standards and specifications.
- Collects software engineering data (for example, defect and effort data).
- Does not examine alternatives or stylistic issues.

Another part of the walkthroughs and inspections strategy is determining who should participate. In this case, we're particularly interested in the role of the testers in the process. It's highly desirable to have system-level testers involved in the requirements and design reviews, but they may or may not be as useful in the code reviews, depending on the skill set of the testers. If the testers don't have any coding experience, their presence in the meeting may not contribute significantly to the review, but can still serve as a useful learning experience for them.

Configuration Management

Another strategic issue that should generally be considered in the *Approach* section of a test plan is how configuration management will be handled during software testing. Alternatively, many companies choose to describe their

10.0
Approach

configuration management processes in an entirely separate document. Configuration management in the context of a Master Test Plan usually includes change management as well as the decision-making process used to prioritize bugs. Change management is important because it's critical to keep track of the version of the software and related documents that are being tested. There are many woeful tales of companies that have actually shipped the wrong (untested) version of the software.

Equally important is the process for reviewing, prioritizing, fixing, and re-testing bugs. The test environment in some companies is controlled by developers, which can be very problematic for test groups. As a general rule, programmers want to fix every bug (in their code) *immediately*. It's as though many programmers feel that if they can fix the bug quickly enough it didn't actually happen. Testers, on the other hand, are famous for saying that "testing a spec is like walking on water – it helps if it's frozen." Obviously, both of the extremes are counterproductive. If every bug fix were immediately promoted into the test environment, testers would never do anything but regression testing. Conversely, if the code is frozen prematurely, the tests will become unrealistic because fixing the bugs that were previously found may change the code now being tested. The key is to mutually agree on a process for reviewing, fixing, and promoting bugs back into the test environment. This process may be very informal during unit and integration testing, but will probably need to be much more formal at higher levels of test.

We recommend that our clients use acceptance testing as a way of validating their software configuration management process. A Change Control Board (CCB) comprised of members from the user community, developers, and testers can be set up to handle this task. They will determine the severity of the bug, the approximate cost to fix and test the bug, and ultimately the priority for fixing and re-implementing the code. It's possible

■■■■■■■■■■■■■■■■
Key Point

If the code is frozen prematurely, the tests will become unrealistic because fixing the bugs that were previously found may change the code now being tested.

■■■■■■■■■■■■■■■■
Key Point

Regression testing is retesting previously tested features to ensure that a change or bug fix has not introduced new problems.

■■■■■■■■■■■■■■■■
Key Point

Confirmation testing is rerunning tests that revealed a bug to ensure that the bug was fully and actually fixed.

– Rex Black

that some bugs discovered, especially in acceptance testing, may be deferred to a future release.

Collection and Validation of Metrics

Another topic often described in the *Approach* section of a test plan is metrics. Since metrics collection and validation can be a significant overhead, it's necessary to discuss which metrics will be collected, what they will be used for, and how they will be validated. All testing efforts will need a way to measure testing status, test effectiveness, software quality, adherence to schedules, readiness for shipment, etc. Refer to Chapter 10 – *The Test Manager* for more information.

Tools and Automation

Another strategy issue that should be addressed in the *Approach* section of the test plan is the use of tools and automation. Testing tools can be a tremendous help to the development and testing staff, but they can also spell disaster if their use isn't carefully planned and implemented. For some types of tools, there can actually be a requirement for more time to develop, implement, and run a test set the first time than there would be if the test cases were executed manually. Alternatively, time may be saved during regression testing. Other types of tools can pay time dividends from the very beginning, but again, it's not our purpose to discuss test tools here (refer to Chapter 7 – *Test Execution* for more information). We only want to emphasize that the use of automated testing tools needs to be well planned and have adequate time allocated for implementation and training.

Changes to the Test Plan

The Master Test Plan should address how changes to the plan itself and its corresponding detailed test plans will be handled. When working to draft the plan, it's desirable to include all of the key people and groups (e.g., developers, users, configuration managers, customers, marketing, etc.) in the development and review cycles. At some point, we hope that these key people will sign off on the plan.

10.0
Approach

It's also important to remember that the test plan will change during the project. Each test manager should include a strategy addressing how to update the plan. Some of the questions that need to be addressed include:

■■■■■■■■■■■■■■■■■
Key Point

The test manager must develop a strategy for updating the test plan.

- Are small changes (e.g., misspelled words) permissible without going through the approval process again?
- Should there be weekly or monthly updates to the test plan?
- Should the test plan go through the regular CM process?
- How should the test plan be published (e.g., electronically, on paper, or both)?
- Should the test plan review be conducted in a "shotgun" fashion, sequentially, in a meeting, or some combination thereof?

Meetings and Communications

It's often a good idea to include a section in the Master Test Plan on meetings, reporting, and communications. If there are to be any standing meetings, they should be described in the *Approach* section of the test plan. Examples of meetings and other methods of communication include the Change Control Board (CCB), status meetings, and presentations to users and/or upper management.

10.0
Approach

Status reporting should also be covered in this section and include details on how often meetings will be held, in what format, and what metrics will be used to monitor and communicate results. Finally, it's useful to describe chains of command and where to go for conflict resolution – the CCB is one obvious choice.

Other Strategy Issues

We've covered a few of the strategy issues that occur frequently. Other topics that might affect the strategy include how to handle:

- multiple production environments
- multi-level security
- beta testing
- test environment setup and maintenance
- use of contractual support
- unknown quality of software
- feature creep
- etc.

The bottom line is that anything that has a *significant* impact on the effectiveness or cost of testing is a candidate for inclusion in the *Approach* section of the test plan.

11.0 – Item Pass/Fail Criteria

This section of the test plan describes the pass/fail criteria for each of the items described in Section 6.0 – *Test Items*. Just as every test case needs an expected result, each test item needs to have an expected result. Typically, pass/fail criteria are expressed in terms of test cases passed and failed; number, type, severity and location of bugs; usability, reliability, and/or stability. The exact criteria used will vary from level to level and organization to organization.

Remember that all test cases are not created equal. Percentage of test cases executed, although a common and often useful metric, can be misleading. For example, if 95% of the test cases pass, but the "nuclear shut-off valve" test fails, the actual percentage may not mean much. Furthermore, all tests don't cover the same amount of the system. For example, it may be possible to have 75% of the test cases cover only 50% of the system. A more effective measure for quantifying pass/fail criteria would relate the test case completion to some measure of coverage (e.g., code, design, requirements, etc.).

If you've never tried to quantify pass/fail criteria before, you may find it a little frustrating at first. But, trying to foresee "what's good enough" can really help crystallize the thinking of the various test planners and reduce contention later. If the software developer is a contractor, this section can even have legal ramifications, since the pass/fail criteria may be tied to bonus or penalty clauses, or client acceptance of the product.

■■■■■■■■■■■■■■■■■
Key Point

Some examples of pass/fail criteria include:

- % of test cases passed
- number, severity, and distribution of defects
- test case coverage
- successful conclusion of user test
- completion of documentation
- performance criteria

12.0 – Suspension Criteria & Resumption Requirements

The purpose of this section of the test plan is to identify any conditions that warrant a temporary suspension of testing and the criteria for resumption. Because testers are often harried during test execution, they may have a tendency to surge forward no matter what happens. Unfortunately, this can often lead to additional work and a great deal of frustration. For example, if a group is testing some type of communications network or switch, there may come a time when it's no longer useful to continue testing a particular interface if the protocol to be used is undefined or in a state of flux. Using our ATM example, it may not be possible to test the *withdraw cash* feature if the *check account balance* feature has not yet been developed.

Metrics are sometimes established to flag a condition that warrants suspending testing. If a certain predefined number of total defects or defects of a certain severity are encountered, for example, testing may be halted until a determination can be made whether or not to redesign part of the system, try an alternate approach, or take some other action.

Gantt charts can be used to clearly show dependencies between testing activities. In Figure 3-10, for example, Task 5.3–*Execute Test Procedures for 8.6* and all subsequent tasks cannot begin until task 5.2–*Load ATM Version 8.6, Build 1* is completed. The Gantt chart clearly shows that Task 5.2 is on the critical path and all subsequent activities will need to be suspended until this task is completed.

Key Point

Frequently used suspension criteria include:
- incomplete tasks on the critical path
- large volumes of bugs
- critical bugs
- incomplete test environments
- and resource shortages.

ID	Work Breakdown	January 26							February 2						
		S	M	T	W	T	F	S	S	M	T	W	T	F	S
27	5.0 Execute System Test														
28	5.1 Validate Hardware Configuration														
29	5.2 Load ATM Version 8.6, Build 1														
30	5.3 Execute Test Procs. for 8.6														
31	5.3.1 Execute Test Procs. 1-15														
32	5.3.2 Execute Test Procs. 17-19														
33	5.3.3 Execute Test Procs. 16, 20-28														
34	5.4 Load Test ATM Version 8.6, Build 2														
35	5.5 Execute Automated Regression Test														
36	5.6 Execute Test Procedure 31														
37	...														

Task   Summary
Critical Task   Milestone
Progress

Figure 3-10

Sample Gantt Chart

13.0 –Test Deliverables

This is a listing of all of the documents, tools, and other components that are to be developed and maintained in support of the testing effort. Examples of test deliverables include test plans, test design specs, test cases, custom tools, defect reports,

Section 13.0

test summary reports, and simulators. One item that is *not* a test deliverable is the software to be tested. The software to be tested should be listed under Section 6.0 – *Test Items*.

Artifacts that support the testing effort need to be identified in the overall project plan as deliverables and should have the appropriate resources assigned to them in the project tracking system. This will ensure that the test process has visibility within the overall project tracking process and that the test tasks used to create these deliverables are started at the appropriate times. Any dependencies between the test deliverables and their related software deliverables should be identified in Section 18.0 – *Schedule* and may be tracked using a Gantt chart. If the predecessor document is incomplete or unstable, the test products will suffer as well.

14.0 –Testing Tasks

This section is called *Testing Tasks* in the IEEE template and it identifies the set of tasks necessary to prepare for and perform testing. All intertask dependencies and any special skills that may be required are also listed here. We often omit this section and include all testing tasks in a matrix under Section 16.0 – *Responsibilities* to ensure that someone will be responsible for the completion of these tasks at a later date.

15.0 – Environmental Needs

Environmental needs include hardware, software, data, interfaces, facilities, publications, security access, and other requirements that pertain to the testing effort, as illustrated in Figure 3-11. An attempt should be made to configure the testing environment as similar to the real-world system as possible. If the system is destined to be run on multiple configurations (hardware, operating system, etc.), a decision must be made

whether to replicate all of these configurations, only the riskiest, only the most common, or some other combination. When you're determining the hardware configuration, don't forget to list your system software requirements as well.

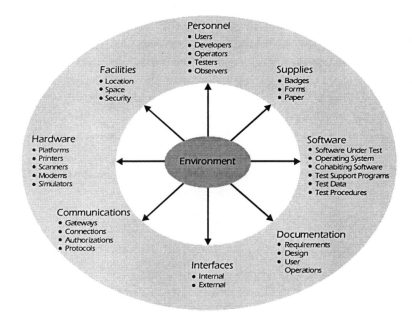

In addition to specifying the hardware and software requirements, it's also necessary to identify where the data will come from to populate the test database. Some possible choices might include production data, purchased data, user-supplied data, generated data, and simulators. At this point, you should also determine how to validate the data and assess its fragility so you know how often to update it. Remember that it's false to assume that even production data is totally accurate.

Undoubtedly, many of our students get tired of hearing that "interfaces are risky," but indeed they are. When planning the test environment, it's very important to determine and define all interfaces. Occasionally, the systems that we must interface with already exist. In other instances, they may not yet be ready and all we have to work with is a design specification or some type of protocol. If the interface is not already in existence, building a realistic simulator may be part of your testing job.

Facilities, publications, and security access may seem trivial, but you must ensure that you have somewhere to test, your tests are properly documented, and you have appropriate security clearance to access systems and data.

Tough Duty

Once, while on active duty in the Marine Corps, I was "loaned" to an Air Force command to help in testing a large critical system. For some reason, my security clearance didn't arrive at the base until two days after I was scheduled to begin work. Since I couldn't logon to the system or even gain access to the building, I was forced to spend a couple of boring days hanging out at the Officer's Club and lounging by the pool – basically doing everything except testing.

— Rick Craig

■■■■■■■■■■■■■■■■■■

Case Study 3-6

Security access may seem trivial, but it's really an important part of the test environment.

Refer to Chapter 6 – *Test Implementation* for more information about the test environment.

16.0 – Responsibilities

We like to include a matrix in this section that shows major responsibilities such as establishment of the test environment, configuration management, unit testing, and so forth. Some people like to list job titles in the responsibilities matrix (i.e., Development Manager) because the staff members holding various jobs change so frequently. We prefer to list the responsible parties by name because we've found that having someone's name next to a task gets their attention more than just listing a department or job title. In Figure 3-12, we hedged our

Section 16.0

bets by listing the responsible parties both by name and by job title.

	Coordinate MTP Development	Develop System Test Plan	Develop Integration/Unit Test Plan	Create Builds	Maintain Test Environment	Automate Scripts 1-22	Develop TDS for Feature A	Develop TDS for Feature B	Develop TDS for Feature C	Task A, Task B, Task C, Etc.
Development Manager (Crissy)			X							
Test Manager (Rayanne)	X									
Test Lead 1 (Lee)						X	X			
Test Lead 2 (Dale)							X	X		
Test Lead 3 (Frances)		X								
Test Environ. Coordinator (Wilton)					X					
Library Manager (Jennifer)				X						

■■■■■■■■■■■■■■■■■

Figure 3-12

Responsibilities Matrix

17.0 – Staffing and Training Needs

The actual number of people required to handle your testing project is, of course, dependent upon the scope of the project, the schedule, and a multitude of other factors. This section of the test plan describes the number of people required and what skills they need to possess. In some cases, you may need 15 journeymen testers and 5 apprentice testers. More often, though, you will have to be more specific. If you already have someone in mind, for example, you could state your requirements as, "We *must* have Jane Smith to help establish a realistic test environment."

Section 17.0

Examples of training needs might include learning how to use a particular tool, testing methodologies, interfacing systems, management systems such as defect tracking, configuration management, or basic business knowledge related to the system under test. Training needs may vary significantly, depending on the scope of the project. Refer to Chapter 10 – *The Test Manager* for more information.

18.0 – Schedule

Section
18.0

The testing schedule should be built around the milestones contained in the Project Plan such as delivery dates of various documents and modules, availability of resources, interfaces, and so forth. Then, it will be necessary to add all of the testing milestones. These testing milestones will differ in level of detail depending upon the level of the test plan being created. In a Master Test Plan, milestones will be built around major events such as requirements and design reviews, code delivery, completion of user manuals, and availability of interfaces. In a Unit Test Plan, most of the milestones will be based on the completion of various software modules.

Initially, it's often useful to build a generic schedule without calendar dates; that is, identify the time required for various tasks, dependencies, and so forth without specifying particular start and finish dates. Normally, this schedule should be portrayed graphically using a Gantt chart in order to show dependencies.

Our template specifies a testing schedule without reference to where the milestone came from, but it's our hope that the milestones are based on some type of formal estimate. If we're ever going to gain credibility in the software development arena, we must be more accurate in estimating time and resources. It's important that the schedule section reflect how the estimates for the milestones were determined. In particular, if the time schedule is very aggressive, estimating becomes even more critical, so that the planning risks and contingencies and priorities for test can be specified. Recording schedules based

■■■■■■■■■■■■■■■■■
Key Point

It's important that the schedule section reflect how the estimates for the milestones were determined.

on estimates also provides the test manager with an audit trail of how the estimates did and did not come to pass, and forms the basis for better estimating in the future.

19.0 – Planning Risks and Contingencies

Many organizations have made a big show of announcing their commitment to quality. We've seen quality circles, quality management, total quality management, and who knows what else. Unfortunately, in the software world, many of these same organizations have demonstrated that their only true commitment is to the schedule. The *Planning Risks and Contingencies* section of Chapter 2 provides a good overview of how to make intelligent and informed planning decisions. Any activity that jeopardizes the testing schedule is a planning risk. Some typical planning risks include:

Section 19.0

- Unrealistic delivery dates
- Staff availability
- Budget
- Environmental options
- Tool inventory
- Acquisition schedule
- Participant buy-in and marketing
- Training needs
- Scope of testing
- Lack of product requirements
- Risk assumptions
- Usage assumptions
- Resource availability
- Feature creep
- Poor-quality software

Possible contingencies include:
- Reducing the scope of the application
- Delaying implementation

- Adding resources
- Reducing quality processes

Refer to Chapter 2 – *Risk Analysis* for more information on planning risks and contingencies.

20.0 – Approvals

The approver(s) should be the person or persons who can declare that the software is ready to move to the next stage. For example, the approver on a Unit Test Plan might be the Development Manager. The approvers on a System Test Plan might be the people in charge of the system test *and* whoever is going to receive the product next, which may be the customer if they're going to perform the Acceptance Testing. Since this is a Master Test Plan, there may be many approvers including developers, testers, customers, QA, configuration management, among others. One of the important parts of the approval section of the test plan is the signature page. Figure 3-13 shows an example of a signature page.

The author(s) should sign in the appropriate block and enter the date that this draft of the plan was completed. In our sample signature page, we've also included a place for the reviewer to sign and date the document and check the block indicating whether or not he/she is recommending approval. The reviewers should be technical or business experts and are usually not managers. If some of the approvers lack the technical or business expertise to understand the entire document, their approval may be based partly upon the expertise and reputation of the reviewers.

Section 20.0

■■■■■■■■■■■■■■■■■
Key Point

The approver(s) should be the person or persons who can declare that the software is ready to move to the next stage.

Signing below indicates that you have read, understand and approve the contents of this document. If you disagree with or have found major discrepancies in the document as written, please return the unsigned document and a description of the discrepancy to the authors named below. If the discrepancy is minor, please sign and check the block called *Conditional Approval* and return this document along with the conditions of your approval.

■■■■■■■■■■■■■■■■■

Figure 3-13

Sample Signature Page

AUTHORS:

Rick Craig   *2-12-02*

Rick Craig, Lead Tester   Date

Stefan Jaskiel   *2-12-02*

Stefan Jaskiel, Tester   Date

REVIEWERS:

☐ Recommend Approval "As-Is"

☐ Do Not Recommend Approval

☐ Comments Attached

Name, Title   Date

☐ Recommend Approval "As-Is"

☐ Do Not Recommend Approval

☐ Comments Attached

Name, Title   Date

APPROVERS:

☐ Approved "As-Is"

☐ Conditional Approval

Name, Title   Date

☐ Approved "As-Is"

☐ Conditional Approval

Name, Title   Date

☐ Approved "As-Is"

☐ Conditional Approval

Name, Title   Date

In our sample signature block, we've included a space for the approver to sign and date the document and indicate approval "as-is" or conditionally. The approver(s) should be the person(s) who have the authority to declare accept/reject the terms of this document. Even though we're anxious to get the approvers to "sign off" on the plan, we really want their buy-in and commitment – not just their signature. If you wait until the plan is written and then circulate the document for approval, it's much harder to get buy-in and the most you can hope for is just a signature. In order to get the commitment we want, the approver(s), or their representatives, should be involved in the creation and/or review of the test plan during its development. It's part of your challenge, as the test planner, to determine how to involve all the approvers in the test planning process.

Ideally, we'd like to have the developers and users actually help write the test plan. For example, convincing the development manager or one of the senior developers to explain how unit testing will be conducted is much more effective than having someone from the testing group try to describe how unit testing will de done. Often, though, the key developer and/or user may not be willing (or may not have enough time) to actually write the plan. We've found that one way to involve developers and users early in the development of the test plan is to invite them to a test planning meeting. While few people like attending meetings, many prefer them over helping write the plan. During the course of the meeting, you should go through the entire template and identify the issues. Then, publish the first rough draft of the plan as the minutes of the meeting. You might want to preface your e-mail with, "Is this what we agreed on?" If you follow these steps, you're well on your way to achieving buy-in for your test plan.

Test planning is a lot of work and can be time consuming. If you're under the gun to get the next release out the door, you

■■■■■■■■■■■■■■■■■
Key Point

In order to get the commitment we want, the approver(s), or their representatives, should be involved in the creation and/or review of the test plan during its development.

may argue that you can't afford to spend time creating a test plan. On the contrary, we hope that you will agree that you can't afford to begin testing without a good test plan.

Chapter 4 –
Detailed Test Planning

"You've got to be careful if you don't know where you're going 'cause you might not get there!"

— Yogi Berra

To be most effective, test planning must start at the beginning and proceed in parallel with software development. General project information is used to develop the master test plan, while more specific software information is used to develop the detailed test plans, as illustrated in Figure 4-1. This approach will target testing to the most effective areas, while supporting and enhancing your development process. When fully implemented, test planning will provide a mechanism to identify improvements in all aspects of the system and development process.

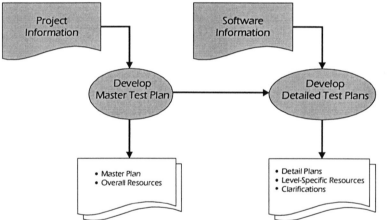

■■■■■■■■■■■■■■■■■

Figure 4-1

Planning Phase Process

A *level* of test is defined by a particular environment, which is a collection of people, hardware, software, interfaces, data, and even the viewpoints of the testers. Table 4-1 lists some sample environmental variables. This list may vary significantly between projects and companies. Some companies, for example, may have only one level of test, while others may have ten or more.

Table 4-1 Sample Environmental Variables

Attribute	Level			
	Unit	Integration	System	Acceptance
People	Developers	Developers & Testers	Testers	Testers & Users
Hardware O/S	Programmers' Workbench	Programmers' Workbench	System Test Machine or Region	Mirror of Production
Cohabiting Software	None	None	None/Actual	Actual
Interfaces	None	Internal	Simulated & Real	Simulated & Real
Source of Test Data	Manually Created	Manually Created	Production & Manually Created	Production
Volume of Test Data	Small	Small	Large	Large
Strategy	Unit	Groups of Units/Builds	Entire System	Simulated Production

What determines the number of levels required? Typically this decision is made based on complexity of the system, number of unique users, politics, budget, staffing, organizational structure and so forth. It's very important that the test manager help define what the levels are and ensure that there aren't too many or too few levels. We can hardly afford to have overlapping levels and, conversely, we don't want to take the risk of having big gaps between levels.

Creating a test plan for a specific *level* requires a clear understanding of the unique considerations associated with that level. Product risk issues, resource constraints, staffing and training requirements, schedules, testing strategy, and other factors must all be considered. Level-specific or detailed test plans are created using the same template that we used for the Master Test Plan (refer to Chapter 3 – *Master Test Planning*), but the amount of detail is greater for a level-specific plan.

■■■■■■■■■■■■■■■■■

Key Point

Cohabiting software is other applications that reside on the same platform.

Figure 4-2 shows the relationship of the Master Test Plan (MTP) to the Project Plan and the Detailed Test Plans.

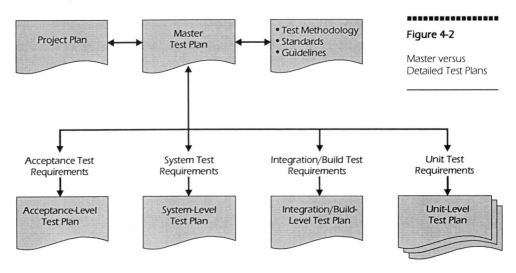

■■■■■■■■■■■■■■■■■

Figure 4-2

Master versus
Detailed Test Plans

There are many names for the levels employed by different groups and companies. Here are only a few that we've encountered recently: unit, component, code, developer, build, string, thread, integration, system, system integration, acceptance, user acceptance, customer acceptance, interoperability, alpha, beta; Verification, Validation, and Testing (VV&T), and others. You see, there are many different names, and you may very well have some that we didn't list here. In the long run, what you name your levels is relatively unimportant. What's important is to define the scope of the level and what that level is supposed to accomplish; then, create a plan to ensure that it happens.

■■■■■■■■■■■■■■■

Key Point

It's important to define the scope of the level and what that level is supposed to accomplish; then, create a plan to ensure that it happens.

Throughout this book, we use the level names defined by the IEEE: Acceptance, System, Integration and Unit. While these names are no better or worse than any others, they are convenient, as they provide a basis for discussion. This chapter will focus on the highest levels first and then progressively move to the lower levels of test. This is done because the level-specific plans should usually be written in reverse order of execution. That is to say, even though the acceptance test is normally the last one to be executed, it should be the first test to be planned. Why? Simply because the acceptance test plan is built on the artifacts that are available first – *the requirements* – and this group of tests is used to model what the system will look like when it's complete. The "V" model of testing in Figure 4-3 shows that the system test should be planned next based on the high-level design (and requirements); integration testing should be planned using the detailed design (and the high-level design and requirements); and unit testing should be planned based on the coding (and the detailed design, high-level design, and requirements).

■■■■■■■■■■■■■■■■■■

Key Point

The level-specific plans should usually be written in reverse order of execution.

――――――――――

■■■■■■■■■■■■■■■■■■

Figure 4-3

The "V" Model of Software Testing

――――――――――

DEVELOPMENT   TESTING

Requirements — planning for — Acceptance

High-Level Design — planning for — System

Detailed Design — planning for — Integration

Coding — planning for — Unit

Without a doubt, some readers may be more concerned with one level of test than the others. However, we encourage you to read about all of the levels of test in this chapter even if you're not directly involved, because it's important to understand all of the types of testing that may be occurring in your company. Also, as a matter of style in writing this book, we sometimes discuss issues in one level of test that are applicable at other levels and may not necessarily be repeated in the other sections of this chapter.

Acceptance Testing ■ ■ ■ ■ ■

Acceptance testing is a level of test that is based largely on users' requirements and demonstrates that those requirements have been satisfied. As illustrated in Figure 4-4, acceptance testing is the first level to be planned because it's built based on the system requirements. Since this group of tests is used to model what the system will look like when it's complete, acceptance testing is most effective when performed by the users or their representatives in the most realistic environment possible.

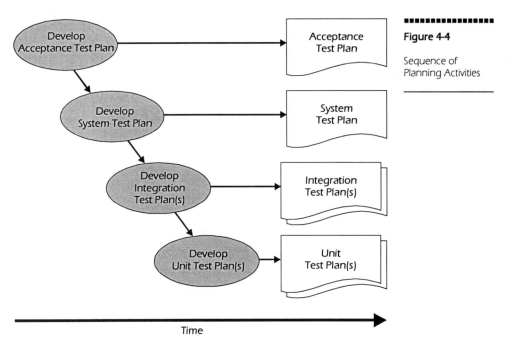

Figure 4-4

Sequence of Planning Activities

Audience Analysis

Obviously the users or customers are part of the audience for the acceptance test plan. Whoever is conducting the system testing is also part of the audience, since their exit criteria must consider the entrance criteria into acceptance testing. The developers will also be anxious to see the acceptance test plan, since it will specify exactly what constitutes success for their development effort. Therefore, the audience for the acceptance test plan may include technical people such as developers, as well as business users who may or may not be very technically adept. In order to accommodate such a diverse audience, the language of this plan should be non-technical.

Activity Timing

The acceptance test planning process should begin as soon as the high-level requirements are known. It's essential that this occur early in the lifecycle because one of the key purposes of the acceptance test plan is to develop the criteria for what constitutes a completed project. In other words, the exit criteria from the acceptance testing provide a basis for acceptance of the product. The acceptance test plan, and later the acceptance test cases, should fairly accurately describe what the finished product will look like. In some of the most progressive companies that we've visited, the acceptance test plan and test cases are actually delivered with the requirements document. In the case of outsourced development, the acceptance test plan and test cases may even be made part of the contract.

■■■■■■■■■■■■■■■■■
When should the test plan be written?

The acceptance test plan would ideally be written by the end-user. This is frequently not possible for a variety of reasons. If, for example, your product is commercial shrink-wrap software or a Web application, you may have thousands or even millions

■■■■■■■■■■■■■■■■■
Who should write the test plan?

of very different and unknown users. In that situation, it's important to find a group of people that represent the final end-users. In many organizations, the acceptance testers are called business associates or some similar name. These people are testers that typically come from the user community. Other organizations employ the users from a particular site or company as testers. Whoever is chosen, they need to have the most complete understanding of the business application as possible.

Figure 4-5 illustrates how the realism of the test environment increases at higher levels of test.

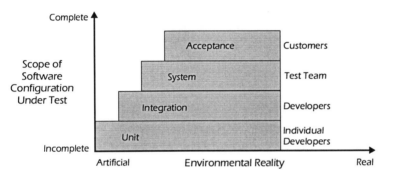

■■■■■■■■■■■■■■■■

Figure 4-5

Typical Test Levels

As we pointed out earlier, the acceptance test is not intended to be comprehensive and, therefore, doesn't last as long as the system test. Sometimes, the acceptance test on extremely large systems may take only a few days or weeks. If your acceptance testing today is going on for weeks and weeks, you may be doing "good" work, but you also may be doing more than what we call *acceptance testing*. In fact, you may be doing some of what we call *system testing*. That's fine, though, because you've just defined your levels differently than we have. The point is that a comprehensive test is not necessary in order to demonstrate that the requirements work.

■■■■■■■■■■■■■■■■

How long should acceptance testing last and how comprehensive should it be?

Of course, anything is possible. Rick used to have a colleague (okay, not a colleague, but his boss) who felt that most acceptance tests were a waste of time (probably because they were often ad hoc) and should be done away with. We believe, though, that the acceptance test is a very valuable way to prove the validity of the requirements and to support buy-in from the users.

Still, with tight time crunches and shortage of personnel, does it make sense to combine system and acceptance testing? Remember that the levels are what define the environment, and each environment can be associated with a level of test. The environment includes the hardware, software, documentation, data, and *people*. One of the most common differences between the system test environment and the acceptance test environment is *who* is doing the testing. Therefore, there are two situations where it might make sense to combine the two levels if necessitated by resource or time constraints:

■■■■■■■■■■■■■■■■■

Can acceptance testing be combined with system testing?

1. *When the users have a very active role in systems test.* It's always desirable to have the users involved in the system test (and throughout the lifecycle). If they're an integral part of the systems test effort and the rest of the test environment is as realistic as possible, then it might make sense to combine acceptance testing with system testing.

2. *When the users have no involvement in testing whatsoever.* If the most frequent difference in the system and acceptance test environments is who is conducting the test and if the test group is conducting both tests in similar environments, then why not combine the two? We've seen situations where organizations had historically conducted both system and acceptance testing and continued to do so even though both tests were virtually identical. In one case, the acceptance test set was a subset of the system test set and was rerun in exactly the same environment by the same people.

Should the execution of one level begin before the execution of the previous level is complete? In order to cut the elapsed time (schedule) from inception to delivery, many organizations overlap various testing levels. The penalty for overlapping the levels, however, is extra effort. Even though the lifecycle is shortened, it will typically take more effort because the higher level of test may find bugs that may have already been found (and sometimes fixed) by the lower level of test. Sometimes, both levels of test may be finding some of the same bugs at the same time and reporting them in slightly different words. This can add overhead to defect and configuration management.

Another issue may be one of first impressions. The first time the users see a nearly complete product is often during the acceptance test. If users receive a product that has not yet completed system testing, it will potentially contain more (possibly many more) bugs, which may cause them to get the feeling that the system is unsound. Hopefully, this attitude doesn't exist in your company, because, ideally, we would like to have the users involved throughout the lifecycle.

In some instances, system testing can be combined with integration testing. Our clients who successfully use this strategy have excellent configuration management, a relatively high level of test automation, and a good working relationship between the developers and testers. The basic strategy is that the integration tests are developed around each build – usually by the test group. That is, each progressively larger build is tested as part of the integration effort. The final build contains the entire system and becomes, in fact, the system test. This technique is not for everyone and depends on a lot of the factors that we explained above. One of the downsides of combining system and integration testing is that it removes part of the developer's responsibility for developing and delivering a finished product and passes that responsibility to the test team.

■■■■■■■■■■■■■■■■
Can acceptance testing begin before the system testing is done?

■■■■■■■■■■■■■■■■
Can the system testing be combined with integration testing?

Sources of Information

The key documents needed to write the acceptance test plan include the project plan, the master test plan and the requirements documentation. Other documents, such as user manuals, are also useful if they're available. The project plan lays out the entire strategy and schedule for the development project, and the acceptance test plan must relate to that document. However, the master test plan is typically based upon the project plan and gets into more detail on specifically how the system will be tested. Therefore, level-specific test planners can typically rely on the master test plan more than the project plan for general guidance. For example, an overall testing schedule is published in the master test plan. Another feature of the master test plan is the characterization of broad goals for each level including the entrance and exit criteria. The acceptance test plan (and all subsequent level-specific test plans) should follow this grand scheme. If significant changes are identified in the course of the detailed test planning, they must be rolled up into the master test plan.

■■■■■■■■■■■■■■■■■■

Key Point

If changes are identified in the course of the detailed test planning, they must be rolled up into the master test plan.

Ideally, the acceptance test cases should be based upon the requirement specification. Unfortunately, many projects do not have a requirements document *per se*. In those instances, other methods or documents must be used to identify the key features and components to test. This is the subject of Chapter 5 – *Analysis and Design*. For acceptance testing in particular, user documentation can be very useful when planning a new release of an existing system. At all levels of test, enhancement requests and defect reports should be treated as requirements documents.

User Responsibilities

The users or their representatives play an important part in the acceptance testing process. Some of their responsibilities may include:

- Defining the requirements
- Identifying the business risks
- Creating, updating, and/or reviewing the Acceptance Test Plan
- Defining realistic scenario-based tests
- Providing realistic test data
- Executing the tests
- Reviewing the documentation
- Reviewing the test output
- Providing acceptance criteria

Usability Testing

In many organizations, customers (users) conduct the acceptance testing on a nearly complete product in a near-production environment. Many organizations are proud of their stance that "the user is always right," but one of the problems associated with this is defining who is the user. Companies that develop and sell commercial software spend lots of thought and money on just this issue. All users are just not the same and have different needs. Some users want to be able to have a powerful system devoid of annoying prompts such as "Do you really want to delete this file?" Other users are a little more timid and after deleting their newly written doctoral thesis would welcome the child-like but annoying question that required a second thought. Sometimes user 'A' wants a feature that is a direct detriment to what user 'B' wants. Who is right and who decides? Maybe you should pay for two systems to satisfy both users? But then what happens if you have a hundred users instead of just two?

■■■■■■■■■■■■■■■■■
What if there are many users and they're not always right?

Another problem is that the users often don't know what they want. That's not pointing the finger at the users. It's simply a challenging task because the software developers also often don't have a clear view of what the system requirements are. Anyone who has ever participated in the creation of a requirements document (which, by the way, is often done by the users) knows just how difficult that task is.

The solution to these problems lies within the entire software engineering process (including requirements formulation and acceptance testing) and the communications between the users, developers, and testers. Fostering clear and concise communications between developers, tester, and users near the beginning of the software development lifecycle can help reduce the problem of "who's right."

Usability testing is one of the hardest kinds of testing to accomplish. Part of the difficulty is that the usability requirements are hard to describe and are often done poorly – and poor requirements can lead to poor testing. For example, a common usability requirement is that the system must be "user-friendly," but what does that mean? An accomplished user might consider a powerful system with shortcuts to other features to be user-friendly, while other users may require extensive menus to drag them from one part of the system to another. This entire problem is compounded because there may be many users with different needs and/or the users may be unknown.

■■■■■■■■■■■■■■■■
Key Point

Usability requirements are hard to describe and are often done poorly – and poor requirements can lead to poor testing.

Another problem with usability testing is that it can be difficult to conduct until very late in the lifecycle (i.e., acceptance test execution). Even if problems are discovered at this late juncture, it may be too late or too expensive to correct them (at least in this release). One approach used by some companies to overcome this problem is to use prototypes to "mock up" the system and let the users see what the finished product will look like earlier in the lifecycle. Sometimes, these prototypes may merely be paper mock-ups of reports or screens. Other companies have more sophisticated tools at their disposal such as usability laboratories, where a cut-down version of the actual system is created to allow the users to interact with it early to get a feel for it.

Usability Labs

A usability lab (Ulab) is a special environment created to evaluate the usability of a prototype product (application). Prospective users are asked to "use" the prototype being evaluated with only the assistance of the normal product documentation. The goal is to discover usability problems before the actual system is built, effectively saving the cost of building the "wrong" system.

■■■■■■■■■■■■■■■■■
Key Point

The goal of a usability lab is to discover usability problems before the actual system is built. Effectively, this saves the cost of building the "wrong" system.

The key actors in any type of usability testing are the *user*, the *observer*, and a *recording mechanism* or method. In the usability lab in Figure 4-6, the *user* sits in an observation room where he or she uses the prototype product. Video cameras record the user activities, facial expressions, body positions, and other factors that may be indications of the usability of the software under test. On the other side of a one-way mirror, the observers are watching the user in his or her attempts to use the system. Occasionally, a user may be asked why he or she did something or be told how to resolve a difficult situation, but overall, communications between the observers and the user are kept to a minimum. Observers may include usability laboratory staff members, developers, and/or testers. The video cameras serve as the principal recording mechanism.

■■■■■■■■■■■■■■■■■
Key Point

One danger of using a prototype is that the users may want to immediately install and use it.

Unfortunately, a prototype is not a complete system and it's not ready to be used in a production environment.

The Ulab staff members record notes as the user works, and these notes will later be reviewed with the videotape. Additionally, the users may be interviewed and/or fill out a questionnaire designed to learn their perception of the usability of the product. The results of the Ulab session (i.e., notes, video, interviews, and questionnaires) are used to identify and correct usability deficiencies.

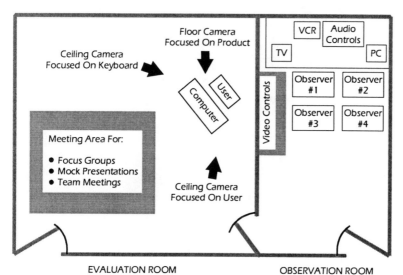

■■■■■■■■■■■■■■■■■

Figure 4-6

Usability Lab Design by Dr. Michael J. Prasse, *Director of OCLC Usability Lab*

Both usability testing and Ulab sessions are designed to discover usability problems that may require correction. The major difference is in *when* they are conducted. Because most usability testing is conducted at the end of the development lifecycle (i.e., system or acceptance testing), usability problems that are discovered are difficult and expensive to correct. Since the Ulab is conducted before the final product is built, usability problems can be addressed early when it's relatively inexpensive to rectify them.

Case Study 4-1 describes an incident that often occurs in usability labs.

Round #1: In the Usability Lab

Perhaps one of the most interesting events to watch is the reaction of the developers to a user's initial attempt to use a prototype in the usability lab. When a user unsuccessfully attempts to use a function, the developer on the other side of the one-way mirror can often be seen fuming at the "stupid" user for not understanding how to handle the problem. When the function doesn't work the way the user thinks it should work, he or she almost always tries the same thing again or pounds the Enter key several times. About that time, the developer starts to see the discrepancies between what he or she has created and what the user is trying to do. The key here, though, is that this usability discrepancy was discovered in the prototype and not in the final product. This means that the development team will have more time and therefore a better shot at fixing the problem.

■■■■■■■■■■■■■■■■■
Case Study 4-1

Are the users really "stupid" or is the user interface difficult to understand?

Alpha and Beta Testing

At best, the terms "alpha testing" and "beta testing" are highly ambiguous or at least mean very different things to different people. We'll try to offer the most common definitions of both. *Alpha* testing is an acceptance test that occurs at the development site as opposed to a customer site. Hopefully, alpha testing still involves the users and is performed in a realistic environment.

Beta testing is an acceptance test conducted at a customer site. Since beta testing is still a test, it should include test cases, expected results, etc. Many companies give the software to their customers to let them "play with it" and call this the beta test. While allowing your customers to play with your software may be a valuable thing to do, it's probably not adequate for a beta test. On the other hand, if a more formal acceptance test has been conducted and you just want some additional assurance that the customers will be happy, it's fine to let the users have a go.

■■■■■■■■■■■■■■■■■
Key Point

Some organizations merely refer to *alpha testing* as testing that is conducted on an early, unstable version of the software, while *beta testing* is conducted on a later, more stable version.

Frequently, though, the users will not conduct a very broad test if they are allowed to proceed in a purely ad hoc fashion without the benefit of a test strategy and test cases.

Requirements Traceability

Requirements traceability is an important concept in testing, especially at the acceptance level. In a nutshell, requirements traceability is the process of ensuring that one or more test cases address each requirement. These are normally presented in a matrix as illustrated in Table 4-2 or done in a spreadsheet, database, or using a commercially available tool.

Table 4-2 Tracing Test Cases to Requirements

Requirement	TC-1	TC-2	TC-3	TC-4
RQ-1	✓	✓	✓	✓
RQ-2	✓			✓
RQ-3		✓	✓	
RQ-4				✓
RQ-5		✓		
RQ-6	✓		✓	
RQ-7	✓	✓		✓

Requirements traceability is a high-level measure of coverage, which in turn is one way that test managers can measure the effectiveness of their testing. The requirements traceability matrix can and normally should be used in concert with the software risk analysis described in Chapter 2 – *Risk Analysis*.

The entire thrust of acceptance testing is to ensure that every requirement is addressed. It may or may not be clear to you that it's possible to test every requirement and still not have tested the "entire" system. Remember, the requirements traceability matrix doesn't show that every requirement is tested completely, only that each requirement has been addressed. Additionally, design characteristics are not specifically addressed during acceptance testing and, therefore, other issues may be left untested. In other words, acceptance testing is not a comprehensive test, nor was it intended to be. Rather, in the perfect world, the acceptance test would demonstrate to (or, even better, by) the user or their representative that the requirements have been met.

Configuration Management

During acceptance testing, configuration management of the software under test (SUT) should be as formal as it is in the production environment. Because the execution of the acceptance test plan (and test cases) is conducted shortly before the scheduled implementation date, finding major defects is a problem because there is little time to fix and test them. Ideally, we want the acceptance test to be largely a demo and hope to find all of the major problems in earlier levels of test. Unfortunately, if the users were not involved throughout the lifecycle in requirements formulation, walkthroughs, and earlier levels of test, prototypes, and so forth, acceptance testing may be their first encounter with the "system" or at least their first time since the requirements were created. Users are almost certain to find things that are incorrect or don't meet their vision. In fact, users may not have a clear vision of what they expected, only that the system doesn't meet their expectations. Hence, the users typically request major requirements changes. The worst thing that can (and frequently does) happen is to discover a major requirements flaw just before shipping and try to make the change on the fly without providing adequate time for analysis, design, implementation, and regression testing. There is a good chance that the change was rushed and may go out without being tested or, at least, tested inadequately. Almost all companies ship their products with known bugs (and unknown bugs) but

■■■■■■■■■■■■■■■■
Key Point

During acceptance testing, configuration management of the software under test (SUT) should be as formal as it is in the production environment.

■■■■■■■■■■■■■■■■
Key Point

Configuration management is covered in more detail later in this chapter under the topic *System Testing*.

there's something about "that last bug" that makes many developers feel that they must correct it before shipping. So, developers fix that last bug and if there is inadequate time to test, then *untested* software is shipped.

Implementing major requirements changes at the end of the lifecycle can turn a project into chaos. That's why it's so important for the Change Control Board (CCB), or its equivalent, to review each major change and determine the impact on the system and the project. Each change must be prioritized and in many cases, the correct choice is to delay certain fixes to a future release. If the change must be done in this release, then the planning risks discussed in Chapter 2 must be revisited. That is, we may have to slip the schedule, not ship a particular feature, add resources, or reduce testing of some relatively low-risk features.

■■■■■■■■■■■■■■■■■
Key Point

It's important for the Change Control Board (CCB), or its equivalent, to review each major change and determine the impact on the system and the project.

Exit Criteria

The categories of metrics for release criteria are pretty much the same for each level of test, but the actual values will be different. The exit criteria for acceptance testing are especially key, since they're also the exit (or release) criteria for the entire system. These exit criteria were originally laid out in general terms in the master test plan and republished in greater detail in the level-specific plans. Case Study 4-2 provides an example of one company's exit criteria for their acceptance testing.

Example Exit Criteria for an Acceptance Test

- There can be no Medium or High severity bugs.
- There can be no more than 2 bugs in any one feature or 50 bugs total.
- At least one test case must pass for every requirement.
- Test cases 23, 25, and 38-52 must all pass.
- 8 out of 10 experienced bank clerks must be able to process a loan document in 1 hour or less using only the on-line help system.
- The system must be able to process 1,000 loan applications/hour.
- The system must be able to provide an average response time of under 1 second per screen shift with up to 100 users on the system.
- The users must sign off on the results.

■■■■■■■■■■■■■■■■■

Case Study 4-2

Some exit criteria may be standard across the organization, while others may be unique to each project.

_____

Release Strategies

When acceptance testing has successfully concluded, the system is typically rolled out to the users. One strategy is to ship and install the entire system at every client site simultaneously. This introduces a significant risk if major problems are encountered in the installation or functionality of the system. In order to reduce this risk, organizations commonly use other rollout strategies such as: pilots, gradual implementation, phased implementation, and parallel implementation.

Pilots

■■■■■■■■■■■■■■■■■

Key Point

The difference between a beta site and a pilot is that the users at the pilot site are actually using the product to do real work, while the beta testers are executing tests.

_____

Pilots are often confused with beta tests. You will remember that a beta test is an acceptance test at a client site where test cases are executed in a very realistic (test) environment. A pilot is a *production* system executed at a single or limited number of sites, as shown in Figure 4-7. The difference between a beta site and a pilot is that the users at the pilot site are actually using the product to do real work. Failures can immediately affect their business.

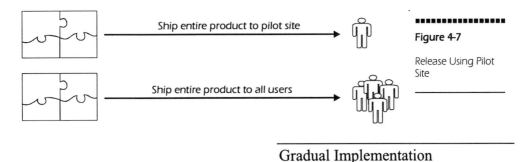

Ship entire product to pilot site

Ship entire product to all users

Figure 4-7

Release Using Pilot Site

Gradual Implementation

Figure 4-8 shows that gradual implementation or shipping the entire product to a few customers at a time is another possible option. This, of course, allows developers to get feedback from the earlier recipients of the product, which may allow them to make changes before the product is generally available. The downside of this technique is that it extends the time until all customers have the product in hand (i.e., general availability). It also means that the developers and testers must maintain more than one version simultaneously.

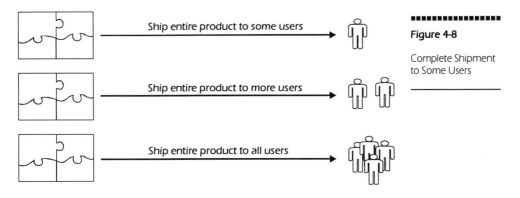

Ship entire product to some users

Ship entire product to more users

Ship entire product to all users

Figure 4-8

Complete Shipment to Some Users

Phased Implementation

Phased implementation is when the product is rolled out to all users incrementally. That is, each successive release contains additional functionality. As a system is being built, functionality is installed for immediate use at the client sites, as it becomes available, as illustrated in Figure 4-9. The beauty of this is that the customers get involved early, get something that they can (hopefully) use, and can provide useful feedback to the developers and testers. The downside is that the overall integration of the system may be more complicated and there will be significantly more regression testing conducted over the entire lifecycle of the product.

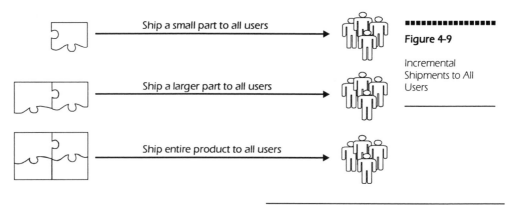

Figure 4-9

Incremental Shipments to All Users

Parallel Implementation

Parallel implementation is another technique used to reduce the risk of implementation. The existing application is run side by side (in production) with the new application. If there are any differences, the existing system is considered correct until proven otherwise. Parallel implementation may require extra hardware, software, and personnel resources.

All of the above implementation techniques (pilots, gradual implementation, phased implementation, and parallel implementation) are done in order to reduce the risk of shipping an entire system to all of your clients and having it fail spectacularly. There is one risk, though, that each of these techniques introduces – the elapsed time for all of the clients to receive the entire system is extended. Remember how sensitive management normally is about getting the product out the door? It seems that in some companies, once the pilot begins, the entire company lets go with a collective sigh of relief.

Test Environment

The environment for acceptance testing should be as realistic as possible. Any differences between the acceptance test environment and the real world are actually risks – things that have not been tested. For each level of testing (especially for acceptance and system), the testers should compare their environment to the real world and look for differences. If possible, the differences should be eliminated or reduced. If this is not possible, then the testers will have to look for other ways to deal with the risk of an unrealistic test environment. Case Study 4-3 compares one of our clients' test environment to their production environment.

An Example Test Environment

Here is an example test environment from one of our clients. (Remember that the environment includes who is doing the testing, hardware, software, interfaces, data, cohabiting systems, etc.)

People:	*Testers (formerly users)*
Hardware:	*"Exact" replica of the most common configuration*
Software Under Test:	*Same*
Interfaces	*Some missing, some simulated*
Data	*Subset of real production data, updated weekly*
Cohabiting Software:	*Unknown*

■■■■■■■■■■■■■■■■■

Case Study 4-3

Example of a Test Environment

This is not a bad test environment, but you can see that differences do exist between the test environment and the real word. Let's analyze each part of the environment to see if it introduces a significant risk. If it does, is there is a way to mitigate the risk?

People: This project had a good strategy of using former users as testers, which helped reduce the risk. As former users, the testers, for the most part, have some business knowledge, but as time goes by, the business changes and memories fade (sounds like a song) and they become testers rather than users. However, these testers will always retain their business viewpoint and empathy for the users. In the example above, the system being developed had many different users with different needs, some of which were not represented by the former user testers. If the team felt that a risk existed (and they did) they might have chosen to bring some users on board as temporary testers or possibly conduct a beta test at one or more customer sites (this client did both).

Hardware: This client/server system had consistent hardware and operating systems for the servers, but the clients were not as closely controlled. The test team addressed this issue by inventorying the hardware used by the customers and creating profiles of the most common client hardware configurations, operating systems, printers, etc.

Software Under Test: Same – no issues.

Interfaces: This was a problem. It was not possible to interface with the live systems, so simulators had to be created to replicate the interaction of the system under test and the other systems and databases it interacted with. The testing is only as good as the simulators were and, in this case, problems were experienced upon fielding the system. Fortunately, this project used a pilot site and the problems were limited to one (volunteer) customer.

Data: Copies of real data were used as much as possible. Some unique data had to be created by hand. Due to the constraints of the test environment, the volume of data used for testing was significantly less than production. This was offset somewhat by using some dynamic load testing tools and techniques. The *data was not particularly "fragile," and the fact that some of the data was quite old did not adversely impact the test.*

Cohabiting systems: This was another problem. Customers were not supposed to load their own software on the client machines, but of course they did. The testers did not test the impact of any other software, because the users were not supposed to load it. Actually, it turned out that another piece of software developed by the company caused the software under test to crash frequently if both were loaded and used at the same time.

System Testing ■ ■ ■ ■ ■

The system test is what most people think about when they think of testing. It is what Rick often calls "The Big Kahuna." The system test is where most of the testing resources normally go because the testing may go on for an extended period of time and is intended to be as comprehensive as the resources allow and the risk dictates. In addition to functional testing, it is typically during system test that load, performance, reliability, and other tests are performed if there is not a special effort or team for those activities. The system test set or a portion of it will normally comprise the bulk of the regression test suite for future releases of the product.

Audience Analysis

If there is an independent test team, their focus is normally on system testing. The manager of this team or a senior test analyst would normally be the primary author of the system test plan. He or she would be responsible for coordinating with the developers and users to get their input on the areas that affect them. If there is no independent test team, the system test plan

■■■■■■■■■■■■■■■■■
Who should write
the system test plan?

may be written by the development team or in some cases by the users.

The system test plan can normally be started as soon as the first draft of the requirements is fairly complete. The software design documentation will also have an impact on the system test plan, so the "completion" of the plan may be delayed until it is done.

■■■■■■■■■■■■■■■■■
When should the
system test plan be
written?
_____

Sources of Information

As in the case of the acceptance test plan, the system test plan must be in agreement with the master test plan and seek to amplify those parts of the MTP that address system testing. The system test plan is built based on the requirements specifications, design documentation, and user documentation, if they exist. Other documents such as functional specifications, training materials, and so on are also useful. Chapter 5 – *Analysis and Design* explains the valuable of creating inventories of functions, states, interfaces, etc. to be used as a basis for the test design.

The requirements traceability matrix that is used for acceptance testing is a good starting point for the system testing traceability matrix, but is generally not comprehensive enough to support the system test design. Generally, the system test group will try to build a matrix that not only covers the requirements, but also includes an inventory of features, design characteristics, states, etc. Other domains that are addressed in systems testing might include capacity, concurrence, configuration, conversion, hardware, installation, interoperability, interfaces, localization, performance, recovery, reliability, resource usage, scalability, sensitivity, software configuration, and usability. However, not all of these domains are applicable for every application.

■■■■■■■■■■■■■■■■■
A traceability matrix
for system testing
may include some or
all of the following
domains:

- requirements
- features
- design
  characteristics
- states
- capacity
- concurrence
- conversion
- h/w configuration
- interoperability
- installation
- interfaces
- localization
- performance
- recovery
- reliability
- resource usage
- scalability
- sensitivity
- s/w configuration
- usability
_____

Software Configuration Management

Software configuration management is critical to the testing effort. It is so important that if the software configuration management is done poorly, the testing effort and indeed the entire project may fail. Normally, we think of software configuration management as a process that has two distinct but related functions, as illustrated in Figure 4-10.

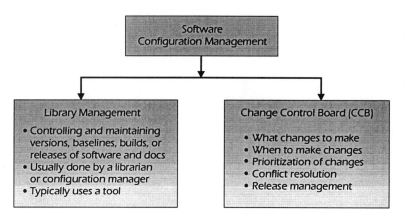

Figure 4-10

Functions of Configuration Management

The first of these is an administrative function that is itself sometimes called configuration management, although library management is probably a more accurate term. This is the function of creating the builds, managing changes to the software, and ensuring that the correct versions of the software and documentation are maintained and shipped. It's frequently done with the aid of commercially available or homegrown tools. The configuration manager may be organizationally independent, or the function may fall under the development organization, the QA team, or the testing team. Configuration management is a difficult and thankless job where you're hardly ever noticed until something goes wrong – kind of like testing.

Key Point

Change Control Board (CCB) members may include:

- testers
- developers
- configuration managers
- database admins
- users/customers
- customer support
- marketing

The other part of software configuration management is more of a management function. This is usually done with a group called the Change Control Board (CCB), Change Management Board (CMB), bug committee, the every-other-Tuesday meeting, or whatever you call it – really, the name is not that important. The purpose of the CCB is to determine how incidents, defects, and enhancements should be handled, as illustrated in Figure 4-11. Basically, the CCB determines what changes should be made and in what order (i.e., the priority).

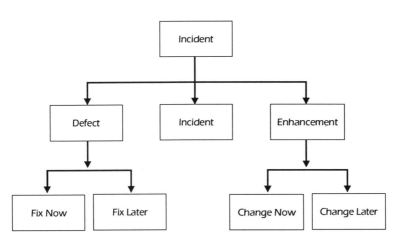

Ideally, the CCB would comprise a group of users, developers, testers, and anyone else with a vested interest in the final product. Normally, priorities are based upon the severity of the bug (users are useful), the effort to fix the bug (developers are useful), the impact on the schedule (managers are useful), and the effort to re-test (testers are useful).

Most companies have some type of formal or informal CCB that looks at production bugs and enhancement requests. Many of these same companies do not have any special process to handle and prioritize bugs and enhancements that occur during the course of the software development lifecycle. This is not necessarily a big problem at the lower levels of test (e.g., unit), where the required degree of formality of configuration management is less, but becomes critical at system and acceptance test times. We're discussing configuration management in greater detail in the section on system testing because it seems that is where some of the biggest configuration management problems occur. Case Study 4-4 describes a configuration management problem that occurs all too often.

The Bug That "Never Existed"

See if this scenario sounds familiar... The systems test is being conducted and Heather, the tester, discovers a defect. She immediately documents the bug and sends it back to the developer for resolution. Bob, the developer, can't stand the thought that someone found a bug in his work, so he fixes it immediately and updates the version of the software under test. Out of sight, out of mind... Many developers feel that if they fix the bug fast enough, it's as if it never happened. But now, Heather and maybe some of her colleagues have to test the bug fix, possibly retest other parts of the system, or even re-run a significant part of the regression suite. If this is repeated over and over with different developers and testers, the testing gets out of control and it's unlikely that the testers will ever finish testing the entire system. At the very least, they will have spent way too much time and money.

On the other hand, testers are also a problem. You may have heard or even said yourself, "How do you expect me to ever get this tested if you keep changing it? Testing a spec is like walking on water, it helps if it is frozen." Well, obviously if the software is frozen prematurely, at some point the testing will become unrealistic. A bug found by tester 'A,' for example, would certainly change what tester 'B' was doing if the first bug had been fixed.

■■■■■■■■■■■■■■■■■■

Case Study 4-4

If a developer fixes a bug really fast and creates a new build, did the bug really exist?

The solution to Case Study 4-4 is not to fix every bug immediately or to freeze the code prematurely, but to manage the changes to the system under test. Ideally, changes should be gathered together and re-implemented into the test environment in such a way as to reduce the required regression testing without causing a halt or slowdown to the test due to a blocking bug. The changes to the software under test should begin to slow down as the system test progresses and moves into the acceptance test execution phase. Case Study 4-5 describes an example of how one company's system test plan identifies a strategy for implementing changes to their software.

An Example Strategy for Implementing Changes

- *For the first two weeks of testing, all change requests and bug fixes will be implemented in a daily build to occur at 5:30 p.m.*

- *For the next two weeks, the test manager, development manager, user representative, and configuration manager will meet at 10:00 every Tuesday and Thursday to prioritize all outstanding or open change requests or bug fixes. They will also decide which completed fixes will be promoted into the System Test Environment.*

- *For the final two weeks of scheduled system test, only "show-stopper" bug fixes will be implemented into the test environment.*

■■■■■■■■■■■■■■■■■
Case Study 4-5

How does your organization manage changes to the software under test?

———————

Many of our students and some of our clients ask about daily builds. Daily builds are not for everyone and not for the entire software development lifecycle. Early in the development phase, unit and integration testing, and even in the early stages of the system test execution phase, daily builds can be a useful tool. However, using daily builds until the very end assures most companies that they have spent too much time doing regression testing and/or shipping a product that isn't fully tested. If the regression test suite is automated, then it is possible to extend the daily builds well into the system test execution phase, but there still needs to be a code freeze (show-stoppers aside) during the later stages of system test and during acceptance testing.

There are very few things that a test manager can do to improve the efficiency of the testing effort that will pay a dividend as much as managing how changes are re-implemented into the test environment. Some managers of testing groups have little or no control over how changes are promoted into the test environment. Other managers may not even have a clear view of what changes are introduced and when (i.e., the developer has total control of the software under test). If you fall into one of these two categories, getting control of how changes are promoted into your test environment should be one of your top priorities. Otherwise, you're not really managing the testing effort – you're only reacting to the changes to your environment.

Key Point

There are very few things that a test manager can do to improve the efficiency of the testing effort that will pay a dividend as much as managing how changes are re-implemented into the test environment.

Exit/Entrance Criteria

Exit and entrance criteria are important issues that should be addressed in the system test plan. If the system test execution is started prior to the conclusion of integration testing (in order to shorten the lifecycle), then many of the bugs that would have been contained during the developmental testing (e.g., unit and integration) may be discovered during system test, where the cost to find and fix them is much greater. For example, in Figure 4-12, the defect found at point 'A' might have been discovered during integration testing had integration testing concluded prior to the start of system testing.

Key Point

Many organizations begin executing one level of test before the prior one completes, in order to field the system sooner. The downside of this strategy is that it typically requires more resources.

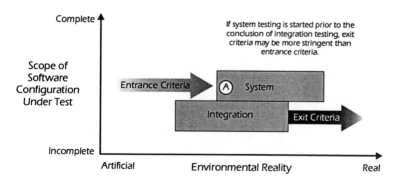

Figure 4-12

Consequences of Overlapping Test Levels

If a developer discovers a bug in his or her code during unit or integration testing, he or she normally just fixes it without advertising the problem. If the same bug is discovered during system test, it has to be documented, prioritized, returned to the developer for correction, and ultimately reintroduced into the system test environment for re-testing and appropriate regression testing. During this time, the developer may have already moved on to something else. Debugging is often significantly more difficult for bugs found by the tester in the *system* as opposed to finding them in unit or integration testing.

Automation of regression test suites (or any other, for that matter) is difficult if the software and, consequently, the test cases have to change frequently. In fact, if the software is too unstable and changing too rapidly, some test automation techniques would probably prove to be counterproductive and it would be easier to test manually. To help solve these problems, it's useful to create exit criteria from the developer's test (unit or integration) and entrance criteria into system test. We would also need to consider exit criteria from system test and entrance criteria into acceptance test. Case Study 4-6 describes one company's exit criteria from their *developmental tests*.

■■■■■■■■■■■■■■■■■
Key Point

Developmental tests are those levels of test that are normally accomplished by the developer. In this book, those levels are Unit and Integration.

Example Exit Criteria from Developmental Tests

- All unit and integration tests and results are documented.
- There can be no High severity bugs.
- There must be 100% statement coverage.
- There must be 100% coverage of all programming specifications.
- The results of a code walkthrough are documented and acceptable.

The exit criteria that this company defined are somewhat of a wish list. Some test managers would be happy if the code just compiled cleanly. At a minimum, test cases and results should be documented, and if it is part of your culture

■■■■■■■■■■■■■■■■■
Case Study 4-6

How does your organization define developmental tests? What are your exit criteria?

(and we hope it is), the results of the code walkthroughs should also be documented.

The entrance criteria should include all or some of the exit criteria from the previous level, plus they may contain statements about the establishment of the test environment, gathering of data, procurement and installation of tools, and if necessary, the hiring or borrowing of testers. If you are having difficulty receiving a stable system, you might want to consider building a "smoke" test as part of the entrance criteria.

Smoke Test

A smoke test is a group of test cases that establish that the system is stable and all major functionality is present and works under "normal" conditions. The purpose of a smoke test is not to find bugs in the software, although you might, but rather to let the system test team know what their starting point is. It also provides a goal for the developers and lets them know when they have achieved a degree of stability.

■■■■■■■■■■■■■■■■■
Key Point

A *smoke test* is a group of test cases that establish that the system is stable and all major functionality is present and works under "normal" conditions.

The smoke test cannot be created autonomously by the testing team, but should be done jointly or at least with the consent of the developers. Otherwise, the developers will feel like the testers are dictating to them how to do their job, and no buy-in will be achieved for the smoke test. Then, all you'll have is a smoke test that may or may not work, and the developer will say, "So what?" Remember that buy-in is the key to success.

The trick to establishing a good smoke test is to create a group of tests that are broad in scope, as opposed to depth. Remember that the purpose is to demonstrate stability, not to find every bug in the system. We like to take our smoke test cases from the regression test set, so the smoke test becomes a subset of the regression test set. We also like to target the smoke tests as the very first tests that we attempt to automate.

It doesn't really matter if the smoke test is run by the developers or testers, but it should be run in the system test environment. The developer may want to try it in his or her environment first, but you must remember that just because it works in the development environment doesn't mean it will work in the system test environment. The test manager might want to make the test environment available to the developers, so they can run the test and have some confidence that it works prior to promoting the code to the test team.

Integration Testing ■ ■ ■ ■ ■

Integration testing is the level of test done to ensure that the various components of a system interact and pass data correctly among one another and function cohesively. Integration testing can be accomplished at various levels. At the lowest level, integration testing is normally done by the development group to ensure that the units work properly together. Higher levels of integration or builds may also be done by the developer or by the test team. Integration testing is the process of examining how the pieces of a system work together, especially at the interfaces. Integration can occur at various levels, as illustrated in the car example in Figure 4-13.

■ ■ ■ ■ ■ ■ ■ ■ ■ ■ ■ ■ ■ ■ ■ ■ ■
Key Point

Integration testing is also known as string, thread, build, subsystem, and by a multitude of other names.

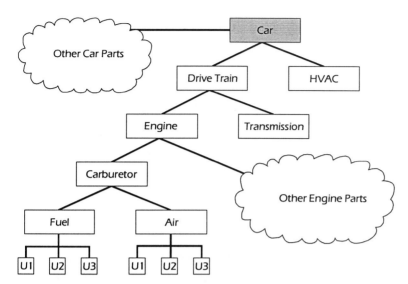

■■■■■■■■■■■■■■■■■■

Figure 4-13

Levels of Integration in a Typical Car

Several units (e.g., U1, U2, U3) are used to make the fuel module, the fuel and the air module make the carburetor, the carburetor and other parts are used to make the engine, and so on. The levels of integration continue up the chain until the entire car is assembled. Different people might do different levels of integration testing. What you call "integration" is dependent on what you call a "system." Consider the example in Figure 4-13. If you define the system as the *car*, then everything below the car is integration that leads to the ultimate system. If the *engine* is seen as the system, then all of the parts leading to the engine are part of the integration testing. The process of testing the engine with the transmission becomes a systems integration task or a job of testing the interface between two systems. The decision of "what is a system" was described in the *Introduction (Scope)* section of the master test plan and may be affected by the structure of the organization, politics, staffing, and other factors.

Audience Analysis

In most organizations, the integration test plan is used primarily by developers as a "road map" to test how all the individual parts of a system fit together. The test group also uses this plan to make sure there's no overlap between what they're testing and what the developers or other test groups are testing.

Many companies that we've visited have never done integration testing *per se* and frequently deliver well-tested systems. In this case the integration testing is probably done as part of an extended unit testing effort or is accomplished as part of system testing. Integration testing can become very important, especially on larger, more complex systems, and in particular on new development. Some bugs that can be discovered as the units are integrated are impossible to find when testing isolated units. The interfaces between modules are the target of integration testing and are normally error-prone parts of the system.

Activity Timing

As always, we're anxious to start the test plan as soon as possible. Normally, this would mean that the integration test planning process could begin as soon as the design is beginning to stabilize.

■■■■■■■■■■■■■■■■■
When should the Integration Test Plan be written?

Developers play an important part in the development of the integration test plan because they'll eventually be required to participate in the testing. We have always felt that the developers are the most logical people to do the integration testing, since the development team really doesn't know if they have created a viable system without doing at least some integration testing. Having the developers do the integration testing also speeds the fixing of any bugs that are discovered.

■■■■■■■■■■■■■■■■■
Who should write the Integration Test Plan and who should do the testing?

Finally, in order to do integration testing, it is frequently necessary to create scaffolding code (stubs and drivers). The members of the test team may or may not have the skill set necessary to create this scaffolding code.

One of the key issues in integration testing is determining which modules to create and integrate first. It's very desirable to integrate the riskiest components or those that are on the critical path (drivers) first, so that we can discover as early as possible if there are any major problems. There's nothing worse than discovering a fatal flaw in one of the most critical components late in the lifecycle. Another reason why the developers are often called upon to do the integration test is because the strategy of how to conduct the integration testing is controlled almost entirely by the strategy for integrating the system, which is done by the developer.

Since systems are frequently built by iteratively combining larger and larger pieces of code (and underlying functionality), there may be various levels of integration tests. The earliest levels are often used to just check the interaction of units. In many companies this is accomplished in a fairly informal fashion and is often seen as just an extension of unit testing. Integration testing is often done by individual developers working together to see how their code works. At some point, entire modules or subsystems need to be built. This is also often known as integration or build testing. Logically, build testing should be done by the developers or, in some cases, the test group.

Sources of Information

Typically, the integration tests are built based upon the detailed design specifications. Higher levels of integration testing may also use the high-level or architectural design specifications. Finally, even in integration testing, an effort should be made to

Key Point

According to Glenford Myers' *The Art of Software Testing*, scaffolding is code that simulates the function of non-existent components.

Drivers are modules that simulate high-level components, while *stubs* are modules that simulate low-level components.

What do you mean by different levels of integration testing?

match the software design and its corresponding test cases to the requirements.

Integration Test Planning Issues

Many strategic issues should be considered before deciding what type of integration testing to perform:

- What modules or objects should be assembled and tested as a group?
- What are the functional subassemblies?
- What are the critical features?
- How much testing is appropriate?
- Are there any implementation-based testing objectives?
- How much scaffolding code or test support code is required?
- How will problems be isolated?
- How is testing coordinated with system and unit testing?

Figure 4-14 illustrates a sample project containing a group of interacting builds. The shaded boxes represent critical-path components that must pass integration testing before the *Make Reservation* function can move to the system testing phase.

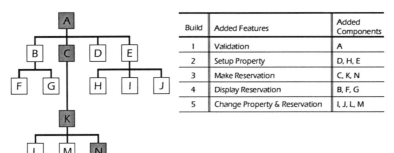

Build	Added Features	Added Components
1	Validation	A
2	Setup Property	D, H, E
3	Make Reservation	C, K, N
4	Display Reservation	B, F, G
5	Change Property & Reservation	I, J, L, M

■■■■■■■■■■■■■■■■■

Figure 4-14

Sample Build Scheme

If any of the components A, C, K, or N are incomplete, the *Make Reservation* function cannot be executed without including stubs or drivers.

Configuration Management

At the earliest stages of integration testing, that is to say, as the first units are being integrated, configuration management is normally done in a fairly informal fashion with the developers and/or program leads handling most of the duty. As the builds get progressively larger, the configuration management should become more formal, as changes to the system can potentially affect the coding and testing of other developers and testers.

Test Environments

In most organizations, the integration test environment will be the development environment. Because the integration testing will commence prior to the total integration of the system, integration test cases often cannot be executed without creating stubs and/or drivers to stub out the missing pieces of code. The effectiveness of the integration testing will be directly affected by the validity of the scaffolding code.

Often the data being used in integration testing will be made up of a subset of the production environment. Since integration testing is focused on testing the internal interfaces of the system, volume testing is not normally attempted and therefore large volumes of test data are not required.

■■■■■■■■■■■■■■■■■
Key Point

"Volume testing is testing that purposely subjects a system to a series of tests where the volume of the data being processed is the subject of the test... Volume testing will seek to verify the physical and logical limits to a system's capacity..."

– The Information Security Glossary

Unit Testing

■■■■■■■■■■■■■■■■
Key Point

A simplified template for a unit test plan is contained in Appendix E.

Over the course of the past several years, we have had the opportunity to present over 300 seminars on various aspects of software testing. During these seminars, one topic that receives more than its share of blank stares is "unit testing." Rick jokingly tells the audience that "there's an IEEE standard (IEEE Std. 1008-1987, Standard for Software Unit Testing) for unit testing, but so far only one copy has been sold and I own it!" Refer to Figure 4-15.

This section will explore some of the reasons why unit testing is done poorly (or not at all), why unit testing is important, and some ideas for implementing formal unit testing within an organization.

■■■■■■■■■■■■■■■■
Figure 4-15

Rick's copy of the Unit Testing Standard

IEEE Std. 1008-1987 for Software Unit Testing

Contents

1. Scope and References
    1.1 Inside the Scope
    1.2 Outside the Scope
    1.3 References

2. Definitions

3. Unit Testing Activities
    3.1 Plan the General Approach, Resources, and Schedule
    3.2 Determine Features to Be Tested
    3.3 Refine the General Plan
    3.4 Design the Set of Tests
    3.5 Implement the Refined Plan and Design

Common Obstacles in Unit Testing

Most developers are quick to learn that their job is to create code. Management may talk about the importance of unit testing, but their actions contradict their words. Developers are measured and rewarded for producing code. It's true that developers may also be penalized for excessive bugs in their code, but the pressure to get the code out the door often outweighs every other concern. Another problem is the attitude of the developers themselves. Most seem to be eternal optimists, and when placed under the gun, they *believe* their code will work correctly and unit testing is something to do only if time permits (which, of course, it never does).

■■■■■■■■■■■■■■■■■

"It's not my job to do unit testing."

An extension of this problem is the normal situation in most companies, where the developers/unit testers have not been trained to do unit testing. Many managers and some developers believe that if you know how to code, you also know how to test – as if testing was some inherent trait existent in every developer. Developers must be trained in the general concepts of testing at all levels (unit, integration, system, acceptance, etc.) and in the specific techniques necessary to effectively perform unit testing.

■■■■■■■■■■■■■■■■■

"I haven't been trained to do unit testing."

Finally, the proper procedures and tools have to be in place in order for developers to conduct unit testing. Documents need to be created that describe unit test plans, test designs, configuration management, etc. Adequate test tools and

■■■■■■■■■■■■■■■■■

"I don't have the tools to do unit testing."

debuggers must also be available. Certainly, each developer needs to have access to debugging tools, code coverage tools, defect tracking systems, and library management systems. Other tools may be necessary in some organizations.

If the three preceding paragraphs describe some of the situations that exist in your organization, please read on. We have described some of the issues that need to be addressed in order to successfully implement and conduct unit testing in an organization.

Education and Buy-In

The first step in implementing effective unit testing is to provide all developers with training on how to test. The training should include general training in testing methodologies as well as training on specific unit testing techniques and tools. Development managers would also benefit from participating in training on testing methodologies and techniques. Not only will the training provide them with an understanding of the discipline, it will also show support to their staff.

■■■■■■■■■■■■■■■■
Key Point

Our testing classes have recently shown an increase in the number of developers attending.

Many companies have independent test teams, often at the system test level. These test groups have a vested interest in the quality of the unit testing, since good unit testing can greatly facilitate the testing at higher levels by finding defects earlier in the lifecycle. Many development managers may find that the testing groups can provide some type of training for their staffs. Often the testing groups are willing (even excited) to provide a trainer or mentor to assist in the creation of unit test plans, test case design, etc.

Standards and Requirements

An effective way to develop standards is to provide company-unique samples of each kind of document required. As a minimum set the following samples should be created: unit test plan, test design, test case/test procedure, defect report, and test summary report. Unless the work is remarkably consistent from project to project, it may be necessary to provide samples for small projects (i.e., 3-4 individuals) and for larger projects, since documentation requirements are generally greater for larger projects. It's important that the samples include only the information necessary to avoid the perceived (and sometimes real) notion that documentation is being created for its own sake.

Often, the only process documentation required in addition to the sample documents is a series of flowcharts that describe how to accomplish certain tasks such as reporting a defect, checking code in and out, where and how to save test cases, when and how to implement an inspection or walkthrough, and how to use a test log. The key is to make all of these activities as simple and painless as possible.

It's important that an individual (or group) be identified as the champion of the testing process and documentation. The champion is a person whom everyone knows they can go to for help. Typically, the champion should be an opinion-leader although not necessarily a manager. In fact, the champion should probably not be in the chain of command.

Developers should be responsible for creating and documenting unit testing processes. If a set of documents or procedures is passed down to the programming staff, they'll often adopt the attitude that "this is just another bureaucratic requirement." Similarly, the practitioners, possibly through the champion, must

■■■■■■■■■■■■■■■■

Key Point

Developers should be responsible for creating and documenting unit testing processes.

feel that the standards can be changed if they're not working. A periodic review of the procedures by a group of practitioners will help facilitate this idea.

Configuration Management

Systematic unit testing is seldom achieved without first establishing procedures for source code control. If developers are allowed unregulated control of their code during unit test, they are unlikely to execute formal unit tests that identify defects in their code, since no one likes to admit that their work is "less than perfect." Placing the code under configuration management is one way to signal that it is time for the execution of unit tests. There is a danger, of course, of establishing controls that are too rigid, especially early in the development process. Initially, it may be adequate to control source code at the team level or even at the individual developer level (if adequate guidelines are provided) rather than through the library manager, but if no procedures are established it will be difficult to differentiate between debugging and unit testing. The successful completion of a code inspection can also be used as a signal for formal unit test execution.

■■■■■■■■■■■■■■■■
Key Point

Systematic unit testing is seldom achieved without first establishing procedures for source code control.

Metrics

Another benefit of formal unit testing is that it allows the collection of unit-level metrics, which help identify problematic areas early in the development process. Although it's not necessarily an intuitive concept, programs or modules that have had large numbers of defects identified in them (and subsequently corrected) generally *still* have abnormally large numbers of undetected defects remaining. One reason that this phenomenon occurs may be because programs with large numbers of defects are complex or not well understood. Another reason might be that some bugs are introduced into the system as

■■■■■■■■■■■■■■■■
Key Point

Defect density is the ratio of defects to size. The most common ratio is the number of defects per thousand lines of code (KLOC).

a result of implementing fixes. Organizations that can identify defect-prone modules during unit testing can tag them as high risk and ensure that they receive adequate attention prior to integration and system testing. High defect density during unit test may also signal that more time needs to be allotted for higher-level testing.

Collecting metrics during unit testing also facilitates estimating testing time and resources for future releases and helps identify areas for process improvement. One word of caution: we are interested in measuring the product and the process, but many developers may feel that they are being measured! Make sure you understand the culture and personality of the development group before you implement measurements that might appear threatening.

They'd Rather Just Fix the Bugs Than Reveal Them

I've always found it difficult to collect metrics on unit testing, since most developers would rather just fix the bugs in their code rather than reveal them. This is unfortunate because knowledge of which units contained the most bugs is lost. Knowing which units had the most bugs is useful for systems testers because those buggy units tend to have more "escapes" than other units.

One test manager explained how she learned of those problematic units without requiring the developers to record their bugs. She merely asked every developer, "Of all the units that you created, which ones were the most difficult?" It turns out that the units identified as difficult had a greater concentration of bugs than the ones that weren't identified.

- Rick Craig

■■■■■■■■■■■■■■■■■
Case Study 4-7

Most developers would rather just fix the bugs in their code rather than reveal them.

Reusing Unit Testware

In this era of tight budgets and schedules, it's absolutely imperative that every effort be made to maximize all resources. One way of doing this is in the reuse of work products such as test cases and procedures, test plans, etc. If unit test cases are properly documented, they can be invaluable in helping to describe the system (i.e., they can be thought of as part of the system documentation). Furthermore, well-documented test cases can be reused during regression testing and sometimes can even be reused at higher levels of test. This idea of reusing some of the unit tests at a higher level of test is a concept that some practitioners have difficulty accepting. We're not suggesting that all of the unit-level tests need to be rerun (say at integration test), or that the unit test set by itself is adequate for higher-level testing. We're only suggesting that if a unit test satisfies a testing objective at integration or system test, it may be possible to reuse it for that purpose. Running the same test case at two different levels frequently results in testing quite different attributes. All of this is a moot point, of course, if the test cases are not *intelligently* documented and saved (by intelligently, we mean that you know what each test case is designed to test, i.e., coverage).

■■■■■■■■■■■■■■■■■
Key Point

Well-documented test cases can be reused during regression testing and sometimes can even be reused at higher levels of test.

Reviews, Walkthroughs, and Inspections

More and more software engineers believe that review techniques (such as inspections) that use the power of the human mind and the dynamics of group interaction are a powerful and effective method of identifying defects. Some organizations agonize over what to inspect (code, test cases, test plans), when to conduct inspections (before unit testing, after unit testing, both before and after), and how to measure their effectiveness, but very few organizations that we have encountered regret choosing

■■■■■■■■■■■■■■■■■
Key Point

Refer to Chapter 3 under *Walkthroughs and Inspections* for more information.

to use inspections. The use of code inspections complements systematic unit testing by helping to flag when to begin unit test execution. Inspections are also effective at finding defects that are difficult to find during unit testing and vice versa.

Buddy Testing

For some time now, we've been recommending that our clients employ a team approach ("*Buddy Testing*") to coding and unit testing. Using this concept, two-person teams are identified and assigned programming tasks. Developer 'A' writes the test cases for Developer 'B's specification *before* Developer 'B' begins coding. Developer 'B' does the same thing for Developer 'A'. There are several advantages to this technique:

- Objectivity is introduced into testing at a very low level, which is seldom achieved during developmental testing.
- By creating the test cases prior to coding, they can serve as models of the program specification requirements. Most developers will find that having the test cases available prior to coding actually *changes* the way they write their code. The test cases are designed to break the code as well as show that it works. Many developers who write test cases after coding merely demonstrate that their code "does what it does." Don't underestimate the power of buddy testing. This is applying the principle of preventative testing at the lowest level.
- Finally, buddy testing provides a certain degree of cross-training on the application. If developer 'A' leaves, then Developer 'B' has knowledge of his or her code.

■■■■■■■■■■■■■■■■
Key Point

Most developers will find that having the test cases available prior to coding actually *changes* the way they write their code.

The downside of buddy testing is the extra time required to write the test cases up front and for the developers to familiarize themselves with each other's specifications and code.

We've been using buddy testing for 20 years or so and first published an introduction to the process in 1995. Most of the methods we espouse as part of buddy testing are also incorporated in a larger discipline now known as *extreme programming*. For more information, we highly recommend *Extreme Programming: Embrace Change (The XP Series)* by Kent Beck.

As we explained throughout this chapter, detailed test planning must start at the beginning and proceed in parallel with the software development lifecycle in order to be effective. We recommend that you start with the basic levels of test defined by the IEEE (acceptance, system, integration and unit) and add or delete levels as necessary. If you use this approach, you'll provide yourself with a good foundation to build your detailed test plans.

Chapter 5 –
Analysis and Design

"Absolute certainty about the fail-proofness of a design can never be attained, for we can never be certain that we have been exhaustive in asking questions about its future."

— Henry Petroski
  To Engineer Is Human

Test Analysis and Design is the process of determining test objectives and how to organize the test objectives in a manner that supports efficient execution. There are many different design techniques available to the tester, and the choice of what technique to use is typically based on the nature of the system, the overall risk of the implementation, the level of test, and the skill set of the testers. It's also likely that on any given system, more than one technique will apply. This chapter will introduce the reader to some of the available techniques and will explain, in detail, how to use one of these techniques: inventories. Using inventories to develop a test design actually embodies several different testing techniques.

■■■■■■■■■■■■■■■■■
Key Point

Test objectives are broad categories of things to test. Test objectives are to testing what requirements are to development.

Creating Inventories ■■■■■

Test objectives are broad categories of things that need to be tested for any given application. For example, the testers of a car insurance program might determine that the following objectives exist: type of car, geographic region, age of driver, age of car, safety features of the car, security features of the car, deductible amount, primary use of the car, and so forth.

The inventory is the actual list of things that need to be tested for each of the test objectives. For example, the inventory for *type of car* might include SUVs, sports cars, vintage cars, off-road vehicles, sedans, etc., as illustrated in Figure 5-1. Many objectives will be unique to the application being tested. Our insurance example used *type of car* as an objective, but this would certainly not be a test objective for an ATM application, or a grocery store point-of-sale application.

Objective: Type of Car

Inventory: {
  SUVs
  Sports Cars
  Vintage Cars
  Off-Road Vehicles
  Sedans
  Etc.
}

Figure 5-1

Inventory of Types of Cars

_____

Some objectives, though, are universal enough that they can be called *common*. For example, one common objective is interfaces. It's highly likely that most applications would need to have all of their interfaces to other systems tested. Consequently, the testers of each application would need to create an inventory of interfaces unique to their particular application.

Creating inventories is a multi-step process that begins with gathering reference materials and "ends" with maintaining the testing matrix. We've developed a process, outlined in Figure 5-2, that uses objectives and inventories as the primary basis for test design.

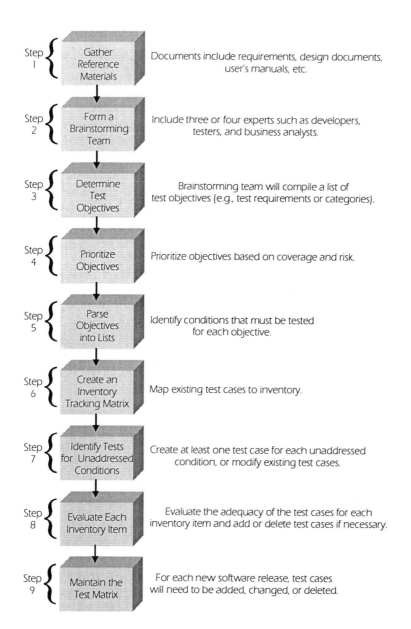

Step 1 — Gather Reference Materials — Documents include requirements, design documents, user's manuals, etc.

Step 2 — Form a Brainstorming Team — Include three or four experts such as developers, testers, and business analysts.

Step 3 — Determine Test Objectives — Brainstorming team will compile a list of test objectives (e.g., test requirements or categories).

Step 4 — Prioritize Objectives — Prioritize objectives based on coverage and risk.

Step 5 — Parse Objectives into Lists — Identify conditions that must be tested for each objective.

Step 6 — Create an Inventory Tracking Matrix — Map existing test cases to inventory.

Step 7 — Identify Tests for Unaddressed Conditions — Create at least one test case for each unaddressed condition, or modify existing test cases.

Step 8 — Evaluate Each Inventory Item — Evaluate the adequacy of the test cases for each inventory item and add or delete test cases if necessary.

Step 9 — Maintain the Test Matrix — For each new software release, test cases will need to be added, changed, or deleted.

Step 1
Gather Reference Materials

The first step in creating an inventory is to gather all of the relevant documentation that you can find about the system. These may include:

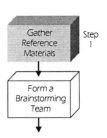

- requirements documentation
- design documentation
- user's manuals
- product specifications
- functional specifications
- government regulations
- training manuals
- customer feedback

Step 2
Form a Brainstorming Team

The brainstorming team should ideally be made up of three or four subject-matter experts (but probably not more than seven or eight). Systems and business expertise are the two most sought areas of experience. Good brainstormers might include developers, testers, users, customers, business analysts, user representatives, system architects, and marketing representatives. The key is to get the people with the most knowledge of the business application and the systemic nature of the application (for existing systems). Our team might look like this:

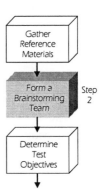

- Cheryl   Test Manager
- Crissy   Systems Architect
- Stefan   Senior Developer
- Rayanne   Business Analyst
- Erika   Marketing Representative

Step 3
Determine Test Objectives

The idea behind the brainstorming session is to create lists of things to test. It's important not to scrutinize the list too closely up front and equally important not to get too detailed. In fact, we recommend that the team first just brainstorm the inventory topics (i.e., objectives). Examples of common requirements objectives include:

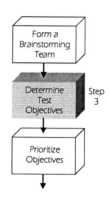

- Functions or methods
- Constraints or limits
- System configurations
- Interfaces with other systems
- Conditions on input and output attributes
- Conditions of system/object memory (i.e., states that affect processing)
- Behavior rules linking input and memory conditions (i.e., object states) to resultant functions
- Critical usage and operational scenarios
- Anything else to worry about, based on an external analysis of the system

Many other test objectives exist, and there will always be some that are unique to a particular system, but the above list gives you an idea of the kinds of things we're looking for. Another word of caution: don't be concerned about the overlap in the objectives or inventories. Remember, we're trying to determine what's possible to test by looking at the system from many viewpoints. We'll worry about eliminating redundancy in future steps.

The following list shows some of the test objectives that we compiled for an insurance company:

- Requirements
- Features
- Screens
- Error Messages
- Transaction Types
- Customers
- States (geographical)
- Type of Policy
- Type of Vehicle
- States (Effective)

Step 4
Prioritize Objectives

Once the high-level objectives have been determined, it's time to prioritize them. Normally we prioritize the objectives based on scope (i.e., breadth) and risk. It's always desirable to choose, as the highest priority, an objective (and its associated inventory) that has broad coverage of the system. Often, that will turn out to be the inventory of features, customer types, the requirements specification itself, or some other similar broad category. In our insurance company example, we took the requirements document and features as our two highest-priority objectives since they had the broadest scope.

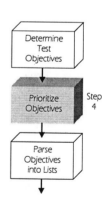

Step 5
Parse Objectives into Lists

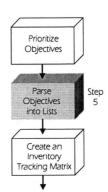

The next step in creating an inventory is to parse the objectives into lists (inventories). You should start with the highest-priority objectives and parse them into more detailed components. Lower-priority objectives will be parsed into more detail when, and if, time allows. The objective *features*, for example, can be parsed into the following inventory:

- Write a policy
- Add a driver
- Add a car
- Submit a claim
- Change address (same locale)
- Change address (different locale)
- Submit a bill
- Amend a policy
- Amend a bill

Later, if more time permits, the inventory could be expanded to a finer level of granularity:

- Write a policy
  - Commercial
  - Individual
  - High-risk
  - Stated Value
- Add a driver
  - Under 16
  - Over 16, under 65
  - Male
  - Female
  - Driving School
  - Record
    - Good

- - Bad
- Add a Car
  - Type
    - SUV
    - Sports
    - Pickup
- Security Devices
  - Club
  - Alarm
  - Tracking Device
- Garaged?
- Etc.

Obviously, this inventory could be broken down even further. We recommend that you initially not try to make them too detailed, because creating the test cases can be overwhelming. If time allows, additional detail can always be added later.

Step 6
Create an Inventory Tracking Matrix

To create the matrix, list the objectives and their corresponding inventories down the left column of Table 5-1, starting with the number 1 priority objective, and then the number 2 objective, and so forth. Then, place any existing test cases from previous releases and testing efforts horizontally across the top of the table. This process of mapping existing test cases to the inventories is known as calibration because we are calibrating the test cases against a "known" entity (i.e., the inventories). If you think you have a pretty good set of test cases, but have never calibrated them, we believe most of you will be surprised to find that the coverage of your tests is not nearly as great as you might have imagined.

Table 5-1 Inventory Tracking Matrix

Objectives / Inventories	Test Cases						
	TC#1	TC#2	TC#3	TC#4	TC#5	TC#6	TC#7
Requirements							
Requirement 1							
Requirement 2	X	X		X			
Requirement 3		X	X		X		
Features							
Feature 1							X
Feature 2							
Feature 3						X	
Feature 4	X	X					X
Objective A							
Objective B							
Objective C							

Requirements Traceability

NOTE: Objectives A, B, C, and so on may be other common objectives such as interfaces, configurations, etc. or they may be application specific objectives.

Notice that the first objective on our list is the requirements specification. The mapping of this inventory to the test cases is known as *requirements traceability* (shown in Table 5-1), which is a preferred practice of virtually every testing methodology. Notice that we've gone beyond just tracing to the requirements specification and have traced to the entire set of inventories. Most people will find that even if they have a good set of requirements, the additional inventories will identify many test scenarios that were "missed." Also note that one test case can cover multiple inventories. In Table 5-1, for example, Test Case #1 covers both Requirement 2 and Feature 4. This also demonstrates how the matrix can help reveal redundancies in the inventories and the test cases.

Key Point

Most people will find that even if they have a good set of requirements, the additional inventories will identify many test scenarios that were "missed."

Step 7
Identify Tests for Unaddressed
Conditions

In Table 5-2, you can see that existing test cases cover Requirements 2 and 3, and Features 1, 3, and 4. However, Requirement 1 and Feature 2 (refer to shaded rows) are not covered by any test. Therefore, it's necessary to create a test case or cases to cover these inventory items.

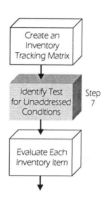

Table 5-2   Inventory Tracking Matrix

Objectives / Inventories	Test Cases						
	TC#1	TC#2	TC#3	TC#4	TC#5	TC#6	TC#7
Requirements							
Requirement 1							
Requirement 2	X	X		X			
Requirement 3		X	X		X		
Features							
Feature 1							X
Feature 2							
Feature 3						X	
Feature 4	X	X					X
Objective A							
Objective B							
Objective C							

NOTE: Objectives A, B, C, and so on may be other common objectives such as interfaces, configurations, etc. or they may be application-specific objectives.

In Table 5-3, notice that Requirement 1 is now covered by Test Case #1. It was possible to modify Test Case #1 to cover

Requirement 1 and still cover Requirement 2 and Feature 4. It wasn't possible to modify an existing test case to cover Feature 2, so Test Case #8 was added and, later, Test Case #9 was added because we felt that Test Case #8 didn't adequately test Feature 2 by itself.

Table 5-3   Inventory Tracking Matrix

Objectives / Inventories	Test Cases								
	TC#1	TC#2	TC#3	TC#4	TC#5	TC#6	TC#7	TC#8	TC#9
Requirements									
Requirement 1	X								
Requirement 2	X	X		X					
Requirement 3		X	X		X				
Features									
Feature 1							X		
Feature 2								X	X
Feature 3						X			
Feature 4	X	X					X		
Objective A									
Objective B									
Objective C									

NOTE: Objectives A, B, C, and so on may be other common objectives such as interfaces, configurations, etc. or they may be application-specific objectives.

Rather than modify existing test cases, it's frequently easier to add new test cases to address untested conditions. Testers also have to be careful about making any one test case cover too many conditions. If the test fails, or has to be modified, it will possibly invalidate the testing of other conditions.

Step 8
Evaluate Each Inventory Item

Evaluate each inventory item for adequacy of coverage and add additional test cases as required – remember that this process will never truly be complete. The testers must use their experience and exercise their judgment to determine if the existing tests for each condition are adequate. For example, in Table 5-3 (above), we see that Requirement 1 is covered by test case #1. Does that one test case adequately cover Requirement #1? If not, Requirement 1 will have to be parsed into greater detail or more test cases will have to be created.

Bug Parties

I once had a student from a well-known company who said they used a similar process in their group. Testers were committed to developing and maintaining a systematic set of test cases. Testers also recognized, though, the value of creative or ad hoc testing, so they conducted something which they called a "bug party," every other Friday. At these bug parties, all test cases were thrown out for the day and the testers (and anyone else that wanted to "play") were urged to look for bugs. Prizes were awarded for the most bugs found, the biggest bug, and the most creative testing technique. The whole thing was a huge morale booster and resulted in finding many bugs, some of which were significant. But finding bugs, as important as it was, was not the purpose of the party. You see, they then wrote the test case that would have found the bug, which improved the coverage of their existing test set. But that wasn't the real reason they had the bug parties either. What they were really looking for were entire categories or lists (inventories) of things that they forgot to test. How interesting, they were using ad hoc testing techniques to validate the effectiveness of their systematic testing. Who says testers are not creative!

— Rick Craig

Case Study 5-1

These creative testers used ad hoc testing techniques to help evaluate their systematic testing process.

Step 9
Maintain the Testing Matrix

As the system matures and changes, so too should the testing matrix.   The testing matrix is a reusable artifact that is particularly valuable in determining what regression tests to maintain and execute for any given release (at least which ones to begin with). The testing matrix is also a valuable tool to help in the configuration management of the test cases, since it helps relate the tests to the system itself. The maintenance of the matrix is a huge undertaking, but without it, the testers must virtually start over with the development of their tests for each new release. Not only is that a waste of time, but there's always the risk that some great test that was created for a previous release will not be remembered for this one.

Commercial tools are available to help document and maintain the inventories and test cases, but the effort required to maintain the testing matrix is still significant.

Design Analysis

The design can be subjected to the same process as described above.   In fact, the design coverage can be added to the requirements traceability matrix as shown in Table 5-4.

Table 5-4 Inventory Tracking Matrix

Objectives / Inventories	Test Cases								
	TC#1	TC#2	TC#3	TC#4	TC#5	TC#6	TC#7	TC#8	TC#9
Requirements									
Requirement 1	X								
Requirement 2	X	X		X					
Requirement 3		X	X		X				
Features									
Feature 1							X		
Feature 2								X	X
Feature 3						X			
Feature 4	X	X					X		
Design									
Design 1			X		X				
Design 2					X				
Design 3	X								X

Black-Box vs. White-Box ■ ■ ■ ■ ■

Black-box testing or behavioral testing is testing based upon the requirements and, just as the name implies, the system is treated as a "black box." That is, the internal workings of the system are unknown, as illustrated in Figure 5-3. In black-box testing the system is given a stimulus (input) and if the result (output) is what was expected, then the test passes. No consideration is given to how the process was completed.

■ ■ ■ ■ ■ ■ ■ ■ ■ ■ ■ ■ ■ ■ ■ ■
Key Point

White-box or black-box (testing) improves quality by 40%. Together, they improve quality by 60%.

– Oliver E. Cole, *Looking Under the Covers to Test Web Applications,* STAR East Conference, 2001

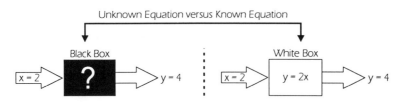

■■■■■■■■■■■■■■■■

Figure 5-3

Black-Box versus
White-Box Testing
_____

In white-box testing, an input must still produce the correct result in order to pass, but now we're also concerned with whether or not the process worked correctly. White-box testing is important for at least two reasons. Without peering inside the box, it's impossible to test all of the ways the system works (i.e., *how* the system works). While both black-box and white-box testing can determine if the system is doing what it's supposed to do, only white-box testing is effective at determining if the "how" part of the equation is correct. Generally speaking, if the result of a test is correct, we can assume that the process was completed successfully. This, however, is not *always* true. In some cases it is possible to get the correct output from a test for the wrong reason. This phenomenon is known as coincidental correctness and is not necessarily discovered using black-box techniques.

■■■■■■■■■■■■■■■■

Key Point

White-box testing is also called *structural testing* because it's based upon the object's structure.
_____

■■■■■■■■■■■■■■■■

Key Point

Coincidental correctness describes a situation where the expected result of a test case is realized in spite of incorrect processing of the data.
_____

Let's say that we have a system that's supposed to estimate hours based upon the complexity of the task being performed. As estimating experts (at least in this fictitious system), we know that the correct algorithm to predict the hours required to complete a certain task might be $y=2x$, where y is the time estimate and x is the complexity of the task. So, we know that if the complexity of a task has a value of 2, the task should take 4 hours to complete.

For example, if we input a value of 2 into the system and get an answer of 4, the system must be correct, right? It may be, or may not be. Suppose your programmer, for whatever reason, miscoded the algorithm and put in the formula $y=x^2$ (instead of y=2x). If the poor tester is unfortunate enough to put in a test value of 2, the system will give the correct answer in spite of the bad code. However, this is only coincidental. If we run another test with a value of x=3, we would find that our system gives a result of 9 instead of 6!

To find bugs like these, we need to look inside the box. White-box testing would have been more effective in finding the sample bug than black-box testing (although probably the most effective way to have found the bug in the example would have been using code inspection). Another important point about white-box testing is that it allows the testers to use their knowledge of the system to create test cases based on the design or the structure of the code. However, in order to conduct white-box tests, the testers must know how to read and use software design documents and/or the code.

Key Point

White-box is also known as *clear-box, glass-box, translucent-box,* or just about any other non-opaque box.

Black-Box Science ■ ■ ■ ■ ■

Several techniques fall into the category of black-box science. Some of these techniques include equivalence partitioning, boundary value analysis, design analysis, decision tables, domain analysis, state-transition diagrams, orthogonal arrays, and others. Some of these techniques are more useful at one level than another, while others can be used at any level of test. Table 5-5 lists the most appropriate use of the various techniques described in this chapter.

Table 5-5 Techniques vs. Levels of Test

Method	Unit	Integration	System	Acceptance
Equivalence Class Partitioning	✓	✓	✓	✓
Boundary Value	✓	✓	✓	✓
Inventories/Trace Matrix			✓	✓
Invalid Combinations and Processes	✓	✓	✓	✓
Decision Table	✓	✓	✓	✓
Domain Analysis	✓	✓	✓	✓
State-Transition Diagrams			✓	✓
Orthogonal Arrays	✓	✓	✓	✓

Equivalence Partitioning

Equivalence partitioning is a technique that is intuitively used by virtually every tester we've ever met. Basically we are identifying inputs that are treated the same by the system and produce the same results. Assume that Figure 5-4 represents a typical domestic passenger jet. We have been asked to help with testing some new software that helps gate agents assign seats. As you probably are aware, most U.S. domestic airlines have two classes of seats: First Class and Coach (or as our colleague Dale would say, "Cattle Class"). If a patron only cares about the class of service, there are only two (partitions) to consider: First Class and Coach. Every First Class seat is like every other First Class seat as far as assigning of seats is concerned. Therefore, if the only consideration for seating were class of service, we would only need two test cases since there are only two equivalence partitions. We would need to test any First Class seat and any Coach seat.

■■■■■■■■■■■■■■■■
Key Point

A group of tests forms an equivalence class if you believe that:

- they all test the same thing
- if one catches a bug, the others probably will too
- if one doesn't catch a bug, the others probably won't either

– Cem Kaner, *Testing Computer Software*

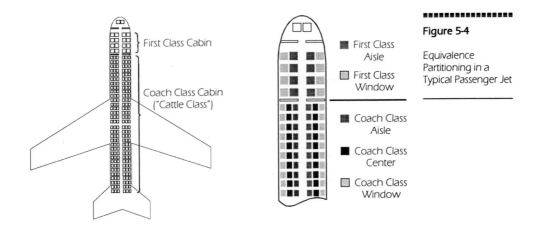

■■■■■■■■■■■■■■■■■

Figure 5-4

Equivalence
Partitioning in a
Typical Passenger Jet

The world is seldom so simple, though. Most people have a preference not only for the class of service but also where they sit in a row: aisle, middle, window. So now we have several more partitions:

- First Class Aisle
- First Class Window
- First Class Middle (at least on some airplanes)
- Coach Aisle
- Coach Window
- Coach Middle

We now have 6 equivalence partitions and would need a minimum of 6 test cases. But wait, some people want the exit row! Now we have First Class or Coach, aisle, middle, window, and exit row, or not. The number of equivalence partitions has grown to 12! As you can see, it's possible that the number can get quite large. Actually, if the seating chart really needed to consider all of these attributes, we would also have to consider the back row (which doesn't recline), smoking or non-smoking (on many non-US carriers), over the wing, next to the lavatory, etc. At some point, we might just think it's easier to test every single seat!

Still, equivalence partitioning can help reduce the number of tests from a list of all possible inputs (e.g., 200+ on a modern jet) to a minimum set that would still test each partition. If the tester chooses the right partitions, the testing will be accurate and efficient. If the tester mistakenly thinks of two partitions as equivalent and they are not, a test situation will be missed. Or on the other hand, if the tester thinks two objects are different and they are not, the tests will be redundant.

As another example, suppose that an ATM will allow withdrawals of cash in $20 increments from $20 to $200 (inclusive). There are three equivalence partitions to consider: one is valid and two are invalid, as illustrated in Figure 5-5.

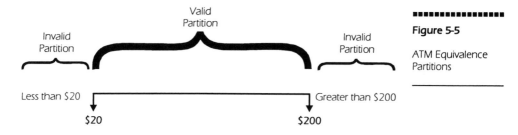

■■■■■■■■■■■■■■■■■

Figure 5-5

ATM Equivalence Partitions

Some testers might decide that since there are so few valid amounts, they will just try them all:

- TC 01 – Withdraw $20
- TC 02 – Withdraw $40
- TC 03 – Withdraw $60
- TC 04 – Withdraw $80
- …
- TC 10 – Withdraw $200

Unfortunately, a tester would have wasted her time if all of these test cases were created and executed. In this example, it's safe to assume that if our ATM can withdraw $20, it can surely withdraw $40, $60, $80, or $200 as long as there are sufficient funds in the account, the account has not already exceeded its daily limit, and there's money in the machine. This tester wasted precious time testing things that were part of an equivalence partition. Of course it's possible that the programmer created some abnormal (disjointed) code and using more than one test case might discover this fault, but there are other more effective techniques for finding this type of bug (such as a code inspection).

As far as equivalence partitioning goes, we would need only one valid and two invalid test cases for adequate coverage. Naturally there are other important test cases to try such as special characters and odd amounts (withdraw $145.78), but you would have to use another technique to discover them (such as error guessing).

Boundary Value Analysis

We know what many of you are thinking. What about the boundaries? In most cases when we use equivalence partitioning, we also use boundary value analysis. Boundary value analysis is important because we have learned from experience that the boundaries are often prone to failure. In the example above, the valid boundaries are $20 (the minimum amount we can withdraw) and $200, the maximum amount we can withdraw, and so we would create test cases for both of these values. You could (successfully) argue that both of these tests are part of the same equivalence partition of $20 to $200 and, therefore, if you test the boundaries you would not need any other tests for this partition. Most testers have been taught to test the boundaries and a valid value in the middle. While most of us were never told why we needed the value in the middle, we just did it. The reason we were taught to take a value somewhere in the middle of the partition is because if the valid boundary values fail, there will still be a test case for the valid partition.

Actually, most experienced testers learn that testing the middle value has a fairly low ROI (i.e., it doesn't really improve the coverage and it has a low likelihood of finding the bug). Still, many of these same experienced testers insist on testing the value in the middle because that's the way they were trained.

Normally when conducting boundary value analysis, the exact boundaries are tested, the value immediately above the upper boundary, and the value immediately below the lower boundary. Some testers also choose a value just above the bottom boundary and just below the top boundary. We think this adds little value to the test coverage and, therefore, we don't recommend it. So for the ATM, we would test the following boundaries:

- $ 0, Below the Bottom Boundary – Invalid
- $ 20, Bottom Boundary   – Valid
- $200, Top Boundary   – Valid
- $220, Above the Top Boundary   – Invalid

You could argue that the invalid boundaries are $19 and $201, or $19.99 and $200.01, but this doesn't make sense from a practical standpoint since we know that any amount that is not in $20 increments is invalid.

This turns out to be a rather trivial example, and in fact, if we were testing the ATM we might decide to test the withdrawal of all valid values, just because it's easy to do and because of the high risk associated with these transactions.

Decision Tables

Decision tables are tables that list all possible "conditions" (inputs) and all possible actions (outputs). Decision tables have been in use for many years. One of the earliest systems that we worked on over 20 years ago used decision tables as the primary design medium, that is to say, the entire system was described with decision tables in lieu of (or in addition to) other design mediums available in that era (i.e., HIPOs, flow charts, etc.). Most engineers today would not even consider using a labor-intensive technique such as decision tables to document an entire system, but they're still particularly useful for describing critical components of a system that can be defined by a set of rules (e.g., payroll, insurance rules, amortization schedules, etc.).

Table 5-6 contains a decision table for computing payroll taxes. There is a "rule" for each possible combination of conditions. For each condition it's identified as a "Yes", a "No", or an "I" for immaterial.

Table 5-6   Decision Table

Condition	Rules			
	Rule 1	Rule 2	Rule 3	Rule 4
Wages Earned	No	Yes	Yes	Yes
End of Pay Period	I	No	Yes	Yes
FICA Salary Exceeded	I	I	No	Yes
Action				
Withhold FICA Tax	No	No	Yes	No
Withhold Medicare Tax	No	No	Yes	Yes
Withhold Payroll Tax	No	No	Yes	Yes

To read the table, go to the first (top) condition and follow the row to the right until the rule that satisfies the condition is met. Then, go to each succeeding rule and follow the column down until the corresponding condition is satisfied. When the last condition is satisfied, apply the actions indicated by the column (rule) that you ended up in.

For example, if the answer to *Wages Earned* is "Yes," we go to Rule 2, 3, or 4. If the answer to the condition *End of Pay Period* is "Yes," then we now go to Rule 3 or 4. If the *FICA Salary*

Exceeded condition is "Yes," then we follow the table down Rule 4 to the actions and know that we must:

- not withhold FICA tax
- withhold Medicare tax
- withhold payroll tax

Table 5-7 summarizes the input conditions for test cases 1 through 4 and lists the expected results.

Table 5-7 Test Cases for Payroll Tax Table

Test Case	Input Condition	Expected Results	
1	No Wages Earned	1.	Don't Withhold FICA Tax
		2.	Don't Withhold Medicare
		3.	Don't Withhold Payroll Tax
2	Wages Earned	1.	Don't Withhold FICA Tax
	Not End of Pay Period	2.	Don't Withhold Medicare
		3.	Don't Withhold Payroll Tax
3	Wages Earned	1.	Withhold FICA Tax
	End of Pay Period	2.	Withhold Medicare
	FICA Not Exceeded	3.	Withhold Payroll Tax
4	Wages Earned	1.	Don't Withhold FICA Tax
	End of Pay Period	2.	Withhold Medicare
	FICA Salary Exceeded	3.	Withhold Payroll Tax

State-Transition Diagrams

State-transition diagrams are an ancient (mid-1900s), but still effective, method of describing system design and guiding our testing. A state machine is a thing (e.g., system, subsystem, component, unit) whose functionality and output is dependent not solely on its current input, but also on its past input. The result of its previous input is called its *state*, and *transitions* are commands that cause changes from one state to another.

■■■■■■■■■■■■■■■■■■

Case Study 5-2

State-transition
diagrams are used in
airline reservations
systems.

Simplified State-Transition Diagram for a One-Way Ticket

I call Southwest Airlines to make a reservation. I provide information about the origin and destination of my travel, and the date and time that I wish to fly. A reservation is made for me and stored in their system. My reservation is now in the "Made" state.

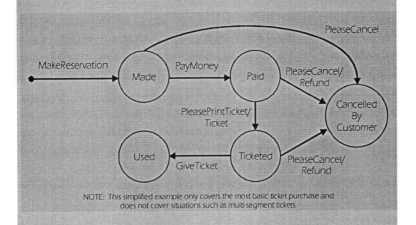

NOTE: This simplified example only covers the most basic ticket purchase and does not cover situations such as multi-segment tickets.

Depending on the various fare rules, I'm given a certain amount of time to pay for the ticket. It could be within 24 hours; or it might be until 1 hour before departure. Once I pay for the ticket, my reservation changes state. It's now "Paid". On the day of travel, I arrive at the airport in plenty of time, stand in the incredibly long lines, and get a printed copy of my ticket. The reservation is now in the "Ticketed" state. When I give my ticket to the agent and get on the plane, the reservation changes to the "Used" state. Of course, I can cancel my reservation at any time before I get on the plane. If I've paid for it, I should be able to get a refund or at least a credit.

Now, let's use this state-transition diagram to guide our testing. At first glance we might decide that the appropriate level of coverage is to create the minimum number of test cases to visit every state (Made, Paid, Ticketed, Used, CancelledByCustomer) at least once. This approach will miss some of the possible execution paths. A second approach is to create the minimum number of test cases to exercise each transition (MakeReservation, PayMoney,

PleasePrintTicket, PleaseCancel, GiveTicket) at least once. This approach will also miss some of the paths.

The recommended approach is to test every state-transition combination (i.e., every arrow on the diagram) at least once. This gives good coverage of the state machine, although it may not cover all the paths. If the diagram has loops back to previous states, then there can be a very large number (infinite) of paths – far too many to test.

— Lee Copeland

Orthogonal Arrays

The orthogonal array shown in our example in Table 5-8 is a two-dimensional array of integers with an interesting property: if you choose any two columns in the array, all of the combinations of the numbers will appear in those columns.

For example, consider the $L_9(3^4)$ orthogonal array shown in Table 5-8. The "9" indicates it has 9 rows. The "3^4" is not an exponent. It indicates the array has 4 columns and each cell in the array contains a 1, 2, or 3.

■■■■■■■■■■■■■■■■■
Key Point

Orthogonal arrays are curious mathematical oddities with an interesting property: if you choose any two columns in the array in Table 5-8, all of the combinations of the numbers will appear in those columns.

Table 5-8   L₉(3⁴) Orthogonal Array

	1	2	3	4
1	1	1	1	1
2	1	2	2	2
3	1	3	3	3
4	2	1	2	3
5	2	2	3	1
6	2	3	1	2
7	3	1	3	2
8	3	2	1	3
9	3	3	2	1

Now, let's test this array. Choose any two columns at random (We'll pick columns 2 and 4, but you can choose another combination if you like). Can you locate all the pairs (1,1), (1,2), (1,3), (2,1), (2,2), (2,3), (3,1), (3,2), (3,3) looking at columns 2 and 4? Yes you can, so this is an orthogonal array.

Do all of the combinations of 1s, 2s, and 3s appear in the table? No, there are 81 combinations (3 x 3 x 3 x 3). For example, (3,3,3,3) is a valid combination, but it's not in the table.

Now, this is all very interesting but what does it have to do with testing? In many testing situations, there are simply too many test cases to write and execute. So, how do we choose a "good" subset? Orthogonal arrays are the answer. Whenever we have a number of variables and each of these variables takes on a defined state, we can map the problem onto an orthogonal array.

Consider the following situation. Suppose you have a Web site that is hosted on a number of servers and operating systems and viewed on a number of browsers with various plug-ins:
- Web Browser (Netscape 6.2, IE 6.0, Opera 4.0)
- Plug-in (None, RealPlayer, MediaPlayer)

- Application Server (IIS, Apache, Netscape Enterprise)
- Operating System (Win2000, WinNT, Linux)

How many distinct combinations should be tested? The answer is 81 (3x3x3x3 = 81). But what if you don't have enough resources to do this level of testing? What other choices do you have? You could test a few combinations chosen at random. Or, you could test a few that are easy. Or, you could test a few that you believe will work. Unfortunately, none of these approaches really inspire confidence.

So, let's map our problem onto the L_9 orthogonal array as shown in Table 5-9. In the first column, let 1=Netscape 6.2, 2=IE 6.0, 3=Opera 4.0. In the second column, let 1=None, 2=RealPlayer, 3=MediaPlayer. In the third column, let 1=IIS, 2=Apache, 3=Netscape Enterprise. In the fourth column, let 1=Win2000, 2=WinNT, 3=Linux.

Table 5-9 $L_9(3^4)$ Orthogonal Array

Test Case	Browser	Plug-In	Server	Operating System
1	Netscape 6.2	None	IIS	Win2000
2	Netscape 6.2	RealPlayer	Apache	WinNT
3	Netscape 6.2	MediaPlayer	Netscape Enterprise	Linux
4	IE 6.0	None	Apache	Linux
5	IE 6.0	RealPlayer	Netscape Enterprise	Win2000
6	IE 6.0	MediaPlayer	IIS	WinNT
7	Opera 4.0	None	Netscape Enterprise	WinNT
8	Opera 4.0	RealPlayer	IIS	Linux
9	Opera 4.0	MediaPlayer	Apache	Win2000

Now, let's take a look at what we've achieved:
- Each browser is tested with every plug-in, with every server, and with every operating system.
- Each plug-in is tested with every browser, every server, and every operating system.

- Each server is tested with every browser, every plug-in, and every operating system.
- Each operating system is tested with every browser, every plug-in, and every server.

Not all combinations of all variables have been tested – that would be 81 combinations – but all pairs of combinations have been tested (and with only 9 test cases).

Orthogonal array testing is extremely useful because most compatibility defects are pair-wise defects. In recent weeks, we installed a commercial software package on Windows 95 (worked), Windows 98 (worked), Windows NT (worked), Win2000 (worked), and Windows ME (didn't work). The Windows ME problem is called a *pair-wise defect*.

Black-Box Art ■ ■ ■ ■ ■

Ad Hoc Testing

Case Study 5-3

How can Mary Brown always find the bugs, just by looking at the system?

Mary Brown Always Finds the Bugs

I've been an advocate of systematic testing for years. In fact, one of the courses that I teach is even called Systematic Software Testing. Still, even in a class with a name like that, someone always asks me about ad hoc testing. The student will say, "Mary Brown can always find bugs, really big bugs, by just looking at the system." For years, I would steadfastly insist that testing should be systematic. Finally, though, a few years ago, I relented. If you have a Mary Brown in your company (and everyone does!), then she's too valuable an asset to waste.

I secretly believe that most of the Mary Browns in the world are actually very systematic in the processes that they employ. They just don't like to document their test cases and sometimes can't even remember how they found a bug. Then, if the situation that found the bug can't be replicated, the bug can't be fixed and everyone just ends up feeling badly because they know there's a bug, but they can't do anything about it.

In the case of Mary Brown, the company decided to install a capture-replay tool on her system so when she stumbled onto a bug, the scenario could be recreated. Unfortunately, the test manager didn't explain to Mary that everything she did would be recreated. When Mary found a bug while doing her ad hoc testing and the execution was replayed, the test manager discovered that Mary spent a great deal of time surfing the Internet (instead of working).

— Rick Craig

Most ad hoc testers will tell you that their tests are based upon experience and, indeed, that's true. However, if we were to analyze their thought processes, we believe it would look a lot like some of the "systematic" techniques addressed in this book. For example, most ad hoc testers focus on the things that have failed in the past (e.g., Pareto analysis), or things that they know are important to the user (e.g., risk analysis), or situations that are always problematic (e.g., zero sums, boundaries), etc. The key to successfully using ad hoc testing is to make sure that when a bug is found, the problem can be replicated. This usually means that when a bug is found using ad hoc methods, you should create the test case that would have found the bug. The test cases are needed to facilitate the debugging, and they'll also need to be rerun after the problem has been rectified.

Key Point

It's a good idea to add the test cases created during ad hoc testing to your repository.

As many of you know, bugs seem to have a way of reappearing, so it's a good idea to add the test cases created during ad hoc testing to your test repository. Probably one of the most important aspects of ad hoc testing is that it allows you to use the expertise of some users/engineers who otherwise would not be willing and/or able to sit down and document tests. It can also be a useful reality check on your systematic testing process. If a bug is found in ad hoc testing, you should ask yourself, "Why didn't I have a test to find this?" Sometimes ad hoc testing will identify an entire class of tests that were missed using other testing strategies. And, finally, ad hoc testing is just plain fun!

Random Testing

Random testing means quite different things to different people. To us, random testing is creating tests where the data is in the format of real data but all of the fields are generated randomly, often using a tool. For example, if we were testing the name field of a system that is supposed to accept up to 20 characters, strings of 20 characters would be randomly generated and input into the system. One 20-character string might be:

> ty5%,,ijs5ajU jjkk kkk

Key Point

Random testing is sometimes called *monkey testing.*

Obviously, no one really has a name like that and, in fact, we probably don't even want to allow certain characters in the name field like the % sign. So we might refine the "random" set to omit certain characters that are not allowed, otherwise we'll end up with lots and lots of negative tests (definitely overkill). But as soon as we begin to refine the input stream, is the data really random? Now, we're beginning to generate test data with (minimally defined) parameters. Often when using random data, we don't necessarily figure out the expected results in advance. This means that we may be spending inordinate amounts of time reviewing the output of random tests to determine if the results are actually correct. Besides, if you remember equivalence partitioning, many of the random strings generated will be from the same equivalence partition, which means that we'll essentially be running the same tests over and over again.

Key Point

A *negative* test is when you put in an invalid input and expect to receive an error message.

A *positive* test is when you put in a valid input and expect some action to be completed in accordance with the specification.

Let's recount some of the weaknesses of random testing:

- The tests are often not very realistic.
- There is no gauge of actual coverage of the random tests.
- There is no measure of risk.
- Many of the tests become redundant.
- A great deal of time may have to be spent in determining the expected results.
- The tests can't be recreated unless the input data is stored or a seed is used to create the random data.

This kind of random testing is really of little use most of the time and at best can be used for "crash-proofing" or to see if the system will "hang together" under adverse impact.

Semi-Random Testing

Let's take the idea of random testing and refine it so that it is a little more useful. Let's say that we are testing an inventory system that has the following parameters:

- There are 400 stores.
- There are 12,000 different products in the stores.
- There are 8 different ways to bill for each product.
- There are 200 different suppliers of the various products.

Assuming that all four variables are mutually independent, the total number of different combinations of the four attributes results in an astronomically large number (in fact, our scientific calculator returned a 'memory overflow' error).

We could (and should) use techniques like equivalence partitioning to reduce the number of combinations to a workable number. Still, we might want to generate some random combinations of the four parameters listed above to possibly stumble onto a defect. Semi-random testing also gives us a little added confidence in our systematic techniques, and it's fairly easy to create large numbers of combinations. Remember, though, many of these semi-random tests probably add little to the functional coverage of the system.

Exploratory Testing

Exploratory testing is a term originally coined in 1988 by Cem Kaner in *Testing Computer Software*. Since that time, Cem Kaner, James Whitaker, James Bach, and others have refined the process and created an alternative (or a complementary process) to more traditional, structured techniques.

In exploratory testing, the test design and execution are conducted concurrently. The results of a test or group of tests will often prompt the tester to delve deeper into that area (i.e., explore). We think the beauty of exploratory testing is that productive areas of test are expanded immediately. In structured testing, the testers often create many tests that don't seem as useful during execution as they did during creation.

Exploratory testing is not the same thing as ad hoc testing. Just as its name implies, ad hoc testing is an unplanned, unstructured, maybe even impulsive journey through the system with the intent of finding bugs. Ad hoc testing, in fact, often does find bugs and can be a useful addition to structured testing, but should never replace structured techniques.

Exploratory testing, on the other hand, can be a viable alternative to more structured testing techniques. Obviously, since we're writing a book that focuses primarily on systematic or structured techniques, we believe that these more traditional techniques are very important to most organizations, and we recommend that exploratory techniques be considered as a complement to (not a replacement for) structured testing. There are, however, many

■■■■■■■■■■■■■■■■
Key Point

The beauty of exploratory testing is that productive areas of test are expanded immediately.

■■■■■■■■■■■■■■■■
Key Point

"Always write down what you did and what happened when you run exploratory tests."

– Cem Kaner
Testing Computer Software

testimonials from testing groups that focus exclusively on exploratory testing techniques.

In fact, exploratory testing is neither ad hoc nor random. Exploratory testers are not merely keying in random tests, but rather testing areas that their experience (or imagination) tells them are important and then going where those tests take them. Even structured testers know that some of the best test cases they run are often precipitated by the results of other tests. This means, of course, that most good "traditional" testers do at least some exploratory testing.

Key Point

There are several excellent articles by James Bach on Exploratory Testing at:

stickyminds.com

satisfice.com

Exploratory testers share some traits with traditional testers too. Good exploratory testers often keep notes or checklists of tests that appear to be useful, to reuse on future releases. These "notes" may (or may not) even look a lot like test scripts.

Definitely Not Ad Hoc Testing

While teaching a testing course at Microsoft in the late 1980s, I remember one student describing the informal bug sessions they conducted in his group and I said, "Oh, ad hoc testing." He replied, "No, creative and unstructured, but not ad hoc testing." He went on to describe how the individual testers, without scripts, tested areas of the code that they thought might contain bugs and then launched the rest of the testing from there. He explained that the best bug-session testers actually had a pretty good testing strategy outlined in their minds when they began the session. As I recall, this group spent 1 day every two weeks or 10% of their time using this technique, and he reported that it was some of their most productive testing time. In spite of their ability to find bugs, these bug sessions didn't totally replace structured testing, because the test group needed the repeatability of an automated regression suite and a gauge of coverage, which was obtained by using the "systematic" test set.

— Rick Craig

Case Study 5-4

A Successful Example of Unstructured Testing

White-Box Science ■ ■ ■ ■ ■

Black-box test cases should be designed before attempting to design white-box test cases, because they can be created from the requirements and high-level design long before any code exists and they may help improve the detailed design and code. Some white-box techniques cannot be done until the code/detailed design exists. But if you wait to do them, you've lost the opportunity to prevent problems.

White-Box Testing

White-box testing allows you to look inside a component being tested and create your test cases based on the component's implementation (code). Unfortunately, you can't see through the color white any better than you can see through black. So, technically, white-box testing should really be called "clear-box" or "glass-box" testing because you're able to see the code. Consider the code illustrated in Figure 5-6, which implements a software module.

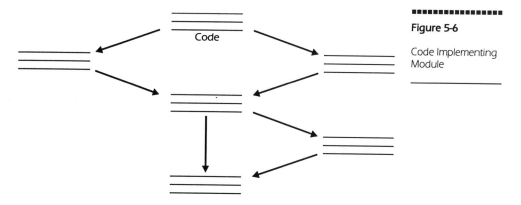

■ ■ ■ ■ ■ ■ ■ ■ ■ ■ ■ ■ ■ ■ ■ ■ ■

Figure 5-6

Code Implementing
Module

How many paths do you see from the top to the bottom of this code? The correct answer is four (4), because you could move left-left, right-right, left-right, and right-left as you execute each statement from top to bottom. If your goal is to achieve path coverage and someone claims to be able to test this module with only three test cases, they're wrong! You must have at least four test cases in order to touch every path at least once.

This diagram was fairly simple to evaluate, but as the paths get more numerous and more complex, you need automated help in determining the number of paths and, thus, the number of test cases to create. There are a number of tools available to help you determine which paths need to be tested.

Cyclomatic Complexity

Tom McCabe developed a metric called *Cyclomatic Complexity*, which is derived from mathematical graph theory and used to describe the complexity of a software module. The complexity *C* is determined by the formula:

$$C = e - n + 2p$$

e = the number of edges in the graph (i.e., the number of arrows)

n = the number of nodes (i.e., the chunks of code that are executed without loops and/or branches)

p = the number of independent procedures

For this single-entry, single-exit example, p is equal to 1. The Cyclomatic Complexity of the example shown in Figure 5-6 is:

$$C = 7 - 6 + 2(1) = 3$$

The Cyclomatic Complexity metric provides a measure of the complexity of a software module. It also allows you to determine the maximum number of tests that are required to reach branch coverage. (Sometimes, branch coverage can be reached with fewer than C tests, but more tests are never needed.) McCabe suggests using the *basis-path test model*, which chooses C test cases for effective test coverage.

Scalability of White-Box Testing

Although white-box testing is almost always viewed as a technique for testing code as a part of unit testing, this approach can also be scaled to accommodate subsystem and system testing. Simply replace each of the chunks of code in Figure 5-6 with rectangles that represent subsystems.

White-box testing is really about path testing, and there are often a number of paths between subsystems. Using white-box techniques during integration testing can help you understand the flow of data and control through subsystems, which, in turn, will help you wisely choose integration test cases. Even at the system level, if the system under test interacts with other systems, white-box techniques can help you determine the number of paths and guide you in choosing test cases.

Coverage Techniques

We believe that many organizations can benefit from white-box testing, especially when using tools to measure code coverage. While obviously valuable for developmental testing (e.g., unit and integration), code coverage can also be useful for high-level testing (e.g., system and acceptance). However, we're sensitive to the fact that some organizations become enamored with code coverage tools and lose sight of functional coverage and risk

■■■■■■■■■■■■■■■■■■
Key Point

We're sensitive to the fact that some organizations become enamored with code coverage tools and lose sight of functional coverage and risk issues.

issues. To avoid this pitfall, we offer the following strategy for testing organizations that use code coverage tools.

Strategy for using "Code Coverage":

1. Design test cases using techniques such as inventories, equivalence partitioning, etc. and the results of the risk analysis.
2. Measure code coverage.
3. Examine unexecuted code.
4. If resources allow and risk dictates, create test cases to execute code previously unaddressed by tests. If the system is of lower risk or the code that is unaddressed is in a low-risk part of the system, the decision may be made not to test every line of code. This will, of course, introduce a risk that the unexecuted code may fail. It's really all about weighing the risk versus the resources available.

■■■■■■■■■■■■■■■■
Key Point

Statement coverage measures are used to determine the number of lines of code that are invoked by the tests.

Decision or branch coverage measures are used to determine the number of decisions or yes/no expressions that are invoked by the tests.

Path coverage measures are used to determine the number of paths that are executed by the tests.

Test Design Documentation ■ ■ ■ ■ ■

Recall that in Chapter 3 we covered the Master Test Plan and, in Chapter 4, we covered the Detailed Test Plan. Here, we'll cover the Test Design Specification, Test Case Specifications, and Test Procedures.

IEEE Test Design Specification

Figure 5-7 shows all of the documents created on the front end (i.e., before execution) of testing using an IEEE Std. 829-1998 Standard for Software Test Documentation. The system test plan shown in this figure is supported by three test design specifications. The integration and acceptance test plans would also be supported by one or more test design specifications. For the sake of simplicity, the test design specifications for these plans are not shown in the diagram.

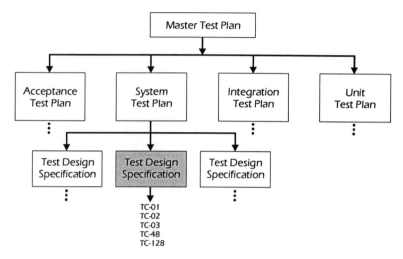

■■■■■■■■■■■■■■■■■

Figure 5-7

Test Design
Specification

When many people think of a test plan, they think about a group of test cases. In this book, we've identified a test plan as a document that outlines the strategy, schedule, risks, responsibilities, and so forth (Refer to Chapter 3 – *Master Test Planning*). Nowhere in this plan did we include test cases. So where are the test cases? In the IEEE model, the test cases are described in a document known as a *Test Design Specification*. We like to think of the test design specification as a miniature test plan that *does* include the test cases necessary to test one or more features. The purpose of the test design specification is to group similar test cases together. Every level of test (except unit) will have one or more test design specifications.

■■■■■■■■■■■■■■■■■

Key Point

We like to think of
the test design
specification as a
miniature test plan
that includes the test
cases necessary to
test one or more
features.

Figure 5-8 shows the IEEE template for the Test Design Specification.

IEEE Std. 829-1998 for Software Test Documentation **Template for Test Design Specification** **Contents** 1. Test Design Specification Identifier 2. Feature(s) to Be Tested 3. Approach Refinement 4. Test Identification 5. Feature Pass/Fail Criteria	■■■■■■■■■■■■■■■■■ **Figure 5-8** Test Design Specification Template from IEEE Std. 829-1998

Test Design Specification Identifier

This is the unique number (and date and version) of the test design specification, which will allow us to change and control the document. Each test design specification should be referenced to its associated test plan.

Feature(s) to Be Tested

This section of the test design specification is called *Feature* (or *Features*) *to Be Tested*. Each test design specification should contain a description of the group of test cases that must be executed in order to test a feature (or features). We've found that it's often useful to have a single test design specification for each feature identified in the section *Features to Be Tested* in the corresponding test plan. For example, there might be a series of test design specifications such as *Withdraw Cash*, *Check Account Balance*, etc. that refer back to the system test plan for our ATM. All of the features identified in the *Features to Be Tested* section of the test plan need to be included in a test design specification.

Approach Refinement

Remember the long explanation we had about the *Approach* section of the test plan in Chapter 3? Since the test design specification is a document that details a part of the system identified in the test plan, the *Approach Refinement* in the test design specification must support the approach in the test plan, but it usually goes into much greater detail. For example, the approach in an acceptance test plan might suggest that cash will be withdrawn from selected ATMs throughout the downtown San Francisco area. The test design specification for *Withdraw Cash* might specify exactly which ATMs will be used, which accounts need to be established or used, and what time of day the transactions will occur. This information provides additional detail that supports the original approach outlined in the test plan.

Test Identification

In this section, the test case identifiers and a short description of the test cases are recorded. There is no need to describe the details of the test cases or their execution, since the test cases will be described in a separate document or program (if automated). The following test cases are used in our ATM example:

- TC 01 –   Withdraw $20 from valid account with $200
- TC 02 –   Withdraw $200 from valid account with $200
- TC 03 –   Withdraw $200 from valid account with $100
- TC 04 –   Withdraw $182.34 from valid account with $200
- TC 05 –   ...
- TC 28 –   ...
- TC 96 –   ...

Each of these test cases will be described in detail in a Test Case Specification. The test case specification will describe which account will be used for each test case, how to set up the test case, what the expected results should be, and so on.

Notice that some of the identified test cases are probably negative tests. Even though we don't have the requirements specification in front of us, TC 03 is probably a negative test or a test designed to do error checking, since it's unlikely that the bank will want someone with only $100 in their account to be able to withdraw $200.

Notice that the test cases are not necessarily sequential (i.e., we go from TC 05 to TC 28). That's because the test design specification describes all of the tests necessary to test a feature. Some of the tests necessary to test this feature (*Withdraw Cash*) will probably already have been created to test some other part of the system. For example, TC 28 may be a test that checks the validity of a user. This is important to the *Withdraw Cash* feature, but there's no reason to create a new test case if one was created for another feature such as *Security*. The test design specification describes a covering set of tests, but it does not describe how those tests will be executed. The Test Procedure Specification, which we'll explain in a moment, is used to actually execute the tests in an efficient manner.

■■■■■■■■■■■■■■■■■
Key Point

The test design specification describes a covering set of tests, but it does not describe how those tests will be executed.

Feature Pass/Fail Criteria

The *Feature Pass/Fail Criteria* establish what constitutes success or failure for the testing of this feature(s). This is similar to the pass/fail criteria in the test plan, but the criteria in the test plan apply to the entire (product) item. The test design specification pass/fail will let us know if the *Withdraw Cash* feature is ready to be used.

We can use some of the same categories of metrics (used in the test plan) to establish the pass/fail criteria for the test design specification:

- The most common metric is the percentage of test cases that passed. For example, "all test cases must pass" or "90% of all test cases must pass, and all test cases that dispense money must pass."
- Criteria can also be built around the number, severity, and distribution of defects.
- Other criteria could include the results of a review, performance characteristics, security characteristics, etc. Remember, though, one good way to handle these other criteria is with performance test cases, security test cases, etc. That way the criteria can be limited to pass/fail of test cases, defects, and possibly a review.

IEEE Test Case Specification

Test cases are at the heart of all testing. They describe exactly *what* will be executed and *what* is being covered. How the test cases are described depends on several things such as the number of test cases, frequency of change, level of automation, skill of the testers, methodology chosen (i.e., exploratory testing, STEP, etc.), staff turnover, and risk.

■■■■■■■■■■■■■■■■■
Key Point

Test cases are at the heart of all testing. They describe exactly *what* will be executed and *what* is being covered.

There are as many ways to document test cases as there are people testing. In this book, we focus on two approaches for documenting test cases: one approach uses the IEEE Std. 829-1998 Standard for Software Test Documentation for a test case, and the other approach uses a spreadsheet. Some of you will also be using automated test tools to describe your tests.

In the hierarchy of the master test plan, Figure 5-9 shows that the test case specification occurs immediately below the test design specification for the system test plan. The integration and acceptance test plans would also be supported by one or more test design specifications and associated test case specifications, but are not shown in the diagram for the sake of simplicity.

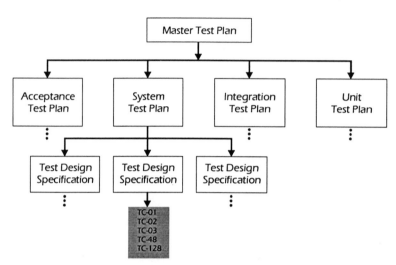

■■■■■■■■■■■■■■■■■■

Figure 5-9

Test Case
Specification

The IEEE template for test case specifications describes each test case in exact detail. It's especially useful for organizations that are working on high-risk, stable systems. It's also a good choice if the testers are less experienced or if there's rapid turnover of the testing staff. Figure 5-10 shows the IEEE template for the Test Case Specification.

IEEE Std. 829-1998 for Software Test Documentation

Template for Test Case Specification

Contents

1. Test Case Specification Identifier
2. Test Items
3. Input Specifications
4. Output Specifications
5. Environmental Needs

■■■■■■■■■■■■■■■■■

Figure 5-10

Test Case
Specification
Template from IEEE
Std. 829-1998

> 6. Special Procedural Requirements
> 7. Inter-Case Dependencies

In particular, the IEEE approach for documenting test cases requires fairly complete documentation of each test case, which is one of the reasons that it's so useful for high-risk systems. This template is not as good a choice for systems that are undergoing rapid change and/or are unstable, since it requires significant effort to create each test case. Changes to the system might invalidate many test cases and require the creation of new tests. It's good, though, for companies that have a lot of rapid turnover or inexperienced staff, since the test cases are very detailed and can be handled by less experienced staff members.

■■■■■■■■■■■■■■■■■
Key Point

The IEEE approach for documenting test cases requires fairly complete documentation of each test case, which is one of the reasons it's so useful for high-risk systems.

Test Case Specification Identifier

This is the date, number, and version of the test case that identifies the test case and any subsequent changes to the test case specification.

Test Items

This describes the items (e.g., requirement specs, design specs, and code) required to run this particular test case.

Input Specifications

This describes what input is required for the test case. This will often describe the values that must be entered into a field, input files, completion of graphic user interfaces, etc. The input can be described in English, as a "picture" of a properly completed screen, a file identifier, or an interface to another system.

Output Specifications

This will describe what the system should look like after the test case is run. Normally, it can be described by examining particular screens, reports, files, etc. One test case may change many different outputs (i.e., multiple files, reports, etc.). The sample output can be a comparator file, screen image, copy of a report, English description, etc.

Environmental Needs

This describes any special environmental needs for this particular test case. Examples might include the need for stubs or drivers (especially at lower levels of test), tools, specific records or files, interfaces, etc.

Special Procedural Requirements

This section describes any special procedural requirements necessary to set up the test environment. For example, Y2K data might have to be converted into YYYYMMDD format before proceeding.

Inter-Case Dependencies

Experienced testers know that one way to set up the environment for a particular test is to run another test to set the state of the environment. In our ATM, for example, we might have a test that requires a deposit of $1,000 that needs to be run before we run another test case that requires a withdrawal, otherwise the account might not have sufficient funds.

Using a Spreadsheet

Table 5-10 shows what simplified test case specifications might look like if you chose to use a spreadsheet to manage your testing. Each of the test cases is listed sequentially along with special notes about how to run each test, what the input variables should look like, and what the acceptable results are.

Table 5-10 Simple Test Case Specifications

Test Cases	Special Notes	INPUTS Var 1 Var 2 Var 3	OK RESULTS Var X Var Y Var Z ....
TC0401			
TC0402			
TC0501			
...			

Using a spreadsheet is one of the most common methods used by our clients to record their test cases. This method is particularly valuable for testers who construct many small test cases where the input is often a few keystrokes and the result is a new screen or report (e.g., testing user interfaces).

As you can see, the template identifies each test case, describes the input required, and the desired results. Other sections included in the IEEE model, such as environmental needs, are handled on an exception basis in the *Special Notes* field. There's room at the end of the template to record the results, which may be recorded as pass/fail or may describe what the actual results were.

IEEE Test Procedure Specification

When all is said and done, the Test Procedure Specification is nothing more than a description of *how* the tests will be run. Test procedures can be described manually or they can be written into scripts using a tool. These scripts are actually code written in a high-level language, and the people who created them may be called *testers*, but now they're also coders. This may have far-reaching ramifications regarding who the testers can be, the skill sets required, and so on.

The structure that we recommend following when developing a test procedure is shown in Figure 5-11. After the test procedures are executed, the results should be evaluated and then the test environment should be restored to its initial condition. Test design procedures should be kept simple and they should use common sub-procedures.

■■■■■■■■■■■■■■■■■
Key Point

We use the word *scripts* to describe automated test procedures. These scripts are actually code written in a high-level language.

Some people use the word *scripts* to describe all test procedures (manual and automated).

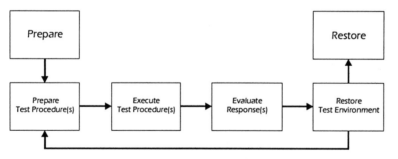

■■■■■■■■■■■■■■■■■
Figure 5-11

Structure of a Test Procedure Specification

Figure 5-12 shows the IEEE template for a test procedure.

IEEE Std. 829-1998 for Software Test Documentation
Template for Test Procedure
Contents

■■■■■■■■■■■■■■■■■
Figure 5-12

Test Procedure Template from IEEE Std. 829-1998

1.0   **Test Procedure Specification Identifier**

Specify the unique identifier assigned to this test procedure. Supply a reference to the associated test design specification.

2.0   **Purpose**

Describe the purpose(s) of the procedure and refer to the test cases being executed.

3.0   **Special Requirements**

Describe any special requirements such as environmental needs, skill level, training, etc.

4.0   **Procedure Steps**

This is the heart of the test procedure. The IEEE describes several steps listed below:

     4.1   **Log**

         Describe any special methods or formats for logging the results of test execution, the incidents observed, and any other events pertinent to the test.

     4.2   **Set up**

         Describe the sequence of actions necessary to prepare for execution of the procedure.

     4.3   **Start**

         Describe the actions necessary to begin execution of the procedure.

     4.4   **Proceed**

         Describe any actions necessary during execution of the procedure.

         4.4.1   Step 1

         4.4.2   Step 2

         4.4.3   Step 3

         4.4.4   Step Z

     4.5   **Measure**

         Describe how the test measurements will be made.

     4.6   **Shut Down**

         Describe the action necessary to suspend testing when unscheduled events dictate.

     4.7   **Restart**

> Identify any procedural restart points and describe the action necessary to restart the procedure at each of these points.
>
> **4.8　Stop**
>
> Describe the actions necessary to bring execution to an orderly halt.
>
> **4.9　Wrap Up**
>
> Describe the action necessary to restore the environment.
>
> **4.10　Contingencies**
>
> Describe the actions necessary to deal with anomalies and other events that may occur during execution.

In the IEEE template, it's not clear that somewhere between Steps 4.3 – *Start* and 4.6 – *Shutdown*, it's necessary to list all of the chronological steps that need to occur. Indeed, this is the key part of the entire test procedure and will normally make up the bulk of the document.

Example Test Procedure

Since we virtually live on airplanes, we decided to show an example from a (fictitious) frequent flyer system using the IEEE template for a test procedure (refer to Figure 5-13).

Example Test Procedure for a Frequent Flyer System Using the IEEE Template

Request for Domestic Award

Contents

1.0	**Test Procedure Specification Identifier**
	5.2
2.0	**Purpose**

Figure 5-13

Example Test Procedure for a Frequent Flyer System Using the IEEE Template

This procedure will execute test cases 2, 28, 35, and 44 in order to validate requesting an award.

3.0   Special Requirements

It's necessary to have at least one record available for a super-duper frequent flyer who has adequate miles to request a domestic award.

4.0   Procedure Steps

4.1   Log.   Results will be compared manually to predetermined responses calculated by customer service representatives.

4.2   Set up. The frequent-flyer program must be loaded and running and the client must be logged into the server.

4.3   Start. Logon to the frequent-flyer program using a password for a valid customer service representative. Note the system log time.

4.4   Proceed.

4.4.1   Go to screen 'X.'

4.4.2   Enter Frequent Flyer number for a super duper frequent flyer.

4.4.3   Double Click the "Check Miles" icon. Note the mileage.

4.4.4   Double click the "Request Domestic Award" icon (screen 'Y' displays).

4.4.5   Enter Tampa for departure city.

4.4.6   Enter San Francisco for destination city.

4.4.7   Enter 6/01/2002 for departure date.

4.4.8   Enter 6/05/2002 for return date.

4.4.9   Hit the Enter key (message "Request accepted" displays).

4.4.10   Go to screen 'X.'

4.4.11   Double Click the "Check Miles" icon.

4.5   Measure. The value for "Check Miles" should be reduced by 25,000 after the successful execution of this procedure. An e-ticket request should be processed. Check this by going to the reservation system.

4.6	Shut Down. Log off the frequent-flyer program.	
4.7	Restart. If necessary, the test procedure will be restarted in Step 4.4.1.	
4.8	Stop. Close the connection to the server.	
4.9	Wrap up (restore). Restore the system to the state identified in Step 4.3.	
4.10	Contingencies. If the frequent-flyer record specified is not available, use record locater 838.78.	

This test procedure or script describes *how* the tests will be executed. It may contain one or more test cases, each of which will describe something (*what*) that needs to be tested. For example, Test Case 2 might be a test case for something as simple as logging on to the system. Test Case 28 might be a test designed to test requesting a domestic award for a super-duper frequent flyer who has more than 25,000 miles in their account. Both of these test cases will be executed by the test procedure shown in Figure 5-13.

The test cases specify *what* needs to be tested and provide us with measures of coverage, but the test procedures specify *how* the test cases will be executed and provide us with efficiency of execution. As Figure 5-14 shows, one test procedure may execute test cases from a single test design specification or from many.

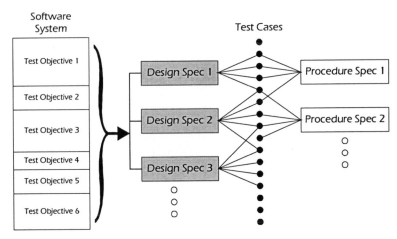

Figure 5-14

Specifications for a Typical System-Level Test

When developing the test design specification, you should start with the testing objectives. Since more than one procedure may be required to run the test cases contained in the test design specification, you may want to work on the test cases first in order to establish a baseline of coverage. Some companies (e.g., medical and pharmaceutical) buy the test design documentation from software developers in order to prove to various government agencies that the software actually meets requirements.

Chapter 6 –
Test Implementation

"Just do it."

— Nike Advertisement

Test implementation is the process of acquiring test data, developing test procedures, preparing the test environment, and selecting and implementing the tools that will be used to facilitate this process. During this phase, test managers and testers are faced with a myriad of questions:

- What setup will be required for the test environment?
- How will the test data be obtained?
- Which test procedures will be automated?
- Which test tools will be used?
- How will the test set be verified?

This chapter describes a systematic approach, which will help you to identify these questions early in the software development lifecycle and plan realistic solutions before reaching the test execution phase.

Test Environment ■■■■■

The test environment is the collection of data, hardware configurations, people (testers), interfaces, operating systems, manuals, facilities, and other items that define a particular level. In the planning chapters, we discussed the importance of choosing the right levels in order to avoid duplication of effort or missing some important aspect of the testing. An important exercise that test managers should undertake is to examine the current levels and attributes at each level of test. Table 6-1 shows some example environmental features and attributes for a product developed by one of our clients.

Table 6-1   Example Test Environment Attributes at Various Levels

Attribute	Level			
	Unit	Integration	System	Acceptance
People	Developers	Developers & Testers	Testers	Testers & Users
Hardware O/S	Programmers' Workbench	Programmers' Workbench	System Test Machine or Region	Mirror of Production
Cohabiting Software	None	None	None/Actual	Actual
Interfaces	None	Internal	Simulated & Real	Simulated & Real
Source of Test Data	Manually Created	Manually Created	Production & Manually Created	Production
Volume of Test Data	Small	Small	Large	Large
Strategy	Unit	Groups of Units/Builds	Entire System	Simulated Production

As you can see in Table 6-1, the realism of the test environment approaches the production environment at higher levels of test. In fact, an important drill that test managers should undertake is to compare every facet of their system and acceptance test environments with the production environment and try to determine the differences (and therefore the risks). If a significant risk exists, the tester should try to find a way to mitigate that risk (refer to the *Planning Risk* section of Chapter 2 – *Risk Analysis* for more information).

Case Studies 6-1 through 6-7 provide a series of examples that compare the acceptance testing environment of an insurance company to the production environment. The people, hardware, cohabiting software, interfaces, source and volume of data, and strategy are all attributes of the test environment. Keep in mind that in this example, the software is released immediately after successful conclusion of the acceptance test. Therefore, any

■■■■■■■■■■■■■■■■■

Key Point

Cohabiting software is other applications that reside in the test environment, but don't interact with the application being tested.

differences between the acceptance test environment and the production environment represent untested attributes of the system.

People

An important part of every test environment is the people who are doing the testing. By testing, we mean not only the execution of the tests, but the design and creation of the test cases as well. There is really no right or wrong answer as to who should do the testing, but it is best be done by people who understand the environment at a given level. For example, unit testing is usually done by the developers because it is based on the program specifications and code, which are typically understood best by the developers. Unit testing also provides the developer with assurance that his or her code functions correctly and is ready to be integrated.

Similarly, integration testing is usually done by groups of developers working in concert to determine if all of the software components and their interfaces function together correctly. Some organizations also use testers instead of, or in addition to, the developers because of a shortage of developers, lack of testing skill, or a problem in the past (i.e., the system was promoted to the test environment without adequate testing). We're advocates of having the developer do the integration testing; otherwise, developers can't be sure they're promoting a viable, integrated system.

At system test, it's not always clear who should do the testing. If there's no test group, the system testing must be accomplished by the developers or possibly the users (or their representatives). If an independent test group exists, their focus is often on system testing, because this is where the bulk of testing occurs. Other people such as developers, QA personnel, users, tech writers,

■■■■■■■■■■■■■■■■■

Key Point

The creation and execution of tests is best be done by the people who understand the environment associated with that level of test.

help desk personnel, training personnel, and others often augment the system test group. This is done to add expertise to the test group or just because extra resources are needed.

Ideally people with knowledge of how the system will be used should do acceptance testing. This might be users, customer service representatives, trainers, marketing personnel as well as testers. If users are employed as testers, the issue is "which users?" If there are many different users of the system, it's likely that every one of them will use the system in a different manner. The key is to get users involved in testing who best represent the general user community, plus any other users that might use the system in a radically different mode.

Test Environment Attribute – People in an Acceptance Testing Environment – for ABC Insurance Company

■■■■■■■■■■■■■■■■

Case Study 6-1

People in an
Acceptance Testing
Environment

Situation:

The testers are mostly former users of the system. Most of them have been testers for many years.

Analysis:

Certainly, turning motivated users into acceptance testers is one way to get business experience and realism in the testing environment. For the most part, these testers retain their empathy and user viewpoint throughout their career. However, as time goes by, the former users tend to have less and less current business experience.

Mitigation:

This company decided to bring in some current users to supplement the test team. Even though they lacked testing experience, they helped to emphasize the current needs of the users. Unfortunately, the three users who were chosen could not possibly represent the actual number of users (about 3,000) of the production system, who each had different needs and skill levels.

Hardware Configuration

An important part of the test environment is the hardware configuration(s). This is always important, but it's particularly important (and difficult) for those companies that are vendors of software. Each customer could potentially have slightly different configurations of hardware, operating systems, peripherals, etc. An excellent approach to take in this case is to develop "profiles" of different customers' environments. One company that we often visit has a Web site that literally has thousands of customers. Each customer potentially has a different configuration. This company, which happens to be a vendor of software, obviously has no control over its customers' environments.

The approach taken by the test group was to survey a sample of the existing customer base and create a series of profiles that describe the various customer configurations. Since it's impossible to replicate thousands of these in the laboratory, the test group looked for common configurations and set up a number of them (about 20) in their laboratory. Even though the bulk of the functional testing was done on just one of these configurations, the automated regression test suite was run on each of the 20 configurations prior to deployment. A lab like this is also worth its weight in gold when a customer calls in with a problem. The help desk, developers, and testers are often able to replicate the customers' environment and therefore facilitate the isolation, correction, and testing of the problem.

Obviously, not every test group has the luxury of creating an entire laboratory of test configurations. In that case, it's desirable to create a profile of a *typical* customer environment. If resources allow, it's also desirable to set up an environment

Key Point

If there are many diverse users of the system, it's useful to create profiles of common customer environments.

that represents the minimum hardware configurations required to run the software under test.

Test Environment Attribute – Hardware in an Acceptance Testing Environment – for ABC Insurance Company

Situation:

This was largely a client-server system. The servers were maintained by data processing professionals at regional sites. The clients were company-provided PCs. The testers used "exact" replicas of the hardware. All systems used the same operating system, but the memory, storage, and peripherals (especially printers and drivers) were different. The testers set up three different environments:

- "High-end," which represented the most powerful configuration found
- "Low-end," which represented the least powerful configuration found
- "Normal" configuration, which represented the average configuration found

Analysis:

This seems like a reasonable approach. On the previous release, the team had only used the "normal" configuration and there were lots of problems with users on "low-end" systems and with some peripherals. This test environment with three hardware configurations worked well for this company.

Mitigation:

Of course, this problem could also have been addressed by upgrading all clients to the same standard. That turned out to be politically impossible, since each region funded its own hardware purchases.

■■■■■■■■■■■■■■■■■
Case Study 6-2

Hardware in an Acceptance Testing Environment

Cohabiting Software

Most applications that you test will ultimately be installed on a machine (PC, mainframe, client/server) that also serves as a host for other applications. This has important implications to the tester:

- Do the cohabiting applications share common files?
- Is there competition for resources between the applications?

The approach we recommend for testing cohabiting software is to make an inventory of the cohabiting applications used by the various users. If there are many users, this may have to be done on a sampling basis. It's also beneficial to create one or more profiles of the most common combinations of cohabiting applications employed by different users. The strategy is to test each of the cohabiting applications in the inventory (unless there are just too many) and the most common and important combinations (profiles). This can be done by having the various cohabiting software applications running during the execution of the system and/or acceptance test. Other organizations conduct a separate testing activity designed just to test the cohabiting software. This is frequently done using the regression test set. Sometimes, the testing of the profiles of cohabiting software can be combined with testing the various hardware profiles.

Test Environment Attribute – Cohabiting Software in an Acceptance Testing Environment – for ABC Insurance Company

Situation:
Company regulations specified what software could be loaded onto the client machines. In reality, most of the users installed whatever additional software they wanted.

Analysis:
The system was tested on machines that had only the software under test (SUT) installed. There were isolated instances where the "additional" software installed by some users crashed the application or hindered its performance.

Case Study 6-3

Cohabiting Software in an Acceptance Testing Environment

Mitigation:

Enforcing the regulations could have solved this problem. The testing solution could be to develop "profiles" of commonly user-installed software and test the interaction of various applications. In the end, the team felt that the problem was not severe enough to warrant the creation of profiles, and their (reasonable) solution was to urge all end-users to conform to company regulations or at least report what software was loaded. Interestingly, though, some of the problematic cohabiting software was unlicensed, which is an entirely different issue.

Interfaces

Testing interfaces (to other systems) is often difficult and is frequently a source of problems once systems are delivered. Interfaces between systems are often problematic because the systems may not have originally been built to work together, may use different standards and technology, and are frequently built and supported by different organizations. All of these things make the testing of interfaces difficult, but the problem is exacerbated because it's frequently necessary to conduct the tests using simulated rather than real interfaces, since the system(s) that are being interfaced may already be in production. Hence, the quality and effectiveness of interface testing is dependent on the quality of the simulated interface. (Do you remember all of the bugs that you found in the application you're testing? The simulated interfaces were created using the same types of tools, methods, and people.)

Test Environment Attribute – Interfaces in an Acceptance Testing Environment – for ABC Insurance Company

Situation:

The only interface that the clients had was with the server. The server interfaced with several other company systems. The test environment normally simulated the interfaces to these various production systems. On previous releases, some of the interfaces did not work correctly after installation in spite of the testing using the simulations.

Analysis:

This is a common and difficult situation. It's frequently impossible to have "live" interfaces with production systems due to the risk of corrupting actual processes or data.

Mitigation:

After the particularly troublesome release, the testers re-evaluated the realism of the interfaces and tried to more closely model the actual interface. This problem was serious enough that on future releases, the system was installed on a pilot site before being installed globally.

Source of Test Data

A goal of testing is to create the most realistic environment that resources allow and the risks dictate – this includes the test data. Data can be in the form of messages, transactions, records, files, etc. There are many sources of data, and most test groups will probably try to use several different sources. Real data is desirable in many instances because it's the most realistic. Unfortunately, there are lots of reasons why real data is inadequate or, in some instances, impossible to use. For example, if the latest release uses radically different data formats from the production data, then production data may not be a viable choice. In some cases (e.g., military), the data could be classified and would require that the test environment also be classified. This can greatly add to the cost of the tests and might mean that some of the staff cannot participate. In other environments, real data, although not classified, may be company sensitive (e.g., financial records) or personally sensitive (e.g., social security numbers). In this case, additional security precautions may be required if real data is used.

If there are a large number of different users who have different profiles of data, it may be more difficult or impossible to accurately model all of the real data. Different users may have different profiles of data (e.g., an insurance company in Colorado may have much more data relating to the insurance of snowmobiles than one in Florida). In any case, even a large sample of production data seldom provides all of the situations that are required for testing, which means that some data must be created by hand or using some type of test data generator.

Table 6-2 lists some sources of data and their testing characteristics.

Table 6-2   Data Source Characteristics

	Production	Generated	Captured	Manually Created	Random
Volume	Too Much	Controllable	Controllable	Too Little	Controllable
Variety	Mediocre	Varies	Varies	Good	Mediocre
Acquisition	Easy	Varies	Fairly Easy	Difficult	Easy
Validation (Calibration)	Difficult	Difficult	Fairly Difficult	Easy	Very Difficult
Change	Varies	Usually Easy	Varies	Easy	Easy

Production data is the most realistic but may not cover all of the scenarios that are required. Additionally, this type of data could be sensitive, difficult to ensure that it is all correct, and sometimes difficult to change. Production data may vary depending on the day of the week, month, or time of year. Similarly, there may be different data mixes at different client sites. Another issue for some organizations is that a copy of the production data may be prohibitively large and would, therefore, slow the execution of the test or require the use of a profiling or extract tool to reduce its size.

■■■■■■■■■■■■■■■■■■
Key Point

Production data may vary depending on the day of the week, month, or time of year.

Generated data typically requires a tool or utility to create it. The variability of generated data depends on the sophistication of the tool and the tester's specification of how the data is to be created. If a tool is used to create very specific types of data, it may almost be like hand-creating the data. A tool, for example, may be used to create large volumes of similar data or data that varies according to an algorithm. Realism of the data depends on the quality of the tool and how it's used.

Captured data is only as good as the source from which it came. No extra effort is required to obtain the data once it has been gathered the first time. Most tools allow testers to modify the data, but the ease of this task varies depending on the particular tool.

Manually created data is, sometimes, the only way to obtain the extremely unique data required by certain test cases. Unfortunately, creating data by hand is time consuming and tedious. Sometimes, this approach is not very realistic if the author of the data doesn't have a good understanding of the functionality of the system (e.g., the data might be in the correct format, but not representative of the real world).

Random data, although easy to obtain, is not very realistic because an unknown amount of data would be required to cover every situation. Random data is useful for stress or load testing, but even here, the type of data can sometimes affect the quality of the load test.

Most testers will probably want to use data from a variety of sources, depending on the level of test and the availability of different types of data. If production data is available, most high-level testers (i.e., system and acceptance) will use this as their primary source of data. However, they may still need to create some data by hand to exercise circumstances not represented by the production data, or use generated data for volume testing, etc.

Volume of Test Data

In our goal of creating a realistic environment (especially during system and acceptance testing), it's necessary to consider the volume of data that will be needed. Most organizations choose to use a limited volume of data during the execution of the structural and functional tests. This is done because the objective of most test cases can be achieved without large volumes of data, and using smaller volumes of data is quicker and uses fewer resources. Unfortunately, the volume of data can have a large impact on the performance of the system being tested and therefore needs to be addressed. Ideally, the test group would use a volume equal to the volume expected in production. This may be possible, but in some instances, resource constraints make this impossible and the test group will have to use smaller volumes (and accept the associated risk), or resort to using a load generation tool.

It's also important to note, though, that sometimes it's not enough to use an equivalent volume of data, but you must also consider the mix of the data. If production data is available, it can sometimes be used to get the correct mix.

Test Environment Attribute – Data (Source and Volume) in an Acceptance Testing Environment – for ABC Insurance Company

Situation:

The team used copies of real production data from one of the regions. This data was the same data used in the previous release.

Analysis:

In this case, this strategy worked fine since the production data had enough variability and volume to satisfy their testing needs. Other companies that we've visited found that the data is different on different days of the week, months, etc., or is different at different client sites, or changes rapidly from release to release.

Mitigation:

None.

■■■■■■■■■■■■■■■■■■

Case Study 6-5

Data in an Acceptance Testing Environment

Strategy

In "Strategy," we discuss any additional considerations that the testing strategy has on the design of the test environment. For example, if *buddy testing* is used for unit testing, the environment must make it easy for programmers to access each other's specifications and code, and provide rules about how recommended changes will be communicated and made.

If the strategy for integration testing is to test progressively larger builds, the environment must support the testing of each successive build with data files that "cover" that build. For example, the test environment for 'Build C' will have to have data to cover the functionality added during that build. An example in the system test environment might be to create a small test environment for functional testing and a larger, more realistic environment for performance testing.

Similarly, if the system or acceptance testing is built around testing specific customer profiles, then the hardware and data in the test environment must match the profiles.

Test Environment Attribute – Strategy in an Acceptance Testing Environment – for ABC Insurance Company

Situation:
The testers decided that the test cases would mirror the instructions that were used in the user's manual (e.g., create a policy, amend a policy, etc.).

Analysis:
This worked pretty well. It turns out that the (well-designed) user's manual covered most of the situations that a user might encounter. In fact, the user's manual itself looked remarkably like a set of high-level test cases or scenarios.

Mitigation:
None.

■■■■■■■■■■■■■■■■■
Case Study 6-6

Strategy in an
Acceptance Testing
Environment
_____

Model Office Concept ■ ■ ■ ■ ■

One concept that we've recently seen several times is the *model office*. The model office is really just what its name implies – a test environment (probably acceptance) that is set up exactly like a real office. If you were in the business of creating software for travel agencies, for example, your model office could be an office that is set up just like a real travel agency, right down to the travel posters on the wall. The office is typically arranged like the real environment and uses testers and customers who are as near the real thing as possible. For our travel agent, for example, the tester would be a real travel agent and the customer would be someone who went into the model office to plan a vacation to Tampa, Florida. The tests are complete, end-to-end processing of the customer's request using actual hardware, software, data, and other real attributes.

Because the model office has the look and feel of a production environment and uses real data, it provides developers and testers the opportunity to make changes to production system code, test it, and move it into the production environment without impacting the current production environment.

What Should Be Automated? ■ ■ ■ ■ ■

We're constantly frustrated when we visit a client site where testing is in its infancy – they have no test cases, no metrics, poor or no defect tracking – and all they want to know is what tool they should buy. Fred Brooks' famous quote says, "There is no silver bullet," and indeed that's the case with test tools.

Is Automation the "Silver Bullet?"

Way back in the early '80s, when I was a (really) young Captain of Marines, Mr. Bill Perry of the Quality Assurance Institute asked me to be a speaker at the Second Annual International Testing Conference. First of all, I was very flattered, but I was also pretty nervous at the thought of speaking in front of a large group of people (especially those very unpredictable civilian types). However, I overcame my fear and gave a presentation on a topic that was near and dear to my heart, "Test Automation."

But let me digress a bit. At that time, I was in charge of an Independent Test Group at the (now non-existent) United States Readiness Command. Even though I had a fairly large staff of testers, the size and importance of the

■ ■ ■ ■ ■ ■ ■ ■ ■ ■

Case Study 6-7

The tool will do all of the work. Or, will it?

application was huge and quite overwhelming. We decided that the answer to our problems was test automation, so we hired a couple of high-powered consultants to help us develop crude (by today's standards) code coverage tools, performance monitors, script recorders, test execution tools, and even a really crude screen capture facility. This was all really cutting-edge stuff for that era. Unfortunately, the tools required huge overhead in the form of effort and computer resources. We soon found ourselves purchasing computer time from the local university and spending almost all of our time "serving the tools," for they had certainly become our masters. I was truly enamored.

So, let's get back to the conference. What did I say? I started off with the antique slide you see below and explained to my audience that if your testing is automated, all you have to do is sit back, have the Corporal turn the crank, and measure the successes and failures. The tool will do all of the work! When I joined SQE a few years later, however, I was surprised to find my slide in one of their note sets with a new title! The cartoon was renamed "Automation is not the Answer," which reversed the meaning of my original slide and speech.

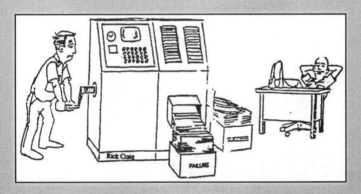

Well, now I'm a wily old Colonel instead of a naive young Captain, and I've learned that as important as testing tools and automation are, they are <u>not</u> THE answer to your problems. They are just one more tool in your bag of testing tricks.

– Rick Craig

A testing tool is a software application that helps automate some part of the testing process that would otherwise be performed manually. In this category, we also include tools that support testing, such as some configuration management tools, project management tools, defect tracking tools, and debugging tools.

Automation is the integration of testing tools into the test environment in such a fashion that the test execution, logging, and comparison of results are done with minimal human intervention. Generally, most experienced testers and managers have learned (in the school of hard knocks) that it's typically not fruitful, and probably not possible or reasonable, to automate every test. Obviously if you're trying to test the human/machine interface, you can't automate that process since the human is a key part of the test. Similarly, usability testing is normally done manually for the same reasons.

■■■■■■■■■■■■■■■■■
Key Point

It's typically not fruitful, and probably not possible or reasonable, to automate every test. Obviously, if you're trying to test the human/machine interface, you can't automate that process since the human is a key part of the test.

Fast Trash

I had a friend who used to work for a large bank in Hong Kong as the Test Automation Director. Once, while I was consulting for his bank, James confided in me about the state of the practice at his bank. He said, "You know, Rick, here at the ABC bank, we do testing very poorly and it takes us a really long time." He went on to say, "My job is to automate all of the tests so that we can do the same bad job, but do it quicker." Naturally, I was a little skeptical, but James made a strong case for using the "extra" time he gained by automation for process improvement.

The next time I arrived in Hong Kong and met with James, he looked rather bedraggled and said, "You know, if you automate a bunch of garbage, all you end up with is fast trash."

– Rick Craig

■■■■■■■■■■■■■■■■■
Case Study 6-8

If you automate a bunch of garbage, all you end up with is fast trash.

Creating automated test scripts can often take more expertise and time than creating manual tests. Some test groups use the strategy of creating all tests manually, and then automating the ones that will be repeated many times. In some organizations, this automation may even be done by an entirely separate group. If you're working in an environment where it takes longer to write an automated script than a manual one, you should determine how much time is saved in the execution of the automated scripts. Then, you can use this estimate to predict how many times each script will have to be executed to make it worthwhile to automate. This rule of thumb will help you decide which scripts to automate. Unless there is very little cost in automating the script (perhaps using capture-replay, but don't forget the learning curve), it's almost always more efficient to execute the test manually if it's intended to be run only once.

Repetitive Tasks

Repetitive tasks, such as regression tests, are prime candidates for automation because they're typically executed many times. Smoke, load, and performance tests are other examples of repetitive tasks that are suitable for automation, as illustrated in Figure 6-1.

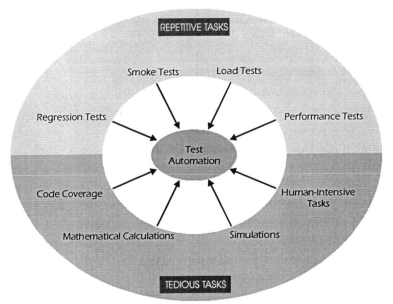

■■■■■■■■■■■■■■■■■

Figure 6-1

Repetitive and
Tedious Tasks Are
Prime Candidates for
Automation

We usually recommend that smoke tests be included as a subset of the regression test set. If there isn't enough time to automate the entire regression test set, the smoke tests should be automated first since they will probably be run more than any other tests. Performance tests are typically much easier to execute using a tool and, in some environments, load testing may not be possible without a tool.

Tedious Tasks

Tedious tasks are also prime candidates for automation. Code coverage, mathematical calculations, simulations, and human-intensive tasks, as listed in Figure 6-1 above, are virtually impossible to do on any sizable scale without using a tool.

Avoiding Testing Tool Traps ■ ■ ■ ■ ■

There are a multitude of reasons why the use of testing tools may fail. While some of these obstacles may seem easy to overcome on the surface, they're often deep-rooted within an organization's culture and may be difficult to resolve. According to a survey conducted at the 1997 Rational ASQ Conference, 28% of respondents said they didn't use automated testing tools due to lack of management support or budget; 18% said adequate tools weren't available; 13% said their current testing effort was too disorganized to use automated tools; 7% said their current manual testing was adequate; 5% said they didn't know that tools were available; and 0% said they didn't see any benefit to using tools. Chapter 11 – *Improving the Testing Process* has more information on how to identify and manage some of these obstacles.

No Clear Strategy

One of the greatest pitfalls is implementing a tool without a clear idea of how the testing tool can help contribute to the overall success of the testing effort. It's important that tools be chosen and implemented so that they contribute to the overall strategy as outlined in the master test plan. For the most part, it's not a good strategy to choose a tool and then modify your procedures to match the tool (well, you will almost always have to do this a little bit). The idea is to get a tool that helps you implement *your* testing strategy, not that of the tool vendor. An exception (there are always exceptions) might be if you have no processes at all in place for a certain function. For example, if your organization has no defect tracking system in place, it might be reasonable to choose a popular tool and create your defect tracking process around that of the tool. We reiterate, though, that in most

■■■■■■■■■■■■■■■■
Key Point

In most instances, it's necessary to first define the process and then choose a tool to facilitate that process.

instances it's necessary to first define the process and then choose a tool to facilitate that process.

Great Expectations

Management (especially upper management) expects that after the purchase of a tool, the testing will be better *and* faster *and* cheaper – usually by an entire order of magnitude and usually immediately. While some projects may achieve this triad of success, most should consider one or two of these a success. The actual level of improvement expected (or required) needs to be quantified, otherwise it's not possible to determine if the tool implementation was actually successful. For more hints on where and how to quantify expectations, refer to Chapter 11 – *Improving the Testing Process*.

Lack of Buy-In

The developers and testers that can potentially benefit from the use of a tool must be convinced that the tool will help them, that it is within their capability to use, and that they'll receive adequate training on how to use the tool. Would-be users are much less likely to enthusiastically learn and use the tool if their requirements and opinions are not taken into account during the tool selection and procurement.

Poor Training

Most test managers understand that testers must be trained on how to use new tools. Unfortunately, the amount of time and training is often underestimated. Similarly, training sometimes occurs too early and a significant time gap exists between the training and the first use of the tool. Training without immediate use is usually not very valuable. In fact, as a rough rule of

■■■■■■■■■■■■■■■■■
Key Point

The amount of time and training required to implement and use tools successfully is frequently underestimated.

thumb, if more than 6 months have passed since the training without using the tool, the potential users can be considered largely untrained.

Another training issue is how to use the tool to actually test software. In this case, we don't mean how to actually set up the tool or press the keys but, rather, we're talking about how the tool helps the testers select the test cases, set up the test cases, and determine the results – in other words, "how to test."

Automating the Wrong Thing

One common pitfall that should be avoided is automating the wrong thing. In the section *What Should Be Automated*, we concluded that there are a variety of human-intensive and repetitive tasks that are good candidates for automation. But there are also situations where automation is not as useful. For example, test cases that are intended to be run only once are not a good choice for automation. When a system is changing rapidly, it usually ends up taking more resources to automate the tests, since even the regression tests are unstable. Obviously, any tests designed to exercise the human interface with the system cannot be automated.

Choosing the Wrong Tool

If an attempt is made to automate the wrong thing, there's a good chance that the wrong tool will be chosen. In order to choose the right tool, it's important that requirements be formulated for the selection and use of the tool. It's important to note that as with all software requirements, it is necessary to prioritize them. There may be no one tool (of a certain type) that fulfills all of the requirements. Different potential users of the tool may also have different needs, so it may be possible (and unfortunate) that more than one of the same kind of tool may have to be selected,

■■■■■■■■■■■■■■■■■
Key Point

Not having a clear idea of the strategy on how to use the tool can result in choosing the wrong tool.

especially if there are many different environments in which the application being tested must run.

Ease of Use

Another major issue in tool selection is ease of use and the technical bent of the testing staff. Some testers may have been (or still are) developers. Some organizations may purposely choose testers with a development background, while other organizations may choose testers based on their business acumen. These testers may or may not like the idea of becoming "programmers," and in spite of what many vendors may say, using some tools requires the users to do some high-level programming.

Using Developers As Test Automation Engineers

We once heard a speaker from a large telecom company describe their test automation efforts. Apparently, their testers came mostly from the user community and weren't comfortable using automated testing tools. The test manager arranged to have a developer assigned to each testing team to help them automate the manual scripts they had written. Not only did it hasten the automation of the tests, but it also sent a very clear message to the testers, "that your time is so important that we've gotten a developer to work with you." Unfortunately, some of the developers that had been sent to help the testers acted like they had received a prison sentence.

Case Study 6-10

Some organizations enlist developers to assist in the automation of tests.

Even if your testers are programmers or former programmers, some tools are just hard to use. This is frustrating and may result in "shelfware."

Choosing the Wrong Vendor

This is a touchy subject, but we have to admit that all vendors do not meet the same standards. When choosing a vendor, it's important to choose one that the group is comfortable working with. The responsiveness of the tool vendor is a key factor in the long-term success of a tool. Another important issue in selecting a vendor is the training/consulting that they supply. Here are some things to consider when choosing a vendor:

- Do they only show the testing staff how to use the tool on "canned" examples, or do they actually provide training on your application?
- Are they available for assistance in the implementation of the tool?
- How difficult is it to get on-site assistance after the tool is purchased?
- When the tool is being demonstrated, does the vendor only send sales people or do they also send technical people who can answer in-depth questions?
- Do the vendors have an annual user's conference and/or regional users' groups? We have found that companies that do often have a greater customer focus than those that don't.
- Can the tool be modified to meet your needs? Some vendors are willing to help modify the tool for your particular needs and environment, while other vendors are not. If the tool works for you "as is" off-the-shelf, then this is not an issue. However, if you do need to have it modified, this can be a disqualifier for that vendor.

Sometimes, it may be easier to choose different tools from the same vendor if they must work together. For example, a defect tracking tool may work with the configuration management tool

■■■■■■■■■■■■■■■■■
Key Point

Ask the tool vendor how they test their own software. This may give you valuable insight into how good their software really is.

■■■■■■■■■■■■■■■■■
Key Point

In a survey conducted at the 1997 Rational ASQ Conference, 64% of respondents stated that what they did not like about automated tools was the effort required to maintain the test cases.

– Ross Collard

from the same vendor, but not with another vendor's. Choosing the same vendor also allows the testers to become more familiar with the vendor's help desk, their personnel, and any particular design quirks of their tools. Some vendors may also provide a price break for buying multiple tools.

It's an excellent idea to ask the tool vendor to explain how *they* test their own software. Are their developers trained in testing methodologies and techniques? Can they explain their measures of test effectiveness? Are they ISO certified? What CMM level have they achieved? We wouldn't disqualify a vendor for not being ISO certified or at a low CMM level, but we might have more interest in one that is.

■■■■■■■■■■■■■■■■
Key Point

It's an excellent idea to ask the tool vendor to explain how *they* test their software.

Another good idea is to ask other testing organizations how they like the vendor and their products. One good place to do this is at testing conferences like Software Testing Analysis and Review (STAR), EuroSTAR, Quality Week, The Test Automation Conference, Quality Assurance Institute (QAI) Conferences, and others. Not only can you see many tools demonstrated, but you'll also have the opportunity to talk to people who have actually purchased and used the tool. Don't forget, though, that their needs are not necessarily the same as yours.

Unstable Software

Another important consideration in deciding whether or not to automate test cases is the stability of the software under test. If the software that is brought into the test environment is of poor quality or is changing rapidly for any reason, some of the test cases will potentially have to be changed each time the software under test (SUT) is changed. And, if the automated scripts take longer to write than manual scripts, then the SUT may not be a good candidate for automation. Some of our clients feel that

■■■■■■■■■■■■■■■■
Key Point

If the application being tested is unstable or changing rapidly, automating the test scripts may be difficult.

automated scripts can be created as quickly as manual ones. In other words, they create the tests using a tool, rather than writing the tests and then automating them. This process is similar to us typing this text as we think of the sentences, rather than writing it down and later transcribing it. For these companies, it's just as easy and more economical to automate most tests (with the exception of some usability tests), including those that may only be executed once or twice.

The first foray many testing groups take into test automation is in the area of regression testing. The idea behind regression testing is that the regression tests are run after changes (corrections and additions) are made to the software to ensure that the rest of the system still works correctly. This means that we would like the regression test set to be fairly constant or stable. Since we know that creating automated scripts can sometimes take longer than creating manual ones, it doesn't make a lot of sense to automate the regression test set for an application that is changing so rapidly and extensively that the regression test cases are in a constant state of flux.

■■■■■■■■■■■■■■■■
Key Point

Regression tests are tests that are run after changes (corrections and editions) are made to the software to ensure that the rest of the system still works correctly.

Doing Too Much, Too Soon

Just as with any process improvement, it's generally a good idea to start small and limit the changes. Normally, we'd like to try the new tool out on a pilot project rather than do a global implementation. It's also generally a good idea to introduce one, or at least a limited number, of tools at one time. If multiple tools are implemented simultaneously, there's a tendency to stretch resources, and it becomes difficult to judge the impact of any one tool on the success of the testing effort.

Underestimating Time/Resources

Poor scheduling and underestimating the amount of time and/or resources required for proper implementation can have a significant impact on the success or failure of a test tool. If a tool is purchased for a particular project, but isn't implemented on that project, there's little chance that it will be implemented on any other project. In reality, the tool will probably sit on the test bench or stay locked in the software cabinet until it's obsolete.

Implementing tools can take a long time. Some of our clients report that they spend years (that's not a typo) implementing a tool across an entire organization. Even implementing a tool in a small organization can take weeks or even months. You have to ensure that you have buy-in for that extended effort.

■■■■■■■■■■■■■■■■■
Key Point

If a tool is purchased for a particular project, but isn't implemented on that project, there's little chance that it will be implemented on any other project.

Inadequate or Unique Test Environment

Now it's time to defend the tool vendors for a moment. Some testing organizations purchase tools that they aren't equipped to use, or their test environment is incapable of effectively utilizing these tools. By environment, we're talking about databases, files, file structures, source code control, configuration management, and so on. It's necessary to get your own development and testing environments in order if you want to successfully implement testing tools.

One common test management issue is, "Should we build, buy, or as we (sometimes jokingly) say, 'steal' the tool?" We recommend that in almost every case it's better to buy the tool than to make it. Just think of all of the things that you don't like to do that are required if you build the tool yourself: document it, test it and maintain it. Joking aside, the vendors have

■■■■■■■■■■■■■■■■■
Key Point

If you build your own tools, you also have to test them, document them, and maintain them.

amortized their development and testing of the tool across multiple users, where you would be making it for a limited audience. You wouldn't normally create your own word processor, would you? Of course, there are exceptions: If you have a very unique environment (embedded systems, for example), it might mean that you have to build the tool since there may not be any commercially available. Another example might be where you want to capitalize on some existing expertise and/or infrastructure. Let's say that your company is accustomed to using some kind of groupware like Lotus Notes. If it's difficult to introduce technical change in your organization, it might be worthwhile to build a defect tracking system on top of the groupware (assuming you can't find an off-the-shelf defect tracking system based on the groupware).

Poor Timing

Timing is everything. Trying to implement a major tool or automation effort in the midst of the biggest software release of all time is not a good strategy. We understand that there never really seems to be a good time to implement a tool (or improve processes or train people), but you have to use your common sense here. For example, many companies were buying (and sometimes using) regression testing tools to help in their Y2K testing. In most instances, starting in the fall of 1998, we stopped recommending that our clients buy these tools for the purpose of reaching their millennium goals, because we felt that implementing the tool at that late juncture would take too much of their remaining time. This time would be better spent on creating and running tests manually.

■■■■■■■■■■■■■■■
Key Point

Timing is everything. Trying to implement a major tool or automation effort in the midst of the biggest software release of all time is not a good strategy.

Cost of Tools

Another reason that tool implementation never gets off the ground is cost. There are the obvious costs of licensing plus the not-so-obvious costs of implementing and training, which may actually exceed the licensing costs. Because some tools may cost thousands of dollars per copy, there may be a tendency to restrict the number of copies purchased, which can be very frustrating if the testers have to take turns to access the tool. While it may not be necessary to have a copy for every tester, there have to be enough to preclude testers from "waiting around" for access to the tool. We know of clients who have had testers queue up to enter defects into the only workstation with the defect tracking tool installed.

■■■■■■■■■■■■■■
Key Point

Some vendors offer network licensing, which may be more economical than buying individual copies of a tool.

Evaluating Testware ■ ■ ■ ■ ■

It should be clear to most testers and test managers that in the process of testing an application, the testers are also evaluating the work of the people who specified the requirements, design, and code. But who evaluates the work of the testers? In some organizations, an evaluation may be done by the QA department, but ultimately, it's the customers or end-users who judge the work done by the testers. Among his clients, Capers Jones states that "...the number of enterprises that have at least some bad test cases is approximately 100%. However, the number of clients that measure test case quality is much smaller: only about 20 enterprises out of 600 or so." Our colleague, Martin Pol, has stated that 20% of all defects are testing defects. Even though we believe that for the most part testers are smarter, better looking, and, in general, just better people than the general population (just kidding), they too are only human and can make mistakes. The intellectual effort in testing an application is often as great as the effort to create it in the first place, and, therefore, someone should evaluate the work of the testers.

■■■■■■■■■■■■■■
Key Point

The intellectual effort in testing an application is often as great as the effort to create it in the first place and, therefore, someone should evaluate the work of the testers.

Quality Assurance Group

Some organizations may have a quality assurance group that evaluates the quality of the testing effort. Other organizations use post-project reviews to evaluate (after the fact) the effectiveness of the development and testing efforts. Measures of test effectiveness such as coverage and defect removal efficiency are important topics in and of themselves. For more information about these topics, refer to the section on *Measuring Test Effectiveness* in Chapter 7 – *Test Execution*. In addition to these topics, however, it's also important to understand that there are a variety of other techniques that can be used to evaluate the effectiveness of testware. Generally speaking, you can evaluate your testware using many of the same techniques that are used to test the software.

Reviews

Reviews of test documents can be a useful way to analyze the quality of the testing. Walkthroughs, inspections, peer reviews, and buddy checks can be used to review test plans, test cases, procedures, etc. These reviews should include interested parties outside of the test group such as users, business analysts, and developers. You'll benefit from the diverse range of ideas while, at the same time, achieving buy-in for the testing effort.

■■■■■■■■■■■■■■■■■
Key Point

Some organizations find it useful to review test documents and the corresponding development documents at the same time.

Dry Runs

It's often useful to conduct a dry run of the test cases, possibly on a previous version of the software. Even though the previous version is different and, therefore, some of the tests will (and should) fail because of these differences, many test cases should

■■■■■■■■■■■■■■■■■
Key Point

A *test set* is a group of test cases that cover a feature or system.

pass. The testers can then analyze the failed tests in order to determine if any of the failures can be attributed to incorrect tests, and subsequently upgrade the test set.

Traceability

Traceability is the process that ultimately leads to the coverage metrics described in the *Test Effectiveness* section. For our particular purposes, we simply want to ensure that the test cases can be mapped to the requirements, design, or code in order to maintain traceability. Tables 6-3, 6-4, and 6-5 list some sample requirements for an ATM, some sample test cases that might be used to test those requirements, and the resulting traceability matrix.

Table 6-3   Requirements for ATM Example

Requirement	Description
1.0	A valid user must be able to withdraw up to $200 or the maximum amount in the account.
1.1	Withdrawal must be in increments of $20.
1.2	User cannot withdraw more than account balance.
1.3	If the maximum amount in the account is less than $200, user may withdraw an amount equal to the largest sum divisible by 20, but less than or equal to the maximum amount.
1.4	User must be validated in accordance with Requirement 16.
2.0	A valid user may make up to 5 withdrawals per day.
...	
...	

Table 6-4   Simplified Description of Test Cases for ATM Example

Test Case	Description
TC-01	Withdraw $20 from a valid account that contains $300.
TC-02	Withdraw $25 from a valid account that contains $300.
	NOTE: This is a negative test and should return an error message.
TC-03	Withdraw $400 from a valid account that contains $300.
	NOTE: This is a negative test and should return an error message.
TC-04	Withdraw $160 from a valid account that contains $165.
...	

Table 6-5 shows a simplified requirements and design traceability matrix for our ATM example. Notice that it takes more than one test case to test Requirement 1.1. Also notice that test cases TC-01 through TC-04 are also used to test Requirement 16.0 in addition to testing the other requirements.

Table 6-5   Traceability of Requirements to Test Cases

Attribute	TC #1	TC# 2	TC #3	TC #4	TC #5
Requirement 1.0					
Requirement 1.1	✓	✓			
Requirement 1.2			✓		
Requirement 1.3				✓	
Requirement 2.0					
...					
...					
Requirement 16.0	✓	✓	✓	✓	✓
Design 1.0					
Design 1.1	✓				
Design 1.2					✓
...					
...					

Defect Seeding

Defect seeding is a technique that was developed to estimate the number of bugs resident in a piece of software. This technique may seem a little more off the wall than other techniques for evaluating testware, and it's definitely not for everyone. Conceptually, a piece of software is "seeded" with bugs and then the test set is run to find out how many of the seeded bugs were discovered, how many were not discovered, and how many new (unseeded) bugs were found. It's then possible to use a simple mathematical formula to predict the number of bugs remaining. The formulae for calculating these values are shown in Figure 6-2.

■■■■■■■■■■■■■■■■■
Key Point

Most articles about defect seeding seem to be written by college professors and graduate students. Perhaps this means that defect seeding is only used in the world of academia?

For example, if an organization inserted 100 seed bugs and later were only able to locate 75 of the seeded bugs, their seed ratio would be 0.75 (or 75%). If the organization had already discovered 450 "real" defects, then using the results from the seeding experiment, it would be possible to extrapolate that the 450 "real" defects represented only 75% of all of the real defects present. Then, the total number of real defects would be estimated to be 600. Since only 450 of the potential 600 real defects have been found, it appears that the product still has 150 "real" defects waiting to be discovered plus 25 seed bugs that still exist in the code. Don't forget to remove the seed bugs!

Figure 6-2

Formulae for
Calculating Seed
Ratio and Estimated
Number of Real
Defects Still Present

Estimated Number of Real Defects Still Present	=	Estimated Total Number of Real Defects	–	Number of Real Defects Found

Seed Ratio = $\dfrac{\text{Number of Seed Bugs Found}}{\text{Total Number of Seed Bugs}}$

Number of Seed Bugs Found = 75

Total Number of Seed Bugs = 100

Seed Ratio = $\dfrac{75}{100}$ = 0.75   Or = 75%

Estimated Total Number of Real Defects	=	$\dfrac{\text{Number of Real Defects Found}}{\text{Seed Ratio}}$

Number of Real Defects Found = 450

Estimated Total Number of Real Defects = $\dfrac{450}{0.75}$ = 600

Estimated Number of Real Defects Still Present = 600 – 450 = 150

In our experience, seeding doesn't work very well as a means of predicting the number of undiscovered bugs, because it's virtually impossible to create the seeded bugs as creatively as programmers do in real life. In particular, seeded bugs seldom replicate the complexity, placement, frequency, etc. of developer-created defects. Still, this technique can be used to "test" the testware. Software with seeded or known bugs is subjected to the test set to determine if all of the seeded bugs are discovered. If some of the bugs are not found, the test set may be inadequate. If all of the bugs are found, the test set may or may not be adequate. (Great, just what we need – a technique that shows us when we've done a bad job, but can't confirm when we've done a good job!)

The Genesis of Defect Seeding

I've been telling a story in my classes for the last several years about the genesis of defect seeding in software. I tell my students that software defect seeding is a technique borrowed from the State Fishery Department. The fishery department would catch a batch of fish, tag them, and then release them. Later, a second batch of fish would be caught and the ratio of tagged to untagged fish was noted. It's then a simple mathematical calculation to determine the population of fish in the lake.

Some wise person, as I tell my class, decided to try this technique with software. After the software is seeded with bugs and tested, the ratio of seeded to unseeded bugs is computed. Using the same mathematical formula as our friends in the fisheries, we should be able to predict the number of bugs in the software. Well, apparently bugs are different from fish, because it didn't work nearly as well with software as it did with fish. No doubt, this technique failed because nobody can seed the software with bugs as creatively as programmers do.

While re-reading the book Software Defect Removal *by Robert H. Dunn, I was surprised to learn that indeed software defect seeding did come from the work of scientists measuring populations of fish. The first suggestion of seeding software with defects seems to come from the work of Harlan Mills around 1970.*

– Rick Craig

Some organizations also use software with known or seeded bugs as a training vehicle for new testers. The neophyte testers are asked to test a piece of software to see if they can find all of the bugs.

For all practical purposes, most of you don't have the time or resources to do defect seeding, and the technique is definitely not at the top of our priority list. Besides, isn't it just a little scary to put bugs in the software on purpose? Can you imagine what would happen if these bugs were shipped to customers by mistake? We know of one company where this actually happened.

Mutation Analysis

Mutation analysis is sometimes used as a method of auditing the quality of unit testing. Basically, to do mutation analysis, you insert a mutant statement (e.g., bug) into a piece of code (e.g., a unit) and run the unit test cases to see if the mutant is detected, as illustrated in Figure 6-3.

If the unit test set is comprehensive, the mutant should always be found. If the mutant is not found, the unit test set is not comprehensive. The converse, however, is not true. Just because the mutant is discovered, doesn't mean the test set is comprehensive.

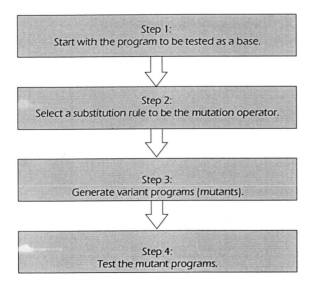

Figure 6-3

Steps in the Mutation
Analysis Process

Mutation analysis is only effective in organizations that have already achieved high levels of code coverage, since mutation analysis is based on the premise that virtually all lines of code have been covered and we're just looking for an anomaly. Our research has shown that only 25% of organizations do any form of formal unit testing. It's very likely that the coverage is so low for the 75% of organizations that don't do any formal unit testing, that it's actually a surprise if the mutant is found rather than if it isn't found.

So, it's our opinion that mutation analysis is primarily of value to organizations that are already doing comprehensive unit testing. We believe that these "advanced" organizations are also likely to be the ones using code coverage tools and therefore don't need mutation analysis anyway. The bottom line on mutation analysis is that unless you have a lot of time on your hands, move on to something more useful, like code coverage.

Key Point

Mutation analysis is only effective in organizations that have already achieved high levels of code coverage, since mutation analysis is based on the premise that virtually all lines of code have been covered and we're just looking for an anomaly.

Testing Automated Procedures

When test procedures are automated, they effectively become software – just like the software under test. You can employ the same techniques for testing automated procedures that you would use for any other piece of software.

Chapter 7 –
Test Execution

"Knowledge must come through action; you can have no test which is not fanciful, save by trial."

— Sophocles

"Take time to deliberate, but when the time for action has arrived, stop thinking and go in."

— Napoleon Bonaparte

Test execution is the process of executing all or a selected number of test cases and observing the results. Although preparation and planning for test execution occur throughout the software development lifecycle, the execution itself typically occurs at or near the end of the software development lifecycle (i.e., after coding).

Before Beginning Test Execution ■ ■ ■ ■ ■

When most people think of testing, test execution is the first thing that comes to mind. So, why is there an emphasis on execution? Well, not only is test execution the most visible testing activity, it also typically occurs at the end of the development lifecycle after most of the other development activities have concluded or at least slowed down. The focus then shifts to test execution, which is now on the critical path of delivery of the software. By-products of test execution are test incident reports, test logs, testing status, and results, as illustrated in Figure 7-1.

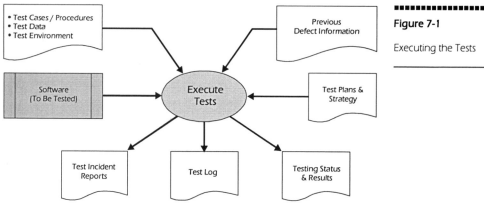

Figure 7-1

Executing the Tests

By now, you should know that we consider testing to be an activity that spans the entire software development lifecycle. According to Martin Pol, "test execution may only consume 40% or less of the testing effort," but it typically has to be concluded as quickly as possible, which means that there is often an intense burst of effort applied in the form of long hours and borrowed resources. Frequently, it also means that the test execution effort will be anxiously scrutinized by the developers, users, and management.

Deciding Who Should Execute the Tests

Who executes the tests is dependent upon the level of test. During unit test it is normal for developers to execute the tests. Usually each developer will execute their own tests, but the tests may be executed by another programmer using techniques like *buddy testing* (refer to Chapter 4 – *Detailed Test Planning* for more information on buddy testing). Integration tests are usually executed by the developers and/or the testers (if there is a test group). System tests could be executed by the developers, testers, end-users, or some combination thereof. Some organizations also use developers to do the system testing, but in doing so, they lose the fresh perspective provided by the test group.

Ideally, acceptance tests should be executed by end-users, although the developers and/or testers may also be involved. Table 7-1 shows one way that test execution may be divided, but there is really no definitive answer as to who should execute the tests. Ideally, we are looking for people with the appropriate skill set, although sometimes we're lucky to find somebody, anybody that's available.

Table 7-1   Responsibilities for Test Execution

Responsible Group	Unit	Integration	System	Acceptance
Testers		✓	✓	✓
Developers	✓	✓	✓	
End-Users			✓	✓

During test execution, the manager of the testing effort is often looking for additional resources. Potential testers might include: members of the test team (of course), developers, users, technical writers, trainers, or help desk staff members. Some organizations even bring in college interns to help execute tests. College interns and new-hires can be used successfully if the test cases are explicit enough for them to understand and they've received training in how to write an effective incident report. We must be cautious, though, or we might spend more time training the neophyte testers than it's worth. On the other hand, having new testers execute tests is one way to quickly make them productive and feel like part of the team.

■■■■■■■■■■■■■■■■■
Key Point

"Newbies" make good candidates for usability testing because they're not contaminated by previous knowledge of the product.

Deciding What to Execute First

Choosing which test cases to execute first is a strategy decision that depends on the quality of the software, resources available, existing test documentation, and the results of the risk analysis. As a rule of thumb, we normally recommend that the regression test set (or at least the smoke test) be run in its entirety early on to flag areas that are obviously problematic. This strategy may not be feasible if the regression set is exceptionally large or totally manual. Then, the focus of the test should be placed on those features that were identified as high-risk during the software risk analysis described in Chapter 2. High-risk features will almost certainly contain all features that were extensively

■■■■■■■■■■■■■■■■■
Key Point

As a rule of thumb, we normally recommend that the regression test set (or at least the smoke test) be run in its entirety early on to flag areas that are obviously problematic.

modified, since we know that changed features are typically assigned a higher likelihood of failure.

Writing Test Cases During Execution

Really, no matter how good you and your colleagues are at designing test cases, you'll always think of new test cases to write when you begin test execution (this is one of the arguments for techniques such as exploratory testing). As you run tests, you're learning more about the system and are in a better position to write the additional test cases. Unfortunately, in the heat of battle (test execution) when time is short, these tests are often executed with no record made of them unless an incident is discovered. This is truly unfortunate, because some of these "exploratory" test cases are frequently among the most useful ones created and we would like to add them to our test case repository, since we have a long-term goal of improving the coverage of the test set. One of our clients includes notes in the test log as a shorthand way of describing these exploratory test cases. Then, after release, they use the test log to go back and document the test cases and add them to the test case repository.

■■■■■■■■■■■■■■■■■■
Key Point

No matter how good you and your colleagues are at designing test cases, you'll always think of new test cases to write when you begin test execution.

Recording the Results of Each Test Case

Obviously, the results of each test case must be recorded. If the testing is automated, the tool will record both the input and the results. If the tests are manual, the results can be recorded right on the test case document. In some instances, it may be adequate to merely indicate whether the test case passed or failed. Failed test cases will also result in an incident report being generated. Often, it may be useful to capture screens, copies of reports, or some other output stream.

Test Log ■ ■ ■ ■ ■

The IEEE Std. 829-1998 defines the test log as a chronological record of relevant details about the execution of test cases. The purpose of the test log shown in Figure 7-2 is to share information among testers, users, developers, and others and to facilitate the replication of a situation encountered during testing.

IEEE Std. 829-1998 for Software Test Documentation

Template for Test Log

Contents

1. Test Log Identifier
2. Description
3. Activity and Event Entries

Figure 7-2

Test Log Template from IEEE Std. 829-1998

In order for a test log to be successful, the people that must submit data into and eventually use the log must want to do so. Forcing participants to use a test log when they don't want to use it is seldom successful. In order to make it desirable, the test log must be easy to use and valuable to its users.

Since the primary purpose of the test log is to share information rather than analyze data, we recommend making the log free form, instead of using fields or buttons, which are desirable in other areas such as defect tracking. If the testing team is small and co-located, the test log might be as simple as a spiral notebook in which testers and/or developers can make log entries. Alternatively, it might be more convenient to have a word-processed document or e-mailed form. If the team members are geographically separated, the test log would

Key Point

Since the primary purpose of the test log is to share information rather than analyze data, we recommend making the log free form.

probably be better served in the form of a Web page or company intranet. Wherever it is, the test log should be easy to access and update. One of our clients, for example, has a continuously open active window on their monitor where a thought can be entered at any time.

Table 7-2 shows an example of a test log sheet. Notice that even though it mentions the writing up of PR#58, it doesn't go into any detail. The purpose of the log is not to document bugs (we have defect tracking systems for that), but rather to record events that you want to share among the team members or use for later recall. The larger the team and/or the project and the more geographically separated they are, the more important the log becomes.

Table 7-2 Sample Test Log

Description: Online Trade   Date: 01/06/2002

ID	Time	Activity and Event Entries
1	08:00	Kicked off test procedure #18 (buy shares) with 64 users on test system.
2	09:30	Test system crashed.
3	10:00	Test system recovered.
4	10:05	Kicked off test procedure #19 (sell shares).
5	11:11	PR #58 written up.
6	12:00	New operating system patch installed.

Test Incident Reports ■ ■ ■ ■ ■

Incidents can be defined as any unusual result of executing a test (or actual operation). Incidents may, upon further analysis, be categorized as defects or enhancements, or merely retain their status as an incident if they're determined to be inconsequential or the result of a one-time anomaly. A *defect* (or *bug*) is a flaw in the software with the potential to cause a failure. The defect can be anywhere: in the requirements, design, code, test, and/or documentation. A *failure* occurs when a defect prevents a system from accomplishing its mission or operating within its specifications. Therefore, a failure is the manifestation of one or more defects. One defect can cause many failures or none, depending on the nature of the defect. An automated teller machine (ATM), for example, may fail to dispense the correct amount of cash, or an air defense system may fail to track an incoming missile. Testing helps you find the failure in the system, but then you still have to track the failure back to the defect.

Defect tracking is an important activity and one that almost all test teams accomplish. Defect tracking is merely a way of recording software defects and their status. In most organizations, this process is usually done using a commercial or "home-grown" tool. We've seen many "home-grown" tools that were developed based on applications such as Infoman, Lotus Notes, Microsoft Access, and others.

■■■■■■■■■■■■■■■■■
Key Point

Some software testing books say, *"The only important test cases are the ones that find bugs."*

We believe that proving that some attribute of the system works correctly is just as important as finding a bug.

The First Computer Bug

I'm very proud of the fact that I got to meet Rear Admiral Grace Murray Hopper, the famous computer pioneer, on two separate occasions. On one of these meetings, I even received one of Admiral Hopper's "nanoseconds," a small piece of colored "bell" wire about a foot or so long, which Grace often gave to her many admirers to show them how far electricity would travel in one nanosecond.

Among Rear Admiral Grace Murray Hopper's many accomplishments were the invention of the programming language COBOL and the attainment of the rank of Rear Admiral in the U.S. Navy (one of the first women to ever reach this rank). But, ironically, Admiral Hopper is probably most famous for an event that occurred when she wasn't even present.

■■■■■■■■■■■■■■■■■
Case Study 7-1

On September 9, 1945, a moth trapped between relays caused a problem in Harvard University's Mark II Aiken Relay Calculator.

Admiral Hopper loved to tell the story of the discovery of the first computer bug. In 1945, she was working on the Harvard University Mark II Aiken Relay Calculator. On September 9 of that year, while Grace was away, computer operators discovered that a moth trapped between the relays was causing a problem in the primitive computer. The operators removed the moth and taped it to the computer log next to the entry, "first actual case of a bug being found." Many people cite this event as the first instance of using the term "bug" to mean a defect. The log with the moth still attached is now located in the History of American Technology Museum.

Even though this is a great story, it's not really the first instance of using the term "bug" to describe a problem in a piece of electrical gear. Radar operators in World War II referred to electronic glitches as bugs, and the term was also used to describe problems in electrical gear as far back as the 1900s. The following is a slide that I used in a presentation that I gave at a testing conference in the early 1980s shortly after meeting Admiral Grace Hopper.

— *Rick Craig*

IEEE Template for Test Incident Report

An incident report provides a formal mechanism for recording software incidents, defects, and enhancements and their status. Figure 7-3 shows the IEEE template for a Test Incident Report. The parts of the template in Figure 7-3 shown in italics are not part of the IEEE template, but we've found them to be useful to include in the Test Incident Report. Please feel free to modify this (or any other template) to meet your specific needs.

IEEE Std. 829-1998 for Software Test Documentation
Template for Test Incident Report

Contents

1. Incident Summary Report Identifier
2. Incident Summary
3. Incident Description
   3.1 Inputs
   3.2 Expected Results
   3.3 Actual Results
   3.4 Anomalies
   3.5 Date and Time
   3.6 Procedure Step
   3.7 Environment
   3.8 Attempts to Repeat
   3.9 Testers
   3.10 Observers
4. Impact
5. *Investigation*
6. *Metrics*
7. *Disposition*

■■■■■■■■■■■■■■■■■■
Figure 7-3

Template for Test Incident Report from IEEE Std. 829-1998

Incident Summary Report Identifier

The *Incident Summary Report Identifier* uses your organization's incident tracking numbering scheme to identify this incident and its corresponding report.

Incident Summary

The *Incident Summary* is the information that relates the incident back to the procedure or test case that discovered it. This reference is often missing in many companies and is one of the first things that we look for when we're auditing their testing processes. Absence of the references on all incident reports usually means that the testing effort is largely ad hoc. All identified incidents should have a reference to a test case. If an incident is discovered using ad hoc testing, then a test case should be written that would have found the incident. This test case is important in helping the developer recreate the situation, and the tester will undoubtedly need to re-run the test case after any defect is fixed. Also, defects have a way of reappearing in production and this is a good opportunity to fill in a gap or two in the test coverage.

■■■■■■■■■■■■■■■■■
Key Point

All identified incidents should have a reference to a test case. If an incident is discovered using ad hoc testing, then a test case should be written that would have found the incident.

Incident Description

The author of the incident report should include enough information so that the readers of the report will be able to understand and replicate the incident. Sometimes, the test case reference alone will be sufficient, but in other instances, information about the setup, environment, and other variables is useful. Table 7-3 describes the subsections that appear under Incident Description.

Table 7-3 Subsections Under Incident Description

Section Heading	Description
4.1 Inputs	Describes the inputs actually used (e.g., files, keystrokes, etc.).
4.2 Expected Results	This comes from the test case that was running when the incident was discovered.
4.3 Actual Results	Actual results are recorded here.
4.4 Anomalies	How the actual results differ from the expected results. Also record other data (if it appears to be significant) such as unusually light or heavy volume on the system, it's the last day of the month, etc.
4.5 Date and Time	The date and time of the occurrence of the incident.
4.6 Procedure Step	The step in which the incident occurred. This is particularly important if you use long, complex test procedures.
4.7 Environment	The environment that was used (e.g., system test environment or acceptance test environment, customer 'A' test environment, beta site, etc.)
4.8 Attempts to Repeat	How many attempts were made to repeat the test?
4.9 Testers	Who ran the test?
4.10 Observers	Who else has knowledge of the situation?

Impact

The *Impact* section of the incident report form refers to the potential impact on the user, so the users or their representative should ultimately decide the impact of the incident. The impact will also be one of the prime determinants in the prioritization of bug fixes, although the resources required to fix each bug will also have an effect on the prioritization.

One question that always arises is, "Who should assign the impact rating?" We believe that the initial impact rating should be assigned by whoever writes the incident report. This means that if the incident is written as a result of an incorrect response to a test case, the initial assignment will be made by a tester.

Many people think that only the user should assign a value to the impact, but we feel that it's important to get an initial assessment of the impact as soon as possible. Most testers that we know can correctly determine the difference between a really critical incident and a trivial one. And, it's essential that incidents that have the potential to become critical defects be brought to light at the earliest opportunity. If the assignment of criticality is deferred until the next meeting of the Change Control Board (CCB) or whenever the user has time to review the incident reports, valuable time may be lost. Of course, when the CCB does meet, one of their most important jobs is to review and revise the impact ratings.

A standardized organization-wide scale should be devised for the assignment of impact. Oftentimes, we see a scale such as Minor, Major, and Critical; Low, Medium, and High; 1 through 5; or a variety of other scales. Interestingly enough, we discovered a scale of 1 through 11 at one client site. We thought that was strange and when we queried them, they told us that they had so many bugs with a severity (or impact) of 10 that they had to create a new category of 11. Who knows how far they may have expanded their impact scale by now (…35, 36, 37)? It's usually necessary to have only four or five severity categories. We're not, for example, looking for a severity rating of 1 to 100 on a sliding scale. After all, how can you really explain the difference between a severity of 78 and 79? The key here is that all of the categories are defined.

If your categories are not defined, but just assigned on a rolling scale, then the results will be subjective and very much depend on who assigns the value. The imprecision in assigning impact ratings can never be totally overcome, but it can be reduced by defining the parameters (and using examples) of what minor, major, and critical incidents look like. Case Study 7-2 shows the categories chosen by one of our clients.

■■■■■■■■■■■■■■■■■
Key Point

It's essential that incidents that have the potential to become critical defects be brought to light at the earliest opportunity.

■■■■■■■■■■■■■■■■■
Key Point

The imprecision in assigning impact ratings can never be totally overcome, but it can be reduced by defining the parameters (and using examples) of what minor, major, and critical incidents look like.

Example of Minor, Major, and Critical Defects

Minor:
Misspelled word on the screen.

Major:
System degraded, but a workaround is available.

Critical:
System crashes.

Case Study 7-2

Example Impact Scale

Investigation

The *Investigation* section of the incident report explains who found the incident and who the key players are in its resolution. Some people also collect some metrics here on the estimated amount of time required to isolate the bug.

Metrics

Initially, most testers automatically assume that every incident is a software problem. In some instances, the incident may be a hardware or environment problem, or even a testing bug! Some of our clients are very careful to record erroneous tests in the defect tracking system, because it helps them to better estimate their future testing (i.e., how many bad test cases are there?) and helps in process improvement. As an aside, one company told us that recording erroneous test cases helped give their testers a little extra credibility with the developers, since the testers were actually admitting and recording some of their own bugs. In most cases, though, testers don't normally like to record their own bugs, just as many developers don't like to record their own unit testing bugs.

Key Point

The *Metrics* section of the incident report can be used to record any number of different metrics on the type, location, and cause of the incidents.

The *Metrics* section of the incident report can be used to record any number of different metrics on the type, location, and cause of the incidents. While this is an ideal place to collect metrics on incidents, be cautious not to go overboard. If the incident report gets too complicated or too long, testers, users, and developers will get frustrated and look for excuses to avoid recording incidents.

Good Initiative, But Poor Judgment

I learned that every bug doesn't have to be a software bug the hard way. In the late 1980's, I was the head of an independent test team that was testing a critical command and control system for the U.S. military. During one particularly difficult test cycle, we discovered an alarming number of bugs. One of my sergeants told me that I should go inform the development manager (who was a Brigadier General, while I was only a Captain) that his software was the worst on the planet. I remember asking the sergeant, "Are you sure all of the tests are okay?" and he replied, "Yes, sir. It's the software that's bad."

In officer training school we were taught to listen to the wisdom of our subordinate leaders, so I marched up to the General's office and said, "Sir, your software is not of the quality that we've come to expect." Well, you can almost guess the ending to this story. The General called together his experts, who informed me that most of the failures were caused by a glitch in our test environment. At that point, the General said to me, "Captain, good initiative, but poor judgment," before I was dismissed and sent back to my little windowless office.

The moral of the story is this: If you want to maintain credibility with the developers, make sure your tests are all valid before raising issues with the software.

— Rick Craig

■■■■■■■■■■■■■■■■■
Case Study 7-3

What happens when there's a defect in the testware?

Disposition (Status)

In a good defect tracking system, there should be the capability to maintain a log or audit trail of the incident as it goes through the analysis, debugging, correction, re-testing, and implementation process. Case Study 7-4 shows an example of an incident log recorded by one of our clients.

Example Incident Log

2/01/01 Incident report opened.

2/01/01 Sent to the CCB for severity assignment and to Dominic for analysis.

2/03/01 Dominic reports that the fix is fairly simple and is in code maintained by Hunter C.

2/04/01 CCB changed the severity to Critical.

2/04/01 Bug fix assigned to Hunter.

2/06/01 Bug fix implemented and inspection set for 2/10/01.

2/10/01 Passed inspection and sent to QA.

2/12/01 Bug fix is re-tested and regression run. No problems encountered.

2/12/01 Incident report closed.

Note: Closed incident reports should be saved for further analysis of trends and patterns of defects.

■■■■■■■■■■■■■■■■■
Case Study 7-4

Example Incident Log Entry

Writing the Incident Report

We are often asked, "Who should write the incident report?" The answer is, "Whoever found the incident!" If the incident is found in the production environment, the incident report should be written by the user – if it's culturally acceptable and if the users have access to the defect tracking system. If not, then the help desk is a likely candidate to complete the report for the user. If the incident is found by a tester, he or she should complete the

■■■■■■■■■■■■■■■■■
Key Point

Most incident tracking tools are also used to track defects, and the tools are more commonly called *defect tracking tools* than incident tracking tools.

report. If an incident is found by a developer, it's desirable to have him or her fill out the report. In practice, however, this is often difficult, since most programmers would rather just "fix" the bug than record it. Very few of our clients (even the most sophisticated ones) record unit testing bugs, which are the most common type of bugs discovered by developers. If the bug is discovered during the course of a review, it should be documented by the person who is recording the minutes of the review.

It's a good idea to provide training or instructions on how to write an incident report. We've found that the quality of the incident report has a significant impact on how long it takes to analyze, recreate, and fix a bug. Specifically, training should teach the authors of the incident reports to:

- focus on factual data
- ensure the situation is re-creatable
- not use emotional language (e.g., bold text, all caps)
- not be judgmental

> **Key Point**
>
> Very few of our clients record unit testing bugs, which are the most common type of bugs discovered by developers.

Attributes of a Defect Tracking Tool

Most organizations that we work with have some kind of defect tracking tool. Even organizations that have little else in the way of formal testing usually have some type of tracking tool. This is probably because in many organizations, management's effort is largely focused on the number, severity, and status of bugs.

We also find that some companies use commercial defect tracking tools, while others create their own tools using applications that they're familiar with such as MS-Word, MS-Access, Lotus Notes, Infoman, and others. Generally, we urge companies to buy tools rather than make them themselves unless the client environment is so unique that there is no tool that will

> **Key Point**
>
> In a survey conducted in 1997, Ross Collard reported that defect tracking tools were the most commonly used testing tools among his respondents (83%).
>
> – Ross Collard
> *1997 Rational ASQ User Conference*

fit their requirements.   Remember that if you build the tool yourself, you also have to document it, test it, and maintain it.

Ideally, a defect tracking tool should be easy to use, be flexible, allow easy data analysis, integrate with a configuration management system, and provide users with easy access.   Ease of use is why so many companies choose to build their own defect tracking tool using some familiar product like Lotus Notes.   If the tool is difficult to use, is time-consuming, or asks for a lot of information that the author of an incident report sees no need for, use of the tool will be limited and/or the data may not be accurate.   Software engineers have a way of recording "any old data" in fields that they believe no one will use.

■■■■■■■■■■■■■■■■

Key Point

Ideally, a defect tracking tool should be easy to use, be flexible, allow easy data analysis, integrate with a configuration management system, and provide users with easy access.

A good defect tracking tool should allow the users to modify the fields to match the terminology used within their organization. In other words, if your organization purchases a commercial tool that lists severity categories of High, Medium, and Low, users should be able to easily change the categories to Critical, Major, Minor, or anything else they require.

■■■■■■■■■■■■■■■■

Key Point

A good defect tracking tool should allow the users to modify the fields to match the terminology used within their organization.

The tool should facilitate the analysis of data.   If the test manager wants to know the distribution of defects against modules, it should be easy for him or her to get this data from the tool in the form of a table or chart. This means that most of the input into the tool must be in the form of discrete data rather than free-form responses. Of course there will always be a free-form description of the problem, but there should also be categories such as distribution, type, age, etc. that are discrete for ease of analysis.   Furthermore, each record needs to have a dynamic defect log associated with it in order to record the progress of the bug from discovery to correction (refer to Case Study 7-4).

Ideally, the incident reports will be linked to the configuration management system used to control the builds and/or versions.

All users of the system must be able to easily access the system at all times. We have occasionally encountered organizations where incident reports could only be entered into the defect tracking system from one or two computers.

Using Multiple Defect Tracking Systems

Although we personally prefer to use a single defect tracking system throughout the organization, some organizations prefer to use separate defect tracking systems for production and testing bugs. Rather than being a planned event, separate defect tracking systems often evolve over time, or are implemented when two separate systems are initially created for separate purposes. For example, the production defect tracking system may have originally been designed for tracking support issues, but later modified to also track incidents. If you do use separate systems, it's beneficial to ensure that field names are identical for production and test bugs. This allows the test manager to analyze trends and patterns in bugs from test to production. Unfortunately, many of you are working in organizations that use entirely different vocabularies and/or metrics for bugs discovered in test versus those found by the user.

It's useful to analyze trends and patterns of the failures, and then trends and patterns of the defects. Generally, part of the process of analyzing an incident report is to determine if the failure was caused by a new bug, or if the failure is just another example of the same old bug. Obviously, the development manager is most concerned about the number of defects that need to be fixed, whereas the user may only be concerned with the number of failures encountered (even if every failure is caused by the same bug).

■■■■■■■■■■■■■■■■■■
Key Point

Part of the process of analyzing an incident report is to determine if the failure was caused by a new bug, or if the failure is just another example of the same old bug.

Testing Status and Results ■■■■■

One of the first issues that a test manager must deal with during test execution is finding a way to keep track of the testing status. How the testing status will be tracked should be explained in the master test plan (refer to Chapter 3 – *Master Test Planning*). Basically, testing status is reported against milestones completed; number, severity, and location of defects discovered; and coverage achieved. Some test managers may also report testing status based upon the stability, reliability, or usability of the system. For our purposes, however, we'll measure these "...*ilities*" based on their corresponding test cases (e.g., reliability test cases, usability test cases, etc.).

Measuring Testing Status

The testing status report (refer to Table 7-4) is often the primary formal communication channel that the test manager uses to inform the rest of the organization of the progress made by the testing team.

Table 7-4 Sample Test Status Report

Project: Online Trade Date: 01/05/02

Feature Tested	Total Tests	# Complete	% Complete	# Success	% Success (to date)
Open Account	46	46	100	41	89
Sell Order	36	25	69	25	100
Buy Order	19	17	89	12	71
...	...	...	...	...	...
...	...	...	...	...	...
...	...	...	...	...	...
Total	395	320	81	290	91

Notice that Table 7-4 shows, at a glance, how much of the test execution is done and how much remains unfinished. Even so, we must be careful in how we interpret the data in this chart and understand what it is that we're trying to measure. For example, Table 7-4 shows that the testing of this system is 81% complete. But is testing really 81% complete? It really shows that 81% of the test cases have been completed, not 81% of the testing. You should remember that all test cases are definitely not created equal. If you want to measure testing status against a timeline, you must weight the test cases based on how long they take to execute. Some test cases may take only a few minutes, while others could take hours.

On the other hand, if you want to measure status against functionality (i.e., how much of the user's functionality has been tested?), then the test cases must be weighted based on how much of the functionality they cover. Some test cases may cover several important requirements or features, while others may cover fewer or less important features.

Test Summary Report

The purpose of the Test Summary Report is to summarize the results of the testing activities and to provide an evaluation based on these results. The summary report provides advice on the release readiness of the product and should document any known anomalies or shortcomings in the product. This report allows the test manager to summarize the testing and to identify limitations of the software and the failure likelihood. There should be a test summary report that corresponds to every test plan. So, for example, if you are working on a project that had a master test plan, an acceptance test plan, a system test plan, and a combined unit/integration test plan, each of these should have its own corresponding test summary report, as illustrated in Figure 7-4.

■■■■■■■■■■■■■■■■■
Key Point

If you want to measure testing status against a time line, you have to weight the test cases based on how long they take to execute, but if you want to measure status against functionality, then the test cases must be weighted based on how much of the functionality they cover.

■■■■■■■■■■■■■■■■■
Key Point

The purpose of the Test Summary Report is to summarize the results of the testing activities and to provide an evaluation based on the results.

In essence, the test summary report is an extension of the test plan and serves to "close the loop" on the plan.

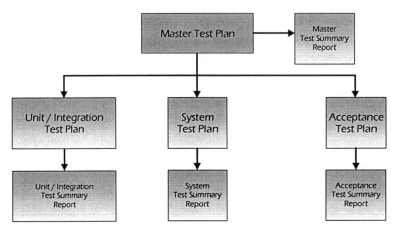

Figure 7-4

There Should Be a Test Summary Report for Each Test Plan

One complaint that we often hear about the test summary report is that, since it occurs at the end of the test execution phase, it's on the critical path of the delivery of the software. This is true, but we would also like to add that completing the test summary report doesn't take a lot of time. In fact, most of the information contained within the report is information that the test manager should be collecting and analyzing constantly throughout the software development and testing lifecycles. You could consider using most of the information in the test summary report as a test status report. Just think of the test summary report as a test status report on the last day of the project.

Key Point

Think of the Test Summary Report as a test status report on the last day of the project.

Here's a tip that you may find useful – it works well for us. Once we begin the execution of the tests, we seldom have time to keep the test plan up-to-date. Instead of updating the plan, we keep track of the changes in the test summary report's *Variances* section, and after the software under test has moved on, we go back and update the plan.

The Test Summary Report shown in Figure 7-5 conforms to IEEE Std. 829-1998 for Software Test Documentation. Sections that are not part of the IEEE template are indicated in italics.

> **IEEE Std. 829-1998 for Software Test Documentation**
> **Template for Test Summary Report**
>
> **Contents**
>
> 1. Test Summary Report Identifier
> 2. Summary
> 3. Variances
> 4. Comprehensive Assessment
> 5. Summary of Results
>   5.1 Resolved Incidents
>   5.2 Unresolved Incidents
> 6. Evaluation
> 7. *Recommendations*
> 8. Summary of Activities
> 9. Approvals

Test Summary Report Identifier

The *Report Identifier* is a unique number that identifies the report and is used to place the test summary report under configuration management.

Summary

This section summarizes what testing activities took place, including the versions/releases of the software, the environment and so forth. This section will normally supply references to the test plan, test-design specifications, test procedures, and test cases.

Variances

This section describes any variances between the testing that was planned and the testing that really occurred. This section is of particular importance to the test manager because it helps him or her see what changed and provides some insights into how to improve the test planning in the future.

Comprehensive Assessment

In this section, you should evaluate the comprehensiveness of the testing process against the criteria specified in the test plan. These criteria are based upon the inventory, requirements, design, code coverage, or some combination thereof. Features or groups of features that were not adequately covered need to be addressed here, including a discussion of any new risks. Any measures of test effectiveness that were used should be reported and explained in this section.

Summary of Results

Summarize the results of testing here. Identify all resolved incidents and summarize their resolution. Identify all unresolved incidents. This section will contain metrics about defects and their distribution (refer to the section on *Pareto Analysis* in this chapter).

Evaluation

Provide an overall evaluation of each test item, including its limitations. This evaluation should be based upon the test results and the item pass/fail criteria. Some limitations that might result could include statements such as "The system is incapable of supporting more than 100 users simultaneously" or "Performance slows to x if the throughput exceeds a certain limit." This section could also include a discussion of failure likelihood based upon the stability exhibited during testing, reliability modeling and/or an analysis of failures observed during testing.

Recommendations

We include a section called *Recommendations* because we feel that part of the test manager's job is to make recommendations based on what they discover during the course of testing. Some of our clients dislike the Recommendations section because they feel that the purpose of the testing effort is only to measure the quality of the software, and it's up to the business side of the company to act upon that information. Even though we recognize that the decision of what to do with the release ultimately resides with the business experts, we feel that the authors of the test summary report should share their insights with these decision makers.

Summary of Activities

Summarize the major testing activities and events. Summarize resource consumption data; for example, total staffing level, total machine time, and elapsed time used for each of the major testing activities. This section is important to the test manager, because the data recorded here is part of the information required for estimating future testing efforts.

Approvals

Specify the names and titles of all persons who must approve this report. Provide space for the signatures and dates. Ideally, we would like the approvers of this report to be the same people who approved the corresponding test plan, since the test summary report summarizes all of the activities outlined in the plan (if it's been a really bad project, they may not all still be around). By signing this document, the approvers are certifying that they concur with the results as stated in the report, and that the report, as written, represents a consensus of all of the approvers. If some of the reviewers have minor disagreements, they may be willing to sign the document anyway and note their discrepancies.

When Are We Done Testing? ■ ■ ■ ■ ■

So, how do we know when we're done testing? We'd like to think that this would have been spelled out in the exit criteria for each level. Meeting the exit criteria for the acceptance testing is normally the flag you're looking for, which indicates that testing is done and the product is ready to be shipped, installed, and used. We believe that Boris Beizer has nicely summed up the whole issue of when to stop testing:

■ ■ ■ ■ ■ ■ ■ ■ ■ ■ ■ ■ ■ ■ ■ ■
Key Point

"Good is not good enough when better is expected."

- Thomas Fuller

"There is no single, valid, rational criterion for stopping. Furthermore, given any set of applicable criteria, how each is weighed depends very much upon the product, the environment, the culture and the attitude to risk."

At the 1999 Application Software Measurement (ASM) Conference, Bob Grady identified the following key points associated with releasing a product *too early*:

- Many defects may be left in the product, including some "show-stoppers."
- The product might be manageable with a small number of customers with set expectations.

- A tense, reactive environment may make it difficult for team members to switch their focus to new product needs.
- The tense environment could result in increased employee turnover.
- Customers' frustration with the product will continue.

Grady also identified the following key points associated with releasing the product *too late*:

- Team members and users are confident in the quality of the product.
- Customer support needs are small and predictable.
- The organization may experience some loss of revenue, long-term market share, and project cancellations, thus increasing the overall business risk.
- The organization may gain a good reputation for quality, which could lead to capturing a greater market share in the long term.

When you consider the implications associated with releasing too early or too late, it's clear that important decisions (such as when to stop testing) should be based on more than one metric – that way, one metric can validate the other metric. Some commonly used metrics are explained in the paragraphs that follow.

Defect Discovery Rate

Many organizations use the defect discovery rate as an important measure to assist them in predicting when a product will be ready to release. When the defect discovery rate drops below the specified level, it's often assumed (sometimes correctly) that the product is ready to be released. While a declining discovery rate is typically a good sign, one must remember that other forces (less effort, no new test cases, etc.) may cause the discovery rate to drop. This is why it is normally a good idea to base important decisions on more than one supporting metric.

Notice in Figure 7-6 that the number of new defects discovered per day is dropping and, if we assume that the effort is constant, the cost of discovering each defect is also rising.

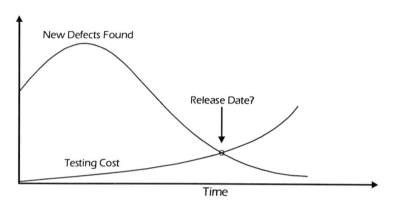

Figure 7-6

Defect Discovery Rate

At some point, therefore, the cost of continuing to test will exceed the value derived from the additional testing. Of course, all we can do is estimate when this will occur, since the nature (severity) of the undiscovered bugs is unknown. This can be offset somewhat if risk-based techniques are used. In fact, another useful metric to determine whether the system is ready to ship is the trend in the severity of bugs found in testing. If risk-based techniques are used, then we would expect not only the defect discovery rate to drop, but also the severity of the defects discovered. If this trend is not observed, then that's a sign that the system is not ready to ship.

Remaining Defects Estimation Criteria

One method of determining "when to ship" is to base the decision on an estimate of the number of defects expected. This can be accomplished by comparing the defect discovery trends with those from other, similar projects. This normally requires that an extensive amount of data has been collected and managed in the past, and will also require normalization of the data to take into account the differences in project scope, complexity, code quality, etc.

Running Out of Resources

It's true, running out of time or budget may be a valid reason for stopping. Many of us have certainly recommended the release of a product that we felt was fairly poor in quality because it was better than what the user currently had. Remember, we're not striving for perfection, only acceptable risk. Sometimes, the risk of not shipping (due to competition, failure of an existing system, etc.) may exceed the (business) risk of shipping a flawed product.

Great Software, But Too Late

One of our clients several years ago made a PC-based tax package. They felt that they had created one of the best, easiest-to-use tax packages on the market. Unfortunately, by the time their product had met all of their quality goals, most people who would normally buy and use their product had already purchased a competitor's product. Our client was making a great product that was of very little use (since it was too late to market). The next year the company relaxed their quality goals (just a little), added resources on the front-end processes, and delivered a marketable product in a timely fashion.

■■■■■■■■■■■■■■■■■

Case Study 7-5

In the world of software, timing can be everything.

Measuring Test Effectiveness

When we ask our students, "How many of you think that the time, effort, and money spent trying to achieve high-quality software in your organization is *too much?*" we get lots of laughs and a sprinkling of raised hands. When we ask the same question, but change the end of the sentence to "…too little?" almost everyone raises a hand. Changing the end of the sentence to "…about right?" gets a few hands (and smug looks). Generally, there may be one or two people who are undecided and don't raise their hands at all.

Next, we ask the same people, "How many of you have a way to measure test effectiveness?" and we get almost no response. If you don't have a way to measure test effectiveness, it's almost impossible to answer question #1 with anything other than, "It's a mystery to me." Knowing what metrics to use to measure test effectiveness and implementing them is one of the greatest challenges that a test manager faces.

We've discovered the following key points regarding measures of test effectiveness:
- Many organizations don't consciously attempt to measure test effectiveness.
- All measures of test effectiveness have deficiencies.
- In spite of the weaknesses of currently used measures, it's still necessary to develop a set to use in your organization.

In this section, we'll analyze some of the problems with commonly used measures of test effectiveness, and conclude with some recommendations. In working with dozens of organizations, we've found that most attempts to measure test

Question #1

Do you think that the time, effort, and money spent trying to achieve high-quality software in your organization is:

❏ *too much?*
❏ *too little?*
❏ *not enough?*

Question #2

Do you have a way to measure test effectiveness?

Gilb's Law

"Anything you need to quantify can be measured in some way that is superior to not measuring it at all."

– Tom Gilb

effectiveness fall into one of the three major categories illustrated in Figure 7-7.

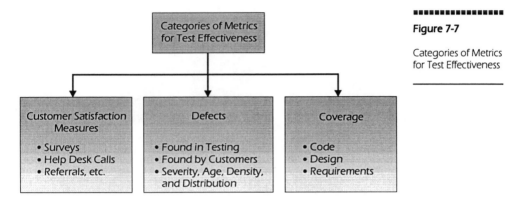

Figure 7-7

Categories of Metrics for Test Effectiveness

Customer Satisfaction Measures

Many companies use customer satisfaction measures to determine if their customers are happy with the software they have received.   The most common customer satisfaction measures are usually gathered by analyzing calls to the help desk or by using surveys.   Both of these measures have general deficiencies and other problems specific to testing.   First, let's examine surveys.

Surveys

Surveys are difficult to create effectively. It's hard for most of us to know specifically what questions to ask and how to ask them.   In fact, there's a whole discipline devoted to creating, using, and understanding surveys and their results. Case Studies 7-6 and 7-7 describe some of the pitfalls associated with designing and administering surveys.

What Do You Mean, "I Need an Expert"?

Case Study 7-6

The Science of Survey Design

When I was working on a large survey effort in the early 1990s, my colleague suggested that I should have a "survey expert" review my survey. I was a little miffed, since I had personally written the survey and I was sure that I knew how to write a few simple questions. Still, I found a "survey expert" at a local university and asked him to review my software survey. I was surprised when he had the nerve to say, "Come back tomorrow and I'll tell you how your respondents will reply to your survey." Sure enough, the next day he gave me a completed survey (and a bill for his services). I thought that he was pretty presumptuous since he was not a "software expert," but after administering the survey to a few of my colleagues, I was amazed that this professor had predicted almost exactly how they would respond!

How a respondent answers a survey is dependent on all kinds of issues like the order of the questions, use of action verbs, length of the survey, and length of the questions used. So, the moral of the story is this: If you want to do a survey, we recommend that you solicit help from an "expert."

— Rick Craig

The Waitress Knows Best

Case Study 7-7

Personal Bias in Survey Design

Another experience I had with a survey occurred several years ago at a restaurant that I own in Tampa called "Mad Dogs and Englishmen." My head waitress decided to create a customer satisfaction survey (on her own initiative). You have to love employees like that! The survey had two sections: one rated the quality of food as Outstanding, Excellent, Above Average, Average, and Below Average, and the other section rated service.

Customer Satisfaction Survey

MadDogs and Englishman

4115 South MacDill Ave.   (813) 832-3037
Tampa, Florida

Quality of Food	Quality of Service
☑ Outstanding	☑ Outstanding
☐ Excellent	☐ Excellent
☐ Above Average	☐ Above Average
☐ Average	
☐ Below Average	

The service scale included Outstanding, Excellent, and Above Average. I asked her about the missing Average and Below Average categories and she assured me that as long as she was in charge, no one would ever get average or below-average service! I realized that the survey designer's personal bias can (and will) significantly influence the survey results!

— Rick Craig

All issues of construction aside, surveys have more specific problems when you try to use them to measure the effectiveness of testing. The biggest issue, of course, is that it's theoretically possible that the developers could create a really fine system that would please the customer even if the testing efforts were shoddy or even non-existent. Customer satisfaction surveys do not separate the quality of the development effort from the effectiveness of the testing effort. So, even though surveys may be useful for your organization, they don't give the test manager much of a measure of the effectiveness of the testing effort. On the other hand, if the surveys are all negative, that gives the test manager cause for concern.

Help Desk Calls

Another customer satisfaction measure that is sometime used is the number of calls to the help desk. This metric suffers from the same problem as a survey – it doesn't separate the quality of the software from the effectiveness of the testing effort. Each call must be analyzed in order to determine the root cause of the problem. Was there an insufficient amount of training? Are there too many features? Although most companies are immediately concerned when the help desk is swamped right after a new release, how would they feel if no one called? If nobody called, there would be no data to analyze and no way to discover (and resolve) problems. Even worse, though, maybe the application is so bad that nobody is even using it.

Key Point

Customer satisfaction measures are useful for your organization and are of interest to the test manager, but don't, in themselves, solve the problem of how to measure test effectiveness.

One final problem with the customer satisfaction measures that we've just discussed (i.e., surveys and help desk calls) is that they're both after the fact. That is, the measures are not available until after the product is sold, installed, and in use. Just because a metric is after the fact doesn't make it worthless, but it does lessen its value considerably.

Customer satisfaction measures are useful for your organization, and are of interest to the test manager, but don't, in themselves, solve the problem of how to measure test effectiveness.

Defect Measures

Another group of measures commonly used for test effectiveness are built around the analysis of defects.

Number of Defects Found in Testing

Some test managers attempt to use the number of defects found in testing as a measure of test effectiveness. The first problem with this, or any other measure of defects, is that all bugs are not created equal. It's necessary to "weight" bugs and/or use impact categories such as all "critical" bugs. Since most defects are recorded with a severity rating, this problem can normally be overcome.

Another problem with defect counts as a measure of test effectiveness is that the number of bugs that originally existed significantly impacts the number of bugs discovered (i.e., the quality of the software). Just as in the customer satisfaction measures, counting the number of bugs found in testing doesn't focus on just testing, but is affected by the initial quality of the product being tested.

Some organizations successfully use the number of defects found as a useful measure of test effectiveness. Typically, they have a set of test cases with known coverage (coverage is our next topic) and a track record of how many bugs to expect using various testing techniques. Then, they observe the trends in defect discovery versus previous testing efforts. The values have to be normalized based upon the degree of change of the system and/or the quantity and complexity of any new functionality introduced.

■■■■■■■■■■■■■■■■■■
Key Point

Another problem with defect counts as a measure of test effectiveness is that the number of bugs that originally existed significantly impacts the number of bugs discovered (i.e., the quality of the software).

Figure 7-8 shows the defect discovery rates of two projects. If the projects are normalized based on size and complexity, one can assume that 'Project B' will contain a number of defects similar to 'Project A'. Consequently, the curves described by each of these projects should also be similar.

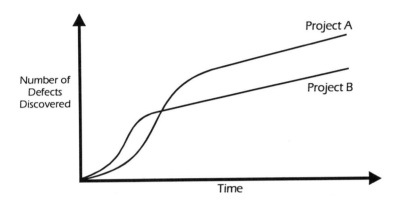

Figure 7-8

Defect Discovery Rates for Projects A and B

If the testing effort on 'Project B' finds significantly fewer bugs, this might mean that the testing is less effective than it was on 'Project A'. Of course, the weakness in this metric is that the curve may be lower because there were fewer bugs to find! This is yet another reason why decisions shouldn't be based solely on a single metric.

Another, more sophisticated, example of measuring defects is shown in Table 7-5. Here, a prediction of the number of bugs that will be found at different stages in the software development lifecycle is made using metrics from previous releases or projects. Both of these models require consistent testing practices, covering test sets, good defect recording, and analysis.

Table 7-5 Bug Budget Example

	Total # Predicted	Predicted (P) Versus Actual (A)									
		P	A	P	A	P	A	P	A	P	A
		Jan		Feb		Mar		Apr		May	
Requirements Review	20	20	14								
Design Review	35	5	0	15		15					
Test Design	65			25		30		10			
Code Inspections	120							60		60	
Unit Test	80										
System Test	40										
Regression Test	10										
Acceptance Test	5										
6 Months Production	15										
Totals	390	25	14	40		45		70		60	

Production Defects

A more common measure of test effectiveness is the number of defects found in production or by the customer. This is an interesting measure, since the bugs found by the customer are obviously ones that were not found by the tester (or at least were not fixed prior to release). Unfortunately, some of our old problems such as latent and masked defects may have appeared.

Another issue in using production defects as a measure of test effectiveness is that it's another "after the fact" measure and is affected by the quality of the software. We must measure severity, distribution, and trends from release to release.

Defect Removal Efficiency (DRE)

A more powerful metric for test effectiveness (and the one that we recommend) can be created using both of the defect metrics discussed above: defects found during testing and defects found during production. What we really want to know is, "How many bugs did we find out of the set of bugs that we could have found?" This measure is called Defect Removal Efficiency (DRE) and is defined in Figure 7-9.

$$DRE = \frac{\text{Number of Bugs Found in Testing}}{\text{Number of Bugs Found in Testing} + \text{Number Not Found}}$$

Figure 7-9

Formula for Defect Removal Efficiency (DRE)

The number of bugs not found is usually equivalent to the number of bugs found by the customers (though the customers may not find all of the bugs either). Therefore, the denominator becomes the number of bugs that could have been found. DRE is an excellent measure of test effectiveness, but there are many issues that you must be aware of in order to use it successfully:

- The severity and distribution of the bugs must be taken into account. (Some organizations treat all defects the same, i.e., no severity is used, based on the philosophy that the ratio of severity classes is more or less constant).
- How do you know when the customer has found all of the bugs? Normally, you would need to look at the trends of defect reporting by your customers on previous projects or releases to determine how long it takes before

Key Point

Dorothy Graham calls DRE Defect Detection Percentage (DDP). We actually prefer her naming convention because it's more descriptive of the metric. That is, Defect Removal Efficiency does not really measure the removal of defects, only their detection.

the customer has found "most" of the bugs. If they are still finding a bug here and there one year later, it probably won't significantly affect your metrics. In some applications, especially those with many users, most of the bugs may be reported within a few days. Other systems with fewer users may have to go a few months to have some assurance that most of the bugs have been reported.

- It's after the fact (refer to the bullet item above). Metrics that are "after the fact" do not help measure the test effectiveness of the current project, but they do let test managers measure the long-term trends in the test effectiveness of their organizations.

- When do we start counting bugs (e.g., during unit, integration, system, or acceptance testing? during inspections? during ad hoc testing?), and what constitutes a bug-finding activity? It's important to be consistent. For example, if you count bugs found in code inspections, you must always count bugs found in code inspections.

- Some bugs cannot be found in testing! Due to the limitations of the test environment, it's possible, and even likely, that there is a set of bugs that the tester could not find no matter what he or she does. The test manager must decide whether or not to factor these bugs out. If your goal is to measure the effectiveness of the testing effort without considering what you have to work with (i.e., the environment), the bugs should be factored out. If your goal is to measure the effectiveness of the testing effort including the environment (our choice), the bugs should be left in. After all, part of the job of the tester is to ensure that the most realistic test environment possible is created.

■■■■■■■■■■■■■■■■■

Key Point

In his book *A Manager's Guide to Software Engineering*, Roger Pressman calls DRE "the one metric that we can use to get a 'bottom-line' of improving quality."

■■■■■■■■■■■■■■■■■

Key Point

Metrics that are "after the fact" do not help measure the test effectiveness of the current project, but they do let test managers measure the long-term trends in the test effectiveness of their organizations.

DRE Example

Figure 7-10 is an example of a DRE calculation. Horizontal and upward vertical arrows represent bugs that are passed from one phase to the next.

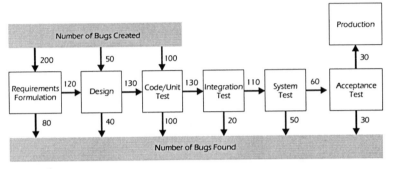

■■■■■■■■■■■■■■■■
Figure 7-10

DRE Example

→ OR ↑ = Bugs Passed on to Next Phase

DRE = $\dfrac{\text{Number of Bugs Found in Testing}}{\text{Number of Bugs Found in Testing + Number Not Found}}$

■■■■■■■■■■■■■■■■
Key Point

In their book *Risk Management for Software Projects*, Alex Down, Michael Coleman, and Peter Absolon report that the DRE for the systems they are familiar with is usually in the range of 65-70%.

Number of Bugs
Found in Testing = 80 + 40 + 100 + 20 + 50 + 30 = 320

Number
Not Found = 30

DRE = $\dfrac{320}{320 + 30}$ = 0.91   OR = 91%

Defect Removal Efficiency (DRE) is also sometimes used as a way to measure the effectiveness of a particular level of test. For example, the system test manager may want to know what the DRE is for their system testing. The number of bugs found in system testing should be placed in the numerator, while those same bugs plus the acceptance test and production bugs should be used in the denominator, as illustrated in the example below.

System Test DRE Example

Figure 7-11 is an example of a system test DRE calculation. Horizontal and upward vertical arrows represent bugs that are passed from one phase to the next.

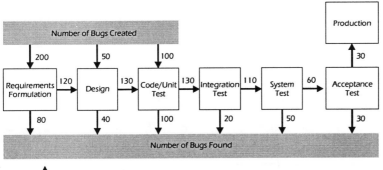

Figure 7-11

System Test DRE Example

$$\text{System Test DRE} = \frac{\text{\# of Bugs Found in System Testing}}{\text{\# of Bugs Found in System Test} + \text{\# of Bugs Found in Acceptance Test and Production}}$$

$$\text{\# of Bugs Found in System Test} = 50$$

$$\text{\# of Bugs Found in Acceptance Test and Production} = 30 + 30 = 60$$

$$\text{System Testing DRE} = \frac{50}{50 + 60} = 0.45 \quad \text{OR} = 45\%$$

Unit Testing DRE

When measuring the DRE of unit testing, it will be necessary to factor out those bugs that could not be found due to the nature of the unit test environment. This may seem contradictory to what we previously recommended, but we don't want the developer to have to create a "system" test environment and, therefore, there will always be bugs that cannot be found in unit testing (e.g., bugs related to the passing of data from one unit to another).

Defect Age

Another useful measure of test effectiveness is defect age, often called *Phase Age* or *PhAge*. Most of us realize that the later we discover a bug, the greater harm it does and the more it costs to fix. Therefore, an effective testing effort would tend to find bugs earlier than a less effective testing effort would.

■■■■■■■■■■■■■■■■■
Key Point

The later we discover a bug, the greater harm it does and the more it costs to fix.

Table 7-6 shows a scale for measuring defect age. Notice that this scale may have to be modified to reflect the phases in your own software development lifecycle and the number and names of your test levels. For example, a requirement defect discovered during a high-level design review would be assigned a PhAge of 1. If this defect had not been found until the Pilot, it would have been assigned a PhAge of 8.

Table 7-6   Scale for Defect Age on Project X

Phase Created	Requirements	High-Level Design	Detailed Design	Coding	Unit Testing	Integration Testing	System Testing	Acceptance Testing	Pilot	Production	
Phase Discovered											
Requirements	0	1	2	3	4	5	6	7	8	9	
High-Level Design		0	1	2	3	4	5	6	7	8	
Detailed Design			0	1	2	3	4	5	6	7	
Coding				0	1	2	3	4	5	6	
Summary											

Table 7-7 shows an example of the distribution of defects on one project by phase created and phase discovered. In this example, there were 8 requirements defects found in high-level design, 4 during detailed design, 1 in coding, 5 in system testing, 6 in acceptance testing, 2 in pilot, and 1 in production. If you've never analyzed bugs to determine when they were introduced, you may be surprised how difficult a job this is.

Table 7-7 Defect Creation versus Discovery on Project X

Phase Created	Phase Discovered										Total Defects
	Requirements	High-Level Design	Detailed Design	Coding	Unit Testing	Integration Testing	System Testing	Acceptance Testing	Pilot	Production	
Requirements	0	8	4	1	0	0	5	6	2	1	27
High-Level Design		0	9	3	0	1	3	1	2	1	20
Detailed Design			0	15	3	4	0	0	1	8	31
Coding				0	62	16	6	2	3	20	109
Summary	0	8	13	19	65	21	14	9	8	30	187

Defect Spoilage

Spoilage is a metric that uses the Phase Age and distribution of defects to measure the effectiveness of defect removal activities. Other authors use slightly different definitions of spoilage. Tom DeMarco, for example, defines spoilage as "the cost of human failure in the development process," in his book *Controlling Software Projects: Management, Measurement, and Estimates*. In their book *Software Metrics: Establishing a Company-Wide Program*, Robert Grady and Deborah Caswell explain that Hitachi uses the word spoilage to mean "the cost to fix post-release problems." Regardless of which definition of spoilage you prefer, you should not confuse spoilage with Defect Removal Efficiency (DRE), which measures the number of bugs that were found out of the set of bugs that could have been found.

■■■■■■■■■■■■■■■■■

Key Point

Spoilage is a metric that uses Phase Age and distribution of defects to measure the effectiveness of defect removal activities.

Table 7-8 shows the defect spoilage values for a particular project, based on the number of defects found weighted by defect age. During acceptance testing, for example, 9 defects were discovered. Of these 9 defects, 6 were attributed to defects created during the requirements phase of this project. Since the defects that were found during acceptance testing could have been found in any of the seven previous phases, the requirements defects that remained hidden until the acceptance testing phase were given a weighting of 7. The weighted number of requirements defects found during acceptance testing is 42 (i.e., 6 x 7 = 42).

Table 7-8   Number of Defects Weighted by Defect Age on Project X

Phase Created	Requirements	High-Level Design	Detailed Design	Coding	Unit Testing	Integration Testing	System Testing	Acceptance Testing	Pilot	Production	Spoilage = Weight/ Total Defects
Requirements	0	8	8	3	0	0	30	42	16	9	116 / 27 = 4.3
High-Level Design		0	9	6	0	4	15	6	14	8	62 / 20 = 2.1
Detailed Design			0	15	6	12	0	0	6	42	81 / 31 = 2.6
Coding				0	62	32	18	8	15	120	255 / 109 = 2.3
Summary											514 / 187 = 2.7

The Defect Spoilage is calculated using the formula shown in Figure 7-12.

$$\text{Spoilage} = \frac{\text{Sum of (Number of Defects} \times \text{Discovered PhAge)}}{\text{Total Number of Defects}}$$

Figure 7-12

Formula for Defect Spoilage

Generally speaking, lower values for spoilage indicate more effective defect discovery processes (the optimal value is 1). As an absolute value, the spoilage has little meaning. However, it becomes valuable when used to measure a long-term trend of test effectiveness.

Defect Density and Pareto Analysis

Defect Density is calculated using the formula shown in Figure 7-13.

■■■■■■■■■■■■■■■■■

Figure 7-13

$$\text{Defect Density} = \frac{\text{Number of Defects}}{\text{Number of Lines of Code or Function Points}}$$

Formula for Defect Density

Unfortunately, defect density measures are far from perfect. The two main problems are in determining *what is a defect* and *what is a line of code.* By asking, "What is a defect?" we mean "What do we count as a defect?"

- Are minor defects treated the same as critical defects, or do we need to weight them?
- Do we count unit testing bugs or only bugs found later?
- Do we count bugs found during inspection? During ad hoc testing?

Similarly, measuring the size (i.e., lines of code or function points) of the module is also a problem, because the number of lines of code can vary based on the skill level of the programmer and the language that was used.

Figure 7-14 shows the defect density per 1,000 lines of code in various modules of a sample project. Notice that Module D has a high concentration of bugs. Experience has shown that parts of a system where large quantities of bugs have been discovered

■■■■■■■■■■■■■■■■■

Key Point

J.M. Duran admonished us to concentrate on the vital few, not the trivial many. Later, Thomas J. McCabe extended the Pareto Principle to software quality activities.

To learn more about the history of the Pareto Principle and see some actual examples, read *The Pareto Principle Applied to Software Quality Assurance* by Thomas J. McCabe and G. Gordon Schulmeyer in the *Handbook of Software Quality Assurance.*

will continue to have large numbers of bugs even after the initial cycle of testing and correcting of bugs. This information can help the tester focus on problematic (i.e., error prone) parts of the system. Similarly, instead of plotting defect density on the histogram as in Figure 7-14, the causes of the defects could be displayed in descending order of frequency (e.g., functionality, usability, etc.). This type of analysis is known as Pareto Analysis and can be used to target areas for process improvement.

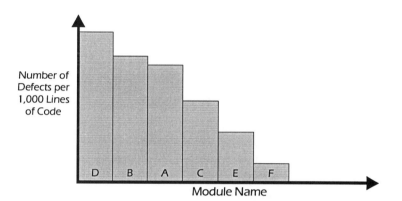

Number of Defects per 1,000 Lines of Code

Module Name

■■■■■■■■■■■■■■■■■
Figure 7-14

Defect Density in Various Modules
_____

The bottom line is that defect measures can and should be used to measure the effectiveness of testing, but by themselves, they're inadequate and need to be supplemented by coverage metrics.

_____
Coverage Measures
_____

Coverage metrics are probably the most powerful of all measures of test effectiveness, since they are not necessarily "after the fact" and are not affected by the quality of the software under test. High-level coverage metrics such as requirements and/or inventory coverage can be done as soon as the test cases are defined. In other words, you can measure the coverage of the test cases created before the code is even written!

■■■■■■■■■■■■■■■■■
Key Point

Requirements coverage can be measured before the code is even written.
_____

Coverage can be used to measure the completeness of the test set (i.e., the test created) or of the tests that are actually executed. We can use coverage as a measure of test effectiveness because we subscribe to the philosophy that a good test case is one that finds a bug *or* demonstrates that a particular function works correctly. Some authors state that the only good test case is the one that finds a bug. We contend that if you subscribe to that philosophy, coverage metrics are not useful as a measurement of test effectiveness. (We reckon that if you knew in advance where the bugs were, you could concentrate on only writing test cases that found bugs – or, better yet, just fix them and don't test at all.)

Requirements and Design Coverage

How to measure requirements, inventory, design, and code coverage was discussed in Chapter 5 – *Analysis and Design*. At the very least, every testing methodology that we are familiar with subscribes to requirements coverage. Unfortunately, it's possible to "test" every requirement and still not have tested every important condition. There may be design issues that are impossible to find during the course of normal requirements-based testing, which is why it's important for most testing groups to also measure design coverage. Table 7-9 shows a matrix that combines requirements and design coverage.

Table 7-9   Requirements and Design Coverage

Attribute	TC #1	TC# 2	TC #3	TC #4	TC #5
Requirement 1	✓	✓		✓	✓
Requirement 2		✓			✓
Requirement 3			✓		✓
Requirement 4				✓	✓
Design 1	✓	✓		✓	✓
Design 2				✓	✓
Design 3		✓			✓

It's quite clear, however, that if requirements coverage is not achieved, there will be parts of the system (possibly very important parts) that are not tested!

Code Coverage

Many testing experts believe that one of the most important things a test group can do is to measure code coverage. These people may be touting code coverage as a new silver bullet, but actually, code coverage tools have been in use for at least as long as Rick has been a test manager (20 years). The tools in use today, however, are much more user-friendly than earlier tools. Table 7-10 is a conceptual model of the output of a code coverage tool. These tools can measure statement, branch, or path coverage.

Table 7-10 Code Coverage

Statement	Test Run			Covered?
	TR #1	TR# 2	TR #3	
A	✓	✓	✓	Yes
B	✓		✓	Yes
C	✓			Yes
D				No
E			✓	Yes
Total	60%	20%	60%	80%

The reports are clearer and easier to interpret, but the basic information is almost the same. Code coverage tools tell the developer or tester which statements, paths, or branches have and have not been exercised by the test cases. This is obviously a good thing to do, since any untested code is a potential liability.

Code Coverage Weaknesses

Just because all of the code has been executed does not, in any way, assure the developer or tester that the code does what it's supposed to do. That is, ensuring that all of the code has been exercised under test does not guarantee that it does what the customers, requirements, and design need it to do.

Figure 7-15 shows a fairly typical progression in software development. The users' needs are recorded as requirements specifications, which in turn are used to create the design, and from there, the code is written. All of the artifacts that are derived from the users' needs can and should be tested. If test cases are created from the code itself, the most you can expect to prove is that the code "does what it does" (i.e., it functions, but not necessarily correctly).

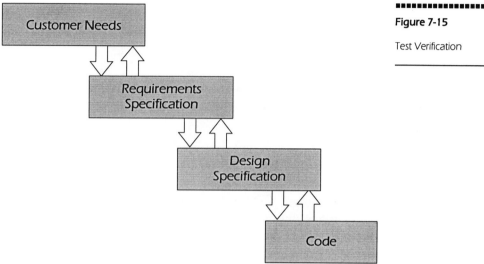

■■■■■■■■■■■■■■■■■■

Figure 7-15

Test Verification

By testing the design, you can show that the system matches the design and the code matches the design, but you can't prove that the design meets the requirements. Test cases based upon the requirements can demonstrate that the requirements have been met and the design matches the requirements. All of these verification steps should be done and, ultimately, it's important to create test cases based upon the code, the design, and the requirements. Just because a code coverage tool is used, doesn't mean that the test cases must be derived solely from the code.

■■■■■■■■■■■■■■■■■■

Key Point

Just because a code coverage tool is used, doesn't mean that the test cases must be derived solely from the code.

In some organizations, code coverage becomes the ultimate metric. Some organizations may be struggling to move from say 85% to 90% coverage regardless of the cost. While that may be good, we think it's important to ensure that we have tested the "right" 90%. That is to say, even using code coverage metrics requires that we use some kind of risk-based approach. This is true even if a goal of 100% code coverage is established, because it's advantageous to test (and fix problems) in the critical components first.

Another issue when using code coverage tools is that the test cases may have to be executed one additional time, since most code coverage tools require the source code to be instrumented. Therefore, if a defect is discovered while using a code coverage tool, the test will have to be run again without the tool in order to ensure that the defect is not in the instrumentation itself.

Generally, we have found that code coverage is most effective when used at lower levels of test (e.g., unit and integration). These levels of test are normally conducted by the developer, which is good because the analysis of the parts of the code that were not tested is best done by the people with intimate knowledge of the code. Even when using a code coverage tool, unit test cases should first be designed to cover all of the attributes of the program specification before designing test cases based on the code itself.

■■■■■■■■■■■■■■■■■■
Key Point

Even when using a code coverage tool, unit test cases should first be designed to cover all of the attributes of the program specification before designing test cases based on the code itself.

As with most projects, you've got to crawl before you run. Trying to get a high level of code coverage is fine in organizations that have already established a fairly comprehensive set of test cases. Unfortunately, many of the companies that we have visited have not even established a test set that is comprehensive enough to cover all of the features of the system. In some cases, there are entire modules, programs, or subsystems that are not tested. It's fine to say that every line of code should be tested, but if there are entire subsystems that have no test cases, it's a moot point.

Code Coverage Strengths

Code coverage measures put the focus on lower levels of tests and provide a way to determine if and how well they've been done. Many companies do little unit testing, and code coverage tools can help highlight that fact. Global coverage can also be used as a measure of test effectiveness.

Global Code Coverage

The global coverage number can be used as a measure of test effectiveness, and it can highlight areas that are deficient in testing. This measure of test effectiveness, like all of the others we've discussed, has some problems. While it is useful to see that the coverage has increased from 50% to 90%, it's not as clear how valuable it is to go from 50% to 51%. In other words, if risk-based techniques that ensure that the riskiest components are tested first are used, then every increase has a more or less "known" value. If tests are not based on risk, it's harder to know what an increase in coverage means. It's also interesting to note that it costs more to go from, for example, 95% to 100% coverage than it did to go from 50% to 55% coverage. If risk-based techniques were used, the last gain might not "buy" us as much, since the last 5% tested is also (we hope) the least risky. Perhaps we're just trying to weigh the value of these added tests against the resources required to create and run them. At the end of the day, though, that's what testing is all about!

■■■■■■■■■■■■■■■■■
Key Point

Global code coverage is the percent of code executed during the testing of an entire application.

Chapter 8 –
The Test Organization

"A house divided against itself cannot stand. Our cause must be entrusted to, and conducted by, its undoubted friends – whose hands are free, whose hearts are in the work – who do care for the result."

— Abraham Lincoln

Most software testing books (this one included) devote a lot of pages to the technical issues of testing, even though most of us realize that the human element may be the most important part of the testing process. It's really understandable why this happens. We focus on the process and technical side of testing in our classes and in this book because most people (especially managers) think that they already understand the art of communicating and interacting with other people. This is in spite of the fact that many of these same people have had no formal management training. It's easier to understand and implement process and technical change, which means that testers (and managers) seem to be more in control.

In our Test Management class, for example, we spend about 1/3 of the class time talking about the structure of a test organization, leadership, management, and how to hire testers. Most of the attendees in the class tell us in advance that this is one of their weakest areas, but in the post-class review many say that they really wanted to spend all three days talking about technical topics and the testing process. In other words, they know that the human side is critical, but they still prefer to talk about "concrete" topics.

■■■■■■■■■■■■■■
Key Point

There are at least a few books that deal with the human dynamics of software development. Tom DeMarco and Tim Lister published a wonderful book called *Peopleware*, which talks about various aspects of the human side of software engineering. An earlier book called *The Psychology of Computer Programming* by Gerald M. Weinberg also has a lot to offer on the subject.

Test Organizations ■■■■■

There are as many ways to organize for software testing, as there are organizations that test. There's really no right or wrong way to organize for test and, in fact, we've seen most of the sample organizational structures discussed below work in some companies and fail in others. How the test organization is internally structured and positioned within the overall organization is very much dependent on politics, corporate

■■■■■■■■■■■■■■
Key Point

"It's easy to get good players. Getting 'em to play together, that's the hard part."

– Casey Stengel

culture, quality culture, skill and knowledge level of the participants, and risk of the product.

Words of Wisdom That Still Hold True

We trained hard, but it seems that every time we were beginning to form up into teams we would be reorganized. I was to learn later in life that we meet any new situation by reorganizing, and a wonderful method it can be for creating the illusion of progress while producing confusion, inefficiency, and demoralization.

– Petronius Arbiter 210 BC

I love the quote above by Petronius Arbiter. After over two millennia, it seems the only thing that is the same is "change." I've used this quote for so long that sometimes I feel like I wrote it. I was surprised to find it in Ed Kit's book Software Testing in the Real World*. It seems likely that I may have started using Petronius' quote (Petronius and I are on a first-name basis) after hearing my friend Ed uses it. Ed, if you're reading this book, thanks. The quote is too good not to share.*

– Rick Craig

Sample Test Organizations

Table 8-1 lists some of the pros and cons of various types of test organizations. It's possible that a company could have more than one organizational style. For example, they could have an independent test team and a SWAT team, or a test coordinator and a QA group that performs testing. There are many other strategies for organizing the testing functions – this is only intended to be a sampling.

■■■■■■■■■■■■■■■■

Key Point

A *SWAT team* is what
our colleague Steven
Splaine calls "a
reserve group of
expert testers that
can be rapidly called
in an emergency to
help put out a testing
fire."

Table 8-1 Pros and Cons of Various Test Organizations

Type of Organization	Pros	Cons
Independent Test Teams	Professional testers with fresh, objective viewpoints	Potential conflict between developers and testers, hard to begin testing early enough
Integrated Test Teams	Teamwork, sharing of resources, facilitates early start	Pressure to ship in spite of quality
Developers (as the principal testers)	Expert on software, no conflict with testers	Lack fresh perspective, lack knowledge of business, may lack software testing skills, pressure to ship, focus on the code, requires rigorous procedures and discipline
SWAT Teams	Extra professional resources	Expensive, hard to create and retain; not for small organizations
Test Coordinator	Don't need permanent test infrastructure	Staffing, matrix management, testing skill, lack of credibility
QA / QC	Existing organization, some existing skill, infrastructure	More to worry about than just testing
Outsourcing	Professional testers (maybe), don't need to hire/retain staff	Still requires management of outsourcers, need to have a good contract
Independent Verification and Validation (IV&V)	Lowers risk, professional testers	Too expensive for most; at the very end

Independent Test Teams

An independent test team is a team whose primary job is testing. They may be tasked with testing just one product or many. The test manager does not report to the development manager and should be organizationally equal (i.e., a peer).

Independent test teams have been around for a long time, but they really gained in popularity starting in the early 1980s. Prior to the creation of independent test teams, most of the testing was done by the programmers or by the QA function, if one existed. All too frequently during that era (and even today), products were shipped that didn't satisfy the user's needs and, in some cases, just flat-out didn't work. One of the major reasons for this failure was the overwhelming pressure to get the product out the door on time, regardless of the consequences. Since the developers did the testing as well as the development, they were pretty much able to ship the software without any oversight. And the software was shipped because it was clear that the date was the most important measure of success. Too many of the developers had received very little (if any) training in testing since their primary job was writing code.

The popularity of independent test teams has grown out of frustration. Independent test teams have allowed testing to move to the status of a discipline within software engineering. Testing techniques, standards, and methodologies were created, and some people became full-time professional testers. These professionals focused on testing and, therefore, became experts in their field. The independent test team provides an objective look at the software being tested. Too often, programmers who test their own code are only able to prove that the code does what the code does, rather than what it's supposed to do.

Key Point

Independent test teams provide an objective look at the software being tested.

On the negative side, the creation of independent test teams often results in the creation of a "brick wall" between the developers and the testers. Developers are less anxious to test their code, since they know that the testers are going to do it anyway. One of the biggest challenges facing managers of independent test groups today is getting started early enough in the product lifecycle. Often, the developers balk at having the testers get involved early because they fear that the testers will slow their progress. This means that the testers may be stuck testing at the end of the lifecycle, where they're the least effective (refer to Chapter 1 for more information about preventive testing).

Integrated Test Teams

Integrated test teams are teams made up of developers and testers who all report to the same manager. Lately, integrated teams seem to be resurging in popularity. We've talked to several testers who indicated that, organizationally, they're trying to move the testing function closer to the development function. We believe that this is occurring because integrated teams are used to working together and are physically collocated, which greatly facilitates communications.

■■■■■■■■■■■■■■■■■

Key Point

Many developers have a tendency to assume that the system will work and, therefore, do not focus on how it might break.

Some organizations also find that it's easier to get buy-in to start the testing early (i.e., during requirements specification) when the teams work together. Independent test teams often find it much more difficult to begin testing early, because developers fear that the testers "will be in the way" and slow down their development effort.

Just as in the Independent Test Teams model, integrated team members who conduct the testing are (or should be) professional testers. We've found that in practice, testers who are part of integrated teams sometimes have to fight harder for resources (especially training and tools) than their counterparts in independent test teams. This is probably due to the fact that there's no dedicated test manager at a level equal to the development manager.

Since the manager is in charge of both development and testing in an integrated team, one of the downsides is that when under schedule pressure he or she may feel compelled to ship the product prematurely.

Developers

In this type of test organization, the developers and testers are the same people. There are no full-time testers. In the good old days, the developers did it all – requirements, design, code, test, etc. Even today, there are a large number of organizations where the same individuals write and test the code. While there has been a lot of negative press written about organizations that don't use independent and/or professional testers, we've encountered several organizations that seem to do a good job of testing using only developers. Most of these organizations tend to be smaller groups, although we've seen larger groups where all of the testing was done (and done well) by the developers.

■■■■■■■■■■■■■■■■■
Key Point

While there has been a lot of negative press written about organizations that don't use independent and/or professional testers, we've encountered several organizations that seem to do a good job of testing using only developers.

On the plus side, when the developers do all of the testing, there's no need to worry about communications problems with the testing group! Another bonus is that the developers have intimate knowledge of the design and code. Decisions on the prioritization of bug fixes are generally easier to make since there are fewer parties participating.

The obvious downside of this organizational strategy is the lack of a fresh, unbiased look at the system. When testing, many developers tend to look at the system the way they do when they're building it. There's often a tendency to assume that the system will work, or that no user would be dumb enough to try "that." It's also asking a lot to expect developers to be expert designers, coders, *and* testers. When the developers do all the testing, there may be less expertise in testing and less push to get the expertise, because most developers we know still see programming as their primary job and testing as an "also ran." Finally, developers may not have a good understanding of the business aspect of the software. This is a frequent complaint even in unit testing, but can be very serious in system or acceptance testing.

For this organizational strategy to be successful, we believe that the following things need to be considered:

- A rigorous test process needs to be defined and followed.
- Adequate time must be allocated for testing.
- Business expertise must be obtained from the users or the training department.
- Configuration management needs to be enforced.
- Buddy testing, XP, or some other type of team approach should be used.
- Training developers about testing is mandatory.
- Exit criteria need to be established and followed.
- The process needs continuous monitoring (e.g., QA) to ensure that it doesn't break down.

Test Coordinator

In this style of organizing for test, there's no standing test group. A test coordinator is hired or selected from the development, QA, or user community. The test coordinator then builds a temporary team, typically by "borrowing" users, developers, technical writers, or help desk personnel (or sometimes any other warm bodies that are available).

We've seen this strategy employed at several organizations, especially at companies that have large, mature, transaction-oriented systems (e.g., banks, insurance companies, etc.) where a major new product or revision has occurred and the existing test organization (if any) is inadequate or there's no permanent testing group. In particular, we saw this happening a lot during Y2K because the existing testing infrastructure was inadequate to conduct both normal business and Y2K testing.

Obviously, the reason this strategy is chosen is because there's an immediate need for testing, but there's no time, money, or expertise to acquire and develop a team. Sometimes, the temporary team that's assembled becomes so valuable that it's made into a permanent test group.

Being the test coordinator in the scenario described above is a tough assignment. If you're ever selected for this position, we recommend that you "just say no," unless, of course, you like a challenge. Indeed, the first major obstacle in using this strategy is selecting a coordinator who has the expertise, communication skills, credibility, and management skills to pull it off. The test coordinator is faced with building a testing infrastructure from the ground up. Often, there will be no test environment, tools, methodology, existing test cases, or even testers. The coordinator has to ask (sometimes beg) for people to use as testers from other groups such as the developers or users. All too often, the development or user group manager will not give the coordinator the very best person for the job. And even if the people are good employees, they may not have any testing experience. Then, there's the issue of matrix management. Most of these temporary testers know that they'll eventually go back to their original manager, so where does their loyalty really lie?

■■■■■■■■■■■■■■■■■
Key Point

Using a test coordinator can be a successful strategy for testing, but hinges on the selection of a very talented individual to fill the role.

Quality Assurance (QA)

In this organizational strategy, the testing function is done all, or in part, by the staff of an existing Quality Assurance (QA) group. Some of the earliest testing organizations were formed from, or within, an existing QA group. This was done because some of the skills possessed by the QA staff members were similar to the skills needed by testers. Today, there are many groups that call themselves QA, but don't do any traditional quality assurance functions – they only do software testing. That is to say, they're not really a QA group, but rather a testing group with the name QA.

The downside of this strategy is that a true QA organization has more to worry about than the testing of software. The additional responsibilities may make it difficult for the QA group to build an effective test organization.

Outsourcing

In this type of test organization, all or some of the testing is assigned to another organization in exchange for compensation. Outsourcing has received a lot of visibility in recent years and is a good way to get help quickly. The key to making outsourcing work is to have a good contract, hire the right outsourcer, have well-defined deliverables and quality standards, and have excellent oversight of the outsourcer's work.

Companies often hire an outsourcer to do the testing because they lack the correct type of funding to do it in-house or lack the correct environment or expertise. These are all valid reasons for outsourcing, but outsourcing the testing effort does not necessarily relieve your company of the responsibility of producing high-quality software or guarantee the results achieved by the outsourcer. We've occasionally encountered a situation where a company develops a system and not only wants to outsource the testing, but they also want to "wash their hands" of the entire testing process and transfer the responsibility for delivering a quality product.

Outsourcers often have great expertise in testing and many have excellent tools and environments, but they rarely have a clear vision of the functional aspects of your business. So even if your testing is outsourced, your organization must maintain oversight

■■■■■■■■■■■■■■■■
Key Point

The key to making outsourcing of testing work is to have a good contract, hire the right outsourcer, have well-defined deliverables and quality standards, and have excellent oversight of the outsourcer's work.

■■■■■■■■■■■■■■■■
Key Point

For more information on outsourcing, refer to the article "Getting the Most from Outsourcing" by Eric Patel in the Nov/Dec 2001 issue of *STQE* Magazine.

of the testing process. Ideally, a liaison will be provided who will take part in periodic progress reviews, walkthroughs or inspections, configuration control boards, and even the final run of the tests.

Outsourcing is ideal for certain kinds of testing, such as performance testing for Web applications. Many organizations may also find that outsourcing of the load testing is economically the right choice. Lower levels of test are also easier to outsource (our opinion) because they are more likely to be based on structural rather than functional techniques.

Independent Verification & Validation (IV&V)

Independent Verification and Validation (IV&V) is usually only performed on certain large, high-risk projects within the Department of Defense (DoD) or some other government agency. IV&V is usually conducted by an independent contractor, typically at the end of the software development lifecycle, and is done in addition to (not instead of) other levels of test. In addition to testing the software, IV&V testers are looking for contract compliance and to prevent fraud, waste, and abuse.

Key Point

Independent Verification and Validation (IV&V) is usually only performed on certain large, high-risk projects within the Department of Defense (DoD) or some other government agency.

IV&V may reduce the risk on some projects, but the cost can be substantial. Most commercial software developers are unwilling or unable to hire an independent contractor to conduct a completely separate test at the end. As we've explained in this book, the end of the lifecycle is usually the most inefficient and expensive time to test. Most of our readers should leave IV&V testing to the contractors who do them on government projects, where loss of life, national prestige, or some other huge risk is at stake.

Office Environment

This may not seem like the most important issue to many testers and managers, but the environment that the testers work in can play an important part in their productivity and long-term success.

Office Space

Testers have certain basic needs in order to perform their job. They need a place to call their own (a cube or office or at least a desk), a comfortable chair, telephone, computer (not a cast-off) and easy access to an area to take a break away from their "home". Offices that are too warm or cold, smoky, poorly lit, too small, or noisy can greatly reduce the effectiveness of the workers. Not only do the situations mentioned above affect the ability of the workers to concentrate, they send a message to the testers that "they are not important enough to warrant a better work environment." If you're a test manager, don't dismiss this issue as trivial, because it will have a big impact on the effectiveness of your group.

Key Point

In their book *Peopleware: Productive Projects and Teams,* Tom DeMarco and Timothy Lister explained that staff members who performed in the upper quartile were much more likely to have a quiet, private workplace than those in the bottom quartile.

The Imprisoned Tester

On one project that I worked on, my desk was situated in a hallway. On another project, we were housed in the document vault of a converted prison – the windows still had bars on them.

– Steven Splaine

Case Study 8-2

Not all workspaces are ideal.

Location Relative to Other Participants

We've had the opportunity to conduct numerous post-project reviews over the years. One opportunity for improvement that we have recommended more than once is to collocate testers with the developers and/or the user representatives. Now, we understand that if your developers are in India and you're located in California, you can't easily move India any closer to California. On the other hand, if you're all located in the same building or campus, it just might be possible to move the teams closer together. Having the testers, developers, and user representatives located within close proximity of each other fosters better communications among the project participants. So if geography and politics allow, you should consider co-locating these staffs. If not, then you'll have to be more creative in coming up with ways to improve communications (e.g., interactive test logs, status meetings, conference calls, intranet pages, site visits, and so on).

■■■■■■■■■■■■■■■■■
Key Point

Having the testers, developers, and user representatives located within close proximity of each other fosters better communications among the project participants.

Cube vs. Office vs. Common Office

This issue is way too sensitive and complicated for us to solve here. It seems that every few years we read an article extolling the virtues of private offices, cubes, common work areas, or whatever the flavor of the month is. Every time we think we understand what the best office design is, someone convinces us that we're wrong. However, we're pretty sure that the style that works for one individual or group is probably not the ideal setup for another.

We're not totally clueless, though. We do know that there are times when engineers need some privacy to do their best work and there are other times when they need the stimulus of their

■■■■■■■■■■■■■■■■■
Key Point

There are times when engineers need some privacy to do their best work and there are other times when they need the stimulus of their coworkers.

coworkers. An ideal setup would provide, even if on a temporary basis, both private and common areas. We'll leave it up to you to determine the best way to set up your office for day-in, day-out operations. Unfortunately, some of you will find that you actually have very little to say about the office arrangement, since it may be an inherent part of your corporate culture or be confined by the layout of your office spaces.

Immersion Time

Managers have learned that most 8-hour days result in much less than 8 hours of actual work from each of their employees. We've had clients that claim that they expect to get 6 hours of work per 8-hour day per employee. Others use 4 hours, or 3 hours, or whatever. We're not sure where the values came from, but we're betting that most of them were guesses rather than measured values. In their book *Peopleware,* Tom DeMarco and Tim Lister introduce a metric known as the *Environmental Factor* or *E-Factor*, which somewhat formalizes the metric described above. The E-Factor shown in Figure 8-1 is one way to quantify what percentage of a workday is actually productive.

$$\text{E-Factor} = \frac{\text{Number of Uninterrupted Hours}}{\text{Number of Body Present Hours}}$$

Figure 8-1

Formula for Calculating the Productive Percentage of a Workday

Multiplying the E-Factor by the number of body-present hours tells you how many productive hours were spent on a particular task. You could just measure uninterrupted work every day, but if the E-Factor is relatively consistent, it's easier to measure this value on a sampling basis, then daily measure the number of hours spent on the job, and multiply the two values.

According to DeMarco and Lister, *"What matters is not the amount of time you're present, but the amount of time that you're working at full potential. An hour in flow really accomplishes something, but ten six-minute work periods sandwiched between eleven interruptions won't accomplish anything."*

No doubt, most of you have experienced days where you seem to accomplish nothing due to constant interruptions. How long it takes you to get fully back into the flow of a task after an interruption depends very much on the nature of the task, your personal work habits, the environment, your state of mind, and many other things we don't pretend to understand. We call the amount of time it takes to become productive after an interruption *immersion time*. It occurred to us that if it were possible to reduce the immersion time for an individual or group through some kind of training (although we certainly don't know where you would go to get this training), then productivity would rise. But since we don't really have any good ideas on how to lessen immersion time, we have to achieve our productivity gains by reducing interruptions.

■■■■■■■■■■■■■■■■■
Key Point

Immersion time is the amount of time it takes to become productive after an interruption.

_____

No More Interruptions, Please!

We visit client sites where they still routinely use the overhead speakers located in every room to blast out every trivial message imaginable: "Connie, please call your mother at home." Now this message is not just broadcast in Connie's work area, it's also sent throughout the building. When the message is broadcast, everyone in the building looks up from their desks and wonders, "What has Connie done now?"

If there are 1,000 engineers in the room and it takes each of them 15 minutes to truly immerse themselves into their work, that little message to Connie may have cost the company up to 250 engineering hours. Actually, it probably cost much less, because it's very likely that many of those workers were not currently immersed in their work at that time because they had probably already been

■■■■■■■■■■■■■■■■■
Case Study 8-3

How long does it take for you to truly immerse yourself in your work?

_____

interrupted for some other reason. But you get the point. If Connie's mother only wanted her to pick up a loaf of bread, the cost to Connie's company made it a very expensive loaf of bread indeed!

Quiet Time

One manager from a large European telecom company that we frequently work with told us that he had noticed that many of his staff members were staying later and later every day. Some others were coming in early each day. When queried about why they had voluntarily extended their days, most of these employees responded with a comment like, "I come in early so I can get some work done." When asked by the manager what they did all day during normal business hours, these employees explained, "The time that wasn't spent attending meetings was spent constantly answering e-mails, phone calls, or responding to colleagues' questions."

Shortly thereafter, the manager implemented a policy whereby every staff member had to designate a daily 2-hour window as quiet time. During quiet time, they couldn't attend meetings, receive phone calls (although they could call another colleague who was not in his or her quiet time), or be interrupted by colleagues. The quiet times were staggered for the staff members so that not everyone was "quiet" at the same time. After all, someone still had to talk to the customers. They also kept one 2-hour window when no one was on quiet time. This was reserved for group meetings and other activities. The manager said it was very successful and productivity rose significantly, although the policy was modified later to only have quiet time three days a week. We guess they didn't really need to do all that much work after all.

■■■■■■■■■■■■■■■■■
Key Point

One innovative test manager that we know required each of his testers to declare a 2-hour period of time each day when no interruptions were allowed.

Another innovative software engineer that we know "borrowed" a "Do Not Cross – Police Line" banner and drapes it across her door when she needs some quiet time (please note that we are not advocating swiping the police banners from a crime scene). Still another engineer had a sign designed like a clock (like you see in a restaurant window), where the hands can be moved to indicate a time – in this case the time when the engineer is ready to talk to her fellow engineers.   These are all different approaches to achieving the same goal of getting a little quiet time to do real work. If you're a test manager, it should be clear to you that your staff already knows the importance of quiet time and so should you!

■■■■■■■■■■■■■■■■■
Key Point

Even though "Do Not Cross" banners and "clocks" may provide needed privacy, we worry that they may also label the individuals who use them as loners, rather than team players.

Meetings

Most test managers and testers spend a great deal of time in meetings, and many of these meetings are, without a doubt, valuable. Some meetings, however, are not as effective as they could be.   Many meetings are too long, have the wrong attendees, start and end late, and some have no clearly defined goal. We offer the following suggestions to make your meetings more productive:

- Start the meeting on time.
- Publish an agenda (in writing, if possible – an e-mail is fine) and objectives of the meeting.
- Specify who should attend (by name, title, or need).
- Keep the attendees to a workable number.
- Limit conversations to one at a time.
- Have someone take notes and publish them at the conclusion of the meeting.
- Urge participation, but prevent monopolization (by the people who just like the sound of their own voice).
- Choose a suitable location (properly equipped and free from interruptions).

■■■■■■■■■■■■■■■■■
Key Point

Many meetings are too long, have the wrong attendees, start and end late, and some have no clearly defined goal.

- Review the results of the meeting against the agenda and objectives.
- Assign follow-up actions.
- Schedule a follow-up meeting, if necessary.
- End the meeting on time.

We realize that there are many times when an impromptu meeting will be called or may just "happen." We certainly approve of this communication medium and don't mean to suggest that every meeting has to follow the checklist above.

Case Study 8-4

Some organizations use meeting critique forms to measure the effectiveness of their meetings.

Nobody Told Me There Would Be a Critique Form

I was conducting a meeting at a client site several years ago. At the conclusion of the meeting, all of the participants began to fill out a form, which I learned later was a meeting critique form. This company critiqued every meeting much as they would critique a seminar or training class. I'm not really convinced that most organizations need to go to this level of formality when conducting meetings, but I do admit that it made me re-evaluate how I conducted meetings in the future. Oh, by the way, I didn't get a great rating on my first meeting, but subsequent meetings were graded higher. Perhaps this is a good example of the Hawthorne Effect at work?

— Rick Craig

Chapter 9 –
The Software Tester

"By the work, one knows the workman."

— Jean de La Fontaine

Characteristics of Good Testers

■■■■■■■■■■■■■■■■

Case Study 9-1

Not all testers need all of the same skills

What Do You Look For in a Tester?

One exercise that we do in every Test Management class is ask the students to make a list of what characteristics they'd like to see in a tester. The results of the exercise are instructive, because everyone quickly realizes that the skills required are extensive and diverse and probably don't exist in any one person, or even in most groups of testers. The good news is that not all testers need all the skills mentioned and some of the skills are not required as much at certain levels of test. For example, programming skills are very useful for unit testers, but may be less important for acceptance testers. Here are the unedited results of a recent class:

Common "serious" answers include:

- *Is inquisitive*
- *Has functional/business knowledge*
- *Is detail-oriented*
- *Is open-minded*
- *Has a good personality*
- *Has a technical background, but does not want to be a programmer*
- *Has testing experience*
- *Is a team player*
- *Is flexible*

- *Is self-reliant*
- *Is self-starting*
- *Has a positive attitude*
- *Is logical*
- *Handles stress well*
- *Is a quick thinker*
- *Knows specific tools*
- *Has good common sense*
- *Is politically astute*
- *Has a sense of humor*
- *Understands the software development lifecycle*

Common "fun" answers include:
- Is still breathing
- Has a destructive, devious nature
- Likes to party
- Possesses a thick skin
- Likes to work long hours
- Likes to say, "gotcha"

Finding Good Testers   ■ ■ ■ ■ ■

Finding and hiring the right people for the right job is a challenge in every organization. Managers of some organizations, such as development managers, may choose to hire mostly recent college graduates who have received a degree in computer science, information technology, software engineering, or some similar discipline. Unfortunately for the test manager, looking for testers is complicated by the fact that very few universities offer a curriculum focused on software testing (but this is beginning to change). So test managers must either hire new graduates and train them, or look to other sources such as development and QA, or poach them from other companies' testing departments.

Developers

Hopefully, all developers are doing unit testing, and maybe some integration testing, so they have some knowledge of the testing discipline. Their knowledge of system design and coding can also help them be effective testers and will afford them credibility with the development group. Even though some developers make good full-time testers, most developers that we know don't want to become testers. Still, there are many reasons why a developer might decide to try his or her hand at becoming a full-time tester. Perhaps, for example, there's an exciting project that needs more testers, or help is required in automating test scripts (which is, after all, a form of programming).

Users

Users, or former users, often make good testers, especially at high levels of test like acceptance testing. Many users will not have any experience in testing, but their knowledge of the business function may make them valuable additions in spite of their lack of experience. Of course, you have to be careful not to alienate the user community by trying to "steal" one or more of their key staff members.

Help Desk / Technical Support

Help desk / technical support personnel are often good testers for all of the same reasons that users are. Plus, help desk personnel may have an even broader vision of the business function than many users, since the view of the help desk personnel is shaped by the views of many different users.

Technical Writers

We had to include technical writers since one of the authors of this book is a trained technical writer. However, even if Stefan were not a technical writer, we think that technical writers can be good testers because they provide great attention to detail. Technical writers are also valuable assets in the creation of testing documentation.

QA Personnel

QA personnel understand the importance of quality and of process use, which makes them an excellent addition to the testing team.

Recent Graduates

You could hire your testers right out of college and train them the way you want them.   Recent college graduates are enthusiastic and willing to study and learn more about the testing discipline.   They aren't afraid to try new things, because they don't suffer from "we always did it this way" syndrome.   In the last few years, some colleges are even teaching their software engineering students about testing, something that very rarely happened a decade or so ago.

Rex Black, author of *Managing the Testing Process*, is working with professors from Polytechnic State University and the Milwaukee School of Engineering to develop testing courses. Professors Cem Kaner and James Whitaker are well-known testing gurus who work at the Florida Institute of Technology, where a degree in software engineering with a specialization in testing is available.   Professor Alan R. Hevner of the University of South Florida teaches a graduate level seminar on software testing that emphasizes many of the concepts detailed in this book.   At the time of this writing, other universities are considering or developing curricula of this nature.

Other Companies (New Hires)

It's a fact of life that some companies are always downsizing, while others are expanding.   It's a real bonus if you can hire a tester who has already been trained by another company (including offering to convert consultants into full-time employees). This is also a good way to acquire expertise on a particular testing tool.

Hiring Testers ■ ■ ■ ■ ■

It used to be that in order to hire a new employee, a manager would interview an entourage of candidates and then select one. Undoubtedly, many of you have taken part in both sides of this process: as the job applicant and as the hiring manager, and you probably remember this as a very time consuming and stressful process. Many managers monopolize the conversation and barely allow the applicant a chance to talk. Hiring a tester is a two-way street – the test manager is hiring the tester, and the tester is "hiring" the manager and his or her organization.

According to Bev Berry, Director of Business Development for ProtoTest LLC, "Many test managers are not given training on how to conduct interviews and hire the right people." Bev has identified several important and helpful techniques to effectively interview and hire testers. We've included many of Bev's tips in this section.

Define Job Requirements

Have your job requirements defined before you start interviewing. Define and prioritize what you are looking for. We're amazed at how often this is not done. Many managers don't fully understand the skills and talents they want and/or need to get the job done well. If you don't define what you're looking for upfront, you won't recognize it when it walks through the door. Spend some time determining what type of tester you need technically, interpersonally, and at what level of career development. If you're not finding that person after

■ ■ ■ ■ ■ ■ ■ ■ ■ ■ ■ ■ ■ ■
Key Point

If you don't define what you're looking for upfront, you won't recognize it when it walks through the door.

several interviews, be open to re-evaluating your job requirements and seeing what parts can be modified.

Read the Candidate's Résumé

Prior to your interview, read the candidate's résumé and take notes on specific areas you want to address. We hear over and over again how often testers experience interviews where the hiring manager never even read their résumés. It's important that the candidates feel they are dealing with someone who understands what they've done in the past; otherwise, they won't have any respect for you or your organization.

Prepare Yourself Mentally

Prepare yourself mentally and be present. Clear your head a few minutes before you meet with the candidate. You must be focused during the interview – if you're off thinking about which meeting you have to go to next, you'll likely miss key indicators and the candidate will sense it. You must listen well and take in as much information as you can about the candidate, technically and personally. If your mind is elsewhere, you can't listen effectively and your powers of discrimination are greatly diminished. Active listening skills are important in conducting good interviews.

■■■■■■■■■■■■■■■■
Key Point

You must be focused during the interview – if you're off thinking about which meeting you have to go to next, you'll likely miss key indicators and the candidate will sense it.

First Impressions Are Important

First impressions are important. Remember, you're selling the candidate on you and your organization as much as they are selling you. Make good eye contact, smile, have a firm handshake, and sense as much as you can about what kind of person you are dealing with. Pay attention to what you're sensing and make note of it.

■■■■■■■■■■■■■■■■
Key Point

Remember, you're selling the candidate on you and your organization as much as they are selling you.

Your goal is to put the candidate at ease so you can learn as much about this person and their genuine characteristics as possible. Create a peer-to-peer environment; make it safe for them to reveal information. It's critical to gain trust if you want an open, honest dialogue.

Learn How to Ask Questions

Your job, as a hiring manager, is to gain as much information about the candidate as possible. Ask open-ended questions. Make notes of how the candidate responds to questions. Do they talk incessantly? Do they answer everything "yes" or "no"? This gives you vital information about their interpersonal skills in the work environment.

Keep the candidate talking. We're amazed at how often testers tell us after they've interviewed with a manager, "Well, they never really asked me any questions." The manager spends most of the interview time talking about the project, the problems, how they are testing, and other topics that aren't directly related to the tester being interviewed. It's important to ask questions – lots of them – and stay away from questions that can have a "yes" or "no" response. Asking a tester, "Have you ever written a master test plan?" gets you nothing. Changing the question to, "Tell me your definition of a master test plan and why it's significant to the testing process" will give you much more information. One of our favorite questions to ask testers is, "What are some of the challenges you've faced as a tester and how did you overcome them?" This single question can give you volumes of information about the candidate. Be thorough. The "tell me about a time when…" questions generally solicit meaningful responses that will help you evaluate the candidate.

■■■■■■■■■■■■■■■■
Key Point

One of our favorite questions to ask testers is, "What are some of the challenges you've faced as a tester and how did you overcome them?"

Ask Candidates to Demonstrate Skills

It's sometimes very difficult to see past the words on a job applicant's résumé and the answers received during an interview. Managers looking to hire a tester who can "hit the ground running" might want to ask candidate testers to review a specification and describe what test cases they would write or what strategy they would use for testing.   In order for this approach to work, the specification must be of a general enough nature that each candidate can understand its meaning.   For example, if you were hiring testers to test an insurance application and you're considering candidates without insurance experience, it might be difficult for them to create viable high-level test cases.   A way around this problem is to choose an application that is understandable to all candidates (we use an ATM application) or have them write unit- or integration-level test cases that don't require intimate knowledge of the business application.   Of course, if one of your considerations is industry expertise (in this case, banking), then by all means use an example from your industry.

■■■■■■■■■■■■■■■■■
Key Point

Managers looking to hire a tester who can "hit the ground running" might want to ask candidate testers to review a specification and describe what test cases they would write or what strategy they would use for testing.

Take Notes

Take notes.   It's important to write as much pertinent information down during the interview as possible. You'll forget things after you've interviewed five candidates for the position. Take notes, but be selective – you don't want to take so many notes that you miss paying attention to the candidate. Create a balance between listening and writing.

Answer the Candidate's Questions

Answer the candidate's questions. Near the end of the interview, you should ask the candidate if he or she has any questions for you. Make sure you understand the inner workings of your organization so that you can accurately address any questions. This is a good time to get them excited about working with your organization. As a hiring manager, you have a responsibility to sell the candidate on your position.

Check References

Always check references. The fact is that people change very little over time, and the best predictor of future performance is past performance. References give you additional and valuable information about your candidate that you may not get during the interview process. They give you a deeper understanding of your candidate's strengths and weaknesses, so you're better able to assess them for your needs. Often, you'll find a theme when checking references on a candidate – listen to it. People generally don't want to provide negative information about another person. They'll soften their choice of words but, if you pay attention closely, you'll be able to hear the underlying message. If the message is consistent among three or more references, it's important to give any negative information heavy weighting in considering that candidate.

■■■■■■■■■■■■■■■■■
Key Point

The best predictor of future performance is past performance. References give you additional and valuable information about your candidate that you may not get during the interview process.

Team Interviews

Some test managers employ team interviews as a way of selecting new testers. This is done because these test managers realize the need for the new candidate to "fit in" with the rest of the group. When team members participate in the selection process, they have a vested interest in helping the new team member be successful. Using team interviews does not, in any way, relieve the test manager of the responsibility of the selection.

From a human resources perspective, remember that it's important to treat all candidates fairly and equally, so if you give one person a "test," you should give all candidates the same or similar test. Similarly, if you're using "group" interviewing techniques, you should use them on all candidates. Spend the time to get the right person. It's always easier to hire a tester than it is to fire one.

■■■■■■■■■■■■■■■
Key Point

When team members participate in the selection process, they have a vested interest in helping the new team member be successful.

How Many Testers Do You Need?   ■ ■ ■ ■ ■

Two of the most common questions that we receive are "How many testers do we need?" and "What is the correct ratio of developers to testers?" Usually, the test managers asking these questions secretly have a number or ratio in mind that they want to hear so they can go back to their manager and use it to justify more testers. We can probably find a reference that would answer this question any way the test manager wants. Some references say that the number of developers should equal the number of testers, or the ratio of developers to testers should be 2:1, 3:1, or some other number.

■■■■■■■■■■■■■■■
Key Point

The correct ratio of developers to testers depends on the quality of the software being tested, the skill of the testers, the level of test automation, and the amount of time that you have to test.

The correct answer to "What should the ratio of developers to testers be?" is, of course, "It depends." In fact, it depends on the quality of the software being tested, the skill of the testers, the level of automation of the testing, and the length of time allowed for testing. For example, if the regression test is largely automated and the regression test set is relatively stable, the number of testers required to do the job would be much less than

■■■■■■■■■■■■■■■
Key Point

In his book *Software Testing in the Real World,* Ed Kit states that the typical ratio of developers to testers is 3:1 or 4:1 (as of 1995).

the number required on a rapidly changing application where the testing is mostly manual.

Even after we give this little speech in class, though, someone still says, "That's all well and good, but what should the ratio be?" Although we know that the ratio at one company is not indicative of what the ratio *should be* at another company, we think that it's instructive and interesting to understand what's happening in other companies. For example, if your ratio of developers to testers is 3:1 and someone else's is 2:1, it's hard to argue that you need more testers based on this data alone (maybe you have better test automation or more experienced testers). But if your ratio is 100:1, then you probably have a strong argument that your ratio of developers to testers is out of balance.

■■■■■■■■■■■■■■■■■
Key Point

Roger Sherman reported that the developer-to-tester ratio at Microsoft is 1 to 1.

– Best Development and Testing Strategies of Microsoft Proceedings from the STAR West 1998 Conference

---

How Many Testers Do You Really Need?

In our Test Management classes, we ask each student what the ratio of developers to testers is in their company. Out of a 25-person class, the breakdown usually looks more or less like this:

Ratio of Developers to Testers	Number of Students Who Raised Their Hand
Fewer Developers than Testers	*1*
1:1	*5*
2:1	*5*
3:1, 4:1, 5:1	*10*
6:1, 7:1, 8:1, 9:1, 10:1	*3*
Some Crazy Number Like 100:1	*1*

Obviously the data shown in the table above cannot stand up to any kind of statistical scrutiny, due to the way it was collected (those spoil-sport mathematicians), but anecdotally, we've seen similar results often enough that at least we're convinced of their accuracy. In his book Software Testing in the Real

■■■■■■■■■■■■■■■■■
Case Study 9-2

Survey Results from a Typical Class of 25 Students

World, *Ed Kit cites examples where the number of testers exceeded the number of developers, but concluded that more typical ratios are in the range from 3:1 to 4:1 [developers to testers].*

Retaining Staff ■ ■ ■ ■ ■

When you consider how much it costs to hire and train new testers, it really behooves organizations to retain effective staff members. We have, on occasion, been asked by some companies to review the results of exit interviews conducted with departing employees. Some of the reasons given for leaving were the normal personal and professional reasons that you would expect, but we were also struck by the incredibly trivial reasons that some employees gave for leaving a company. One tester identified as a key employee, for example, was leaving because she felt that she had been "cheated" out of two days of vacation and the system was too rigid to make it up to her. The manager had to go through the entire hiring and training process because of two days of vacation! And of course, it's not known if the new employee will also turn out to be a "key" employee.

Here are some of the typical and not-so-typical reasons given for choosing employment elsewhere:
- No one appreciated the work that I was doing.
- No recognition was given for all of the extra hours that I put in.
- The developers got all of the training.
- Testers are seen as second-class citizens.
- The hours are too long.
- They don't understand how important testing is.

■ ■ ■ ■ ■ ■ ■ ■ ■ ■ ■ ■ ■ ■ ■
Key Point

There is a strong correlation between increased training and improved worker productivity, profitability, and shareholder value. An American Management Association study discovered that companies with increased training are 66% more likely to report productivity improvements, <u>twice as likely to reduce turnover rates</u>, and 150% more likely to improve the quality of their products and services.

- Dick Grote and John Boroshok, *Are Most Layoffs Carried Out Fairly?*

- I was asked my opinion, but no one really listened to my answer.
- My salary was too low.
- I wanted to telecommute one or two days a week, but they said, "No."
- This company was too bureaucratic.
- My manager wouldn't let me do my job.
- Everyone said our work was important, but they would ship the release whether we were done testing or not.
- I was not hired to be a programmer (no doubt, a testing tool issue).
- QA gets stuck with all the SLJ (we think "SLJ" means trivial jobs).

We had intended to write an entire section on how to retain employees, but we believe the list above says it all. To summarize, employees (testers) expect:

- To be recognized for their effort and contribution.
- To be seen as part of the overall team that delivers a quality product.
- To be treated as professionals.
- To be heard.
- To receive pay commensurate with their experience and the job that they perform.
- To receive appropriate and adequate training.
- To perform the job they were hired for.
- To be treated as individuals with personal as well as professional needs.

Working Overtime

It's a fact of life that most projects have periods of time where the resource requirements exceed the availability of staff members. One way to solve the problem is to acquire additional resources in the form of temporary testers drawn from the development group, QA, the user community, or from other sources. But if the need for additional resources comes unexpectedly, as it frequently does, and if the deadline is near, adding more people to a late project may just delay it further due to the training curve of the new people brought on board. So that, of course leads us to overtime. Having your staff work over-time is the best way to obtain small doses of extra resource. Overtime, though, is a resource that needs to be carefully managed. If overtime is just a way of life day in and day out, the test manager will have nothing in reserve when an emergency arises.

■■■■■■■■■■■■■■■■■
Key Point

Adding more people to a late project may just delay it further due to the training curve of the new people brought on board.

And if overtime is the norm, it loses some of its effectiveness as the adrenalin rush subsides and the staff members realize that there's no light at the end of the tunnel. Soon, you'll find yourselves doing in 9 or 10 hours what you used to do in 8 hours. Initially, staff effectiveness may begin to drop, and if "routine" overtime is continued long enough, morale will begin to decline. Managers must remember that overtime is like the reserve in a military campaign – once it's committed, there's no further reserve available.

■■■■■■■■■■■■■■■■■
Key Point

Managers must remember that overtime is like the reserve in a military campaign – once it's committed, there's no further reserve available.

If, in fact, overtime is routine in your organization, this may be indicative of a bigger problem and is an indication that a downward spiral toward inefficient and unhappy workers has begun. Are you understaffed? Are you ineffective? Are you trying to do too much? Remember the concept of risk analysis? Software risk analysis helps determine the priority of testing and planning risks, which help us determine what we can and cannot do with available resources. If you find yourself in the situation described above, we recommend that you go back and re-read Chapter 2 – *Risk Analysis*.

Finally, testers must be shown appreciation for their overtime. A simple "thank you" is a good start. Future time off, or even extra pay, should not be out of the question, even for salaried workers.

And finally, if your entire staff (or a large part of it) is working overtime, so should you, even if only for a show of support. There's nothing worse than working day and night and watching your boss go home every night at the stroke of 5:00 PM.

Beware of the testers who always want to work overtime only because they need the extra money. Just because they're willing participants doesn't ensure that their efficiency and morale will not suffer with extended overtime.

Software Tester Certifications ■ ■ ■ ■ ■

Over the years, we've received many queries from testers and test managers who were interested in some type of technical certification. We've always thought that the concept of certification is sound and offers a lot of benefits to organizations that urge their employees to become certified and to the individuals who participate in this endeavor. Specifically, certification is a way to recognize professional achievement, provide a career path, and introduce an incentive to learn about testing and related fields. We've also worried, though, that there's not a *single* industry-wide certification program for software testers. Several different certification programs have emerged that have gained a certain degree of recognition, but the mere fact that there are multiple certifications available waters down the recognition one gets for achieving any one of them. On balance, though, the benefits of achieving any one of the certifications described below far outweigh any negative perception caused by the lack of standardization.

The comments above are based on the opinions of the authors of this book. The rest of this section on certification draws heavily

■ ■ ■ ■ ■ ■ ■ ■ ■ ■ ■ ■
Key Point

The concept of certification is sound and offers a lot of benefits to organizations that urge their employees to become certified and to the individuals who participate in this endeavor.

from an excellent article by Darin Kalashian and one of the reviewers of this book, Eric Patel.

According to Kalashian and Patel, *"Certification is commonly defined as formal recognition by an institution that an individual has demonstrated proficiency within and comprehension of a specified body of knowledge at a point in time. It's important to note that certification is not registration or a license. It implies that you have fulfilled the requirements to become certified and that you have passed an exam. Once you become certified, it will be important to maintain your certified status by performing approved re-certification activities within a fixed timeframe."*

There are several categories of certification shown in Figure 9-1. Perhaps the most familiar type is the *product-based certification*, such as Novell's Certified Novell Engineer (CNE) and Microsoft's Certified Systems Engineer (MCSE). The other major category of certification is *software certifications*, which come in two basic flavors: vendor-specific and organization-based. Vendor specific programs have some merit, but a broader aspect is gained through what are known as organization-based software certifications, and that will be the focus in this book.

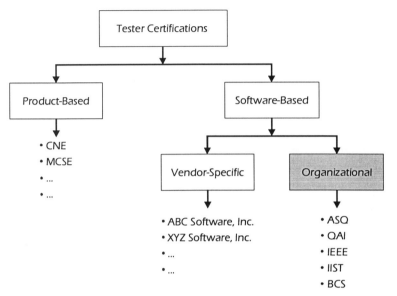

The most widely recognized organization-based software certifications include:

- American Society for Quality's (ASQ) Certified Software Quality Engineer (CSQE)
- Quality Assurance Institute's (QAI) Certified Software Test Engineer (CSTE)
- International Institute for Software Testing's (IIST) Certified Software Test Professional (CSTP)
- Institute of Electrical and Electronic Engineers' (IEEE) Certified Software Development Professional (CSDP)
- British Computer Society's (BCS) Information Systems Examination Board (ISEB)

Table 9-1 provides a comparison of various elements of each software-quality-centric and software-test-centric certification program.

Table 9-1 Comparison of Software Quality and Test Certifications

(Reprinted with permission from *Certification: A Win-Win Investment for Employees and Employers* by Darin Kalashian and Eric Patel)

	Software-Quality-Centric		Software-Test-Centric	
Certification	CSQE	CSDP	CSTE	CSTP
Organization	ASQ	IEEE	QAI	IIST
First Started Certifying	1996	2002[1]	1996	2000
Total Number of Active Certifications[2]	1,969	167	2,200+	153+
Work Experience	3 – 8 years	4-½ years	0 – 6 years	1 year
Exam	4 hours, 160 multiple choice questions[1]	3-½ hours, 180 multiple choice questions[1]	4 hours, true/false, multiple choice, essay[1]	10 short essay exams (within 5 years)
Type of Exam	Open book	Closed book	Closed book	Closed book
Exam Dates	June, December	Spring, Fall	Periodically	Periodically
Passing Score	73% (550/750)	Unknown	75% (in each of 4 parts)	80% (in each exam)
Recertification Period	3 years	3 years	1 year	None[5]
Average Salary Increase	3%[6]	Unknown	19%[7]	Unknown
For More Information	www.asq.org	computer.org	www.qaiusa.com	www.softdim.com/iist
Certification Costs (est.)				
Exam Fee(s)	$180 - $285[3]	$450 - $600[3]	$250	$4,500[8]
Study Materials	$190[4]	$120	$75 - $500	Included
Exam Refresher / Test Prep Course	$355 - $415[3]	To Be Determined	$300 - $400	N/A
Travel	$25	$25	$25	$100 - $4,000
Total	$760 - $925	$595 - $745	$650 - $1,175	$4,600 - $8,500

(1) IEEE is scheduled to offer exams in 2002   (2) As of December 2001   (3) Higher fee is for non-members
(4) CSQE Primer ($65), CSQE CD-ROM ($70), textbook ($55)   (5) IIST is currently identifying recertification requirements
(6) ASQ 2001 Salary Survey, Quality Progress, December 2001   (7) CSTE brochure, QAI, all active CSTEs 1997-2000
(8) $2,225 for five courses

Value of Certification to Testers

If certification is to be successful, the individual testers must find that there's value in it for them. This value may be the hope of a better job, promotion, prestige, or more pay. Testers will also be motivated to strive for certification if they feel that it will help them do a better job and demonstrate their proficiency in testing.

Help in Getting a Job

We won't say that if you get this certification or that certification you'll automatically get any job that you want, but some companies do look favorably upon certification when seeking candidates for testing jobs. Certifications show employers that the candidate has the motivation to learn more about testing, treats testing as a profession, and has a certain body of knowledge on the topic.

Salary Increase or Promotion

Some companies use certification as an indication that the employee is ready for greater responsibility (and maybe more money!). On the other hand, even if your company does not immediately and directly compensate you for your achievement, in the long term, we hope that your increased knowledge will help you improve your work skills to such a degree that you'll be recognized for increasingly more responsible positions. Of course, if your company totally ignores your effort, you may want to refer to the paragraph above entitled *Help in Getting a Job*.

Do a Better Job

Most people receive great satisfaction from doing a job well. Certification, and the training that goes with it, helps most testers perform their jobs better. Unfortunately, we are not aware of any studies that have been done to measure the increase in quality or productivity of work resulting from certification.

Value of Certification to Test Managers

Test managers are anxious for their staffs to become more knowledgeable and proficient testers, and most agree that certification is one way to achieve that goal. Most test managers also welcome a program that provides structure and goals to the training of their staffs.

Certain Level of Knowledge

If a tester has received one of the certifications mentioned above, that will assure the test manager that the employee possesses at least a certain minimal level of testing knowledge. Certification of all employees on the staff can help the test manager introduce common terms and methods, which can improve communications within the group and help the organization become more consistent in its processes.

Using the same certification program for the entire staff is more effective at introducing a commonality of terms than using multiple programs. That is, if one of the goals of the test manager is to establish a common vocabulary and philosophy of testing within the organization, he or she would do well to choose just one of the certification programs explained in this chapter and urge their staff to use that program over the others. If some employees wish to get another certification in *addition* to your organization's standard, then good for them.

■■■■■■■■■■■■■■■■■
Key Point

If one of the goals of the test manager is to establish a common vocabulary and philosophy of testing within the organization, he or she would do well to choose just one of the certification programs explained in this chapter and urge their staff to use that program over the others.

Incentive to Study

Time and money for training are often in short supply, so anything that encourages an employee to study on his or her own time is an obvious plus. Employees who pursue training such as certification on their own initiative are usually more motivated to learn than employees who are forced or "urged" to learn on their own, or to attend a class that they really don't want to attend. The incentive to learn can be further enhanced by offering employees some additional reward for completing the program. One of our clients, for example, presented newly certified testers with a gift certificate and honorable mention in the company newsletter. Other companies award extra vacation or "comp" time to successful individuals, or at least agree to pay for the study fees and course exam. These rewards not only are an incentive to study, but also show support of the certification program and of the employees who participate in it.

Motivation

Training is often a motivator for employees. Pursuing a formal regimen, such as one of the certification programs addressed in this book, can be a motivator for all participating employees.

Career Path

Test managers can use a certification program as a basis for creating a career path for their employees. For example, certification might be one of the criteria for being promoted from one level to another, or for moving from one job to another (e.g., from "tester" to "test analyst"). Since all candidates for promotion are required to complete the same standardized certification program, the promotion process is seen as fair and impartial.

Show of Support

Encouraging staff to participate in a certification program shows the employees that you support their careers and you care about their success. You can reinforce this support by allowing employees who are seeking certification some "company time" to work toward the certification.

Value of Certification to the Company

Everything discussed above that provides value to the individual and the manager ultimately helps the company that employs them. One added bonus for the company is that they can point to the certifications as "evidence" of the quality of the staff (and therefore the products) that they produce (okay, we'll say it, "Some companies may use certification of their employees as a marketing tool"). Employee certifications can also play an important role in helping an organization achieve ISO certification, since the ISO certification process requires managers to maintain employee training records.

How to Prepare for Certification

The first step in obtaining a certification is to complete an application and submit it to the organization to see if you qualify to sit for the exam. The next step is to prepare for the exam itself. This can be done through self-study, formal education, or some combination of the two. Most of the organizations that provide certification also provide training to help students achieve the prescribed goals.

All certification programs have a *Body of Knowledge* (BOK), which is assembled by industry experts and identifies best practices for professional performance. For example, ASQ's Certified Software Quality Engineer (CSQE) certification requires expertise within the following areas:
- Software Standards and Ethics
- Software Quality Management
- Software Processes
- Software Project Management

- Software Test Engineering
- Software Metrics and Measurement Methods
- Software Auditing
- Software Configuration Management

The IEEE's Certified Software Development Professional (CSDP) certification requires knowledge in:
- Software Standards and Ethics
- Software Requirements
- Software Design
- Software Construction
- Software Testing
- Software Maintenance
- Software Configuration Management
- Software Engineering Management
- Software Engineering Process
- Software Engineering Tools and Methods
- Software Quality

QAI's Certified Software Test Engineer (CSTE) body of knowledge covers:
- Quality Principles and Concepts
- Verification and Validation Methods
- Test Approach and Planning
- Test Design and Execution
- Test Analysis, Reporting, and Improvement

IIST's Certified Software Test Professional (CSTP) domain consists of:
- Principles of Software Testing
- Test Design
- Test Management
- Test Execution and Defect Tracking
- Requirements Definition, Refinement, and Verification
- Test Automation
- Verification Testing

BCS's Information Systems Examination Board (ISEB) body of knowledge consists of:

- Principles of Testing
- Testing Terminology
- How Much Testing Is Enough?
- Testing Throughout the Lifecycle
- Dynamic Testing Techniques
- Static Testing Techniques
- Test Management
- Organizational Structures for Testing
- Configuration Management
- Test Estimation
- Test Monitoring
- Incident Management
- Standards for Testing
- Tool Support for Testing

Recertification

Each of the certification programs listed in Table 9-1 requires recertification on a periodic basis. Usually, you can accomplish this by re-sitting for the exam (ugh!) or performing other activities that will earn you recertification credit. Examples include:

- Continuing education courses and/or tutorials
- Attend or present at seminars and/or conferences
- Professional meetings
- Committees
- Publishing
- Speaking engagements, presentations

How Certification Has Benefited Me

I'm glad that I made the decision to pursue certification. Being certified has benefited me on many levels. Being quite active in the software quality community, I have gained additional distinction and credibility with writing articles, speaking at conferences, and teaching courses. I'm a firm believer in continuing education. I enjoy the endless learning aspect of my continuing education efforts, and certification not only has supplemented my knowledge base, but also motivates me to remain certified. By continuing with my professional development activities, which I enjoy doing anyway, I now obtain the additional benefit of recertification credits that I can apply towards my future recertification efforts. Also, when I went to college there were no SQA or testing courses. Certification has helped me fill the void that traditional education left me with.

During a recent job hunt, one of my certifications was a key competitive advantage that helped me land job offers. In addition, with my newly acquired certifications since I got hired, I now have additional leverage during my next performance review. I have effectively increased my worth and value to my employers and in the marketplace. Moreover, certification has given me additional visibility and recognition within my company and has made me the de facto quality "expert" in my business unit. Mostly, I enjoy the personal satisfaction from achieving my career goals and inspiring others to follow the path and enjoy the benefits of becoming certified.

— Eric Patel

■■■■■■■■■■■■■■■■■
Case Study 9-3

Certification Can Benefit You on Many Levels

Certification: Making My Life Easier

I have found that software quality certification is one of the best ways to complement a software engineering degree. An engineer by trade solves problems. A quality engineer attempts to solve problems in the most effective and efficient means while assuring quality. Organizations typically pay software quality engineers to drive end-product quality by testing prior to delivery. Some organizations realize that focusing on activities earlier on and throughout the development process can help achieve software quality. The tools and skills that I developed have allowed me to increase customer satisfaction, reduce development time, and have a team that upon project completion was sane enough to succeed in the future.

Another reason why certification adds value is that it makes my daily functions easier. If I identify a process improvement that saves months of overtime or a metric that aids in resolving a real issue, my life is easier and, more importantly, less chaotic. I was recently discussing this issue with a manager of a Software Quality Department in a very successful company. We were discussing how their products come to "releasable quality levels." His answer was that quality is achieved by extensive testing. Furthermore, we talked about how although testing may be a necessity, it can be a very ineffective process.

As part of the certification program of study, tools and techniques are identified and applied with the goal of preventing defects from being inserted into the product in the first place. This allows the entire team to be more effective and produce a higher quality product or service. The team is not solely dependent upon testing to produce high quality software. We also acknowledged that subjects like prototyping, modeling, and project management weren't new ideas but ones that are hard to implement. Certification taught me to "tool-smith" my abilities and develop skills to fit the right tool to the job.

Attaining certification is the first step. Certifications must be renewed. This means constant learning, demonstration, and application, all of which require ongoing commitment. As a hiring manager, I have found that there is no better way to reward this professional commitment than to recognize individuals' professional certification and accomplishments.

— Darin Kalashian

Chapter 10 –
The Test Manager

"A writer asked me, 'What makes a good manager?' I replied, 'Good players.'"

— Yogi Berra

What Is Management?   ■ ■ ■ ■ ■

Henry Mintzberg wrote a classic article called "The Manager's Job: Folklore and Fact" for the *Harvard Business Review* in 1975. In his article, Mintzberg concluded that many managers don't really know what they do. When pressed, many managers fall back on the mantra many of us have been taught that managers plan, organize, coordinate and control, and indeed managers do spend time doing all of these things.

Rather than discuss management in light of tasks or activities, Mintzberg has defined management by a series of roles that managers fulfill. A manager, states Mintzberg, is vested with formal authority over an organization. From this authority comes status that leads the manager into the various interpersonal roles shown in Figure 10-1, which allow the manager to gain access to information, and ultimately allow him or her to make decisions. It's instructional to take this model and apply it to a software testing manager.

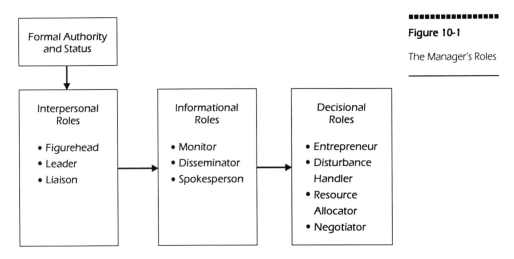

■■■■■■■■■■■■■■■■

Figure 10-1

The Manager's Roles

Interpersonal Roles

The test manager is the figurehead for the testing group and, as such, can affect the perception people outside the test group have of the testing group and the people in it. In most companies, the test manager is very visible within the entire Information Technology (IT) division and may even be well known in other organizations outside of IT. Examples of this visibility are the manager's role on the Configuration Control Board, Steering Council, or Corporate Strategy Group.

Because of the unique nature of testing software (i.e., evaluating the work of another group – the developers – for use by a third group – the users), the testing manager will have to coordinate and work with people from many organizations throughout the company and even with groups and individuals outside of the company. Figure 10-2 shows just a few of the people with whom a test manager may have to deal on a daily basis.

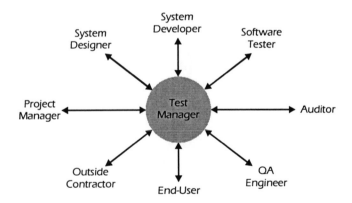

■■■■■■■■■■■■■■■■■

Figure 10-2

Interpersonal Roles of a Test Manager

Another interpersonal role that the test manager plays is, of course, the leader. As such, the manager is trusted to accomplish the mission of the organization and ensure the welfare of the staff. Refer to the section below on the Test Manager as a Leader.

Informational Roles

The test manager is in a position to present information on a daily basis. He or she will be expected to provide status reports, plans, estimates, and summary reports. Additionally, the test manager must fulfill a role as a trainer of the testing staff, upper management, development, and the user community. In this role, the test manager will act as the spokesperson for the testing group.

Decisional Roles

Test managers make hundreds of decisions every day:
- Which tester should get this assignment?
- What tool should we use?
- Should we work overtime this weekend?
- And so on…

One of the major decisional roles that the test manager may take part in is the decision on what to do at the conclusion of testing. Should the software be released or should it undergo further testing? This is primarily a business decision, but the test manager is in a unique position to participate in this decision-making process by advising (the CCB, users, or management) on the quality of the software, the likelihood of failure, and the potential impact of releasing the software.

Management vs. Leadership

According to Robert Kreitner and Angelo Kinicki in their book *Organizational Behavior*, "Management is the process of working with and through others to achieve organizational objectives in an efficient and ethical manner." Effective managers are team players that have the ability to creatively and actively coordinate daily activities through the support of others. Management is about dealing with complexity. Test managers routinely have to work within complicated organizations that possess many formal and informal lines of communication. They deal with complex processes and methodologies, staffs with varying degrees of skill, tools, budgets and estimates. This is the essence of management.

Key Point

Management is about dealing with complexity.

Leadership is about dealing with change.

Kreitner and Kinicki state that leadership is "a social influence process in which the leader seeks the voluntary participation of subordinates in an effort to achieve organizational goals." It's about dealing with change. Leadership is what people possess when they are able to cope with change by motivating people to adopt and benefit from the change. Leadership is more than just wielding power and exercising authority. Leadership depends on a million different little things (e.g., coaching, effectively wandering around, consistency, enthusiasm, etc.) that work together to help achieve a common goal. Management controls people by pushing them in the right direction; leadership motivates them by satisfying basic human needs. In his essay "What Leaders Really Do," John Kotter explains that "management and leadership are complementary." That is, test managers don't need to become test leaders instead of test managers, but they do need to be able to lead as well as manage their organization.

Key Point

"Leadership is a potent combination of strategy and character. But if you must be without one, be without strategy."

- General H. Norman Schwartzkopf

Leadership Styles

A debate that has been going on for thousands of years (if you read Thucydides' *The Peloponnesian War*, you'll see that they were debating the issue over 2000 years ago) is whether leaders are made or born. There are many references to this topic, but, at the end of the day, most conclude that while there are certain personal characteristics that make it easier to be a leader, almost everyone has the potential to be a leader. For example, some people are naturally better communicators than others. Good communications skills are a definite asset to any leader. Still, a determined person can overcome or compensate for a personal deficiency in this area and most others. Certainly, the Marine Corps believe that all Marines are or can become leaders.

We think that what's important for you is to determine what style of leadership best fits your personality. If you're naturally quiet and prefer one-on-one communications, then your leadership style should focus on this strength (of course, you'll still have to talk in front of groups and should work on this skill). If you're naturally extroverted, your leadership style should reflect this trait.

■■■■■■■■■■■■■■■■■

Case Study 10-1

Choosing the correct leadership style is an important part of being an effective leader.

Leadership As a Platoon Commander

As a young Lieutenant stationed in Japan in the 1970s, I was getting my first real taste of leadership as a platoon commander in charge of 30 or so hard-charging Marines. Even after 4 years at the Naval Academy and the Training Program for Marine Lieutenants (appropriately enough, called The Basic School), my leadership style was still very much in the formative stages. There was, however, one Captain who I thought was a really good leader. The one thing I remember about him was that he yelled a lot at his troops. "Move that cannon over there! Do it now! Hurry up!" You get the picture. At that point, I assumed that one of the reasons he was a good leader was because he was very vocal and yelled at his Marines. So, for the first time in my life, I began yelling.

After a couple of days of this surprising tirade, one of my sergeants came up to me and said, "Sir, you know all that yelling crap? Cut it out, it ain't you" (these may not have been his exact words). Now, it takes some courage for a Sergeant to criticize his platoon commander, especially in light of the fact that many new Lieutenants are not yet all that confident in their leadership skills anyway. But, of course, he was right. Yelling was not my style. So I (almost) never yelled at my Marines again and I like to think that I was a better leader for it. Thank you, Sergeant.

P.S. There's another lesson hidden in the story above: Good leaders learn from their employees.

— Rick Craig

Marine Corps Principles of Leadership

The following list contains a set of leadership principles used by the Marine Corps, but pertinent to every leader:

- Know yourself and continually seek self-improvement.
- Be technically and tactically proficient (know your job).
- Develop a sense of responsibility among your subordinates.
- Make sound and timely decisions.
- Set the example.
- Know your Marines and look out for their welfare.
- Keep your Marines informed.
- Seek with responsibility and take responsibility for your actions and the actions of your Marines.

- Ensure that tasks are understood, supervised, and accomplished.
- Train your Marines as a team.
- Employ your command (i.e., testing organization) in accordance with your team's capabilities. (Set goals you can achieve.)

* Derived from *NAVMC 2767 User's Guide to Marine Corps Leadership Training*

It's easy to see that these principles are as valid for your organization as they are for the Marine Corps. Rick wrote these principles down in his day-timer so he could review them periodically, and apply them to his daily routine. It always seems to help him keep what's really important in perspective.

The Test Manager As a Leader   ■ ■ ■ ■ ■

Military-style training for business executives seems to be all the rage these days. There are boot camps and training programs for executives and numerous books on using military leadership skills in the corporate setting. This section uses the model of leadership taught by the Marine Corps.

Cornerstones of Leadership

Over the years, as a Marine officer, Rick has had the opportunity to teach many leadership forums for enlisted personnel and officers of various ages and ranks. Authority, responsibility, and accountability (Figure 10-3) are the cornerstones that the Marine Corps uses to teach Marines how to become leaders.

Accountability   Responsibility

Marine Leaders

Authority

■■■■■■■■■■■■■■■■■

Figure 10-3

Cornerstones of
Marine Leaders
_____

Authority

Authority is the legitimate power of a leader. In the case of the test manager, this authority is vested in the manager as a result of his or her position in the organization and the terms of employment with the company that he or she works for. In some test organizations, informal leaders also exist. For example, in the absence of an appointed test lead, an experienced tester may take over the management of a small group of testers and their work. Informal leaders don't receive any kind of power from the organizational hierarchy, but rather they're able to lead due to their influence over the people they're leading. This influence normally exists due to the experience level of the informal leader and his or her willingness to employ some or all of the principles of leadership outlined in this chapter.

■■■■■■■■■■■■■■■■■
Key Point

Some military books are now commonly found in the business section of many libraries and book stores:

- *Sun Tzu: The Art of War*
- *Fleet Marine Force Manual I (FMFM I)*
- *The Peloponnesian War* by Thucydides

Other popular "business" books have a military theme or background:

- *Leadership Secrets of Attila the Hun*
- *Semper Fi: Business Leadership the Marine Way*

_____

Responsibility

Responsibility is the obligation to act. The test manager is obligated to perform many actions in the course of each day. Some of these actions are mandated (i.e., daily meetings, status reporting, performance appraisals, etc.). Other responsibilities are not mandated, but are required because the leader knows and understands that they will support the ultimate satisfaction of the mission of the organization and its people. Examples include developing metrics and reports to manage the testing effort, rewarding staff members for a job well done, and mentoring new employees.

Accountability

Accountability means answering for one's actions. Test managers are held accountable for maximizing the effectiveness of their organization in determining the quality of the software they test. This means that the manager must test what's most important first (i.e., risk management); they must make use of innovations to achieve greater effectiveness (i.e., tools and automation); they must have a way to measure the effectiveness of their testing group (i.e., test effectiveness metrics); they must ensure the training, achievement, and welfare of their staff; and they must constantly strive to improve the effectiveness of their efforts.

■■■■■■■■■■■■■■■■■
Key Point

Test managers are held accountable for maximizing the effectiveness of their organization in determining the quality of the software they test.

Politics

To many people, the word *politics* evokes an image of some slick, conniving, controlling person. Really, though, there's nothing negative about the word or business we know as politics. One of the definitions of politics in Webster's Dictionary is *"the methods or tactics involved in managing a state or government."*

For our purposes, we can replace the words "state or government" with "organization" and we'll have a workable definition of politics.

Politics is how you relate to other people or groups. If you, as a manager, say, "I don't do politics," you're really saying, "I don't do any work." Politics is part of the daily job of every manager and includes his or her work to secure resources, obtain buy-in, sell the importance of testing, and generally coordinate and work with other groups such as the development group.

Span of Control

There's a limit to the number of people that can be effectively managed by a single person. This span of control varies, of course, with the skill of the manager and the people being managed, and the environment in which they work. Several years ago, a government agency conducted a study to determine what the ideal span of control is for a proficient leader. Their conclusion was that a typical effective leader can successfully manage the work of 4 direct reports and some leaders can effectively manage up to 8 (note that "direct reports" do not include administrative personnel such as clerks and secretaries). The Commandant of the U.S. Marine Corps ultimately has over 200,000 active-duty and reserve "employees," but he directs them through only four (three active-duty and one reserve) Division Commanders (i.e., his span of control is four). We know that some of you are already saying, "That rule doesn't apply to me. I have 20 direct reports and I'm a great manager." Well then, good for you. But we believe that if you have large numbers of direct reports and you're a good and effective manager, there's something else happening. Informal leaders have emerged to coordinate, mentor, counsel, or even supervise some of their colleagues. There's nothing inherently wrong with these informal "chains of command," other than the extra burden they put on the informal leaders. These informal leaders have to function without organizational authority and prestige, and consequently have to work even harder to succeed. They are also, of course, not receiving pay for this extra work, which can itself have long-term implications on their overall morale. One last thought on the subject: This is an opportunity to create the career path that we talked about in the *Software Tester Certifications* section of Chapter 9.

Effective Communication

Poor communication is one of the more frequently cited frustrations of testers. It's important to establish good communications channels to resolve conflicts and clarify requirements. Some of these communications channels will naturally develop into an informal network, while others (e.g., configuration management, defect reporting, status reporting) need to be made formal.

One of the most important jobs of the test manager is to provide feedback to the team members. Testers are anxious to know when they've done a good job or, on the other hand, if they missed a critical bug. In particular, testers need feedback on the metrics that they're required to collect. Without the feedback loop, they'll feel like they're feeding a "black hole." If no feedback is provided, some testers will stop collecting metrics and others will record "any old data."

Feedback loops don't just go down through the ranks. Staff members must feel comfortable communicating with their manager. One way to foster this communication is to establish

■■■■■■■■■■■■■■■■■■
Key Point

" The most important element in establishing a happy, prosperous atmosphere was an insistence upon open, free, and honest communication up and down the ranks of our management structure."

- Harold Geneen

an open-door policy. Basically, the test manager should make it known that any staff member can visit him or her at any time to discuss job-related or personal issues. This open-door policy goes a long way toward developing rapport with the staff and creating the loyalty that all leaders need.

The Test Manager's Role in the Team ■ ■ ■ ■ ■

Test managers play an important role in the testing team. These managers are responsible for justifying testers' salaries, helping to develop career paths, building morale, and selling testing to the rest of the organization.

Equal Pay for Equal Jobs

Traditionally, test engineers have received less pay than their counterparts in the development group. Lately, we've seen a gradual swing toward parity in pay between the two groups. If your test engineers receive less pay than the developers, it's important to determine why:

■ ■ ■ ■ ■ ■ ■ ■ ■ ■
Key Point

A good source for salary information can be found at:

www.salary.com

- Is it because the developers have more experience?
- Is it because the developers require more training or have to be certified?
- Is it because software development is seen as a profession and testing is not?
- Or is it just culture or tradition that developers receive more pay?

As a test manager, you should determine if a pay disparity exists. If it does exist and the reason is only culture or tradition, you should fight the battle for parity of pay for your staff. Even if you don't succeed, your fight will help instill loyalty and respect from your staff. If your engineers receive less pay because they have less training or are perceived as less professional, you have some work to do before lobbying for equal pay. You might consider:

- implementing a formal training curriculum for your testers.
- providing an opportunity for certification using one of the programs described in the *Software Tester Certifications* section of Chapter 9.
- developing a career path so that test engineers have a logical way to advance in the organization without transferring out of the testing organization.
- embarking on a "marketing" campaign that extols the benefits and return on investment of testing to the rest of the company.
- developing and using metrics that measure the value of testing and measure test effectiveness.

The only way you can fail is to throw up your hands and declare, "This is the way it has always been and this is the way it will always be!"

Career Path Development

It's desirable to have a clear career path within the testing organization. If the only way testers can advance in pay and prestige is by transferring to development or some other area within your organization, many of your best people will do just that. In larger organizations, it may be possible to establish different testing roles or positions with established criteria for moving move from one role to another. For example, one company that we visit frequently has established the formal positions listed in Table 10-1 for various testing jobs.

Table 10-1 Testing Positions at XYZ Company

Position	Primary Function
Tester	Executes tests.
Test Engineer	Develops and executes test cases.
Test Analyst	Participates in risk analysis, inventories, and test design.
Lead Test Analyst	Acts as a mentor and manages one of the processes above.
Test Lead	Supervises a small group of testers.
Test Manager	Supervises the entire test group.

Even if you work in a smaller test organization with only one or two testers, it's possible to create different job titles, advancement criteria, and possibly step increases in pay to reward testers for their achievements and progress toward becoming a testing professional.

Desktop Procedures

It is the mark of a good manager if his or her subordinate can step in and take over the manager's job without causing a disruption to the organization. One tool that Rick uses in the Marine Corps (when he's stuck at a desk job) to help ease this transition is the *desktop procedure*. Desktop procedures are simple instructions that describe all of the routine tasks that must be accomplished by a manager on a daily or weekly basis. These tasks may include reports that must be filed, meetings attended, performance appraisals written, etc.

■■■■■■■■■■■■■■■■
Key Point

Desktop procedures are simple instructions that describe all of the routine tasks that must be accomplished by a manager on a daily or weekly basis.

Desktop procedures are often supplemented by what are called *turnover files*. Turnover files are examples of reports, meeting minutes, contact lists, etc. that, along with the desktop procedures, facilitate a smooth transition from one manager to another. We're certain that many of our readers already use similar tools, possibly with different names. But if you don't, we urge you to create and use these simple and effective tools.

Staying Late

Many managers have reached their position because they're hard workers, overachievers, or in a few cases just plain workaholics. For them, becoming a manager is an opportunity to continue the trend to work longer and longer hours. This may be done out of love for the job, dedication, inefficiency, or for some other reason. No matter what the reason is for the manager routinely putting in 12-hour days, it sends a signal to the staff that needs to be understood. How does your staff "see" you? Are you seen as:

- dedicated for working long hours?
- inefficient and having to work late to make up for this inefficiency?
- untrusting of the staff to do their job?

Are you sending a signal that if they become managers, they will have to forgo their personal lives altogether, which will no doubt discourage some of them from following in your footsteps?

One final thought on this subject. There's a culture that exists in a few organizations (including some parts of the military) that urges staff members to arrive as early as the boss and not leave until he or she departs. This is a true morale buster. Often staff members stay late just because the boss is there, even if they have nothing to do or are too burned out to do it. This can foster resentment, plummeting morale, and eventually lower efficiency. Luckily, this culture is not too prevalent, but if it describes your culture and you're the boss, then maybe it's time to go home and see your family!

Motivation

In a Marine Corps Leadership symposium, motivation was simply defined as "the influences that affect our behavior." In his essay "What Leaders Really Do," John Kotter explains that leaders motivate by:

- articulating the organization's vision in a manner that stresses the value of the audience they are addressing.
- involving the members in deciding how to achieve the vision.
- helping employees improve their self-esteem and grow professionally by coaching, feedback and role modeling.
- rewarding success.

We believe that John Kotter's model of what motivates people is accurate and usable. We hope, though, that test managers will remember that different people are motivated by different things. Some people are motivated by something as simple as a pat on the back or an occasional "well done." Other people expect something more tangible such as a pay raise or promotion. Test managers need to understand what motivates their testers in general and, specifically, what motivates each individual staff member. Good leaders use different motivating techniques for different individuals.

■■■■■■■■■■■■■■■■■

Key Point

Good leaders use different motivating techniques for different individuals.

At testing conferences, we often hear discussions about what motivates testers as opposed to developers. Developers seem to be motivated by creating things (i.e., code), while testers are motivated by breaking things (i.e., test). While we agree that some testers are motivated by finding bugs, we don't think they're really motivated by the fact that a bug was found as much as they're motivated by the belief that finding that bug will ultimately lead to a better product (i.e., they helped build a better product).

While we're talking about rewards and motivation, we would like to reward you for taking the time to read this book. Send an e-mail to ColonelRCraig@aol.com and we'll send you a coupon good for 25% off your next bill at Rick's restaurant, *MadDogs and Englishmen*, located in Tampa, Florida. Sorry, plane tickets are not included.

■■■■■■■■■■■■■■■■■
Key Point

Don't forget to e-mail Rick to get a free coupon for 25% off your next bill at his restaurant, MadDogs and Englishmen.

Building Morale

Morale can be defined as "an individual's state of mind," or morale can refer to the collective state of mind of an entire group (e.g., the testing organization). The major factor affecting the morale of an organization is the individual and collective motivation of the group. Test managers need to be aware of the morale of their organization and be on the lookout for signs of poor morale, which can rob an organization of its effectiveness. Signs of declining morale include:

■■■■■■■■■■■■■■■■■
Key Point

Morale can be defined as "an individual's state of mind" or refer to the collective state of mind of an entire group (e.g., the testing organization).

- Disputes between workers.
- Absenteeism (especially on Friday afternoon and Monday morning).
- An unusual amount of turnover in staff.
- Requests for transfer.
- Incompletion of work.
- Poor or shoddy work.
- Change in appearance (dress, weight, health).
- Lack of respect for equipment, work spaces, etc.
- Disdain for authority.
- Clock-watching.

Just because some of these signs exist, doesn't necessarily mean that you have a morale problem. But if the trend of one or more of these signs is negative, you may have cause for concern.

Managers who see morale problems should discuss them with their staff, try to determine the causes, and try to find solutions. Sometimes, morale can be affected by a seemingly trivial event that an astute test manager can nip in the bud. For example, we encountered one organization that had a morale problem because a new performance appraisal system was instituted without adequately explaining it to the staff members who were being measured. Another organization had a morale problem because the testers thought that the way bonuses were allocated discounted their efforts when compared to the developers. Promoting frequent and open dialogue between the test manager and his or her staff can go a long way toward maintaining the morale of the group. Or, as the Marines would say, "Keep your Marines informed."

■■■■■■■■■■■■■■■■■
Key Point

Promoting frequent and open dialogue between the test manager and his or her staffs can go a long way toward maintaining the morale of the group.

Selling Testing

An important part of the test manager's job is to sell the importance of testing to the rest of the Information Technology (IT) division, the user community, and management. This is obviously an instance of trying to achieve buy-in from the aforementioned groups and others. The test manager should always be on the lookout for opportunities to demonstrate the value of testing. This might mean speaking up in a meeting, making a presentation, or customizing metrics for the developer, user, or whomever.

■■■■■■■■■■■■■■■■■
Key Point

If a test manager has a mentor, he or she may be able to use the mentor as a sponsor (i.e., a member of management who supports and promotes the work of the test group).

The test manager must focus on the value of testing to the entire organization and show what testing can do for each of the various organizational entities. For example, not only does creating test cases support the testing of future releases, but the test cases themselves can also be used as documentation of the application. When selling testing, many managers fail to emphasize the larger role that testing can play in producing and maintaining quality software.

This job of promoting the value of testing will have an impact on staffing and budget requests, morale of the testing group, the role of the test manager in decision-making groups such as the Change Control Board (CCB), working relationships with other groups such as development, and just the general perception of the testing group to the rest of the organization.

Manager's Role in Test Automation

It's not the job of the test manager to become an expert on testing tools, but he or she does have an important role in their implementation and use. There was a fairly extensive discussion in Chapter 6 on the pitfalls of testing tools and, essentially, it's up to the test manager to avoid those pitfalls. Additionally, the test manager should:

- be knowledgeable on the state of the practice.
- obtain adequate resources.
- ensure that the correct tool is selected.
- ensure that the tool is properly integrated into the test environment.
- provide adequate training, identify and empower a champion.
- measure the return on investment (ROI) of the tool.

Knowledgeable on State of Practice

Each test manager should understand the basic categories of tools and what they can and cannot do. For example, a test manager should know what the capabilities and differences are between a capture-replay tool, a load testing tool, a code coverage tool, etc. This knowledge of tools should include an awareness of the major vendors of tools, the various types of licensing agreements available, and how to conduct tool trials.

Obtain Adequate Resources

Part of the test manager's job is to obtain the funding necessary to procure the tool, implement it, maintain it, and provide training and ongoing support. Remember that the cost of implementing the tool and providing training often exceeds the cost of the tool itself. While a large part of the training costs are typically incurred early on, the manager must budget for ongoing training throughout the life of the tool due to staff turnover and updates in the tool.

Ensure Correct Tool Is Selected

Even if your company has an organization that is assigned the primary job of selecting and implementing testing tools, the test manager must still ensure that the correct tool is chosen for his or her testing group. We know of many test managers who have had very bad experiences with some tools that were "forced upon them" by the resident tool group. A tool that works well for one testing group may not work well for another.

■■■■■■■■■■■■■■■■■
Key Point

Just because a tool works well for one testing organization doesn't mean that it will work well for your organization.

The good news for those of you who don't have a tools group in your company is that you don't have to worry about having the tools gurus force you to use the wrong tool. On the other hand, it's now up to you to do everything:

- Formulate the requirements for the tool.
- Develop the strategy for the tool use.
- Create the implementation, maintenance, and training plans.
- And so forth…

Ensure Proper Integration of Tool

In tool implementation, one of the most important roles of the test manager is to ensure that the tool is properly integrated into the test environment. For the tool to be successfully used, it must support the testing strategy outlined by the testing manager in the organizational charter and in the master test plan(s). This will require the testing manager to determine what's most useful to automate, who should do the automation, and how the automated scripts will be executed and maintained.

Provide Adequate Training

Many tools are difficult to use, especially if the testers who will be using them don't have any experience in programming or have a fear of changing the way they do business. Training should include two things:

1. Teaching testers how to use the tool (literally, which keys to push).
2. Teaching testers how to use the tool to support the testing strategy outlined by the test manager.

■■■■■■■■■■■■■■■■
Key Point

"Training is everything. The peach was once a bitter almond; cauliflower is nothing but cabbage with a college education."

- Mark Twain

The first type of training (mentioned above) will most likely be provided by the vendor of the tool. The second type of training may have to be created and conducted within the testing organization, since it's very specific to the group that's using the tool.

Identify and Empower a Champion

Tool users, especially less experienced ones, can easily get frustrated if there's no one readily available to answer their questions. The tool vendor's customer service can help with routine questions regarding the mechanics of the tool, but many of them are incapable of answering questions relating to how the tool is being used at a particular company or organization. That's where the champion comes in. The test manager should seek an enthusiastic employee who wants to become an expert on the tool, and then provide that employee with advanced training, time to help in the tool implementation, and ultimately the time to help their peers when they encounter difficulty in using the selected tool(s).

Measure the Return on Investment

We've already explained that tools are expensive to purchase and implement. A surprising number of tools that are purchased are never used or are used sporadically or ineffectively. It's up to the test manager to determine if the cost and effort to continue to use the tool (e.g., maintenance, upgrades, training, and the actual use) are worthwhile.

It's very painful to go to management and present a powerful argument to spend money for the procurement of a tool and then later announce that the return on investment of that tool doesn't warrant further use. Unfortunately, some test managers throw good money after bad by continuing to use a tool that has proven to be ineffective.

The Test Manager's Role in Training ■ ■ ■ ■ ■

According to the Fleet Marine Force Manual 1 (FMFM1), commanders should see the development of their subordinates as a direct reflection on themselves. Training has been mentioned repeatedly in this book under various topics (e.g., test planning, implementation of tools, process improvement, etc.). This section deals specifically with the test manager's role in training, common areas of training, and some useful training techniques.

One common theme that appears repeatedly in most leadership and management books is that *the leader is a teacher.* Ultimately a manager or leader is responsible for the training of his or her staff. This is true even in companies that have a training department, formal training curriculum, and annual training requirements. Just because the manager is responsible for the training doesn't mean that he or she must personally conduct formal training, but it does mean that he or she should ensure that all staff members receive adequate training in the required areas, using an appropriate technique.

■■■■■■■■■■■■■■■■■
Key Point

According to the Fleet Marine Force Manual 1 (FMFM1), commanders should see the development of their subordinates as a direct reflection on themselves.

Topics That Require Training

The topics that managers should provide training in include software testing, tools, technical skills, business knowledge, and communication skills.

Testing

Many of us are proud to proclaim that we're professional testers and, certainly, testing is now regarded by some as a "profession." Since this is the case, it only follows that testers, as professionals, should be trained in their chosen career field. There are formal training seminars, conferences on testing and related topics, Web sites, certification programs and books that deal specifically with testing. In fact, a few universities are now providing classes with a strong testing or QA focus. Managers need to provide the time, money, and encouragement for their testers to take advantage of these and other opportunities.

■■■■■■■■■■■■■■■■■
Key Point

"... A good rule of thumb is that software engineering staff should receive at least 1 and as many as 3 weeks of methods training each year."

– Roger Pressman

Tools

In order to be effective, testing tools require testers to obtain special training. Test managers will want to arrange formal training classes with the vendor of the tools they use, as well as informal coaching from the vendor and/or champion. On-site training will need to be conducted to show your team how the tool is supposed to be used to support the organization's testing strategy.

Technical Skills

Testers that possess certain skills, such as programming, are often more effective testers because they better understand *how* a system works rather than just *if* it works. Some testers have also told us that they have more confidence speaking to developers and other technical people if they understand exactly what the developers do. Other testers have also told us that even though they never had to use their programming skills, just having those skills seemed to give them more credibility when talking with developers. Programming skills can also help testers understand how to automate test scripts.

■■■■■■■■■■■■■■■■■
Key Point

Some types of applications (e.g., Web) require testers to have some technical knowledge just to be able to properly do functional testing.

Business Knowledge

A common complaint that we hear about testers (usually from the business experts) is that they don't really understand the business aspects of the software that they're testing. In particular, doing risk analysis, creating inventories and employing preventive testing techniques require testers to understand the underlying business needs that the application is supporting. To alleviate this problem, test managers should arrange to have their staffs trained in the business functions. A test manager at an insurance company that we often visit, for example, encouraged his staff members to study insurance adjusting and underwriting. Other test managers arrange to have their staff visit customers at their site, work the customer support desk for a day or two, or attend a college course related to their company's industry.

Communication Skills

Testers have to communicate with people (e.g., developers, QA, users, managers, etc.) who have a wide range of backgrounds and viewpoints in both verbal and written forms. Providing training in speaking and writing skills can help facilitate the interaction of the testing staff with each other, and with people throughout the rest of the company and even other companies. One good way to improve the communication skills of the testers (and test manager) is to urge them to submit papers and participate as speakers at a conference. Nothing improves communication skills better than practice.

Methods of Training

Test managers have several options available to them in choosing a method for training their staff members: mentoring, on-site commercial training, training in a public forum, in-house training, and specialty training.

Mentoring

Mentoring is a powerful technique for training staff members, especially newer ones. It's a process where a less experienced person (e.g., a new-hire in a discipline such as testing) works with a more experienced staff member. The mentor's job is to help train and promote the career of his or her understudy. Mentoring includes teaching understudies about the politics of the organizations, rules, etc., as well as teaching them about the methods, tools, and processes in place within the organization. Assigning a mentor to a new hire also sends a clear message to the new employee, "You're important to us." There are few things worse than reporting to a new organization or company and sitting around for days or weeks without anything productive to do.

In some companies, mentors are assigned. In this case, mentors have to be trained in how to be mentors and what they have to teach their understudies. Some people seem to be naturally good mentors, while others are less effective. No one should be forced to be a mentor if they don't want to be one. If they're assigned against their wishes, unwilling mentors will almost always be ineffective in their roles because they impart a negative attitude to their understudies.

Some people voluntarily (and without any organizational support) seek out understudies to mentor. Similarly, some employees will seek out a person to be their mentor. Both of these scenarios are signs of motivated employees and normally exist in organizations with high morale.

On-Site Commercial Training

It's possible to contract with an individual or another company to bring training into your organization. This training can be particularly valuable because it allows the employees of a test group to train as a team. Sometimes, the training can even be customized to meet the unique needs of the group being trained. Even if the training materials are not customized in advance, a good commercial trainer should be able to customize the training/presentation to a certain degree based on the interaction of the participants.

Key Point

Understudies are not the only ones who benefit from mentoring programs. People who volunteer or are chosen to be mentors also benefit by gaining recognition as experts in their field and the opportunity to hone their communication and interpersonal skills.

Key Point

Even if the training materials are not customized in advance, a good commercial trainer should be able to customize the training/presentation to a certain degree based on the interaction of the participants.

One common problem with on-site training is that participants are often "pulled out" of the class to handle emergencies (and sometimes just to handle routine work). The loss of continuity greatly degrades the value of the training for the person who is called out of class, and also reduces the effectiveness of the training for the other participants by disrupting the flow of the presentation. One way to overcome this problem is to conduct "on-site" training at a local hotel conference room or some other venue removed from the workplace.

Training in a Public Forum

In some cases, it's a good idea to send one or more of your staff members to a public training class. This is especially useful if your group is too small to warrant bringing in a professional instructor to teach your entire team, or if you have a special skill that only one or two staff members need (e.g., the champion of a testing tool). The downside of public training classes is that the instructor has little opportunity to customize the material for any one student, because the audience is composed of people from many different backgrounds and companies. On the positive side, public forum training classes allow your staff to interact with and learn from people from other companies. Some employees will also feel that their selection to attend a public training class is a reward for a job well done, or recognition of the value of the employee.

■■■■■■■■■■■■■■■■
Key Point

Some employees will feel that their selection to attend a public training class is a reward for a job well done, or recognition of the value of the employee.

In-House Training

Sometimes, due to budget constraints, the uniqueness of the environment, or the small size of an organization, it may be necessary to conduct in-house training. The obvious drawback here is that it can be expensive to create training materials and to train the trainer. Another drawback is that an in-house trainer may not be as skilled a presenter as a professional trainer.

Remember that the biggest cost of training is usually the time your staff spends in class, not the cost of the professional trainer. So, having your staff sit through an ineffective presentation may cost more in the long run than hiring a professional trainer. Also, just like on-site commercial training, in-house training is subject to disruptions caused by participants leaving to handle emergencies in the workplace.

On the positive side, having one of your team members create and present the training class can be a great learning experience and motivator for the person doing the presentation.

Test managers from larger companies may have an entire training department dedicated to IT or even software testing. In that case, your in-house training will bear more resemblance to commercial training that happens to be performed in-house, than it does to typical in-house training.

■■■■■■■■■■■■■■■■
Key Point

Remember that the biggest cost of training is usually the time your staff spends in class, not the cost of the professional trainer. So, having your staff sit through an ineffective presentation may cost more in the long run than hiring a professional trainer.

Specialty Training

There are many types of specialty training programs available today: Web-enabled training, virtual training conferences, and distance learning are just a few. While all of these are valuable training techniques, they seldom replace face-to-face training.

Is Distance Learning a Viable Solution?

To: Mr. James Fallows
   The Industry Standard
September 20, 2000

Dear James,

I always read your column with interest, and the one on September 18 really grabbed my attention. I travel every week to a different city, state, or country to

■■■■■■■■■■■■■■■■
Case Study 10-2

Will distance learning ever truly replace face-to-face learning in a classroom setting?

give seminars on software testing. You would think that being a consultant and trainer in a technical area would encourage me to buy in to some of the new "distance learning" techniques, but so far I am unimpressed. And believe me when I say that I'm tired of traveling and want to be convinced that there is a better way of communicating than having me board a plane every week.

Over the years, I have seen several stages of evolution that were going to replace face-to-face meetings and training. First we had programmed learning in the old "green screen" days. This was useful for rote learning but didn't encourage much creative thought. Next my talks were videotaped. Most of my students think I'm a fairly dynamic speaker, but occasionally they doze when I'm there in person interacting with them – you can imagine how effective a two-dimensional CRT is. So video didn't work – at least not very well. We tried the live video feed with interactive chat rooms. That was only marginally more successful. Recently, I was asked to speak at a virtual computer conference. I can't even imagine how that would succeed...

Still, I'm not totally a Neanderthal. I have participated in many successful video-teleconferences. These seem to work best with people who are comfortable on the phone and in front of a camera. A well-defined agenda is a must, and the meetings have to be short. My biggest complaint about all forms of "interactive" distance communications is the tendency for many of the participants (okay, I'm talking about me) to lose their train of thought without the visual and emotional stimulation of a human being in close proximity.

I do have high hopes for distance education as opposed to training. By this I mean where assignments, projects, and research are inter-dispersed among short recorded or interactive lectures, which ultimately leads to a broad understanding of a topic or even a degree. For a traveler like me, this is an ideal way to continue to learn without having to be physically present. I could, for example, continue my education while in my hotel room in Belfast or Copenhagen or wherever. The idea is to use short periods of time at the convenience of the student. Training, on the other hand, often requires a fairly intensive infusion of information on a specific topic geared particularly to the audience at hand. To me, this needs to be highly interactive and face-to-face.

Even in the area of sales, I have found no substitute for face-to-face meetings. We have a reasonable record of closing training/consulting deals using the Internet, mail, etc. but have an almost perfect record when we have actually gone to visit the client in person. Is it the medium? Is it training in how to use the technology? Is it that by actually arriving on the client's doorstep, we show that we're serious? I don't really know. But for the moment, I'm going to rack up some serious frequent-flier miles. I personally believe there will never come a time when advanced technology replaces face-to-face human interaction.

– Rick Craig
Published in the Industry Standard, *September 2000.*

Metrics Primer for Test Managers ■ ■ ■ ■ ■

It's very difficult for a test manager do his or her job well without timely, accurate metrics to help estimate schedules, track progress, make decisions, and improve processes. The test manager is in a very powerful position, because testing is itself a measurement activity that results in the collection of metrics relating to the quality of the software developed (usually by a different group). These metrics, though, can be a double-edged sword for the manager. It's relatively easy to create dissatisfaction or organizational dysfunction, make decisions based on incorrect metrics, and cause your staff to be very, very unhappy if metrics are not used judiciously.

Software Measurements and Metrics

Many people (including us) do not normally differentiate between the terms *software measurement* and *software metrics*. In his book *Making Software Measurement Work*, Bill Hetzel has defined each of these terms as well as the terms *software meter* and *meta-measure*. While we don't think it's imperative that you add these terms to your everyday vocabulary, it is instructive to understand how each of the terms describes a different aspect of software measurement.

Software Measure   A quantified observation about any aspect of software – product, process or project (e.g., raw data, lines of code).

Software Metric   A measurement used to compare two or more products, processes, or projects (e.g., defect density [defects per line of code]).

Software Meter   A metric that acts as a trigger or threshold. That is, if a certain threshold is met, then some action will be warranted as a result (e.g., exit criteria, suspension criteria).

Meta-Measure   A measure of a measure. Usually used to determine the return on investment (ROI) of a metric. Example: In software inspections, a measure is usually made of the number of defects found per inspection hour. This is a measure of the effectiveness of another measurement activity (an inspection is a measurement activity). Test effectiveness is another example, since the test effectiveness is a measure of the testing, which is itself a measurement activity.

Benefits of Using Metrics

Metrics can help test managers identify risky areas that may require more testing, training needs, and process improvement opportunities. Furthermore, metrics can also help test managers control and track project status by providing a basis for estimating how long the testing will take.

Lord Kelvin has a famous quote that addresses using measures for control:

> *"When you can measure what you are speaking about and express it in numbers, you know something about it; but when you cannot measure, when you cannot express it in numbers, your knowledge is of a meager and unsatisfactory kind: it may be the beginning of knowledge, but you have scarcely, in your thoughts, advanced to the stage of science."*

It seems that about half of the speakers at software metrics conferences use the preceding quote at some point in their talk. Indeed, this quote is so insightful and appropriate to our topic that we too decided to jump on the bandwagon and include it in this book.

Identify Risky Areas That Require More Testing

This is what we called the *Pareto Analysis* in Chapter 7. Our experience (and no doubt yours as well) has shown that areas of a system that have been the source of many defects in the past will very likely be a good place to look for defects now (and in the future). So, by collecting and analyzing the defect density by module, the tester can identify potentially risky areas that warrant additional testing. Similarly, using a tool to analyze the complexity of the code can help identify potentially risky areas of the system that require a greater testing focus.

■■■■■■■■■■■■■■■■
Key Point

By collecting and analyzing defect density by module, the tester can identify potentially risky areas that warrant additional testing.

Identify Training Needs

In particular, metrics that measure information about the type and distribution of defects in the software, testware, or process can identify training needs. For example, if a certain type of defect, say a memory leak, is encountered on a regular basis, it may indicate that training is required on how to prevent the creation of this type of bug. Or, if a large number of "testing" defects are discovered (e.g., incorrectly constructed test cases), it may indicate a need to provide training in test case design.

Identify Process Improvement Opportunities

The same kind of analysis described above can be used to locate opportunities for process improvement. In all of the examples in the section above, rather than providing training, maybe the process can be improved or simplified, or maybe a combination of the two can be used. Another example would be that if the test manager found that a large number of the defects discovered were requirements defects, the manager might conclude that the organization needed to implement requirements reviews or preventive testing techniques.

Provide Control/Track Status

Test managers (and testers, developers, development managers, and others) need to use metrics to control the testing effort and track progress. For example, most test managers use some kind of measurement of the number, severity, and distribution of defects, and number of test cases executed, as a way of marking the progress of test execution.

■■■■■■■■■■■■■■■
Key Point

You can't control what you can't measure.

– Tom DeMarco

Provide a Basis for Estimating

Without some kind of metrics, managers and practitioners are helpless when it comes to estimation. Estimates of how long the testing will take, how many defects are to be expected, the number of testers needed, and other variables have to be based upon previous experiences. These previous experiences are "metrics," whether they're formally recorded or just lodged in the head of a software engineer.

Justify Budget, Tools, or Training

Test managers often feel that they're understaffed and need more people, or they "know" that they need a larger budget or more training. However, without metrics to support their "feeling," their requests will often fall on deaf ears. Test managers need to develop metrics to justify their budgets and training requests.

Provide Meters to "Flag" Actions

One sign of a mature use of metrics is the use of meters or flags that signal that an action must be taken. Examples include exit criteria, smoke tests, and suspension criteria. We consider these to be mature metrics because for meters to be effective, they must be planned in advance and based upon some criteria established earlier in the project or on a previous project. Of course, there are exceptions. Some organizations ship the product on a specified day, no matter what the consequences. This is also an example of a meter because the product is shipped when the date is reached.

Rules of Thumb for Using Metrics

Ask the Staff

Ask the staff (developers and testers) what metrics would help them to do their jobs better. If the staff don't believe in the metrics or believe that management is cramming another worthless metric down their throats, they'll "rebel" by not collecting the metric, or by falsifying the metric by putting down "any old number." Bill Hetzel and Bill Silver have outlined an entire metrics paradigm known as *the practitioner paradigm*, which focuses on the observation that for metrics to be effective, the practitioners (i.e., developers and testers) must be involved in deciding what metrics will be used and how they will be collected. For more information on this topic, refer to Bill Hetzel's book *Making Software Measurement Work*.

■■■■■■■■■■■■■■■■■
Key Point

Taxation without representation is tyranny and so is forcing people to use metrics without proper explanation and implementation.

Use a Metric to Validate the Metric

Rarely do we have enough confidence in any one metric that we would want to make major decisions based upon that single metric. In almost every instance, managers would be well advised to try to validate a metric with another metric. For example, in Chapter 7 where we discussed test effectiveness, we recommended that this key measure be accomplished by using more than one metric (e.g., a measure of coverage and Defect Removal Efficiency [DRE], or another metric such as defect age). Similarly, we would not want to recommend the release of a product based on a single measurement. We would rather base this decision on information about defects encountered and remaining, the coverage and results of test cases, and so forth.

Normalize the Values of the Metric

Since every project, system, release, person, etc. is unique, all metrics will need to be normalized. It's desirable to reduce the amount of normalization required by comparing similar objects rather than dissimilar objects (e.g., it's better to compare two projects that are similar in size, scope, complexity, etc. to each other than to compare two dissimilar projects and have to attempt to quantify [or normalize] the impact of the differences).

As a rule of thumb, the further the metric is from the truth (i.e., the oracle to which it's being compared), the less reliable the metric becomes. For example, if you don't have a reservoir of data, you could compare your project to industry data. This may be better than nothing, but you would have to try to account for differences in the company cultures, methodologies, etc. in addition to the differences in the projects. A better choice would be to compare a project to another project within the same company. Even better would be to compare your project to a previous release of the same project.

■■■■■■■■■■■■■■■■
Key Point

As a rule of thumb, the further the metric is from the truth (i.e., the oracle to which it's being compared), the less reliable the metric becomes.

Measure the Value of Collecting the Metric

It can take a significant amount of time and effort to collect and analyze metrics. Test managers are urged to try to gauge the value of each metric collected versus the effort required to collect and analyze the data. Software inspections are a perfect example. A normal part of the inspection process is to measure the number of defects found per inspector hour. We have to be a little careful with this data, though, because a successful inspection program should help reduce the number of defects found on future efforts, since the trends and patterns of the defects are rolled into a process improvement process (i.e., the

■■■■■■■■■■■■■■■■
Key Point

"Each measurement must have a linkage to need."

– Howard Rubin

number of defects per inspector hour should go down). A more obvious example is the collection of data that no one is using. There might be a field on the incident report, for example, that must be completed by the author of a report that no one is using.

Periodically Revalidate the Need for Each Metric

Even though good test managers may routinely weigh the value of collecting a metric, some of these same test managers may be a little lax in re-evaluating their metrics to see if there's a continuing need for them. Metrics that are useful for one project, for example, may not be as valuable for another (e.g., the amount of time spent writing test cases may be useful for systematic testing approaches, but has no meaning if exploratory testing techniques are used). A metric that's quite useful at one point of time may eventually outlive its usefulness. For example, one of our clients used to keep manual phone logs to record the time spent talking to developers, customers, etc. A new automated phone log was implemented that did this logging automatically, but the manual log was still used for several months before someone finally said, "Enough is enough."

■■■■■■■■■■■■■■
Key Point

"Not everything that counts can be counted, and not everything that can be counted counts."

– Albert Einstein

Make Collecting and Analyzing the Metric Easy

Ideally, metrics would be collected automatically. The phone log explained in the previous paragraph is a good example of automatically collecting metrics. Another example is counting the number of lines of code, which is done automatically for many of you by your compiler. Collecting metrics as a by-product of some other activity or data collection activity is almost as good as collecting them automatically. For example, defect information must be collected in order to isolate and correct defects, but this same information can be used to provide

■■■■■■■■■■■■■■
Key Point

Collecting metrics as a by-product of some other activity or data collection activity is almost as good as collecting them automatically.

testing status, identify training and process improvement needs, and identify risky areas of the system that require additional testing.

Finally, some metrics will have to be collected manually. For example, test managers may ask their testers to record the amount of time they spend doing various activities such as test planning. For most of us, this is a manual effort.

Respect Confidentiality of Data

It's important that test managers be aware that certain data may be sensitive to other groups or individuals, and act accordingly. Test managers could benefit by understanding which programmers have a tendency to create more defects or defects of a certain type. While this information may be useful, the potential to alienate the developers should cause test managers to carefully weigh the benefit of collecting this information. Other metrics can be organizationally sensitive. For example, in some classified systems (e.g., government) information about defects can itself be deemed classified.

Look for Alternate Interpretations

There's often more than one way to interpret the same data. If, for example, you decide to collect information (against our recommendation) on the distribution of defects by programmers, you could easily assume that the programmers with the most defects are lousy programmers. Upon further analysis, though, you may determine that they just write a lot more code, are always given the hardest programs, or have received particularly poor specifications.

■■■■■■■■■■■■■■■■■
Key Point

We highly recommend that anyone interested in metrics read the humorous book *How to Lie with Statistics* by Darrell Huff.

Consider the defect discovery rate shown in Figure 10-4. Upon examining this graph, many people would be led to believe that the steady downward trend in the graph would indicate that the quality of the software must be improving, and many would even go so far as to say that we must be approaching the time to ship the product. Indeed, this analysis could be true. But are there other interpretations? Maybe some of the testers have been pulled away to work on a project with a higher priority. Or maybe we're running out of valid test cases to run. This is another example of where having more than one metric to measure the same thing is useful.

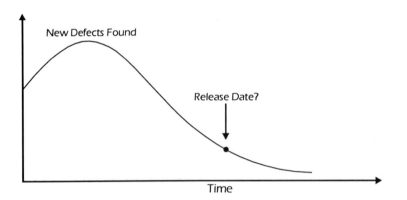

■■■■■■■■■■■■■■■■

Figure 10-4

Declining Defect
Discovery Rate

Present the Raw Data

Presenting the raw data is really a continuation of looking for alternative ways to interpret the data. We've found it very useful to present the raw data that we collected, in addition to the processed or interpreted data. As a matter of style, we often ask our audience (whoever we're presenting the data to) to tell us what the raw data means to them. Sometimes, their interpretation is something that we haven't thought of. At the very least, though, the raw data makes the audience reflect on the results and gives the test manager some insight into how their audience is thinking. This insight is very useful if you're trying

■■■■■■■■■■■■■■■■

Key Point

There are three kinds of lies: lies, damned lies, and statistics.

– Benjamin Disraeli

to use the data to achieve buy-in for some aspect of the product or process.

Format the Data for the Audience

No doubt, the test manager will have occasion to brief developers, users, upper management, marketing, and many other interested parties. When presenting the data, it's important for the manager to consider the background of the audience and their needs. For example, if you're presenting data that shows testing progress, the data might be presented to the users in a different format than it would to the developers. The users may want to know how much of the functionality has passed the test, while developers might want to see the data presented with respect to the amount of code that was tested.

Beware of the Hawthorne Effect

The test manager has at his or her disposal a powerful weapon – metrics – for good or evil due to a phenomenon called the Hawthorne Effect.

Does Lighting Affect Productivity?

Between 1924 and 1927, Harvard professor Elton Mayo conducted a series of experiments at the Western Electric Company in Chicago. Professor Mayo's original study was to determine the effect of lighting on the productivity of workers. The work was expanded from 1927 through 1932 to include other topics such as rest breaks, hours worked, etc. Before each change was made, the impact of the change on the workers and their work was discussed with them. It seemed that no matter what change was implemented, the productivity of the workers continuously improved. Mayo eventually concluded that the mere process of observing (and therefore showing concern) about the workers spurred them on to greater productivity. We have encountered many definitions of the

■■■■■■■■■■■■■■■
Case Study 10-3

Showing people that you care about them spurs them on to greater productivity.

so-called Hawthorne Effect, but most of them sound something like this: Showing people that you care about them spurs them on to greater productivity.

Now I'm not a professor at Harvard and I have not conducted any formal experiments on productivity, but I have observed a more far-reaching phenomenon – basically, observing (measuring) people changes their behavior. The Hawthorne study shows that people are more productive when someone observes them (and sends the message that "what you're doing is important"). I have found that observing or measuring some activity changes the behavior of the people conducting that activity — but the change is not always for the better. It depends on what you're measuring. For example, if you spread the word in your company that "defects are bad; we're finding way too many defects," the number of defects reported would surely drop. People would try to find another way to solve the problem without recording a defect. Notice that the number of defects didn't really go down, just the number reported.

In particular, for those of you who specify individual objectives or goals for your staff, you'll probably discover that your staff will focus on achieving those objectives over other tasks. If you were to tell the developers that the most important goal is to get the coding done on time, they would maximize their efforts to meet the deadline, and this may be done without regard to quality (since quality was not stressed).

So you see, any time you measure some aspect of a person or their work, the mere process of collecting this metric can change the person's behavior and therefore ultimately change the metric measuring their behavior.

So, let's define the Hawthorne Effect for Software Engineers as "The process of measuring human activities can itself change the result of the measurement." Okay, maybe we're not ready for Harvard, but this observation is often true and needs to be considered by test managers every time they implement a new metric.

– Rick Craig

■■■■■■■■■■■■■■■■■

Key Point

Hawthorne Effect for Software Engineers:

The process of measuring human activities can itself change the result of the measurement.

Provide Adequate Training

To many software engineers, metrics are mysterious and even threatening. It's important that everyone affected by a metric (i.e., those who collect them, those whose work is being measured, and those who make decisions based upon them) receive training. The training should include why the metric is being collected, how it will be used, the frequency of collection, who will see and use it, and how to change the parameters of the metric. One good training aid is a metrics worksheet such as described below.

Create a Metrics Worksheet

The metrics worksheet shown in Table 10-2 takes much of the mystery out of each metric and, therefore, is a useful tool to assist in training and buy-in for metrics. It also helps gain consistency in the collection and analysis of metrics, and provides a vehicle to periodically review each metric to see if it's still necessary and accurately measures what it was designed to measure.

Table 10-2 Metrics Worksheet

Item	Description
Handle	Shorthand name for the metric (e.g., number of defects or lines of code could be called the quality metric).
Description	Brief description of what is being measured and why.
Observation	How do we obtain the measurement?
Frequency	How often does the metric need to be collected or updated?
Scale	What units of measurement are used (e.g., lines of code, test cases, hours, days, etc.)?
Range	What range of values is possible?
Past	What values have we seen in the past? This gives us a sense of perspective.
Current	What is the current or last result?
Expected	Do we anticipate any changes? If so, why?
Meters	Are there any actions to expect as a result of hitting a threshold?

NOTE: Adapted from a course called *Test Measurement*, created by Bill Hetzel.

What Metrics Should You Collect?

We're often asked, "What metrics should I collect?" Of course, the correct answer is, "It depends." Every development and testing organization has different needs. The Software Engineering Institute (SEI) has identified four core metrics areas:

- Schedule
- Quality
- Resources
- Size

The Air Force has a similar list, but they've added another metric, "Rework," to the SEI's list. Even though it's impossible for us to say exactly what metrics are needed in your organization, we believe that you'll need at least one metric for each of the four areas outlined above. The Air Force metrics

■■■■■■■■■■■■■■■■■

Key Point

In *Software Metrics: Establishing a Company-Wide Program*, Robert Grady and Deborah Caswell define rework as "*all efforts over and above those required to produce a defect-free product correctly the first time.*"

shown in Table 10-3, for example, were designed more for a development or project manager, but with a few changes they're equally applicable to a testing effort. These metrics are only examples. You could come up with many other valid examples for each of the five metrics outlined in the table.

Table 10-3 Example Metrics

Metric	Development Example	Test Example
Size	Number of modules or lines of code.	Number of modules, lines of code, or test cases.
Schedule	Number of modules completed versus the timeline.	Number of test cases written or executed versus the timeline.
Resources	Dollars spent, hours worked.	Dollars spent, hours worked.
Quality	Number of defects per line of code.	Defect Removal Efficiency (DRE), coverage.
Rework	Lines of code written to fix bugs.	Number of test cycles to test bug fixes.

Metrics Used by the "Best" Projects

It's interesting to look at the metrics actually employed at various companies. Bill Hetzel and Rick Craig conducted a study in the early 1990s to determine what metrics were being collected and used by the "best" projects in the "best" companies. Part of the summary results included a list of those metrics seldom used by the "best" projects and those metrics used by all or most of the best projects involved in the study.

The projects chosen for this study were based on the following criteria:
- Perceived as using better practices and measures.
- Perceived as producing high-quality results.
- Implemented recently or in the final test, with the project team accessible for interview.

Key Point

"Although measurement continues to demand increasing attention, measurement initiatives continue to exhibit a high failure rate, and the value of the measurement goes unrealized."

– David Pitts

- Had to have one of the highest scores on a survey of practices and measures.

Were these truly the very best projects? Maybe not. Were they truly superior to the average project available at that time and therefore representative of the best projects available? Probably.

The data in Table 10-4 is based upon the results of a comprehensive survey (more comprehensive than the one used to select the participants of the study), interviews with project participants, and a review of project documentation. The data from the survey is now a decade old. And, even though we have no supporting proof, we believe that the viability of the data has probably not changed remarkably since 1991.

Table 10-4 Metrics Used by the "Best" Projects

Common Metrics	Uncommon Metrics
• Test Defects	• Code Coverage
• Defects After Release	• Complexity
• Open Problems	• Cost of Rework
• Open Issues	• Cost of Quality
• Schedule Performance	
• Plan and Schedule Changes	
• Test Results	
• Reliability	
• Time Spent Fixing Problems	
• Defects From Fixes	
• Lines of Code	
• Process Compliance	

We don't offer any analysis of this list and don't necessarily recommend that you base your metric collection on these lists. They are merely provided so you can see what some other quality companies have done.

Measurement Engineering Vision

For those readers who have studied engineering, you know that metrics are an everyday part of being an engineer and *measurement is a way of life*. In fact, some of the distinguishing characteristics of being an engineering discipline are that there is a repeatable and measurable process in place that leads to a predictable result. For those of us who call ourselves software engineers, we can see that we don't always meet the criteria specified above. We're confident, though, that as a discipline, we're making progress. This book has outlined many repeatable processes (e.g., test planning, risk analysis, etc.), but to continue our evolution toward a true engineering discipline, we have to reach the point where metrics are an integral part of how we do business – not just an afterthought.

■■■■■■■■■■■■■■■■■
Key Point

The distinguishing characteristics of being an engineering discipline are that there is a repeatable and measurable process in place that leads to a predictable result.

This vision includes:
- Building good measurements into our processes, tools and technology.
- Requiring good measurements before taking action.
- Expecting good measurements.
- Insisting on good measurement of the measurement.

Chapter 11 –
Improving the Testing Process

"The minute you're through changing, you're through."

— Jack Tramiel

"There is nothing more difficult to take in hand, more perilous to conduct, or more uncertain in its success, than to take the lead in the introduction of a new order of things."

— Niccolo Machiavelli

Getting a software testing process on paper is a challenge, but getting the people in the organization to commit to making the required changes is an even bigger challenge. People commit to change for their own reasons, not for someone else's reasons. Therefore, when people are asked to commit to change, their first concern is often "What do I have to gain or lose?" Successful software implementation is predominantly a people management exercise and not an engineering management exercise. Most of us do what we do (whether it's testing software or driving a car) because we feel most comfortable doing things our way. So, it shouldn't be a surprise that persuading people in the software world to do things someone else's way (e.g., the organization's way) can be a daunting challenge full or surprises. The key to success is to make the organization's way "their" way.

Improving the Testing Process   ■ ■ ■ ■ ■

The problem that many organizations face is how to identify the areas that could be improved and how to implement the changes (successfully). Figure 11-1 outlines the steps that we typically follow when suggesting and implementing process improvement for our clients.

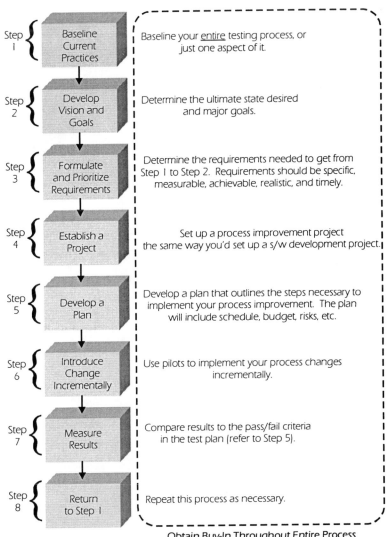

■■■■■■■■■■■■■■■

Figure 11-1

Process Improvement
Steps

_____

Step 1	Baseline Current Practices	Baseline your <u>entire</u> testing process, or just one aspect of it.
Step 2	Develop Vision and Goals	Determine the ultimate state desired and major goals.
Step 3	Formulate and Prioritize Requirements	Determine the requirements needed to get from Step 1 to Step 2. Requirements should be specific, measurable, achievable, realistic, and timely.
Step 4	Establish a Project	Set up a process improvement project the same way you'd set up a s/w development project.
Step 5	Develop a Plan	Develop a plan that outlines the steps necessary to implement your process improvement. The plan will include schedule, budget, risks, etc.
Step 6	Introduce Change Incrementally	Use pilots to implement your process changes incrementally.
Step 7	Measure Results	Compare results to the pass/fail criteria in the test plan (refer to Step 5).
Step 8	Return to Step 1	Repeat this process as necessary.

Obtain Buy-In Throughout Entire Process
Metrics, feedback loops, training, and sponsors can
help you obtain buy-in for your changes.

Step 1
Baseline Current Practices

The first step in improving the testing process is to baseline the current practices. This will give you a point of comparison to measure the success of your process improvements. It's possible to baseline the entire software development process (including test), the entire testing process, or a subset of the testing process (e.g., defect tracking, test planning, etc.). We believe that it's generally beneficial for most testing organizations to baseline their entire testing process, rather than just one aspect of it.

If your organization is undergoing a formal assessment using ISO Standards or the CMM (Capability Maturity Model), your testing group may be able to piggyback onto these efforts. For a quick baseline of your current testing practices, you can have a questionnaire (refer to Appendix B for a sample) completed by a knowledgeable person or group of people in the testing organization. A word of caution, however, is needed here. *The results you get in completing the questionnaire will depend on who fills it out, as you'll learn in Case Study 11-1.* The results will be much more accurate if the form is filled out by a cross-section of the entire testing group and others who work alongside testers, such as developers, configuration managers, business representatives, and others.

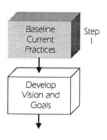

■■■■■■■■■■■■■■■■■

Key Point

A *baseline* is a measurement of where your processes are at any given point in time (i.e., a line in the sand). Baselines are used to compare the processes of one group at a given time to the same group at another point in time.

■■■■■■■■■■■■■■■■■

Key Point

A *benchmark* is a measurement of where your processes are compared directly to other companies or to a static model (e.g., CMM). It's possible that the results of a process assessment might be both a baseline and a benchmark.

Benchmark Study of Best Practices

■■■■■■■■■■■■■■■■■

Case Study 11-1

The results of a benchmark study depend on whom you ask.

In the early 1990s, Bill Hetzel and I undertook a project to develop a benchmark of best practices in use at leading companies. One of the surprises that I received was the disparity in answers on the level of use of any given process from individual to individual. The graph below shows a percentile plot of processes used from one of the companies in the study.

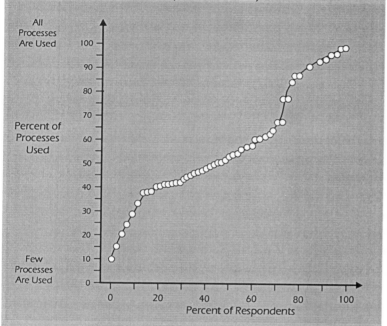

Each dot on the graph represents a person. You can see that there are people at the bottom of the graph who profess to use very little in the way of formal process and there are people at the top who claim to do almost everything. Obviously, if you're trying to benchmark your processes using a single person (or a small number of people), the results will very much depend on whom you ask. By the way, each questionnaire in the study was confidential, but after interviewing many of the respondents I'm pretty sure that the people at the top were often managers.

— Rick Craig

Step 2
Develop Vision and Goals

It's been said that if you don't know where you're going, any road will get you there. The complement to the baseline is a vision of where you want to be or what you want to become sometime in the future. Just as in completing an estimate, it's difficult to know exactly what your testing processes should look like at some point in the future, and it's equally difficult to estimate the return on investment (ROI) of moving from the current state to the desired state. So, be prepared to update your vision as you go.

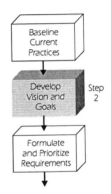

One way to determine the desired end state is to model your vision after a testing organization that you admire. Of course it's important to remember that every organization has its own unique set of priorities, risks, politics, skill sets, etc., which may require a modification of their model to match your environment. Alternatively, a vision statement can be created based upon achieving a desired level of maturity (i.e., controlled, efficient, optimizing) on a Test Process Improvement (TPI) assessment (refer to Table 11-2). Whatever method you choose to use, the vision statement of the testing organization must support the vision of the corporation that it supports, and the statement itself will typically be supported by a series of high-level goals.

Vision Statement and Goals of the System Test Group for ABC Software Company

Vision Statement:
The system testing strategy of the ABC Software Company will employ state-of-the-practice testing techniques and tools in order to effectively and efficiently measure the quality of all systems of the company.

■■■■■■■■■■■■■■■■■

Case Study 11-2

Sample Vision Statement and Goals

Goals #1:

A regression test bed will be established and maintained that covers all requirements and design attributes.

Goals #2:

The testing organization will achieve a DRE of 80% or greater, and there cannot be any Class 3 (critical) escapes.

Goals #3:

An entire test cycle can be performed in 1 week or less.

Goals #4:

The TPI process maturity level for the system test group will be "efficient" or better (refer to Table 11-1).

■■■■■■■■■■■■■■■■■
Key Point

An *escape* is a defect that is not discovered by the current evaluation activity and is pushed on to the next phase.

The point of a vision statement and its supporting goals is to keep everyone focused on the same target. Instead of creating a vague and useless vision statement about leveraging synergies and creating a world-class organization, you should focus on concrete goals and formulate a statement that everyone understands and is willing to uphold.

Step 3
Formulate/Prioritize Requirements

The baseline establishes where the testing organization is today, and the vision describes the desired end state. The actual requirements to get from point 'A' to point 'B' should be developed next. The requirements should follow all of the basic rules of software requirements. They need to be specific, measurable, achievable, realistic, and timely. The requirements must also support the goals and vision of the organization.

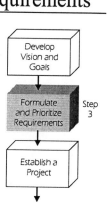

Step 4
Establish a Project

Many process improvement efforts fail due to under-commitment of resources. We frequently encounter a tester or test manager at a training class who has been told to "implement test automation, establish metrics, create a methodology, and implement software metrics in your 'spare' time." Those of you who have tried to implement process changes into your organization in the past know that the scenario described above is largely *wishful thinking*.

We feel that one way to give a process improvement effort the focus that it needs is to establish a project for the process improvement. This means that a project team needs to be established, a budget formulated, people assigned, and a project plan created. If you're part of a smaller organization, it seems unlikely that you could form an entire team, so the project team will probably be only one or two people or perhaps one person part-time. If this is the case, it's important that this one part-time person actually have some of his or her time allocated specifically to the process improvement project.

The team member(s) should ideally be enthusiastic volunteers. (Pointing at someone and saying, "Hey you, you're the project leader" is not a way to get enthusiastic volunteers – with the possible exception of the military.) If there are no enthusiastic volunteers, the project may be in jeopardy from the very beginning. Why are there no volunteers? Was the process change being forced from the top? Do the developers and testers think the change is bad? Or, is this just another "great idea" that will pass? If this is happening, then there's a selling job that must be accomplished before moving on.

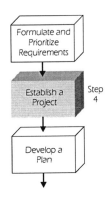

■■■■■■■■■■■■■■■■
Key Point

One way to give a process improvement effort the focus that it needs is to establish a project for the process improvement..

It's not enough that the volunteers be enthusiastic, though. Volunteers must also have technical competency and the respect of their peers. Choosing the person who has the most time on his or her hands is not a good approach. Ironically, the person that is always the busiest is often the person that you need. There must be a reason why they're always busy.

Step 5
Develop a Plan

If you've never written a project plan, we recommend that you use the template for a test plan as a starting point. Everything in this template may not be applicable (e.g., test items), but generally it will work. Figure 11-2 shows what the test plan template might look like if modified for a process improvement project.

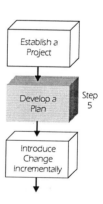

Figure 11-2

Test Plan Template Modified for Process Improvement

Template for Process Improvement

Contents

1. Test Plan Identifier

2. Introduction

    2.1 Genesis of Process Improvement Initiative

    2.2 Scope of Initiative

3. Planning Risks

    3.1 Schedule

    3.2 Budget

    3.3 Staffing

    3.4 Buy-In

4. Approach

    4.1 Major Strategy Decisions

5. Pass/Fail Criteria

    5.1 Describe what constitutes success and how to measure progress and results.

6. Suspension Criteria

    6.1 What should cause us to temporarily suspend our efforts?

7. Deliverables

    7.1 Project Status

    7.2 Reports

    7.3 Metrics

    7.4 Post-Project Review

8. Environmental Needs

    8.1 Hardware and Software

    8.2 Tools

    8.3 Office Space

9. Staffing and Training Needs

    9.1 In-House

    9.2 Contracted

10. Responsibilities

    10.1 Team Members

    10.2 Sponsor

    10.3 Champion

    10.4 Training Department

    10.5 Test Environment Group

    10.6 Process Group

11. Schedule

    11.1 Project Initiative

    11.2 Incremental Milestones

    11.3 Post-Project Review

12. Approvals

    12.1 Person(s) Approving the Plan

Plan on periodically reviewing the progress of the program. It may be useful to use the organization's quality group to help in the reviews, or groups of peers can be used to review the strengths and weaknesses of the implementation. Certainly, post-project reviews will assist in the evaluation of the effectiveness of the program. Careful collection and analysis of metrics is an absolute must to determine if the program is on track.

Step 6
Introduce Change Incrementally

One sure way to derail a process improvement effort is to try to do too much too soon. Rick says this reminds him of when he gets badly out of shape and tries to get back into shape for his next Marine Physical Fitness Test – virtually overnight! The result is inevitable: he gets so sore and discouraged that it puts his workout regimen in jeopardy.

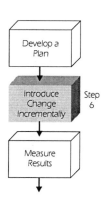

Implementing multiple changes simultaneously requires a greater concentration of resources, which is one of the problems that many process improvement teams often face. Also, when many different changes are implemented at the same time, it's difficult to assess the impact of each change. For example, if your organization implemented software code inspections and preventive testing techniques on the same project at the same time, it would be difficult to determine how much each of these two changes contributed. That is to say, it would be difficult to know what the ROI is of each of these techniques.

One possible model that shows the effects of incrementally implementing process improvements is shown in Figure 11-3. Adaptive change is the lowest in complexity, cost, and uncertainty because it involves re-implementation of a change in the same test group at a later time or imitation of a similar change by another group. For example, an adaptive change for a test group would be to institute mandatory 10-hour workdays during the acceptance testing phase. Similarly, the company's

■■■■■■■■■■■■■■■■
Key Point

An *influence leader* is a person whose example is followed by his or her peers because the influence leader is perceived to be exceptionally innovative, authoritative, or technically astute.

engineering department could initiate the same change in work hours during the unit testing phase. Adaptive changes are not particularly threatening to employees because they're familiar changes.

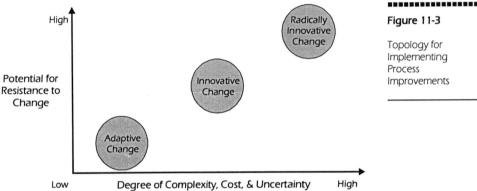

Figure 11-3

Topology for Implementing Process Improvements

Innovative changes fall midway on the horizontal scale of complexity, cost, and uncertainty. An experiment with flexible work schedules by a software development company qualifies as an innovative change if it entails changing to the way that other firms in the industry already operate. Unfamiliarity, and hence greater uncertainty, make fear of change a significant problem when implementing innovative changes.

At the high end of the complexity, cost, and uncertainty scale are radically innovative changes. Changes of this sort are the most difficult to implement and tend to be the most threatening to managerial confidence and employee job security. Changing a development or testing methodology midway through a project, for example, can tear the fabric of a test department's culture. Resistance to change tends to increase as changes go from adaptive to innovative to radically innovative.

Pilots

Pilots are an important vehicle for implementing process improvements. They allow the change team and the project team to more closely control the implementation of the change and assess the impact it had on the project. If the new process turns out to be a disaster, a pilot can help reduce the risk and the damage can be contained within the pilot project.

Pilots also allow multiple changes to be implemented simultaneously, since different pilots can be used for different process improvements. When choosing a pilot, it's important that the team members who are chosen for the project have a sincere desire to participate. As in choosing the process improvement team, unwilling participants can jeopardize the effort. It's also important that the sample project be a real project, not a "toy." The best project for a pilot would be a representative (and real) project on the smaller scale.

■■■■■■■■■■■■■■■■■■
Key Point

"The application (pilot) must be large enough to demonstrate that the approach is applicable to development of large systems, but not so large that the prototypers, who are gaining experience, encounter problems on account of the size of the project."

– Roland Vonk
Prototyping: The Effective Use of Case Technology

Step 7
Measure Results

In order to determine the partial or total success or failure of a process improvement initiative, it's necessary to compare the results of the initiative to the pass/fail criteria established in the plan. This will let you know if you've met the requirements specified in Step 3.

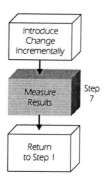

Step 8
Return to Step 1

Process improvement is a continuous process that will never truly be completed. Once the overall vision has been achieved, it's time to re-establish the baseline and start all over again.

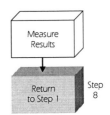

Obtain Buy-In
Throughout the Process

Buy-in is key to success. Without the support of all stakeholders, the process improvement effort will almost always fail. Upper management, line management, and supporting groups must also buy in to the proposed changes. It's sometimes possible to achieve grass-roots change (i.e., bottom up), but it's much more difficult and time-consuming.

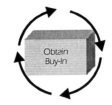

Staff buy-in and effective communication are crucial to the success of any testing effort. Team members need to see the seriousness of the efforts being made and have to perceive the importance of the end-goal in their daily work. Project leaders, particularly, have to feel involved in producing procedures and modifying those procedures that they disagree with. It's also very important to get the most senior buy-in that you can in order to improve your chances of getting the resources that you need.

The Case of the Bogus Metrics

■■■■■■■■■■■■■■■■
Case Study 11-3

Without achieving buy-in, process improvement initiatives are usually worthless.

A few years ago, I had the opportunity to speak at an awards banquet for the software division of a large American company. The banquet began in the normal fashion with cocktails and a hotel-like meal of cold prime rib, rubbery green beans, and chocolate "something." The Director moved to the podium to begin his comments. His comments praised the staff and described in gory detail how the company was benefiting from the hard work of everyone present.

To demonstrate his point, he pontificated at great length about the success of the new corporate software metrics program (that he had implemented). He went on to describe how the collection of project metrics on the expenditure of effort had provided the information necessary to accurately predict the effort required to develop and test new products. It was at this point that the Director introduced me to present awards to the people responsible for this great success.

The first and highest award went to a man whom I'll call "Joe." Joe and his staff, I had been told, had done "great things" in their project. It turns out that the Director's definition of "great things" meant that Joe had supported the Director's metrics program. In fact, Joe's team had a perfect record of reporting all metrics every week right on time.

After describing the feats of Joe and his team, I called him forward to receive his award and say a few words. Joe came forward and rather sheepishly declined to make any comments, which surprised me because Joe was known to be a rather loquacious individual who relished the spotlight.

Later, I learned that Joe met with the Director and returned the award. It seems that Joe thought the Director's entire metrics program was a waste of time and was taking his team away from their primary mission of writing code. So in order to spare his team the anguish of reporting "worthless" metrics, Joe wrote a little program to fill out the weekly metrics form with more or less random (but reasonable) values. Then, these metrics were automatically e-mailed to the Director every Friday exactly at noon when they were due.

As if the story weren't sad enough already, the Director was using Joe's bogus metrics to estimate resource needs and to allocate personnel to projects. The Director even reported that estimation had improved by 30%.

The moral of this story (okay, one moral of this story) is that without buy-in, metrics (and everything else for that matter) are usually worthless.

— Rick Craig

Ask the Practitioners

The first step in achieving buy-in and even enthusiasm from the software developers and testers is to ask them to participate in forming the requirements. If they are not involved until the project is well underway, many will suffer from the "not invented here" syndrome.

Effective Communications

Test managers can communicate to their team members and the entire organization through a variety of media such as face-to-face conversations, phone calls, e-mail, voice mail, written memos and letters, drawings, meetings, computer data, charts, or graphs. Choosing the appropriate media depends on many factors, including the nature of the message, its intended purpose, its audience, its proximity to the audience, and its time frame.

The most important consideration, though, is that the test manager maintain a constant and open dialogue with his or her staff. Staff members who recommend changes to the process must be confident that their recommendations will be seriously considered.

Metrics

One key to achieving buy-in early is to supply metrics that describe the benefits of the proposed change.   Early on, these metrics may often be industry metrics or testimonials.   For example, if you were trying to implement code inspections into your organization, it would be useful to show what the benefits of such a move had been in other companies or organizations. For detailed information on industry software metrics, refer to *Applied Software Measurement* by Capers Jones.

■■■■■■■■■■■■■■■■■

Key Point

Applied Software Measurement by Capers Jones is an excellent source for industry software metrics.

Information from the pilots can be used to garner buy-in as well. Once the pilot has completed, the results of the process change may be useful in getting buy-in for widespread implementation of the change (assuming, of course, that the pilot was a success).

Develop Feedback Loops

The practitioners not only need to have the opportunity to participate in the formulation of the requirements, but they must also have the opportunity to provide feedback, on a continuous basis, on what is and is not working. This feedback loop should extend to practitioners on projects other than the pilot, if they will eventually be affected.

■■■■■■■■■■■■■■■■■

Key Point

The practitioners not only need to have the opportunity to participate in the formulation of the requirements, but they must also have the opportunity to provide feedback, on a continuous basis, on what is and is not working.

Just because a developer or tester has provided feedback doesn't mean that every suggestion has to be implemented, but every suggestion does have to be acted on, even if the only action is to explain why the suggestion was not used.   If the practitioners don't feel that the feedback loop is truly working, they'll often withdraw their support of the project.

Provide Training

Another key component of buy-in is to provide training on the process improvement process and initiatives. Notice that we said training should be supplied *on the process improvement process*. All practitioners need to understand how changes were nominated, chosen, and eventually implemented. The new processes that are implemented will also require training. Some of this training may be commercial (e.g., how to use a new tool), but often the training will have to be conducted in-house.

Pick a Champion and Sponsor

It's vital to have a champion and a sponsor for every change that is implemented. The champion should be an influence leader who is willing to serve as the on-site oracle for the new process. For example, if a new defect tracking system is implemented, the champion should be capable of becoming an expert on the system and how it's used; and he or she should have the time and communication skills needed to help other users when asked. A sponsor is usually a senior manger who can help to secure resources and get buy-in from other senior managers.

■■■■■■■■■■■■■■■■■
Key Point

The *champion* should be an influence leader who's willing to serve as the on-site oracle for the new process.

A *sponsor* is usually a senior manager who can help fight for resources and get buy-in.

Post-Project Reviews

One alternative to Steps 1 and 2 of our process improvement model (baseline current practices and develop goals) described in this chapter is to use a post-project review. The purpose of the post-project review is to identify opportunities for improvement and also to identify any "strengths" or successful processes that need to be repeated on future projects. At the conclusion of the post-project review, the process improvement team can then proceed to Steps 6 through 8.

Post-project reviews can be conducted in many different ways. One of our clients, for example, brings all the participants into a room, where each participant has the opportunity to identify three project strengths and three opportunities for improvement. The most common strengths and opportunities are then reported as the findings of the post-project review. The beauty of this method is that it's done at a single sitting and includes all participants. On the downside, it doesn't really compare the results to the project objectives.

When we conduct project reviews, we administer a questionnaire (similar to the one in the Appendix) to every participant. We then compile the results and compare them to an industry database. This lets us know, in very broad terms, what the participants did before we arrived on site. Upon arrival we personally interview all (or most) project participants (including everyone who wants to be included) and review copies of their work products (i.e., project plans, requirement specifications, test plans, etc.). After analyzing the results of the questionnaires, our interviews, and the documentation review, we present our findings to (1) the project manager, (2) the project participants, and (3) the executive steering committee.

We have conducted many post-project reviews (post-mortems) over the years and have compiled some useful guidelines:
- Conduct the post-project review soon after the conclusion of the project. Don't start on the day that the project ends – give the staff a day or two to relax – but don't wait too long. One to three weeks after the conclusion of the project is an ideal time to begin the review.
- Conduct post-project reviews on every project, or announce at the time of project initiation whether or not

a project will be subjected to a review. Waiting until the project is finished and then deciding to do a review makes the whole process look like a "witch hunt."

- Get an outsider to lead the post-project review team. Since the test manager is in the business of evaluating things, the task is often given to him or her. Other organizations assign the responsibility of conducting the review to the project manager. Both of these are bad ideas. The test manager is already evaluating the work of the development team, so having him or her also evaluate the processes can strain even a good working relationship. The project manager is too close to the project and lacks the fresh perspective to do the job right. An ideal candidate might be the project manager from another project, the QA manager, or an outside consultant.

- Make sure that all project participants have an opportunity to voice their opinions. It's equally important that participants feel that their opinions are heard and seriously considered. Even if all ideas are not used, they should be considered.

- Keep it objective. Compare the results of the project to the objectives and requirements of the project.

- Don't make it personal. Don't report findings that address individuals and personalities.

- When reporting results, always list the "strengths" of the project first. Every project has something good about it, even if it was only that they all wore "cool t-shirts."

- Report the "weaknesses" of the project as "opportunities for improvement" and limit them to 5 or less (it's unlikely that more than 5 opportunities will be acted on anyway).

- Capture objective data when possible, but remember that perceptions are also important.

- Assign to a team the responsibility of analyzing and prioritizing the results. The team can then use the

■■■■■■■■■■■■■■■■■
Key Point

You should consider getting an outsider to lead the post-project review team. An ideal candidate might be the project manager from another project, the QA manager, or an outside consultant.

process improvement flowchart (refer to Figure 11-1) to implement changes, if necessary.

ISO Certification ■ ■ ■ ■ ■

The International Organization for Standardization (ISO) is a worldwide federation of national standardization bodies from 140 countries. Their mission is to develop standards to facilitate the international exchange of goods and services. ISO standards are documented agreements containing technical specifications or other precise criteria to be used consistently as rules, guidelines, or definitions of characteristics to ensure that materials, products, processes, and services are fit for their purpose.

The ISO 9000 series of standards is used to establish a quality management system. ISO 9000-3 describes how ISO 9001 standards apply to software. *TickIt* is a certification scheme (primarily used in the United Kingdom) tuned to deal with the special requirements associated with applying ISO 9000 to software development.

Companies choose to seek ISO registration for a variety of reasons: to improve their quality processes, to baseline improvement efforts, and even to use ISO as a marketing ploy. Becoming ISO certified always warrants a mention in the business news and makes the company look better in the eyes of the stockholders and the business community.

ISO emphasizes the basic elements of quality management and assesses an organization's process using a rigorous auditing model. An ISO 9000 registration effort can be a very involved process that might take a year or more to implement. Periodic

■ ■ ■ ■ ■ ■ ■ ■ ■ ■ ■ ■ ■ ■ ■
Key Point

Shouldn't the acronym for International Organization for Standardization be "IOS" instead of "ISO?" Yes, if it were an acronym, which it is not.

"ISO" is derived from the Greek word *isos*, which means "equal."

■ ■ ■ ■ ■ ■ ■ ■ ■ ■ ■ ■ ■ ■ ■
Key Point

ISO emphasizes the basic elements of quality management and assesses an organization's process using a rigorous auditing model.

reviews by auditors ensure that the outlined processes are being maintained.

ISO audits are at a much higher level than this book (i.e., the entire organization versus the testing organization). So why do we bother to mention them here? For this one simple reason: companies that undergo quality audits such as ISO are usually more receptive to process improvement activities throughout the organization. If your company is undergoing ISO certification, it may be possible to use this effort as a springboard to improve the testing processes. One could even argue that improving the testing process could help your organization achieve ISO certification.

■■■■■■■■■■■■■■■■
Key Point

If your company is undergoing ISO certification, it may be possible to use this effort as a springboard to improve the testing processes.

ISO Checklists

The following checklists provide typical questions that auditors would ask a test manager during the ISO certification process. The bottom line is, "Do you have a procedure in place to handle each of your daily tasks and is that procedure repeatable?" If you can answer "yes" to all of the questions on the auditor's checklist (and prove compliance), then you'll achieve ISO certification. A sample checklist is shown in Table 11-1.

Table 11-1 ISO Certification Process Checklists

Pass	Fail	Checklist for Testing
☐	☐	Are test plans and procedures created and reviewed?
☐	☐	Are test results recorded?
☐	☐	Are defects or problems recorded, assigned, and tracked to closure?
☐	☐	Is there an adequate test process to ensure that areas impacted by changes are retested?

Table 11-1 (Continued)

Pass	Fail	Checklist for Measurement
☐	☐	Is the software validated (tested) as a complete system in an environment as similar as possible to the final operating environment? Is this done prior to delivery and acceptance?
☐	☐	If field-testing is required, are the responsibilities of the supplier and the purchaser defined? Is the user environment restored following the test?
☐	☐	Are product metrics collected and used to manage the testing effort?
☐	☐	Are product defects measured and reported?
☐	☐	Is corrective action taken if metric levels exceed established target levels?
☐	☐	Are improvement goals established in terms of metrics?
☐	☐	Are process metrics collected to measure the effectiveness of the testing process in terms of schedule and in terms of fault prevention and detection?
Pass	**Fail**	**Checklist for Tools / Techniques**
☐	☐	Are tools and techniques used to help make testing and management processes more effective?
☐	☐	Are the used tools and techniques reviewed, as required, and improved upon?
Pass	**Fail**	**Checklist for Training**
☐	☐	Are training needs identified according to a procedure?
☐	☐	Is training conducted for all personnel performing work related to quality?
☐	☐	Are personnel who are performing specific tasks qualified on the basis of appropriate education, training, and/or experience?
☐	☐	Are records kept of personnel training and experience?

Table 11-1   (Continued)

Pass	Fail	Checklist for Documentation
☐	☐	Are test plans, requirements, and other documents revision controlled?
☐	☐	Do procedures exist to control document approval and issue?
☐	☐	Are changes to controlled documents reviewed and approved?
☐	☐	Are current versions of test documents identifiable by a master list or document control procedures?

Pass	Fail	Checklist for Configuration Management
☐	☐	Is there a Configuration Management (CM) system that identifies and tracks versions of the software under test, software components, build status, and changes? Does the system control simultaneous updates?
☐	☐	Does the configuration management plan include a list of responsibilities, CM activities, CM tools and techniques, and timing of when items are brought under CM control?
☐	☐	Is there a mechanism and procedure that enables software, hardware, and files to be uniquely identified throughout the entire software development lifecycle?
☐	☐	Is there a documented mechanism to identify, record, review, and authorize changes to software items under configuration management? Is this process always followed?
☐	☐	Are affected personnel notified of software changes?
☐	☐	Is the status of software items and change requests reported?

Pros and Cons of ISO Certification

There is considerable controversy throughout the software industry over the value of ISO 9000 certification in determining the ability of an organization to consistently produce "good" software. Many people who have been directly involved in the ISO certification process (including Stefan) have seen the effects years later and often ask themselves, "If we're ISO certified, why does this company still suffer the consequences of quality

■■■■■■■■■■■■■■■■■

Key Point

Much of the success of the ISO is dependent upon the motivation for achieving the certification in the first place.

and delivery problems?" A common answer is, "ISO is just a paper trail that we have to follow in order to maintain our certification and compete in the global marketplace."

Philip Crosby (*Quality Is Still Free, Making Quality Certain in Uncertain Times*) minces no words in his assessment of the value of ISO certification:

> *"With a properly run quality management process, there will be no difficulty meeting ISO 9000 requirements. It's really a very old-fashioned Quality Assurance kind of thing. But it is not oriented toward the needs of today and the next century. It's only to provide a living for consultants and for quality people who do not want to think for themselves."*

On the other hand, many organizations report successfully using ISO as a valuable tool for improving processes. Much of the success of ISO is dependent upon the motivation for achieving the certification in the first place.

Capability Maturity Model (CMM) ■■■■■

The quality of software systems depends, to some degree, on the quality of the corresponding software engineering processes. A software buyer is usually interested in getting to know the level of maturity of the vendor's software engineering process in order to be able to draw conclusions about the software system's quality.

The Capability Maturity Model (CMM) was created for the Software Engineering Institute (SEI) based on the vision of Watts Humphrey. The CMM is a framework, distinguished by five different maturity levels, for evaluating the maturity of a

■■■■■■■■■■■■■■■■
Key Point

Finding out the level of maturity of a vendor's software engineering process can help you draw conclusions about the quality of their testing software.

company's software engineering process. With the help of an evaluation process, the maturity of a company's software engineering processes can be assigned to one of these levels. The levels are based on each other, which means that if an engineering process fulfills the requirements of a level, it also fulfills all of the requirements of all of the levels below it. With an increase in the CMM level, the development risk can be reduced and the productivity of the development as well as the quality of the product can be increased.

Figure 11-4 shows the five levels of the CMM. The CMM is only a guide (i.e., not a cookbook) for evolving toward a culture of software engineering excellence. It's a model for organizational improvement because it provides guidelines not only for improving process management, but also for introducing new technology into an organization. In fact, process capability interacts with people, technology, and measurement across all five levels of the CMM.

A frequent complaint of people in the testing business is that the CMM largely ignores testing until Level 3. This is the primary reason why Martin Pol and Tim Koomen created the Test Process Improvement (TPI) model (refer to the section entitled *Test Process Improvement [TPI] Model* for more information). Others have also addressed this issue.

In his article "Growth of Maturity in the Testing Process" Roger Drabick has outlined testing activities that he feels should be performed at each level of the CMM. His comments are indicated in the *shaded boxes* within the description of each level of the CMM.

■■■■■■■■■■■■■■■■■■

Key Point

For more information on the CMM, see *The Capability Maturity Model, Guidelines for Improving the Software Process* from the Carnegie Mellon University's Software Engineering Institute.

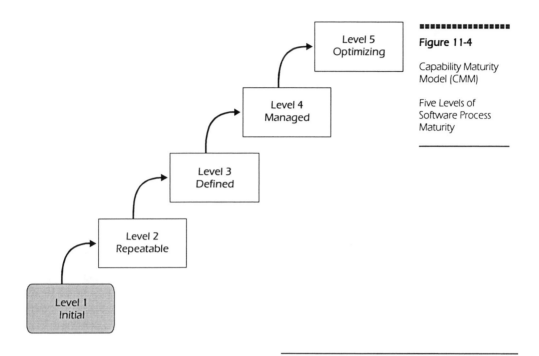

■■■■■■■■■■■■■■■■■

Figure 11-4

Capability Maturity
Model (CMM)

Five Levels of
Software Process
Maturity

CMM Level 1 – Initial

A Level 1 organization's process capability is unpredictable and often chaotic because the software process is constantly changed as the work progresses. The process is, essentially, ad hoc and generally undisciplined, making the organization an unstable environment for developing software. Level 1 performance depends on the individual capabilities of the staff and managers and varies with their innate skills, knowledge, and motivations. During times of crises, project managers typically abandon planned procedures and revert to ad hoc coding and testing.

CMM Level 2 – Repeatable

Level 2 organizations focus on project management, and their process capabilities are usually elevated by the establishment of disciplined processes under sound management control. Realistic project schedules are developed based on requirements and results observed from previous projects. Software requirements and work products are typically baselined and their integrity controlled. In contrast to a Level 1 organization, a repeatable process exists for software projects at Level 2.

At Level 2, test managers should strive toward developing specific testing and debugging goals and initiate a test planning process for the organization.

CMM Level 3 – Defined

Documentation is the primary focus of organizations at Level 3. Organization-wide processes are established for all management and engineering activities. Level 3 processes evolve from the processes that were developed and the successes that were achieved while at Level 2. At Level 2, one or two projects may have repeatable processes. But at Level 3, all projects have repeatable processes.

■■■■■■■■■■■■■■■■■■
Key Point

Level 3 is the first level where formal testing processes are introduced.

This is the first level where formal software testing processes are actually introduced. In his book *Software Testing Techniques*, Boris Beizer explains, "*Although programmers, testers, and programming managers know that code must be designed and tested, many appear to be unaware that tests themselves must be designed and tested – designed by a process no less rigorous and no less controlled than used for code.*" As an evaluation activity, software testing processes are created at Level 3 in order to verify that requirements are satisfied at each phase of the software development lifecycle. At Level 3, test managers should strive to establish a formal software test organization. Test plans should be integrated into the software development lifecycle, and test processes should be controlled and closely monitored.

CMM Level 4 – Managed

At Level 4, the measurements that were put in place at Levels 2 and 3 are used to understand and control software processes and products quantitatively.

At this level, test managers should strive to establish organization-wide programs for software review, technical training, test measurement, and software quality evaluation.

CMM Level 5 – Optimizing

At Level 5, continuous process improvement is enabled by quantitative process feedback and technology insertion.

At this level, test managers should strive to apply process controls to prevent future defects and focus on quality control activities.

Pros and Cons of the CMM

While the CMM focuses on process improvement and has a high visibility within the software industry, it also has some drawbacks. The CMM does not focus on the practitioner or the customer and, consequently, lacks their input on process improvements. This model also requires the implementation of major process changes in order to introduce mature processes.

One issue, in particular, with the CMM is the idea many people have that there's always a direct correlation between the level of process-use and the quality of the product developed. While we certainly believe that improving processes usually also improves that product (or we wouldn't have written this book), it's *not* clear to us that *all* of the processes outlined in the CMM will necessarily be worth implementing in *all* organizations. We believe that some organizations (especially small entrepreneurial companies) might actually be better off operating at CMM Level 3 or 4, rather than Level 5. Level 5 processes may be too demanding and may require too much control for some groups.

Test Process Improvement (TPI) Model

Unfortunately, the CMM does not (in our opinion) adequately address testing issues at levels 1 and 2 (which is where most companies are today). Martin Pol and Tim Koomen have developed a test process improvement process known as TPI, which provides a roadmap to CMM level 3 (for testing). This process is well documented in their book *Test Process Improvement*, and a hands-on class on how to use this model is taught by each author.

The TPI model allows users of the model to determine the current state of their testing process (e.g., baseline), the next logical area for process improvement, and recommended steps to get there.

Once We Were Skeptics, But Now We're Believers

Our initial reaction to the TPI model was outright skepticism. We thought that it would be difficult, if not impossible, to create a single model that could recommend next steps for any organization, regardless of the size, skill level, and techniques employed. But after reading Test Process Improvement *and attending Mr. Pol's class, we became believers. The model is not perfect, but it will accomplish the goal of helping most organizations to baseline their processes and determine targets for continued process improvement.*

For the most part, the TPI model uses CMM-like language. Most of the TPI terms have meanings similar to those used by the CMM, facilitating the use of the TPI model by current CMM advocates. It's not necessary, however, to subscribe to the CMM model in order to use the TPI. Figure 11-5 shows the principal pieces of the TPI model, which include key areas, levels, checkpoints, and improvement suggestions.

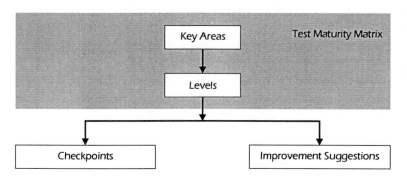

■■■■■■■■■■■■■■■■■■

Figure 11-5

Test Process Improvement (TPI) Model

Key Areas of the TPI

The testing process is broken into twenty key areas that need to be addressed by the testing organization. The baseline and improvement suggestions are based on the following twenty key areas:

- Test Strategy
- Lifecycle Model
- Moment of Involvement
- Estimating and Planning
- Test Specification Techniques
- Static Test Techniques
- Metrics
- Test Automation
- Testing Environment
- Office Environment

- Commitment and Motivation
- Test Functions and Training
- Scope of Methodology
- Communication
- Reporting
- Defect Management
- Testware Management
- Test Process Management
- Evaluation
- Low-Level Testing

Levels of Maturity

Examination of each key area leads to classification of the test process into certain levels of maturity. There can be one to four maturity levels for each of the twenty key areas in the TPI model, and each of these maturity levels is represented by an A, B, C, or D. The ascending levels indicate increasingly more mature processes (e.g., 'B' is more mature than 'A').

A value is assigned (by shading in the template) of A, B, C or D for each key area. One key area (office environment) has only one level and the others have up to four. Office environment, for example, has only one level that you can assign because you either have a usable office environment or you don't. Other key areas such as test strategy have up to four levels because there are more "degrees" of process maturity in the area of test strategy.

Checkpoints

Checkpoints are questions (found in *Test Process Improvement*) that must be answered in order to determine the maturity of each key area. If a key area passes all of the checkpoints of a certain level, then the key area is classified at that level. To make sure that the classification into levels is done objectively, one or more checkpoints are assigned to each level.

Test Maturity Matrix

All of the key areas and levels in the test maturity matrix are not equally important for the performance of the complete test process, and dependencies exist between the different key areas and levels. Consequently, all key areas and levels are mutually linked in a test maturity matrix.

Table 11-2 Blank TPI Assessment

(Reprinted from *Test Process Improvement* by Martin Pol and Tim Koomen with permission of IQUIP)

	Key Area	Controlled						Efficient				Optimizing			
		0	1	2	3	4	5	6	7	8	9	10	11	12	13
1	Test Strategy		A					B				C		D	
2	Lifecycle Model		A			B									
3	Moment of Involvement			A				B				C		D	
4	Estimating and Planning				A							B			
5	Test Specification Techniques		A		B										
6	Static Test Techniques					A		B							
7	Metrics						A			B			C		D
8	Test Automation				A				B			C			
9	Testing Environment				A				B						C
10	Office Environment				A										
11	Commitment and Motivation		A				B						C		
12	Test Functions and Training				A			B			C				
13	Scope of Methodology					A						B			C
14	Communication			A	B								C		
15	Reporting		A		B		C						D		
16	Defect Management		A			B		C							
17	Testware Management			A	B						C				D
18	Test Process Management		A		B								C		
19	Evaluation						A			B					
20	Low-Level Testing					A		B		C					

NOTE: The **blank** test maturity matrix template shown above is completed based on the answers to the questions or checkpoints. Note that this is a copy of the blank TPI template, not a completed one! The initial reaction of many people is confusion when they see this template, but it really does make sense.

The levels (A, B, C, and D) do not line up vertically in the model because the first level for one key area may occur naturally before the same level in another key area. For example, level 'A' for Defect Management occurs before level 'A' for Metrics because you need to collect the defect information in order to use the defect metrics.

Improvement Suggestions

Even though the TPI model shows the next logical step for process improvement based on the checkpoints for each key level, the authors of the TPI have also included additional improvement suggestions (refer to Figure 11-5) to facilitate the process.

Example TPI Assessment

Table 11-3 shows the results of a TPI assessment at an organization. The shaded area represents the level of maturity achieved in each key area. A value of '0' for a key area indicates the minimal requirements to achieve level 'A' have not been met.

Table 11-3 Example TPI Assessment

(Reprinted from *Test Process Improvement* by Martin Pol and Tim Koomen with permission of IQUIP)

	Key Area	Controlled						Efficient				Optimizing			
		0	1	2	3	4	5	6	7	8	9	10	11	12	13
1	Test Strategy		A					B				C		D	
2	Lifecycle Model		A		B										
3	Moment of Involvement			A				B				C		D	
4	Estimating and Planning				A							B			
5	Test Specification Techniques		A	B											
6	Static Test Techniques					A		B							
7	Metrics						A			B			C		D
8	Test Automation				A				B			C			
9	Testing Environment				A				B						C
10	Office Environment				A										
11	Commitment and Motivation		A					B					C		
12	Test Functions and Training				A			B			C				
13	Scope of Methodology					A						B			C
14	Communication			A	B								C		
15	Reporting		A			B	C						D		
16	Defect Management		A				B		C						
17	Testware Management			A			B				C				D
18	Test Process Management		A		B								C		
19	Evaluation						A				B				
20	Low-Level Testing					A		B		C					

Notice the three "levels" of maturity at the top of Table 11-3: *Controlled, Efficient,* and *Optimizing.* These levels were added to the TPI model to give participants (especially upper management) a feel for their testing maturity level. This is an imprecise measurement because an organization is rated as controlled, efficient, or optimizing based on where most of the shading appears on the chart. This organization, for example, is aiming for better control of their testing process, because the controlled area is still largely unshaded.

The model works left to right. In order to improve the testing process (i.e., expand the shaded area), we must first look at the lowest level (A, B, C, D) that appears in the left-most unshaded box. In our example, Test Strategy and Test Specification Techniques are both unshaded, so you must now look at a dependency chart (refer to Table 11-4) to see if any dependencies exist. The dependency chart shows that level 'A' of the Test Strategy is dependent on 11A (Commitment and Motivation) and 5A (Test Specification Techniques). Notice that 11A is already shaded, so you don't have to worry about it. This means that the next logical area for process improvement is level 'A' for *Test Specification Techniques*. After addressing Test Specification Techniques, you would then target level 'A' of the Test Strategy.

Table 11-4 Overview of Dependencies

(Reprinted from *Test Process Improvement* by Martin Pol and Tim Koomen with permission of IQUIP)

	Key Area	**Level A**	**Level B**	**Level C**	**Level D**
1	Test Strategy	Strategy for single high-level test (5A, 11A)	Combined strategy for high-level tests (2A, 5B, 11B, 14B, 18B)	Combined strategy for high-level tests plus either low-level tests or evaluation (20C or (3C, 19B))	Combined strategy for all test and evaluation levels (3C, 19, 20C)
2	Lifecycle Model	Planning, specification, execution (11A)	Planning, preparation, specification, execution, and completion (6A, 17A)		
3	Moment of Involvement	Completion of test basis (2A)	Start of test basis (2B)	Start of requirements definition	Project initiation (11C)
4	Estimating and Planning	Substantial estimating and planning (2A)	Statistically substantiated estimating and planning (7B, 15B)		
5	Test Specification Techniques	Informal techniques	Formal techniques (12A, 17A)		
6	Static Test Techniques	Inspection of test basis	Checklists		

Table 11-4 (Continued)

(Reprinted from *Test Process Improvement* by Martin Pol and Tim Koomen with permission from IQUIP)

	Key Area	Level A	Level B	Level C	Level D
7	Metrics	Project metrics (product) (11B, 15B, 16A, 18B)	Project metrics (process) (15c, 16b)	System metrics (13B, 14C, 18C)	Organization metrics (> 1 system)
8	Test Automation	Use of tools	Managed test automation (5A or 5B, 12A)	Optimal test automation	
9	Test Environment	Managed and controlled test environment (12A)	Testing in the most suitable environment (1B)	'Environment on-call'	
10	Office Environment	Adequate and timely office environment			
11	Commitment and Motivation	Assignment of budget and time	Testing integrated in project organization (2A, 15B, 16A, 18B)	Test engineering (1C, 3C, 8B, 15C)	
12	Test Functions and Training	Test manager and testers	(Formal) methodical, technical, and functional support, management	Formal internal quality assurance (13A)	
13	Scope of Methodology	Project specific (2A, 5B, 16A, 17A, 18B)	Organization generic	Organization optimizing, R&D activities (11B, 18C)	
14	Communication	Internal communication	Project communication (defects, change control) (2A, 15B, 16A)	Communication in organization about the quality of the test processes (13B)	
15	Reporting	Defects	Progress (status of tests and products), activities (costs and time, milestones), defects with priorities (2A, 16A, 18B)	Risks and recommendations, substantiated with metrics (1A, 5B, 7A, 16B)	Recommendations have a *software process improvement* character (1C, 11C)
16	Defect Management	Internal defect management	Extensive defect management with flexible reporting facilities	Project defect management	
17	Testware management	Internal testware management	External management of test basis and test object	Reusable testware (5B)	Traceability of system requirements to test cases
18	Test Process Management	Planning and execution	Planning, execution, monitoring, and adjusting	Monitoring and adjusting within organization (13B)	
19	Evaluation	Evaluation techniques	Evaluation strategy		
20	Low-Level Testing	Low-level test lifecycle model (planning, specification, and execution)	White-box techniques	Low-level test strategy	

	Description for
	Test Spec. Techniques (5A)

The use of informal techniques means that the person writing the test specification has a lot of freedom in inventing test cases. This causes the test quality to be highly dependent on the (subject matter) skills of the person writing the specification and blurs the level of coverage compared to the test basis. However, this is far better than each tester thinking up test cases for themselves, without worrying about the documentation of these test cases.

Making predictions in the specifications of the test cases is very important, because the judging of test results afterwards under the pressure of time is often insufficiently thorough (e.g., the result is 990; I expected something between 800 and 1,000, so that number is probably correct).

	Checkpoints for
	Test Spec. Techniques (5A)

Test Process Improvement shows that the following checkpoints must be satisfied in order to achieve a maturity level of 'A' for the key area *Test Specification Techniques*:
- The test cases are specified by means of a described technique.
- The technique requires at least a description of:
  - the starting situation.
  - the change process and the test actions to be performed.
  - the expected end result.

Since the checkpoints for Test Specification Techniques in Table 11-3 were not satisfied, a value of '0' was assigned.

Improvement Suggestions for
Test Spec. Techniques (5A)

Based on the results of the TPI assessment example in Table 11-3, the checkpoints along with the following improvement suggestions should be followed to get from maturity level '0' to level 'A' for the key area *Test Specification Techniques*:

- Make testers aware of the importance of predictions.
- Describe the specification technique. Try to include as many practical instructions as possible, so that the person writing the specification stays focused.

Continuous Improvement ■■■■■

Whether your organization chooses to use the process improvement model described at the beginning of this chapter, CMM, ISO, TPI, or some combination of these, or an entirely different model, it's necessary that you constantly strive to improve the effectiveness of your testing. If you're not improving, you're probably going backwards. Goals must be constantly raised, and when achieved, raised again.

Static organizations become stale and ineffective, and suffer from declining morale. It's unfortunate that organizations that have achieved a pinnacle of success might actually have to work harder to retain their position than they did to achieve it in the first place.

Chapter 12 –
Some Final Thoughts…

"Once you eliminate your number-one problem, number two gets a promotion."

— Rudy's Rutabaga Rule
Gerald M. Weinberg's Secrets of Consulting

After reading a book like this or attending a seminar or training session, you no doubt ask yourself, "What now?" Hopefully you realize that very few readers of this book need to do *everything* that we've suggested. Similarly, the implementation of each topic in this book will produce a different ROI than every other topic. The number-one priority for one organization might not necessarily be as important to other organizations.

We feel that models such as TPI (refer to Chapter 11) can help most organizations choose the next logical step in the quest for process improvement. Some of you, though, are still not satisfied. You want to know what you can do now. Today! Naturally, we can't answer that question without knowing a lot more about your organization's processes, skills, budget, politics, quality of software produced, and a multitude of other things. There is, though, a short list of things that we think have a high return on investment for almost every organization. These are the things that we believe every testing organization should strive to do:

- Use Preventive Testing Techniques
- Conduct Software Risk Analysis
- Determine Planning Risks
- Develop a Testing Strategy
- Use Inventories
- Use Testing Tools When Appropriate
- Analyze Defect Trends and Patterns
- Measure Test Effectiveness
- Conduct Training Continually
- Sell the Idea of Testing

Use Preventive Testing Techniques

There's nothing a testing organization can do that will provide a greater return on investment than actually preventing defects or finding them very early in the software development lifecycle. Chapter 1 describes the concept of preventive testing, and the rest of this book is based upon the concept that testing activities will occur in advance of or parallel to the software development.

Key Point

See Chapter 1

Conduct Software Risk Analysis

It's a fact of life. It's just not possible to test everything, so what you test is much more important than how much you test. Analyzing software risks can help testing organizations prioritize their tests and determine where to focus their testing effort.

Key Point

See Chapter 2

Determine Planning Risks

We've never taken part in a project where everything went according to the original plan. Requirements change, testers get sick, the code is late, and the list goes on. Since we can't create a perfect plan, we have to identify potential planning risks and formulate viable contingencies. These contingencies will always involve one or more of the following actions: adding resources, changing the schedule, reducing the scope of the project, or reducing some quality activities (like testing). The key is to decide and agree upon the best contingency for each planning risk in advance.

Key Point

See *Planning Risks* in Chapter 2

Develop a Testing Strategy

There are many issues that need to be considered when planning a testing effort. Who should do the testing? When should we start? How will we know when we're done? What should be automated? Do we need training? What metrics are required to measure the effectiveness of our effort?

Key Point

See Chapters 3 & 4

Test planning helps address questions like these and helps in obtaining buy-in from key parties by involving them in the test planning early in the development lifecycle.

Use Inventories

Many organizations struggle to determine what actual conditions should be tested. Inventories are one way of analyzing a product in order to develop lists of potential test conditions. The inventory tracking matrix that is a by-product of developing inventories facilitates the maintenance of the test set and provides a method of determining coverage. When coupled with software risk analysis (see above), inventories can provide the basis for a sound testing strategy.

Key Point

See Chapter 5

Use Testing Tools When Appropriate

Testing tools are not a panacea and are certainly not the answer to all the problems that test teams might encounter, but there are many times when the appropriate use of a tool can help the test team be more effective or productive. You may or may not, in

Key Point

See Chapter 6

fact, choose to use tools on any given project, but their use should always be considered when creating your testing strategy. When trying to decide whether or not to use tools, remember to consider the pitfalls we discussed in Chapter 6.

Analyze Defect Trends and Patterns ■ ■ ■ ■ ■

There is a great deal that one can learn by analyzing the trends, patterns, type, source, severity, age, etc. of defects discovered and missed by the testers. Specifically, testers can identify process improvement and training opportunities and discover risky components that warrant a greater dose of testing.

Key Point

See Chapter 7

Measure Test Effectiveness ■ ■ ■ ■ ■

It's very difficult for the manager of a testing team to determine how well his or her team is doing if the manager does not have a way to measure test effectiveness. Chapter 7 outlines several different metrics for measuring test effectiveness. We believe that every test manager should measure coverage and use at least one other measure of test effectiveness such as Defect Removal Efficiency (DRE).

Key Point

See Chapter 7

Conduct Training Continually ■ ■ ■ ■ ■

Key Point

See Chapters 8 & 10

Testing is now recognized by most software engineers as a discipline. In testing, as in every discipline, there's a body of knowledge and certain skills that every professional should possess. Additionally, some testers will require special or advanced skills or knowledge based upon the kind of testing they perform.

Chapter 10 lists many of the types of training that are available and explains some of the pros and cons of each. Remember that training needs to be timely, appropriate, and ongoing.

Sell the Idea of Testing ■ ■ ■ ■ ■

Key Point

Topics that pertain to selling the idea of testing to your organization are presented throughout this book.

There are still a lot of "nay sayers" in this world who are not truly sold on the benefits of testing. It's up to the test manager and test teams to sell developers, users, and management on the value of testing. Testers need to make effective use of metrics, pilots, and public forums to advance their cause.

"It ain't over till it's over...."

- Yogi Berra

Appendix A – Glossary of Terms

"The words I use are everyday words and yet are not the same."

— Paul Claudel

Glossary of Terms ■ ■ ■ ■ ■

Acceptance Testing: A level of test conducted from the viewpoint of the user or customer, used to establish criteria for acceptance of a system. Typically based upon the requirements of the system.

Ad Hoc Testing: Testing conducted without written or formal plans or test cases.

Alpha Test: An acceptance test conducted at the development site.

Approach: A description of how testing will be conducted. Includes any issues that affect the effectiveness or efficiency of testing. See *Strategy*.

Assumption: A presumed activity or state. If the assumption is false, it's a planning risk. See *Planning Risk*.

Attribute: A characteristic of the system that spans the breadth of the system (e.g., performance, usability).

Baseline: A measurement of where your processes are at any given point in time. Used to compare the processes of one group at a given time to the same group at another point in time.

Benchmark: A measurement of where your processes are compared directly to other companies or to a static model such as the CMM.

Beta Test: An acceptance test conducted at a customer site.

Black-Box Testing: A type of testing where the internal workings of the system are unknown or ignored (i.e., functional or behavioral testing). Testing to see if the system does what it's supposed to do.

Boundary Value Analysis: Testing at or near the boundaries of a system or subsystem.

Brainstorming: A group problem-solving technique that involves the spontaneous contribution of ideas from all members of the group.

Buddy Testing: A technique where two programmers work together to develop and test their code. Preventive techniques are used (i.e., the test cases are written prior to the code).

Bug: A flaw in the software with potential to cause a failure. See *Defect.*

Calibration: The measurement of coverage of test cases against an inventory of requirements and design attributes.

Capability Maturity Model (CMM): A framework used for evaluating the maturity of an organization's software engineering process. Developed by the Software Engineering Institute (SEI) at Carnegie Mellon University.

Certification: Any of a number of programs that lead to formal recognition by an institution that an individual has demonstrated proficiency within and comprehension over a specified body of knowledge.

Champion: An influence leader who's willing to serve as the on-site oracle for a new process.

Change Control Board (CCB): A board typically composed of developers, testers, users, customers, and others tasked with prioritizing defects and enhancements. Also called *Configuration Control Board (CCB)*.

Code Freeze: A time when changes to the system (requirements, design, code, and documentation) are halted or closely managed.

Configuration Control Board (CCB): See *Change Control Board (CCB)*.

Confirmation Testing: Rerunning tests that revealed a bug to ensure that the bug was fully and actually fixed (Derived from Rex Black).

Cohabiting Software: Applications that reside on the same platform as the software being testing.

Coincidental Correctness: A situation where the expected result of a test case is realized in spite of incorrect processing of the data.

Contingency: An activity undertaken to eliminate or mitigate a planning risk.

Coverage: A metric that describes how much of a system has been (or will be) invoked by a test set. Coverage is typically based upon the code, design, requirements, or inventories.

Cut Line (in software risk analysis): The dividing line between *features to be tested* and *features not to be tested*.

Cyclomatic Complexity: A technique using mathematical graph theory to describe the complexity of a software module.

Debugging: The isolation and removal or correction of a bug.

Decision Tables: Tables that list all possible conditions (inputs) and all possible actions (outputs).

Defect: A flaw in the software with potential to cause a failure. See *Bug*.

Defect Age: A measurement that describes the period of time from the introduction of a defect until its discovery.

Defect Density: A metric that compares the number of defects to a measure of size (e.g., defects per KLOC). Often used as a measure of defect quality.

Defect Discovery Rate: A metric describing the number of defects discovered over a specified period of time, usually displayed in graphical form.

Defect Removal Efficiency (DRE): A measure of the number of defects discovered in an activity versus the number that could have been found. Often used as a measure of test effectiveness.

Defect Seeding: The process of intentionally adding known defects to those already in a computer program for the purpose of monitoring the rate of detection and removal, and estimating the number of defects still remaining. Also called *Error Seeding*.

Desktop Procedures: Simple instructions that describe all of the routine tasks that must be accomplished by a manager on a daily or weekly basis.

Driver: Modules that simulate high-level components.

Dry Run: Executing test cases designed for a current release of software on a previous version.

E-Factor: Number of uninterrupted hours versus number of body-present hours.

Entry Criteria: Metrics specifying the condition that must be met in order to begin testing at the next stage or level.

Environment (Test): The collection of hardware, software, data, and personnel that comprise a level of test.

Equivalence Partitioning: A set of inputs that are treated the same by a system.

Escape: A defect that is undetected by an evaluation activity and is therefore passed to the next level or stage.

Evaluation: All processes used to measure the quality of a system. In the STEP methodology, these processes consist of testing, analysis, and reviews.

Exit Criteria: Metrics specifying the conditions that must be met in order to promote a software product to the next stage or level.

Exploratory Testing: A testing technique where the test design and execution are conducted concurrently.

Failure: Any deviation of a system that prevents it from accomplishing its mission or operating within specification. The manifestation of a defect.

Feature: A functional characteristic of a system.

Fragility: A measure of how quickly test data becomes outdated.

Glass-Box Testing: See *White-Box Testing*.

Global Code Coverage: The percentage of code executed during the testing of an entire application.

Hawthorne Effect: The observed phenomenon that showing concern for employees improves their productivity.

IEEE: The Institute of Electrical and Electronic Engineers, Inc. Publisher of engineering standards.

Immersion Time: The amount of time it takes a person to become productive after an interruption.

Impact: The effect of a failure.

Incident: Any unusual result of executing a test (or actual operation).

Independent Testing: An organizational strategy where the testing team and leadership is separate from the development team and leadership.

Independent Verification and Validation (IV&V): Verification and validation performed by an organization that's technically, managerially, and financially independent of the development organization (derived from *IEEE Glossary of Terms*).

Influence Leader: A person whose influence is derived from experience, character, or reputation, rather than by organizational charter.

Inspection: A formal evaluation technique in which software requirements, design, or code are examined in detail by a person or group other than the author to detect faults, violation of development standards, and other problems (definition from *IEEE Glossary of Terms*).

Integrated Test Team: An organizational strategy where testers and developers both report to the same line manager.

Integration Testing: A level of test undertaken to validate the interface between internal components of a system. Typically based upon the system architecture.

Interface Testing: Testing to see if data and control are passed correctly between systems. Also called *Systems Integration Testing*.

International Organization for Standards (ISO): A group of quality standards developed to help organizations assess their processes using a rigorous auditing model.

Inventory: A list of things to test.

Inventory Tracking Matrix: A matrix that relates test cases to requirements and/or design attributes. It's used as a measure of coverage and to maintain test sets.

Latent Defect: An existing defect that has not yet caused a failure because the exact set of conditions has not been met.

Level: A testing activity defined by a particular test environment.

Lifecycle: The period of time from the conception of a system until its retirement.

Likelihood: The chance that an event will occur.

Masked Defect: An existing defect that hasn't yet caused a failure because another defect has prevented that part of the code from being executed.

Master Test Planning: An activity undertaken to orchestrate the testing effort across levels and organizations.

Maturity Level: A term coined by Watts Humphrey to denote the level of process use in software organizations, based on a five-tiered static model that he developed.

Measurement: A quantified observation about any aspect of software (derived from Dr. Bill Hetzel).

Mentoring: Using an experienced person (tester) to help introduce a newer staff member to the processes, culture, and politics of an organization.

Meta-Measure: A measure of a measure. Usually used to measure the effectiveness of a measure, e.g., number of defects discovered per inspector hour (derived from Dr. Bill Hetzel).

Meter: A metric that acts as a trigger or threshold. That is, if some threshold is met, then an action is warranted, e.g., exit criteria (derived from Dr. Bill Hetzel).

Methodology (Test): A description of how testing will be conducted in an organization. Describes the tasks, product, and roles.

Metric: A measurement used to compare two or more products, processes, or projects (derived from Dr. Bill Hetzel).

Milestone: A major checkpoint or a sub-goal identified on the project or testing schedule.

Mitigation: An activity undertaken to reduce risk.

Model Office: An (acceptance) test environment created to closely mirror the production environment, including the use of real data.

Morale: An individual or group's state of mind.

Motivation: The influences that affect behavior.

Mutation Analysis: Purposely altering a program from its intended version in order to evaluate the ability of the test cases to detect the alteration.

Negative Test: Testing invalid input.

Objective: A broad category of things to test. An objective is to testing, what a requirement is to software.

Orthogonal Arrays: A technique used to choose test cases by employing arrays of integers.

Parallel Implementation: Installing and using a new system (or a newer version of an existing system) at the same time the old system (or a previous version) is installed and running.

Parallel Testing: A type of testing where the test results of a new system (or a newer version of a previous system) are compared to those from an old or previous version of the system.

Pareto Principle: 80% of the contribution comes from 20% of the contributors.

Phased Implementation: Shipping a product to the entire customer base in increments.

Pilot: A production system installed at a single or small number of client sites.

Planning Risk: A risk that jeopardizes the (testing) software development schedule.

Politics: The methods or tactics involved in managing an organization.

Positive Test: Testing valid input.

Preventive Testing: Building test cases based upon the requirements specification prior to the creation of the code, with the express purpose of validating the requirements.

Prototype: An original and usually working model of a new product or new version of an existing product, which serves as a basis or standard for later models.

QA: Quality assurance. The QA group is responsible for checking whether the software or processes conform to established standards.

Quality: Conformance to requirements.

Quiet Time: A period of time set aside from all meeting and other interruption in order to improve productivity

Random Testing: Testing using data that is in the format of real data, but with all of the fields generated randomly.

Regression Testing: Retesting previously tested features to ensure that a change or bug fix has not affected them.

Release: A particular version of software that is made available to a group or organization (i.e., a customer, the test group, etc.).

Requirements Traceability: Demonstrating that all requirements are covered by one or more test cases.

Resumption Criteria: Metrics that describe when testing will resume after it has been completely or partially halted.

Review: Any type of group activity undertaken to verify an activity, process or artifact (i.e., walkthrough, inspection, buddy check, etc.).

Risk: The chance of injury, damage or loss; a dangerous chance or hazard.

Risk Management: The science of risk analysis, avoidance, and control.

Safety Critical (System): A system that could cause loss of life or limb if a failure occurred.

Scaffolding Code: Code that simulates the function of non-existent components (e.g., stubs and drivers).

Script: An automated test procedure.

Semi-Random Testing: Testing using data that's in the format of real data, but with the fields generated with minimally defined parameters.

Smoke Test: A test run to demonstrate that the basic functionality of a system exists and that a certain level of stability has been achieved. Frequently used as part of the entrance criteria to a level of test.

Software: The requirements, design, code, and associated documentation of an application.

Software Configuration Management: A discipline of managing the components of a system.   Includes library management and the process of determining and prioritizing changes.

Software Risk Analysis: An analysis undertaken to identify and prioritize features and attributes for testing.

Software Under Test (SUT):   The entire product to be tested, including software and associated documentation.

Span of Control: The number of people directly reporting to a manager.

Spoilage: (1) A metric that uses defect age and distribution to measure the effectiveness of testing.   (2) According to Grady and Caswell, at Hitachi, spoilage means "the cost to fix post-release bugs."

Sponsor: Usually a senior manager who can help obtain resources and get buy-in.

State: The condition in which a system exists at a particular instance in time (e.g., the elevator is on the bottom floor).

State-Transition Diagram: A diagram that describes the way systems change from one state to another.

STEP (Systematic Test and Evaluation Process):   Software Quality Engineering's copyrighted testing methodology.

Strategy: A description of how testing will be conducted. Includes any issues that affect the effectiveness or efficiency of testing. See *Approach*.

Stress Testing: Testing to evaluate a system at or beyond the limits of its requirements.

Stubs: Modules that simulate low-level components.

Suspension Criteria: Metrics that describe a situation in which testing will be completely or partially halted (temporarily).

SWAT Team: A reserve group of expert testers who can be rapidly called, in an emergency.

System Testing: A (relatively) comprehensive test undertaken to validate an entire system and its characteristics. Typically based upon the requirements and design of the system.

Systems Integration Testing: See *Interface Testing*.

TBD (To Be Determined): A placeholder in a document.

Test Automation: Using testing tools to execute tests with little or no human intervention.

Test Bed: See *Environment*.

Test Case: Describes a particular condition to be tested. Defined by an input and an expected result.

Test Coordinator: A person charged with organizing a testing group including people, infrastructure, and/or methodologies. Often used for a one-time or limited-time testing effort. An organizational style using a test coordinator.

Test Data: Data (including inputs, required results, and actual results) developed or used in test cases and test procedures.

Test Deliverable: Any document, procedure, or other artifact created during the course of testing that's intended to be used and maintained.

Test Design Specification: A document describing a group of test cases used to test a feature(s).

Test Effectiveness: A measure of the quality of the testing effort (e.g., How well was the testing done?).

Test Implementation: The process of acquiring test data, developing test procedures, preparing the test environment, and selecting and implementing the tools that will be used to facilitate this process.

Test Incident Report: A description of an incident.

Test Item: A programmatic measure of something that will be tested (i.e., a program, requirement specification, version of an application, etc.).

Test Log: A chronological record of relevant details about the execution of test cases.

Test Procedure: A description of the steps necessary to execute a test case or group of test cases.

Test Process Improvement (TPI): A method for baselining testing processes and identifying process improvement opportunities, using a static model developed by Martin Pol and Tim Koomen.

Test Set: A group of test cases.

Test Suite: According to Linda Hayes, a test suite is a set of individual tests that are executed as a package in a particular sequence. Test suites are usually related by the area of the application that they exercise, by their priority, or by content.

Test Summary Report: A report that summarizes all of the testing activities that have taken place at a particular level of test (or the entire testing process in the case of a master test plan).

Testing: Concurrent lifecycle process of engineering, using, and maintaining testware in order to measure and improve the quality of the software being tested.

Testing Tool: A hardware or software product that replaces or enhances some aspect of human activity involved in testing.

Testware: Any document or product created as part of the testing effort.

Testware Configuration Management: The discipline of managing the test components of a system. Includes library management and the process of determining and prioritizing changes.

Turnover Files: Examples of reports, meeting minutes, contact lists, and other documents that, along with desktop procedures, facilitate a smooth transition from one manager to another.

Unit: A piece of code that performs a function, typically written by a single programmer. A module.

Unit Testing: A level of test undertaken to validate a single unit of code. Typically conducted by the programmer who wrote the code.

Usability Laboratory: A specially equipped laboratory designed to allow potential users of a system to "try out" a prototype of a system prior to its completion.

Use-Case: A use-case describes a sequence of interactions between an external "actor" and a system, which results in the actor accomplishing a task that provides a benefit to someone.

Validation: Any of a number of activities undertaken to demonstrate conformance to requirements (stated and implied) (i.e., building the right product). Often done through the execution of tests or reviews that include a comparison to the requirements.

Verification: Any of a number of activities undertaken to demonstrate that the results of one stage are consistent with the previous stage (i.e., the design is verified against the requirements specification). Typically done using reviews (i.e., doing the thing right).

Walkthrough: A peer review of a software product that is conducted by sequentially "walking through" the product. A type of verification.

Waterfall Model: A model of software development based upon distinct, sequential phases.

White-Box Testing (also known as *Glass-Box*, or *Translucent-Box*): Testing based upon knowledge of the internal (structure) of the system. Testing not only *what* the system does, but also *how* it does it (i.e., Structural Testing).

Appendix B – Testing Survey

"It's better to know some of the questions than all of the answers."

— James Thurber

The following survey was designed to be used at a testing conference to measure industry trends in test and evaluation process use. We've also found it to be a useful tool to baseline current practices within an organization.

Additionally, a gap analysis can be used to identify and prioritize process improvement opportunities. A large difference between the perceived value and usage value indicates a process that, if improved, could yield a large return on investment (ROI).

Test and Evaluation Practices Survey ■ ■ ■ ■ ■

Tables B-1 through B-4 contain a list of some test and evaluation activities that might be employed in your software activities. For each activity, indicate the degree of use in your division/area and how valuable or important you consider it to be towards producing good software. If you do not know the usage or have no opinion on the value, leave it blank. Table B-5 contains a list of some questions that pertain to trends and perspectives in testing.

Usage		Value	
0	No Usage – Not used.	0	Unimportant – Not needed or waste of time.
1	Infrequent Use – Used some of the time.	1	Limited Value – Would be nice.
2	Common Use – Used most of the time.	2	Significant Value – Recommended practice.
3	Standard Use – Used all of the time.	3	Critical – Should be a standard practice for everyone.

Table B-1   Management and Measures

	Description of Activity	Enter 0, 1, 2, or 3	
		Usage	Value
M1	An overall quality and/or test and evaluation plan is produced		
M2	A person is responsible for the testing and evaluation process		
M3	A capital budget is provided each year for the testing and evaluation process		
M4	A record of the time spent on testing and evaluation is produced		
M5	The cost of testing and reviews is measured and reported		
M6	A record of faults and defects found in each review or test stage is produced		
M7	A record of what is missed in each review or test stage is produced		
M8	Test and review effectiveness/efficiency is measured and reported		
M9	The cost of debugging is separated from testing		
M10	Defect density (defects per thousand lines of code) is measured		
M11	A person or department is responsible for managing the test environment and tools		
M12	The pattern of faults and defects found is regularly analyzed		
M13	Full-time testers are used for high-level testing (system and/or acceptance)		
M14	Full-time testers are used for low-level testing (unit and object)		
M15	Full-time reviewers are used in formal reviews and inspections		
M16	Compliance/adherence to the test and evaluation process is monitored		

Usage		Value	
0	No Usage – Not used.	0	Unimportant – Not needed or waste of time.
1	Infrequent Use – Used some of the time.	1	Limited Value – Would be nice.
2	Common Use – Used most of the time.	2	Significant Value – Recommended practice.
3	Standard Use – Used all of the time.	3	Critical – Should be a standard practice for everyone.

Table B-2 Evaluation Process

	Description of Activity	Enter 0, 1, 2, or 3	
		Usage	Value
E1	Review and inspection points are well-defined and documented		
E2	Specialized training is provided for specific roles (moderator, recorder, reader)................		
E3	Requirements documents are formally reviewed and inspected		
E4	Design documents are formally reviewed and inspected		
E5	Code is formally reviewed and inspected		
E6	Changes are formally reviewed and inspected		
E7	Testing plans and documents are formally reviewed...		
E8	Guidelines are used to control review length and review item size		
E9	A standard set of outcomes is used for formal reviews and inspections...............................		
E10	Statistics are kept for time spent by reviewer and review effectiveness...............................		
E11	Standard review reports are used for recording issues and summarizing results.................		
E12	Defects and review issues missed are measured and tracked..		
E13	Risk analysis is formally performed		
E14	Safety/hazard analysis is formally performed...		
E15	Specialized evaluation/analysis training is provided..		
E16	Defects are analyzed as to phase introduced and root cause		
E17	Review process adherence/compliance is monitored and tracked		

Usage		Value	
0	No Usage – Not used.	0	Unimportant – Not needed or waste of time.
1	Infrequent Use – Used some of the time.	1	Limited Value – Would be nice.
2	Common Use – Used most of the time.	2	Significant Value – Recommended practice.
3	Standard Use – Used all of the time.	3	Critical – Should be a standard practice for everyone.

Table B-3 Testing Process and Activities

	Description of Activity	Enter 0, 1, 2, or 3	
		Usage	Value
P1	Unit testing plans and specifications are documented...		
P2	Unit testing defects are tracked and analyzed...		
P3	Unit test summary reports are tracked and analyzed		
P4	System-level test plans and specifications are documented		
P5	System-level defects are tracked and analyzed..		
P6	System-level reports are produced		
P7	Test objectives are systematically inventoried and analyzed		
P8	Risk is acknowledged and used to design, organize, and execute tests		
P9	Requirements test coverage is tracked and measured..		
P10	Design test coverage is tracked and measured (traced)..		
P11	Code coverage is analyzed or traced...		
P12	Tests are rerun when software changes		
P13	Unit-level test sets are saved and maintained		
P14	System-level test sets are saved and maintained		
P15	Test cases and procedures are assigned unique names..		
P16	Tests are specified before the technical design of the software		
P17	Test cases and procedures are formally documented...		
P18	Test documents and test programs are reviewed like software		
P19	Defects found are analyzed as to phase introduced and root cause..		
P20	Test process adherence/compliance is monitored and measured		
P21	Testware is considered an asset and assigned a value..		

Usage		Value	
0	No Usage – Not used.	0	Unimportant – Not needed or waste of time.
1	Infrequent Use – Used some of the time.	1	Limited Value – Would be nice.
2	Common Use – Used most of the time.	2	Significant Value – Recommended practice.
3	Standard Use – Used all of the time.	3	Critical – Should be a standard practice for everyone.

Table B-4 Test and Evaluation Tools

	Description of Activity	Enter 0, 1, 2, or 3	
		Usage	Value
T1	Comparator (file output) is used to support testing		
T2	Simulators (hardware, software, or communications) are part of our test environment		
T3	Capture/playback tools are used for retesting		
T4	Coverage measurement tools are used in unit testing		
T5	Coverage measurement tools are used in system testing		
T6	Data or file generator (parameter or code-driven) tools are available		
T7	Data analyzer tools are used to profile test sets and files		
T8	A test database (bed of tests which simulate the test environment) is available		
T9	Test case or procedure generator (parameter or code-driven) tools are available		
T10	Static code analyzers are used to analyze risk and change		
T11	Test management tools to track and record execution results are used		
T12	Tools are used to estimate test and evaluation effort and/or schedule		

Identify any major commercial tools that you or your division/area *used regularly*:

Tool _____   **Vendor** _____

_____   _____

_____   _____

Table B-5   Trends and Perspectives

Compared with several years ago...	Worse	About Same	A Little Better	A Lot Better	Don't Know
Our overall software effort and quality is.................................					
The effectiveness of our reviews and inspections program is...					
The effectiveness of our unit-level testing is............................					
The effectiveness of our build/integration level testing is					
The effectiveness of our system-level testing is					
The effectiveness of our acceptance-level testing is					
The use of automation/tools to support test and evaluation is ..					
Our choice of what to measure and track is...............................					

Your estimate of the percentage of the total time spent in your division/area on software development and maintenance that is spent on...	Low%	Best Guess	High %	Don't Know
Quality management activities..				
Reviews and inspections (requirements, design, code).............				
Low-level testing (unit and integration)				
High-level testing (system and acceptance)...............................				

The one thing I wish my division/area would do or change regarding our test and evaluation effort is:

_____

_____

_____

_____

_____

Appendix C – IEEE Templates

"Innovate! Follow the standard and do it intelligently. That means including what you know needs to be included regardless of what the standard says. It means adding additional levels or organization that make sense."

— IEEE Computer Society,
Software Engineering Standards Collection

IEEE Templates   ■ ■ ■ ■ ■

For your convenience, we've included in this section all of the IEEE templates (and variations) used in this book. Some templates have been modified based on the experiences of the authors and as described in the text of this book. These changes (additions) are presented in italics. If you delete all of the italicized words in each template, the original IEEE template would remain.

For a complete description of each template, please refer to the corresponding section of the book indicated in the right margin. The complete IEEE guidelines can be purchased from the IEEE Web site at www. ieee.org.

Test Documents

IEEE Std. 829-1998 Standard for Software Test Documentation

Template for Test Documents

Contents

1. Test Plan

   Used for the master test plan and level-specific test plans.

2. Test Design Specification

   Used at each test level to specify the test set architecture and coverage traces.

3. Test Case Specification

   Used as needed to describe test cases or automated scripts.

4. Test Procedure Specification

   Used to specify the steps for executing a set of test cases.

5. Test Log

   Used as needed to record the execution of test procedures.

6. Test Incident Report

   Used to describe anomalies that occur during testing or in production. These anomalies may be in the requirements, design, code, documentation, or the test cases themselves. Incidents may later be classified as defects or enhancements.

7. Test Summary Report

   Used to report completion of testing at a level or a major test objective within a level.

■■■■■■■■■■■■■■■■■

Figure C-1

Template for Test Documents from IEEE Std. 829-1998

Refer to Chapter 1 for more information.

Test Plan

IEEE Std. 829-1998 Standard for Software Test Documentation

Template for Test Planning

Contents

1. Test Plan Identifier
2. *Table of Contents*
3. *References*
4. *Glossary*
5. Introduction
6. Test Items
7. *Software Risk Issues*
8. Features to Be Tested
9. Features Not to Be Tested
10. Approach
11. Item Pass/Fail Criteria
12. Suspension Criteria and Resumption Requirements
13. Test Deliverables
14. Testing Tasks
15. Environmental Needs
16. Responsibilities
17. Staffing and Training Needs
18. Schedule
19. Planning Risks and Contingencies
20. Approvals

■■■■■■■■■■■■■■■■■

Figure C-2

Template for Test
Planning from IEEE
Std. 829-1998

Refer to Chapter 3 for
more information.

Unit Testing

IEEE Std. 1008-1987 for Software Unit Testing

Contents

1. Scope and References
    1.1 Inside the Scope
    1.2 Outside the Scope
    1.3 References

2. Definitions

3. Unit Testing Activities
    3.1 Plan the General Approach, Resources, and Schedule
    3.2 Determine Features to Be Tested
    3.3 Refine the General Plan
    3.4 Design the Set of Tests
    3.5 Implement the Refined Plan and Design
    3.6 Execute the Test Procedures
    3.7 Check for Termination
    3.8 Evaluate the Test Effort and Unit

■■■■■■■■■■■■■■■■■

Figure C-3

Rick's copy of the
Unit Testing Standard

Refer to Chapter 4 for
more information.

Test Design Specification

IEEE Std. 829-1998 for Software Test Documentation

Template for Test Design Specification

Contents

1. Test Design Specification Identifier
2. Features to Be Tested
3. Approach Refinement
4. Test Identification
5. Feature Pass/Fail Criteria

■■■■■■■■■■■■■■■■■

Figure C-4

Test Design
Specification
Template from IEEE
Std. 829-1998

Refer to Chapter 5 for
more information.

Test Case Specification

IEEE Std. 829-1998 for Software Test Documentation

Template for Test Case Specification

Contents

1. Test Case Specification Identifier
2. Test Items
3. Input Specifications
4. Output Specifications
5. Environmental Needs
6. Special Procedural Requirements
7. Inter-Case Dependencies

■■■■■■■■■■■■■■■■■

Figure C-5

Test Case
Specification
Template from IEEE
Std. 829-1998

Refer to Chapter 5 for
more information.

Test Procedure

■■■■■■■■■■■■■■■■■

Figure C-6

Test Procedure
Template from IEEE
Std. 829-1998

Refer to Chapter 5 for
more information.

IEEE Std. 829-1998 for Software Test Documentation
Template for Test Procedure

Contents

1.0   Test Procedure Specification Identifier
Specify the unique identifier assigned to this test procedure.
Supply a reference to the associated test design specification.

2.0   Purpose
Describe the purpose(s) of the procedure and refer to the test cases
being executed.

3.0   Special Requirements
Describe any special requirements such as environmental needs,
skill level, training, etc.

4.0   Procedure Steps
This is the heart of the test procedure. The IEEE describes several
steps listed below:

4.1   Log
Describe any special methods or formats for logging the
results of test execution, the incidents observed, and any
other events pertinent to the test.

4.2   Set up
Describe the sequence of actions necessary to prepare
for execution of the procedure.

4.3   Start
Describe the actions necessary to begin execution of the
procedure.

4.4   Proceed
Describe any actions necessary during execution of the
procedure.
4.4.1   Step 1

4.4.2   Step 2

4.4.3   Step 3

4.4.4   Step Z

4.5   Measure

Describe how the test measurements will be made.

4.6   Shut Down

Describe the action necessary to suspend testing when unscheduled events dictate.

4.7   Restart

Identify any procedural restart points and describe the action necessary to restart the procedure at each of these points.

4.8   Stop

Describe the actions necessary to bring execution to an orderly halt.

4.9   Wrap Up

Describe the action necessary to restore the environment.

4.10   Contingencies

Describe the actions necessary to deal with anomalies and other events that may occur during execution.

Test Log

IEEE Std. 829-1998 for Software Test Documentation

Template for Test Log

Contents

1.   Test Log Identifier

2.   Description

3.   Activity and Event Entries

■■■■■■■■■■■■■■■■■

Figure C-7

Test Log Template from IEEE Std. 829-1998

Refer to Chapter 7 for more information.

Test Incident Report

IEEE Std. 829-1998 for Software Test Documentation
Template for Test Incident Report

Contents

1. Incident Summary Report Identifier
2. Incident Summary
3. Incident Description
   3.1 Inputs
   3.2 Expected Results
   3.3 Actual Results
   3.4 Anomalies
   3.5 Date and Time
   3.6 Procedure Step
   3.7 Environment
   3.8 Attempts to Repeat
   3.9 Testers
   3.10 Observers
4. Impact
5. *Investigation*
6. *Metrics*
7. *Disposition*

■■■■■■■■■■■■■■■■

Figure C-8

Template for Test
Incident Report from
IEEE Std. 829-1998

Refer to Chapter 7 for
more information.

Test Summary Report

IEEE Std. 829-1998 for Software Test Documentation
Template for Test Summary Report
 	
Contents
 	
1. Test Summary Report Identifier
2. Summary
3. Variances
4. Comprehensive Assessment
5. Summary of Results
    5.1 Resolved Incidents
    5.2 Unresolved Incidents
6. Evaluation
7. *Recommendations*
8. Summary of Activities
9. Approvals

■■■■■■■■■■■■■■■■■

Figure C-9

Template for Test
Summary Report
from IEEE-829-1998

Refer to Chapter 7 for
more information.

Test Plan for Process Improvement

Template for Process Improvement
 	
Contents
1. Test Plan Identifier
2. Introduction
    2.1 Genesis of Process Improvement Initiative
    2.2 Scope of Initiative
3. Planning Risks
    3.1 Schedule

■■■■■■■■■■■■■■■■■

Figure C-10

Test Plan Template
MODIFIED for
Process Improvement

Refer to Chapter 11
for more information.

3.2 Budget

3.3 Staffing

3.4 Buy-In

4. Approach

4.1 Major Strategy Decisions

5. Pass/Fail Criteria

5.1 What constitutes success? How are progress and results measured?

6. Suspension Criteria

6.1 What should cause us to temporarily suspend our efforts?

7. Deliverables

7.1 Project Status

7.2 Reports

7.3 Metrics

7.4 Post-Project Review

8. Environmental Needs

8.1 Hardware and Software

8.2 Tools

8.3 Office Space

9. Staffing and Training Needs

9.1 In-House

9.2 Contracted

10. Responsibilities

10.1 Team Members

10.2 Sponsor

10.3 Champion

10.4 Training Department

10.5 Test Environment Group

10.6 Process Group

11. Schedule

11.1 Project Initiative

11.2 Incremental Milestones

11.3 Post-Project Review

12. Approvals

12.1 Person(s) Approving the Plan

Appendix D – Sample Master Test Plan

"Planning is a process that should build upon itself – each step should create a new understanding of the situation which becomes the point of departure for new plans."

— Planning, MCDP 5
   U.S. Marine Corps

Sample Master Test Plan   ■ ■ ■ ■ ■

Below is a sample master test plan that was created to test the STQE.net Web site, which later became known as StickyMinds.com.

STQE.net Master Test Plan, Release 1
Version 1.5

1.   Test Plan Identifier

STQE.net MTP 1.5

2.   References

The following documents have been used in the preparation of this document:
   a.   SQE.NET Requirements Definition, Version 3.2
   b.   SQE.NET Web Site Control Structure, Version 1.00
   c.   SQE.NET Test Objectives, Version 1.5
   d.   SQE Systematic Software Testing Course Notes
   e.   STQE.NET Issue form

3.   Introduction

Software Quality Engineering has contracted with an outside software development vendor to create a World Wide Web (WWW) site to function as a knowledge and information sharing site for software testing and quality engineering professionals. The target audience will be the same as the *Software Testing and Quality Engineering* magazine, software managers (development, testing, and quality) and test professionals, and software engineers who are interested in building and delivering better software.

Unlike many WWW sites, this site, to be known as SQE.net, is a software-driven database application using Microsoft Site Builder with ASP coding and the MS-SQL database. **This Master Test Plan (MTP) covers the testing activities of the <u>software</u> and does not cover the initial or on-going tasks of adding, editing, publishing, and verifying the content.**

The SQE.net site will be introduced in releases with each release having increasing functionality:

- **Release 1.0**, also known as "Live Beta," will be an opportunity for the interest area moderators and product providers (vendors) to begin to enter data into the databases. Formal testing of SQE.net's initial capabilities will begin with this release. After formal testing and loading content, the site will be accepted into production and the public "Grand Opening" of the site will be announced. After all functionality for Release 1.0 has been delivered, internal bug fix releases will be denoted with a letter suffix, i.e. 1.0a, 1.0b, etc.

Future enhancements, such as job postings, banner ad management, a "What's new" feature, and a comprehensive site search engine, will take place in subsequent releases. This master test plan, covering the testing for Release 1 includes the following testing levels:

- <u>Unit and Integration Testing</u>: the vendor as part of its development of the site software will perform these levels. This plan will not discuss these levels of testing.
- <u>Smoke Test:</u> The smoke test will be conducted by the SQE test team. The test plans are written in a manner which can easily be automated. The purpose of the

smoke test is to verify that the software is stable enough to conduct further functional testing.

- Functional Test: The functional test is designed to verify that the functions at each user level work as designed. Many of the tests designed in the smoke test may be re-used along with some additional tests to create the functional test plan. These tests will also be written in a format that can be easily automated. It is at this level of test that the data will be verified to be in the correct state, updated to the appropriate database, etc. This level of test will be conducted at a more detailed level due to lack of formal testing in the unit test phase.

- System Testing: This level of test will test the functions of the system as a whole system. Again, many tests from previous test phases may be reused in the system test phase along, with new tests. The approach will be to verify the functional test plan utilizing more than one browser, operating system and monitor size.

- Performance Test: This level of test will verify that the system can perform adequately with a high volume of users. This test will be performed manually, utilizing the tests from previous test phases. The tests are being designed in a manner such that they can be reused and automated. Performance tests will be performed on the live production site.

- Acceptance Testing: This level of test is to test the Web site from an end-user perspective. The scenarios should be constructed from different types of users entering the site, what they would likely do and the questions they would likely ask. This test can be constructed using the tests from previous test phases and adding additional tests as needed.

- Beta Testing: This level occurs on the live SQE.NET site and is performed concurrently with acceptance testing. The content providers (moderators and product providers), who will be adding data to the site, will provide feedback on the performance and functionality of the site.

The philosophy of the testing is risk-based testing. All test objectives and tests will be prioritized for each level of testing as critical, high, medium, or low priority.

---

4.   Test Items

The software items to be tested include the following:

a. **SQE.NET site software:** Testing will be on the latest version available from the development vendor. Each version will be identified with an internal version code. The testing will be done with the software using the SQL Server database only and not with the Access database used for development.

b. **Netscape Navigator Version 3.02 and Internet Explorer (IE) Version 4.02:** We have specified that SQE.NET is to work with Netscape 3.0 and IE 4.0 and above with frames. Testing may be done on any version, but formal system and acceptance testing will be performed using these versions. Additional browser testing will be done on the latest MS-Windows browsers, including Netscape 4.0 and the upcoming IE 5.0.

c. **Microsoft Windows Platform:** Most testing will be performed on PCs running a minimum of Microsoft Windows 95, OSR 1. However, the reference platform for testing is Microsoft Windows 98 with the latest service pack.

d. **Macintosh Platform**: Minimal testing will be performed on the Macintosh platform with Netscape running the latest version of Mac OS Version 8.0. SQE will recruit and rely on Beta testing on the Mac platform.

e. **UNIX:** No formal testing will be done on UNIX workstations. SQE will recruit and rely on Beta testing for UNIX.

---
5.   Software Risk Issues

As this is the initial release of the STQE.net, testing will be required to verify all requirements of the site. Software risk issues are identified and prioritized in the STQE.net Test Objectives spreadsheet that is included in Appendix A of this plan.

---
6.   Features and Functions to Test

Test objectives are listed as requirements-based, design-based, or code-based and further separated into groups:

Requirements Based

RB-FN	Features - Navigation Bar
RB-FH	Features - Home
RB-UM	Features - User Member Management (Join, Sign-In, Update Profile)
RB-FI	Features - Interest Areas
RB-FB	Features - Books
RB-FT	Features - Tools and Services
RB-FC	Features - Calendar of Events
RB-FD	Features - Disclosures and Terms
RB-FS	Features - Sponsors and Advertisers
RB-FA	Features - Administrators
RB-SG	Scenarios - Guests
RB-SU	Scenarios - User Members (Logged-In)
RB-SM	Scenarios - Moderators
RB-SP	Scenarios - Providers (Vendors)

RB-SA   Scenarios - Administrator

Design Based
DB-US   Usage
DB-SC   Security
DB-ML   Multi-Language
DB-PF   Performance (Volume and Stress)
DB-BC   Browser Configurations
DB-SR   Site Failure/Restart
DB-BK   Backup/Recovery

Code Based
CB-LK   Links
CB-HS   Syntax (HTML and ASP Code)
CB-TG   Metatags and Graphics Tags

7.   Features Not to Test

We expect to test all of the objectives in the Test Objectives Inventory (Appendix A). However, if time does not permit, some of the low-priority items may be dropped.

8.   Approach

The testing will be done manually until the site is sufficiently stable to begin developing automatic tests. The testing will cover the requirements for all of the different roles participating in the site: guests, members, vendors, moderators, and administrators.

Automated Testing Tools

We are going to implement automated testing using commercially available, off-the-shelf tools. A tool will be used for feedback/defect tracking. A tool will be implemented for test scripting using a mix of manual and automated tests. Capture/playback tools will be used on a limited basis for automating parts of the smoke test. Other utilities, such as link testers and HTML syntax checkers, will be used as needed. We do not plan any automated performance testing for Release 1.

The smoke tests will be the first series of tests to automate. Work will begin when the GUI interface and database are stable.

Defect Tracking

Testing issues and feedback from beta users will be reported on the STQE.net Issue Form and entered into a tool. Within one business day, we will analyze and classify any new issue as a software defect, enhancement, could not reproduce, not a problem, or failure. Severity level and fix priority of software defects will be set. Issue classes, severity categories, and fix priorities are listed in Appendix B.

Change Management

When the vendor turns the software over to SQE for testing, all changes to the site software will come under change control. The project manager will approve all changes moved into the test environment. A change notice must define the modules being changed and the reason for the change, including all repaired defects. Except for critical fixes that are blocking current testing efforts, changes will be scheduled not to impact testing.

Except for emergency repairs, changes will not be moved into the live environment until the test manager approves a new version for production. After the software is moved to the live environment, testing will confirm that the software matches the configuration in test and perform a smoke test.

Test Cycles

Each time a new version is released to the test environment, the following process will be undertaken:

- Configuration will be checked and recorded.
- Smoke test will be run.
- If successful, the system and/or acceptance test suite will be updated to account for changes uncovered by the Smoke Test and then run. The incidents will be analyzed and software defects reported.
- Ad hoc testing will be performed by the testers of new or changed functionality or functionality that has been error prone.
- New tests will be developed.

While Release 1 is in the "live beta" status, updates that "pass" a test cycle will be moved to the production host and made "live."

Metrics

Metrics will be kept for test effort, incidents, defects, and test cases executed for each test cycle.

9.   Item Pass/Fail Criteria

The entrance criteria for each level of testing are defined in Appendix C. The exit criteria are the entrance criteria for the following test level. The Web site will not be opened for content providers when any critical defects exist in those functions involved with the addition of content.

Release 1 of the site will not be opened to the general public until all critical and high-severity defects have been resolved. The project manager will have the discretion to determine that some critical and high defects may be deferred, where the effects of their failures do not affect guests and members in the use of the site.

10. Suspension Criteria and Resumption Req'mts

With each update from the vendor, a smoke test will be performed. If this test does not pass, further testing is halted until a version is delivered that will pass that test. Testing will resume when an update that can pass the smoke test has been delivered.

11. Test Deliverables

The following documents will be prepared:
- Master Test Plan (this document)
- Test Design
- Test Procedures
- Test Logs
- Test Summary Report
- Test Data
- Automated Test Scripts
- Incident Reports
- Incident Log

12. Remaining Test Tasks

The vendor will perform the unit and integration testing. The browsers and the operating systems are accepted, as is.

13.   Test Environment

Testers will identify the browser used during all tests. Four Web sites will be used in this development process:

- **Development:** This site, located on the developer network, is the vendor's development environment. *NOTE: The development uses an Access database for SQL tables for faster development. All other sites use MS-SQL databases.*
- **Development Staging:** Updates to the software will be moved to the Development Staging site for the Smoke Test. This site, located on the developer network, uses the MS-SQL database (same as production).
- **SQE Test:** This site, located at SQE, will be used for Functional, System, and Acceptance testing.
- **Live Production:** This site will be located at an ISP supporting 24x7 operations. Performance testing will be done on this site.

A separate test site may be needed for automated testing.

14.   Staffing and Training Needs

The following roles are identified:

- **Project Manager:** Responsible for managing the total implementation of the SQE.NET Web site.   This includes creating requirements, managing the vendor relationship, overseeing the testing process, and reporting to senior management.
- **Test Manager:** Responsible for developing the master test plan, reviewing the test deliverables, managing the test cycles, collecting metrics and reporting status to the

Project Manager, and recommending when testing is complete.

- **Test Engineer:** Responsible for designing the tests, creating the test procedures, creating the test data, executing tests, preparing incident reports, analyzing incidents, writing automated test procedures, and reporting metrics to the test manager.
- **PC/Network Support:** Responsible for maintaining the PCs and network at the SQE office to support the testing.

The test manager and test engineers should be familiar with the STEP methodology from having taken the SST course.

15.　Responsibilities

Role	Candidate	Timing
Project Manager	Jennifer Brock	All, Part-Time
Test Manager	John Lisle	All, Part-Time
Test Engineers	Jennifer Brock, John Lisle, Paul Danon	All, Part-Time
PC / Network Support	Jim Sowder	All, Part-Time

16.　Schedule

See Appendix D for the schedule to develop the test planning and design documents. The following table represents the plan for the expected test cycles.

Testing Cycle	Event	Who	Milestone
Test Cycle 1	Start		3/8/1999
	Run Smoke Test	JB, JD, WM	3/8/1999
	Complete System Test (except performance)	JB, JD, WM	3/12/1999
	Complete Acceptance	JB, JD, WM	3/12/1999
Turnover	Content Providers	WM	3/15/1999
Test Cycle 2	Start		3/22/1999
	Run Smoke Test	JB, JD, WM	3/22/1999
	Complete Acceptance	JB, JD, WM	3/26/1999
Test Cycle 3	Start		4/5/1999
	Run Smoke Test	JB, JD, WM	4/5/1999
	Complete Acceptance	JB, JD, WM	4/9/1999
Test Cycle 4	Start		4/12/1999
	Run Smoke Test	JB, JD, WM	4/12/1999
	Complete Acceptance	JB, JD, WM	4/16/1999
Test Cycle 5	Start		4/19/1999
	Run Smoke Test	JB, JD, WM	4/19/1999
	Complete System Test	JB, JD, WM	4/23/1999
	Complete Acceptance	JB, JD, WM	4/23/1999
Turnover	General Public	WM	5/3/1999

17.   Planning Risks and Contingencies

a. Web Site Not Ready for Content Providers – This will cause a delay to the live beta. We need to give the content providers at least four weeks to enter data before opening the site to the public.

b. Web Site Not Ready for Content Addition and General Public – This could be because the software is not ready or because insufficient content is available. This will cause a delay to the opening of the site.

c. Web Testing Software Not Available – This will delay the introduction of automated testing, and more manual testing will be required. May need to recruit more staff to do the testing.

d. Test Staff Shortages – All of the test staff are part-time and have other priorities. No slack time is allocated for illness or vacation.

e. Host Web Site for Live Production – The search for the Host of the live site is a separate project and not completed.

f. Configuration Management Problems – The project team has experienced problems with the development vendor's configuration/change management.

18. Approvals

This plan needs to be approved by the project manager for the Web site and the SQE project sponsor.

Appendix A for STQE.net MTP

Refer to electronic spreadsheet for Test Objectives Inventory.

Appendix B for STQE.net MTP

Incident Classification	Definition
Software Defect	Clearly a defect in the software, maybe requirements based, code based, or design based.
Enhancement	An enhancement to existing application. It could be code related, data, or process.
Could Not Reproduce	Could not recreate situation; made several attempts before categorizing as such.
Not a Problem	Could reproduce and determined application, process, and data were intentionally designed to behave as they are.
Failure – Environment	Failure occurred and has been determined to be due to a problem with the environment. Same failure does not occur when the environment has been corrected.
Failure – Testware Defect	Failure occurred and determination made. Testware was incorrect. Testware needs to be corrected.
Failure – Test Execution	Failure occurred and determination made was related to improper execution of the test.
Failure – Other	Failure occurred and does not fit into above categories.

Severity	Definition
Low	Minor flaw not affecting operation or understanding of feature.
Medium	Feature is usable, but some functionality is lost or user may misinterpret and use improperly.
High	Important functionality is lost or feature is not usable, but there is a work-around or feature is not critical to the operations.
Critical	Important feature is not usable. Emergency fix is authorized.

Fix Priority	Response
Low	Correct in next scheduled enhancement release or update documentation and do not fix.
Medium	Fix after high-priority defects and enhancements. Document work-around or affect on users.
High	Fix within 72 working hours, stop work on enhancements, if necessary.
Critical	Fix ASAP, within 12 hours; overtime authorized; skip full acceptance testing, if necessary. Don't go home until fixed.

Appendix C for STQE.net MTP

Test Level	Description
Unit Test	Component/Module for unit test is 100% complete: • Items to test are outlined; unit tester should know expected results. • All programs in unit test compile cleanly. • A listing of all unit-tested programs exists.
Functional Test	Components/Modules for integration test are 100% complete: • Unit tests are executed and all open high or critical severity level defects are closed. • Unit tests are executed and all high or emergency priority to fix defects are closed. • All programs scheduled for integration test compile cleanly. • A listing of all integration programs is complete. • High-level integration test plan complete and peer reviewed.
System Test	Components/Modules for System test are 100% complete: • Integration and unit tests are complete and all open high or critical severity level defects are closed. • Integration and unit tests are complete and all open high or emergency priority to fix defects are closed. • All programs scheduled to run as part of the system test execute with no failures. This will be verified by running the smoke test. • System test plan is complete and reviewed. • Change management process is in place and adhered to.
Performance Test	Components/Modules for Performance test are 100% complete: • System tests are complete and all open high or critical severity level defects are closed. • All programs scheduled to run as part of the system test execute with no failures. • Performance test plan is complete and reviewed. • Change management process is in place and adhered to.

(Continued)

Test Level	Description
Acceptance Test	Components/Modules for Acceptance test are 100% complete: • System test is complete and all high or critical severity level defects are closed. • System test is complete and all high or emergency priority to fix defects are closed. • All programs scheduled to run as part of the acceptance test execute with no failures. This will be verified by running the smoke test. • Acceptance test plan is complete and reviewed. • Change management process is in place and adhered to.
Live Beta	Components/Modules for Live Beta are 100% complete: • Acceptance test is complete and all high or critical severity level defects are closed. • Acceptance test is complete and all high or emergency priority to fix defects are closed. • All programs scheduled to run as part of the live beta execute with no failures. This will be verified by running the smoke test. • Data is refreshed. • Change management process is in place and adhered to.

Appendix D for STQE.net MTP

Deliverable	Event	Who	Milestone
Master Test Plan	First Draft	JBL	2/8/1999
	Review	JBL, JB, WM	2/9/1999
	Version 1.0	JBL	2/12/1999
	Review	JBL, JB, WM, DG	2/24/1999
	Version 1.1	JBL	3/1/1999
Test Objectives	First Draft (Partial)	JBL	2/8/1999
	Version 0.9 (Partial)	JBL	2/12/1999
	Review	JBL, JB, WM, DG	2/24/1999
	Version 1.0	JBL	3/1/1999
	Review	JBL, JB, WM	3/3/1999
	Version 1.1	JBL	3/8/1999
Web Control Structure	First Draft (Partial)	JBL	2/11/1999
	Review	JBL, JB, WM, DG	2/15/1999
	Version 1.0	JBL	3/1/1999
	Review	JBL, JB, WM	3/3/1999
	Version 1.1	JBL	3/9/1999
Smoke Test Design	First Draft	JBL	3/8/1999
	Review	JBL, JB, WM	3/12/1999
	Version 1.0	JBL	3/15/1999
	Review	JBL, JB, WM	3/18/1999
	Version 1.1	JBL	3/24/1999
System/Acceptance Test Design	First Draft	JBL	3/12/1999
	Review	JBL, JB, WM	3/15/1999
	Version 1.0	JBL	3/24/1999
	Review	JBL, JB, WM	3/27/1999
	Version 1.1	JBL	3/31/1999

Appendix E – Simplified Unit Test Plan

"KISS – Keep It Simple, Sir!"

— Anonymous

Simplified Unit Test Plan

Created By: Dale Perry
Version 2.1

This unit test plan template was created by our colleague Dale Perry in order to clarify and simplify the tasks needed to perform unit testing.

1. Identification

Version/release information and configuration identification.

2. References

Any supporting documentation including:
- Requirements specifications
- Design specifications
- Other documents/diagrams

3. Module/Component/Unit

Owner	Identification	Type	New	Modified

- Owner of the module/component
- Module identification (e.g., name, etc.)
- Type of module (e.g., C program, DLL, etc.)
- Is this a new module or a modified existing module?

---

4.   Functions/Features (Attributes, Sub-Functions)

Function	Sub-Function/Attribute	Test Aspect/Risk	New	Modified

---

- Identify all modified functions/features and the attributes of those features.
- Test Aspect/Risk:
  - Why does this need to be tested and what is the risk associated with the feature or function?
    - Business Risk
      - Risk to business if feature does not function correctly or causes faults
    - Technical Risk
      - Complexity, technology or other software concerns
- Is this a new function or a modification to an existing function?
- Add as many entries as required.

5.   Shared Elements

Element	Sharing Element	Type	Risk	New	Modified

- Identify any shared constructs and what they are shared with (e.g., constructs, transactions, messages, objects, classes). This will help focus regression test efforts.
- What are the risks to the shared elements?
- Is the shared element new or being modified?
- Add as many entries as required.

6.   Interfaces/Communications

Interface	Type	Risk	New	Modified

- Identify all interfaces and the type of interface:
  - Communication
  - Database
  - Transaction
  - Network
  - Other
- What are the risks to the shared interfaces?
- Is the interface new or being modified?
- Add as many entries as required.

7.   Non-Modified or Other Functions and Attributes

Function	Sub-Function/Attribute	Risk

- Identify all other functions/features and their sub-functions and attributes that are part of the modified component. This does not apply to new features or functions unless they are added to an existing module or to other existing features/functions.
- What are the risks to those non-modified elements?
- This will also help identify elements that require regression testing.

8.   External Updates

Element	Type/Category	Version

Identify any external elements that were updated or modified to support the change:

- These can include DLLs, object classes, shared libraries, vendor packages, etc.
- This will allow identification of those elements that vary from those in the final production environment, and may indicate where a more advanced version was used during development than will be used in production.

9.   Approach

- How will unit testing be accomplished?
  - Debugged
  - Coverage tool
  - Other tool
- How will proof of test be provided to show unit test was completed?
  - Trace reports
  - Coverage reports
  - Debug printouts
  - Other

10.   Pass/Fail Criteria

How will test results be evaluated prior to build/integration testing?

Appendix F – Process Diagrams

"One picture is worth a thousand words."

— Old Chinese Proverb

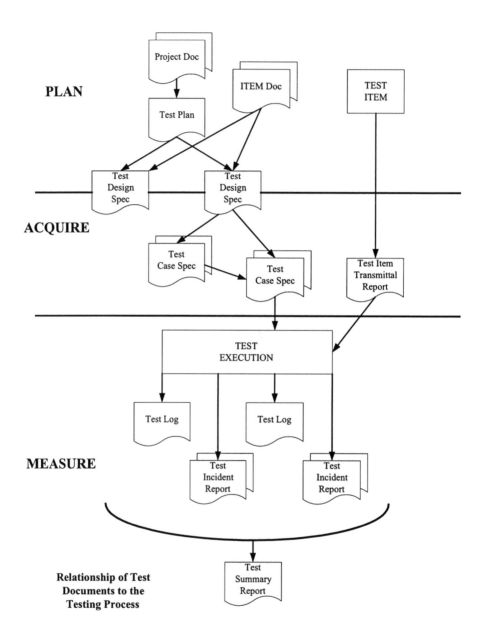

Relationship of Test Documents to the Testing Process

Figure F-1 Test Process and Documentation Relationship

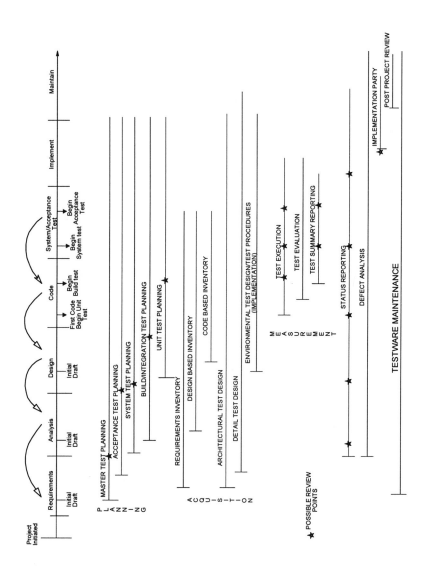

Figure F-2 STEP Process Flow, Timing, and Lifecycle Relationship

Appendix G – Bibliography

"The next best thing to knowing something is knowing where to find it."

— Samuel Johnson

Bibliography ■ ■ ■ ■ ■

Allison, Anna S. W. "Conveying the Context of Your Numbers, Meaningful Metrics"; *Software Testing & Quality Engineering*, Jan/Feb 2002.

Beck, Kent (1999). *Extreme Programming: Embrace Change (The XP Series)*. Addison Wesley. ISBN 0-201-61641-6.

Beizer, Boris (1983). *Software Testing Techniques.* Van Nostrand Reinhold Company. ISBN 0-442-24592-0.

Beizer, Boris (1995). *Black-Box Testing, Techniques for Functional Testing of Software and Systems*. John Wiley & Sons. ISBN 0-471-12094-4.

Berbert, Todd. "Extreme Testing"
http://www.ayeconference.com/articles/estremetesting.shtml

Berra, Yogi, Joe Garagiola, and Dale Berra (1998). *The Yogi Book*. Workman Publishing. ISBN 0-761-11090-9.

Bersoff, Edward H., Vilas D. Henderson, Stanley G. Siegel, (1980). *Software Configuration Management, An Investment in Product Integrity*. Prentice-Hall. ISBN 0-13-821769-6.

Black, Rex. "Effective Status Reporting"; *Software Testing & Quality Engineering*, March/April 2000.

Black, Rex (1999). *Managing the Testing Process*. Microsoft Press. ISBN 0-7356-0584-x.

Block, Robert (1983). *The Politics of Projects*. Yourdon Press. ISBN 0-13-685553-9.

Boehm, Barry W. (1989). *Software Risk Management.* IEEE Computer Society Press. ISBN 0-8186-8906-4.

Brooks, Frederick P. "No Silver Bullets – Essence and Accidents of Software Engineering"; *Computer.* April 1987.

Brooks, Jr., Frederick P. (1995). *The Mythical Man-Month.* Addison Wesley. ISBN 0-201-83595-9.

Carrison, Dan and Rod Walsh (1998). *Semper Fi: Business Leadership the Marine Corps Way.* AMACOM. ISBN 0-814-40413-8.

Charette, Robert N. (1989). *Software Engineering Risk Analysis and Management.* McGraw-Hill. ISBN 0-07-010661-4.

Cockburn, Alister. "Goals and Use Cases"; *Object-Oriented Programming.* 1997.

Cole, Oliver E. "Looking Under the Covers to Test Web Applications"; *Proceedings of STAR East Conference, 2001.*

Collard, Ross. "Small Change, Big Trouble"; *Software Testing & Quality Engineering*, January/February 2002.

Collard, Ross. "Test Design, Developing Test Cases From Use Cases"; *Software Testing & Quality Engineering*, July/August 1999.

Collard, Ross. "What People Like About Automated Test Tools"; *Proceedings of Rational ASQ User Conference, 1997.*

Compton, Stephen B. and Guy R. Conner (1994). *Configuration Management for Software.* Van Nostrand Reinhold. ISBN 0-442-01746-4.

Craig, Rick D. "Independent Test Teams"; *Quality Data Processing*, July 1989.

Craig, Rick D. "Is Distance Learning a Viable Solution?"; *Industry Standard*, Sept 2000.

Craig, Rick. "The Case of the Bogus Metrics"; *Software Quality Management*, New Year 1995, p. 4.

Craig, Rick D. "Using the 'Buddy System' for Unit Testing"; *Management Issues & Software Development*; *Application Development Trends*, Dec 1995.

Craig, Rick D. and Bill Hetzel (1990). *Software Measures and Practices Study*. STQE Press.

Crosby, Philip B. (1992). *Quality Is Free: The Art of Making Quality Certain*. Mentor Books. ISBN 0-451-62585-4.

Crosby, Philip B. (1995). *Quality Is Still Free: Making Certain in Uncertain Times*. McGraw-Hill. ISBN 0-07-014532-6.

Crosby, Philip B. (1997). *The Absolutes of Leadership*. Jossey-Bass Publishers. ISBN 07879-0942-4.

Daich, Gregory T. "Effective Acquirer/Supplier Software Document Reviews"; *Crosstalk*, Aug 1999.

Davis, Alan M. (1995). *201 Principles of Software Development*. IEEE Computer Society. ISBN 0-07-015840-1.

Dedolph, F. Michael. "Why Testers Should Participate in Early Reviews"; *Software Testing & Quality Engineering*, March/April 2001.

DeMarco, Tom and Timothy Lister (1999). *Peopleware: Productive Projects and Teams.* Dorset House. ISBN 0-93263343-9.

Donaldson, Scott E. and Stanley G. Siegel (2001). *Successful Software Development.* Prentice-Hall. ISBN 0-13-086826-4.

Down, Alex, Michael Coleman, and Peter Absolon (1994*). Risk Management for Software Projects.* McGraw-Hill. ISBN 0-07-707816-0.

Drabick, Rodger. "Growth of Maturity in the Testing Process"; International Software Testing Institute. http://www.softtest.org/articles

Draper, Stephen W. "The Hawthorne Effect"; University of Glasgow, Department of Psychology. http://staff.psy.gla.ac.uk/~steve/hawth.html.

Dunn, Robert H. (1984). *Software Defect Removal.* McGraw-Hill. ISBN 0-07-018313-9.

Dunn, Robert H. (1999). "The Quest for Software Reliability" in *Handbook of Software Quality Assurance* edited by G. Gordon Schulmeyer, and James I. McManus, Prentice Hall. ISBN 0-130-10470-1.

Dustin, Elfriede. "Orthogonally Speaking"; *Software Testing & Quality Engineering*, Sept/Oct 2001.

Dyes, Tim. "Tracking Severity"; *Software Testing & Quality Engineering.* March/April 1998.

Eisenberg, Abne M. (1979). *Job Talk.* Macmillan Publishing Company. ISBN 0-02-535120-6.

Fenton, Norman E. "Software Measurement Programs"; *Software Testing & Quality Engineering*, May/June 1999.

Fenton, Norman E. (1991). *Software Metrics, A Rigorous Approach*. Chapman & Hall. ISBN 0-412-40440-0.

Fisk, Jim and Barron, Robert (1984). *Official MBA Handbook of Great Business Quotations*. Simon & Schuster, Inc. ISBN 0-671-50318-9.

Franklin, Benjamin (1976). *Poor Richard's Almanac*. David McKay Co. ISBN 0-679-50072-3.

Freeman, Peter (1987). *Software Perspectives, The System Is the Message*. Addison-Wesley. ISBN 0-201-11969-2.

Freedman, Daniel P. and Gerald M. Weinberg (1990). *Handbook of Walkthroughs, Inspections, and Technical Reviews: Evaluating Programs, Projects, and Products*. Dorset House Publishing. ISBN 0-932633-19-6.

Gause, Donald C. and Gerald M. Weinberg (1989). *Exploring Requirements, Quality Before Design*. Dorset House Publishing. ISBN 0-932633-13-7.

Gause, Donald C. and Gerald M. Weinberg (1990). *Are Your Lights On?* Dorset House Publishing. ISBN 0-932-63316-1.

Gilb, Tom (1988). *Principles of Software Engineering Management*. Addison-Wesley. ISBN 0-201-19246-2.

Gilb, Tom and Dorothy Graham (1993). *Software Inspection*. Addison-Wesley. ISBN 0-201-63181-4.

Goodman, Paul (1993). *Practical Implementation of Software Metrics*. McGraw-Hill. ISBN 0-07-707665-6.

Grady, Robert B. (1992). *Practical Software Metrics for Project Management and Process Improvement.* Prentice-Hall. ISBN 0-13-720384-5.

Grady, Robert B. and Deborah L. Caswell (1998). *Software Metrics: Establishing a Company-Wide Program.* Prentice-Hall. ISBN 0-13-821844-7.

Graham, Dorothy R. "Measuring the Value of Testing"; *Proceedings of STAR East, Software Quality Engineering, 2001.*

Grayson, Dawn and Amy Ostrom. "Customer Satisfaction Fables"; *Sloan Management Review,* Massachusetts Institute of Technology; Summer 1994.

Grote, Dick and Jonb Boroshok. "Are Most Layoffs Carried Out Fairly?"; *Optimize Magazine* (Information Week), Dec 2001.

Hayes, Linda G. (1995). *Automated Testing Handbook.* Software Testing Institute. ISBN 0-970-74650-4.

Hendrickson, Elisabeth. "Writing Effective Bug Reports"; *Software Testing & Quality Engineering,* July/Aug 2001.

Hetzel, Bill (1993). *Making Software Measurements Work.* John Wiley & Sons. ISBN 0-471-56568-7.

Hetzel, Bill (1984). *The Complete Guide to Software Testing.* QED Information Sciences. ISBN 0-89435-110-9.

Hetzel, Bill. *The Systematic Test and Evaluation Process Summary Guide,* Software Quality Engineering.

Huff, Darrell (1954). *How to Lie with Statistics.* W.W. Norton. ISBN 0-393-31072-8.

IEEE Standards Software Engineering 1999 Edition, Volume 2, Process Standards. The Institute of Electrical and Electronics Engineers. ISBN 0-7381-1560-6.

IEEE Standards Software Engineering 1999 Edition, Volume 4, Resource and Technique Standards. The Institute of Electrical and Electronics Engineers. ISBN 0-7381-1562-2.

Jeffries, Ronald E. "Extreme Testing: Why Aggressive Software Development Calls for Radical Testing Efforts"; *Software Testing & Quality Engineering*, March/April 1999.

Joch, Alan. "How Software Doesn't Work"; *Byte*, Dec 1995.

Johnson, Jim. "Chaos Into Success"; *Software Magazine*, Dec 1999.

Johnson, Mark. "Matching ISO 9000 Registration to Your Organization"; *Software Testing & Quality Engineering*, July/August 1999.

Jones, Capers (1991). *Applied Software Measurement, Assuring Productivity and Quality.* McGraw-Hill. ISBN 0-07-032813-7.

Jones, Capers (1994). *Assessment and Control of Software Risks.* Prentice Hall. ISBN 0-13-741406-4.

Jones, Capers (1997). *Software Quality, Analysis and Guidelines for Success.* International Thomson Computer Press. ISBN 1-85032-867-6.

Kaner, Cem. "Rethinking Software Metrics"; *Software Testing & Quality Engineering*, March/April 2000.

Kaner, Cem (1988). *Testing Computer Software*. TAB Professional and Reference Books. ISBN 0-8306-9563-x.

Kit, Edward (1995). *Software Testing in the Real World, Improving the Process*. Addison Wesley. ISBN 0-201-87756-2.

Koomen, Tim and Martin Pol (1999). *Test Process Improvement*. ACM Press. ISBN 0-201-59624-5.

Kotter, John P. (1998). "What Leaders Really Do" in *Harvard Business Review on Leadership*. Harvard Business School Press. ISBN 0-87584-883-4.

Kreitner, Robert and Angelo Kinicki (1998). *Organizational Behavior*. McGraw-Hill. ISBN 0-256-22512-5.

Laporte, Claude Y. and Sylvie Trudel. "Addressing People Issues When Developing and Implementing Engineering Processes"; *Crosstalk*, Nov 1999.

Levenson, Nancy and Clark S. Turner. "An Investigation of the Therac-25 Accidents"; *IEEE Computer*, Vol. 26, No. 7, July 1993, pp. 18-41.

Leveson, Nancy G. (1995). *Safeware, System Safety and Computers*. Addison-Wesley. ISBN 0-201-11972-2.

Levine, Robert. "A Special Report on the Office of the Future"; *The Industry Standard*, May 7, 2001, p. 88.

Lewis, William E. (2000). *Software Testing and Continuous Quality Improvement*. CRC Press. ISBN 0-8493-9833-9.

Lindgaard, Gitte (1994). *Usability Testing and System Evaluation, A Guide for Designing Useful Computer Systems*. Chapman & Hall. ISBN 0-412-46100-5.

Lizotte, Renee. "The NQA and ISO 9000"; *Software Quality Management Magazine*, Autumn 1994.

Lohr, Claire. "Mastering Test Design, Course Notes" *Software Quality Engineering, 2001*.

Lubar, David (1995). *It's Not a Bug, It's a Feature!* Addison-Wesley. ISBN 0-201-48304-1.

Martin, Charles F. (1988). *User-Centered Requirements Analysis*. Prentice-Hall. ISBN 0-13-940578-x.

McCabe, Thomas J. and G. Gordon Schulmeyer (1999). "The Pareto Principle Applied to Software Quality Assurance"; *Handbook of Software Quality Assurance*. Prentice-Hall. ISBN 0-13010470-1.

McCabe, Thomas J. and Arthur H. Watson. "Software Complexity"; *Crosstalk*, Dec 1994.

McCabe, Tom. "Successful Tool Usage"; *Software Quality Management Magazine*, Spring 1994.

McConnell, Steve (1996). *Rapid Development*. Microsoft Press. ISBN 1-55615-900-5.

Metzger, Philip W. and John Boddie. (1995). *Managing a Programming Project*. Prentice-Hall. ISBN 0-13-554239-1.

Möller, K. H., and D. J. Paulish (1993). *Software Metrics, A Practitioner's Guide to Improved Product Development*. IEEE Press. ISBN 0-7803-0444-6.

Myers, Glenford (1979). *The Art of Software Testing*. John Wiley & Sons. ISBN 0-471-04328-1.

Neumann, Peter G. (1995). *Computer Related Risks*. Addison-Wesley. ISBN 0-201-55805.

Ould, Martyn A. (1999). *Managing Software Quality and Business Risk*. Wiley. ISBN 0-471-99782-X.

Ould, Martyn A. and Unwin, Charles (1988). *Testing in Software Development*. Cambridge University Press. ISBN 0-521-33786-0.

Packard, David (1996). *The HP Way: How Bill Hewlett and I Built Our Company*. Harperbusiness. ISBN 0-887-30817-1.

Pajerek, Lori. "Bought Any Good Shelfware Lately?"; *Crosstalk*, Dec 1997.

Patel, Eric, "Getting the Most From Outsourcing"; *Software Testing & Quality Engineering*, Nov/Dec 2001.

Patton, Ron (2001). *Software Testing*. Sams Publishing. ISBN 0-672-31983-7.

Paulk, Mark C. et al. (1995). *The Capability Maturity Model, Guidelines for Improving the Software Process*. Addison-Wesley. ISBN 0-201-54664-7.

Petroski, Henry (1982). *To Engineer Is Human*. St. Martin's Press. ISBN 0-312-80680-9.

Pettichord, Bret. "Testers and Developers Think Differently"; *Software Testing & Quality Engineering*, January/February 2000.

Phillips, Donald T. (1992). *Lincoln on Leadership*. Warner Books. ISBN 0-446-39459-9.

Pitts, David. "Why Is Software Measurement Hard?"; *Proceedings of the 1999 Applications of Software Measurement Conference.*

Pol, Martin and Eric van Veenendaal (1998). *Structured Testing of Information Systems.* Kluwer, Deventer, The Netherlands. ISBN 90-267-2910-3.

Pontin, Jason. "The Future of Electronic Education"; *Red Herring*, January 2002.

Prasse, Dr. Michael J. "It Works, But Is It Usable?"; *Partner's Progress, SQE.* Second Quarter, 1993.

Preece, Jenny, et al. (1993). *A Guide to Usability.* Addison-Wesley. ISBN 0-201-62768-x.

Pressman, Roger S. (1996). *A Manager's Guide to Software Engineering.* McGraw-Hill. ISBN 0-070-52229-4.

Schmauch, Charles H. (1994). *ISO 9000 for Software Developers.* American Society Quality Press. ISBN 0-87389-246-1.

Sherman, Roger. "Best Development and Testing Strategies of Microsoft"; *Proceedings of STAR West Conference, 1998.*

Smith, Lt. Col. Robert W. (1979). *Guidebook for Marines.* Marine Corps Association.

"Space Events Diary"; April - June 1999. http://www.ssc.se/ssd/dia992.html

Splaine, Steven and Stefan P. Jaskiel (2001*). The Web Testing Handbook.* Software Quality Engineering. ISBN 0-9704363-0-0.

Stahl, Bob. "Usability Testing"; *Software Testing & Quality Engineering*, Sept/Oct 2001.

Starbuck, Ronald. "How to Control Software Changes"; *Software Testing & Quality Engineering*, November/December 1999.

Suzuki, John. "Distributed Teams"; *Software Testing & Quality Engineering*. Sept/Oct 2001.

Teal, Thomas (1998). "The Human Side of Management" in *Harvard Business Review on Leadership*. Harvard Business School Press. ISBN 0-87584-883-4.

Tingey, Michael O. (1997). *Comparing ISO 9000, Malcolm Baldrige, and the SEI CMM for Software*. Prentice-Hall. ISBN 0-13-376260-2.

Tzu, Sun and Samuel B. Griffith (translation) (1984). *The Art of War*. Oxford University Press. ISBN 0-195-01476-6.

U.S. Marine Corps (1984). *NAVMC 2767 User's Guide to Marine Corps Leadership*. U.S. Marine Corps Association. PCN 100 013456 00.

U.S. Marine Corps (1997). *MCDP 5 Planning*. U.S. Marine Corps Association. PCN 142 000004 00.

Vonk, Roland (1990). *Prototyping: The Effective Use of Case Technology*. Prentice-Hall. ISBN 0-137-31589-9.

Waters, John K. "Extreme Method Simplifies Development Puzzle"; *Application Development Trends*, July 2000.

Weatherill, Terry. "In the Testing Maturity Model Maze"; *Journal of Software Testing Professionals*, March 2001.

Weinberg, Gerald M. (1986). *Becoming A Technical Leader, An Organic Problem-Solving Approach*. Dorset House Publishing. ISBN 0-932633-02-1.

Weinberg, Gerald M. (1992). *Quality Software Management, Volume 1, Systems Thinking*. Dorset House Publishing. ISBN 0-932633-22-6.

Weinberg, Gerald M. (1993). *Quality Software Management, Volume 2, First-Order Measurement*. Dorset House Publishing. ISBN 0-932633-24-2.

Weinberg, Gerald M. (1998). *The Psychology of Computer Programming*. Dorset House Publishing. ISBN 0-932-63342-0.

Weinberg, Gerald M. (1985). *The Secrets of Consulting, A Guide to Giving and Getting Advice Successfully*. Dorset House Publishing. ISBN 0-932633-01-3.

Wiegers, Karl E. (1999). *Software Requirements*. Microsoft Press. ISBN 0-7356-0631-5.

Yakich, Joe. "Interviewing Your Interviewer"; *Software Testing & Quality Engineering*, March/April 1999.

Yourdon, Edward (1989). *Structured Walk-Throughs*. Prentice-Hall. ISBN 0-13-855289-4.

Index

"Let your fingers do the walking."

— The 'Yellow Pages'

Recent Titles in the Artech House Computing Library

Practical Process Simulation Using Object-Oriented Techniques and C++,
  José Garrido

Secure Messaging with PGP and S/MIME, Rolf Oppliger

Software Fault Tolerance Techniques and Implementation,
  Laura L. Pullum

Software Verification and Validation for Practitioners and Managers,
  Second Edition, Steven R. Rakitin

Strategic Software Production with Domain-Oriented Reuse,
  Paolo Predonzani, Giancarlo Succi, and Tullio Vernazza

Systematic Software Testing, Rick Craig and Stefan Jaskiel

Systems Modeling for Business Process Improvement, David Bustard,
  Peter Kawalek, and Mark Norris, editors

User-Centered Information Design for Improved Software Usability,
  Pradeep Henry

Workflow Modeling: Tools for Process Improvement and Application
  Development, Alec Sharp and Patrick McDermott

For further information on these and other Artech House titles,
including previously considered out-of-print books now available through our
In-Print-Forever® (IPF®) program, contact:

Artech House   Artech House
685 Canton Street   46 Gillingham Street
Norwood, MA 02062   London SW1V 1AH UK
Phone: 781-769-9750   Phone: +44 (0)20 7596-8750
Fax: 781-769-6334   Fax: +44 (0)20 7630-0166
e-mail: artech@artechhouse.com   e-mail: artech-uk@artechhouse.com

Find us on the World Wide Web at:
www.artechhouse.com